Philanthropy in the Shaping of American Higher Education

MERLE CURTI *and* RODERICK NASH

•

Philanthropy in the Shaping of American Higher Education

RUTGERS UNIVERSITY PRESS

New Brunswick · · · *New Jersey*

Preface

In seeking to understand the significance of private, voluntary giving to public purposes, the University of Wisconsin History of Philanthropy Project decided, shortly after its inception in 1958, that American higher education presented one of the most promising subjects for investigation. To be sure, many forces working together gave higher learning in the United States its present shape. The state and federal governments along with the administrators, faculties, and student bodies of college and university communities figured prominently. So did precedent and tradition. And the subtle influence of ideas and educational theories, emanating from both foreign and domestic sources, has been powerful. But philanthropy as a shaping force had a special importance. In many cases it created the models that publicly supported universities and colleges later followed. Philanthropy financed the developments that helped make the tradition, and it paid for the implementation of policies, ideas, and theories. Gifts and bequests made possible an expansion of higher education as the nation grew; at the same time private benefactions took an active part in setting the standards that encouraged quality as well as quantity in higher learning. Yet philanthropy sometimes proved to be a liability to its recipient. Today, for better and for worse, our colleges and universities bear the marks left by philanthropy to an extent that is rare among American institutions.

This book consists of a series of studies on specific topics of importance in the history of philanthropy to American higher education. A central concern gives them cohesion, namely, "What difference did the giving of billions of dollars to American colleges and

v

universities make?" In assessing the achievement of philanthropy, we used broad strokes to paint the main patterns of its relation to higher education over the entire course of American history. No single institution has been treated completely. We hope that selection and interpretation of representative relationships between philanthropists and colleges will be of more value than either exhaustive discussion or a quantitative catalog of gifts and bequests.

The chapters are in roughly chronological order but occasionally overlap, since we have sought in several instances to trace a single theme across several decades in the hope of discovering and interpreting its convolutions. As coauthors we have written separate chapters but have read and criticized them together in an attempt to weld them into a single book.

Our acknowledgments are many: to Jesse Brundage Sears, whose doctoral dissertation of 1919 pioneered in the field; to the authors of numerous college and university histories from which we have drawn to write this synthesis; to Mark Haller, David Allmendinger, Gail Bremer, and Paul Mattingly, whose labor as research assistants and critics has saved both work and face; to Irvin G. Wyllie and Sandra Jackson Nash for their comments and suggestions on the entire manuscript and to F. Emerson Andrews for his criticism of Chapters X and XI; and finally to Mildred Lloyd for her skill as a typist which transformed chaos into order. A generous grant from the Ford Foundation aided substantially in the preparation of this book.

Madison, Wisconsin   MERLE CURTI
Hanover, New Hampshire   RODERICK NASH
January, 1965

Contents

Contents

Philanthropy in the Shaping of American Higher Education

Chapter I

John Harvard to Thomas Hollis

Since 1638, when John Harvard began it all, higher education has attracted a major portion of American philanthropy. Income from gifts and bequests went a long way toward paying the expenses involved in founding and nourishing Harvard and, later, eight other colonial colleges. The colonists thought of these institutions as being vital to the process of bringing civilization and Christianity into a wilderness. The colleges also assumed importance as a means of training a learned leadership in the professions to succeed the leaders of the first generation. Significant, too, in giving precedence to higher education as an object of philanthropy was the driving ambition of the settlers, especially in New England, to build an exemplary society in the New World. Benefactions to colleges fitted perfectly into these plans for progress, while poor relief, which in Tudor and Stuart England received the most philanthropy,[1] was in the American context an admission of defeat.

Socially prominent professional groups—clergymen, merchants and magistrates—founded and supported Harvard and the later colleges.[2] The higher education these leaders knew was the type that had been offered in England with few modifications since the Middle Ages. For the most part they were content with this tradition and wanted it preserved. This conservative bias appeared in the curricula and administrative practices adopted by the colonial colleges as well as in patterns of philanthropy. With few exceptions, the benefactions that nourished higher education in its New World

3

beginnings were given and applied in such a way as to sustain traditional forms. When philanthropy did pioneer new departures it was primarily because the college administration felt them harmless to established values. In some instances governing boards watered down or blatantly defied new ideas that had received philanthropic support. But most colonial benefactors regarded *having* a college as paramount. With a few notable exceptions, questions of what or how a college taught its students were not of primary concern.

The conservative nature of philanthropy to higher education was in part responsible for the failure of the first colleges to alter in response to the changed demands of a new environment.[3] Yet of greater significance was the positive achievement of educational philanthropy: its vital role in establishing and sustaining a series of colleges that served the colonies and provided a solid basis for future expansion. If at this time philanthropy did not patronize departures in curriculum or throw open the doors of higher learning to new groups, it did erect the buildings, fill the libraries, and support in large part several generations of students and professors. These were basic tasks. On the edge of a wilderness and in a society with relatively little money to give or bequeath, the accomplishment was remarkable. A successful start convinced many skeptics of the value of higher education, and those who gave created a bond of sympathy and interest between themselves and the struggling colleges. In the field of philanthropy itself, techniques of fund-raising and a habit of generosity were established that later had important effects.[4]

From the bequest of John Harvard in 1638 to the many gifts in the second decade of the eighteenth century that made Thomas Hollis one of the leading benefactors in the colonial period, Harvard College commanded the major share of philanthropic attention. Although the College of William and Mary was founded in 1693 and the Collegiate School of Connecticut (which was renamed in honor of its first major benefactor, Elihu Yale) in 1701, their stories are part of later colonial foundings. The experience in Massachusetts Bay set a pattern for later colleges in matters of philanthropy, and many of the problems of fund-raising faced by Harvard in the seventeenth and early eighteenth centuries have continued.

Appeals to private individuals for funds were present in the earli-

est attempts to found colleges in the New World, and most donations in the colonial period were the result of active solicitation.
John Eliot, a missionary to the Indians and early member of the
Massachusetts Bay Colony, addressed the first such appeal to a
well-to-do English antiquarian named Simonds D'Ewes. Eliot's letter dated September 18, 1633, was a masterpiece of the philanthropic appeal. After reminding D'Ewes of their acquaintance in
England, Eliot made the point that "if we norish not Larning both
church & common wealth will sinke." From this idealistic beginning,
he appealed to D'Ewes on more personal grounds for patronizing
a colonial college: "God hath bestowed upon you a bounty full
blessing; now if you should please, to imploy but one mite, of that
greate welth which God hath given, to erect a schoole of larning,
a college among us; you should doe a most glorious work, acceptable
to God & man; & the commemoration of the first founder of the
means of Larning, would be a perpetuating of your name & honour
among us. . . ."[5]

The idea that the wealthy owed their fortunes to God and consequently had a duty to perform to society that could be best exe-
cuted by supporting good works was fully exploited in English
appeals of the time.[6] In reminding D'Ewes of the stewardship of
wealth, Eliot brought the force of religion behind his appeal. The
final suggestion of perpetuating the donor's name was directed to
personal vanity and pride. It was to become a favorite bait of
later fund-raisers when major benefactions were the quarry. For
the price of only three hundred pounds, the amount Eliot suggested, D'Ewes might have had his name attached to the institution bearing that of another philanthropist, John Harvard. But
possibly because of his distaste for the extreme varieties of Congregationalism prevalent in New England, he allowed the opportunity to pass untouched.[7]

Little is known about the son of a family of London butchers
who bequeathed half of his estate to the college that was founded
in 1636 at Newtowne (later Cambridge) in Massachusetts Bay.[8]
John Harvard's association with Emmanuel College, Cambridge
University, in the course of which he received two degrees, probably convinced him of the importance of higher education. Quite
possibly he was familiar with the fact that Walter Mildmay's benefactions had founded Emmanuel late in the sixteenth century.[9] He

may also have visited the humble college in Newtowne in the company of Nathaniel Eaton, its first master and also a Cambridge University man.[10] When he died of consumption in Charlestown, Massachusetts Bay on September 14, 1638, Harvard left no known written will and the indefinite nature of his bequest made it easy for the money to be misappropriated. Although half of his estate amounted to £779 17s 2d, only £395 3s was entered as received in the college records.[11] Possibly Eaton, whose reputation was dubious, squandered part of the bequest, but some of Harvard's estate may have been in England, making it difficult to secure entirely.[12] This unfortunate experience at the very dawn of philanthropic support of higher education in America suggested the need for carefully drawn and specific deeds of conveyance. Harvard also bequeathed about three hundred volumes for the college library, which were received without complication.[13]

In 1639 the name of Harvard was conferred on the object of his benefactions. Cotton Mather recalled some years later that although the commonwealth and several individuals contributed to the college, "the memorable MR. JOHN HARVARD, led the way by a generosity exceeding the most of them that followed, *his* name was justly aeternized, by its having the name of HARVARD COLLEDGE imposed upon it." [14] But Harvard's bounty was quickly spent or stolen, the appropriation of the General Court was slow in being paid, and hard times visited the college. The depression that struck New England in the early 1640's retarded philanthropy. The infant college faltered, its students withdrew, and instruction was suspended.

With the college tottering on the brink of collapse, the General Court and Henry Dunster, who succeeded Eaton as president, looked frantically for sources of support. Like John Eliot several years before, they settled on England as the most promising, and launched in the mother country the first of many campaigns on behalf of colonial higher education. The choice was well calculated. England had been exceedingly generous to higher education, contributing over two hundred thousand pounds since 1480 and almost forty thousand pounds in the single decade from 1621–1630.[15]

Thomas Weld, Hugh Peter and William Hibbins were chosen as agents for college and colony and were instructed to raise what funds they could without engaging in dishonorable begging. Ar-

riving in London late in September, 1641, the solicitors met with
moderate success, and Hibbins returned the following year with
several hundred pounds. But the fund-raisers felt a need for promotional literature to arouse interest. In 1642, Peter, Weld, and
President Dunster prepared a tract that, when published the following year, carried the ingenious title *New England's First Fruits*.[16]
Its second part concerned Harvard College and was the first of
thousands of brochures that American educational institutions have
issued in the hope of stimulating contributions. Besides describing
the college program in some detail, it noted how God had been
pleased "to stir up the heart of one Mr. Harvard" to support the
college.[17]

Armed with *New England's First Fruits*, Weld visited several
prospects, one of whom was Anne Mowlson, the childless, wealthy,
and elderly daughter of Anthony Radcliffe. Weld obtained a hundred pounds, and on May 9, 1643 signed a bond stating the terms
of the gift. Following the wishes of Lady Mowlson, the money
was to constitute an endowment for the support at Harvard of
"some poore scholler" through the master of arts degree.[18] Such
scholarships were common at Oxford and Cambridge, some five
hundred having been established since the end of the fifteenth
century.[19] Lady Mowlson further stipulated that the scholarship
should go to a kinsman if one chanced to attend Harvard. Demon-
strating a careful sort of philanthropy, she even made provision for
the transfer of the income to her relative in the event that another
student held it at the time of his entrance. Weld apparently looked
out for his own interests, because the bond stated that one John
Weld, a son, should have the benefit of the first scholarship. This
might have come about had not young Weld been apprehended
while burglarizing a Cambridge house and expelled.[20] Finally,
Weld formally promised Lady Mowlson that the college would
uphold the donor's wishes in regard to the use of the gift.

Several years later an occasion arose to test the integrity of
Weld's promise. In 1655 the General Court, which directed Harvard's affairs, appealed for funds to supplement the meager income
of the college. The request went to the Deputies of the colony,
who pointed out that £150—the Mowlson and other scholarship endowment that Weld had collected—was due the college from England. This money should be applied to repairs, the Deputies said.

The college officials replied that this was impossible "because the £150 was given by the Lady Mowlson, and others, for scholarships annually to be maintained there, which this Court cannot alter." [21] Such integrity in philanthropic matters set a high example for later colleges to follow. But even Harvard could not resist using the Mowlson endowment for general revenue at various times in the next two centuries. In 1893, however, the Corporation took five thousand dollars from its capital and established the Lady Mowlson Scholarship in accord with the original intentions of the donor. [22]

The author of a subscription prospectus circulated for Harvard about 1663 realized that the seventeenth century in the colonies was "our day of small things in a wilderness." While appreciating that the public was poor, with little to spare for philanthropy, he urged "let us creep as we can" in the support of higher education "lest degeneracy, Barbarism, Ignorance and irreligion doe by degrees breake in upon us." [23] In these ideas was an indication of the importance of the higher learning to the colonists as well as the assumption that the first philanthropic support would be small both in total quantity and in the amount of each donation. And Harvard's early records contain references to gifts such as one by a Mr. Venn, "fellow commoner," in 1644 of "one fruit dish, one silver sugar spoon, and one silver tipt jug." [24] The sacrifice of such items, brought carefully from the mother country, suggests the devotion of the colonists to the ideal of higher education. [25] The "widow in Roxbury" who in 1656 spared a single pound for the college probably sacrificed more than the wealthy merchant who gave several hundred. [26]

A remarkable example of grass-roots philanthropy was the "colledge corne" collections made in the late 1640's and early 1650's. The New England Confederation, to which Harvard appealed in 1644, asked every family to make an annual voluntary donation of one-quarter bushel of grain or its equivalent in money to the college. [27] The response of some fifty pounds annually continued for over a decade. It included contributions from distant Hartford and New Haven and was sufficient to support most of the faculty and student body at a time when the college's existence was precarious. [28]

In 1669 Harvard solicited subscriptions for the erection of a new building. As in the campaign for "colledge corne," small donations trickled in from several dozen communities. The inhabitants of Portsmouth declared that "the loud groanes of the sinking colledge, in its present low estate, came to our eares" and in a gesture of appreciation for those scholars "whose care and studdy is to seeke the welfare of our Israell" promised sixty pounds annually for seven years.[29] This was the largest per-capita contribution in the campaign and testified to the profitable lumber business that Portsmouth was enjoying at the time. Understandably, the "Piscataqua Benevolence," as Portsmouth's gift was called, was paid in lumber. The frontier fur-trading post of Springfield also had a large per-capita contribution.[30] Other communities answered Harvard's "loud groanes," and the final proceeds of £2,697 paid for the construction of Harvard Hall.[31] It was such philanthropy from the plain people of the colonies that kept the early Harvard from sinking into oblivion.

The larger donations of the period, frequently accompanied by written deeds of conveyance, present greater opportunity for the study of philanthropic motives, methods, and achievements than do those of small amounts. On the whole the larger contributions were unconditional. When directions for use were attached, they specified such traditional purposes as the erection of buildings, the support of worthy students, or the payment of faculty salaries. The largest single donation to the college in the seventeenth century, for example, was placed unconditionally in the hands of Harvard's directors for use "as they shall judg best for ye promoting of learning and promulgation of ye Gospell. . . ."[32] Similarly, Henry Webb, a merchant, in 1660 bequeathed real estate to the college "either for the maintainance of some poor scholar or for the best Good of the College,"[33] and Joseph Cogan, also a merchant, gave sixty acres of land for the "use benifitt and behoffe" of the president and fellows, attaching only the condition that the proceeds support his descendants if and when they attended Harvard.[34] In 1699 an alumnus of the college and a prominent magistrate, William Stoughton, paid a thousand pounds for the construction of a hall bearing his name. In his will Stoughton remembered Harvard with a bequest of land and suggested the motive for his philanthropy: "my desire to promote good Literature and ye Education of such therein, as may be serviceable to God and these churches."[35] Most philanthropic donations were made simply for the good of the college or for the propagation of learning and piety. Philanthropy in the seventeenth century was not considered a tool with which to effect changes in higher education, and Harvard's administrators chose to let tradition be their guide in its application.

While unconditional donations could be a boon to hard-pressed college officials in search of revenue for current expenses, sometimes the vagueness of a bequest caused chronic litigation. Such was the case with Edward Hopkins, an Englishman and sometime governor of the colony of Connecticut who returned to England in his later years. In a will written in 1657, Hopkins bequeathed an unspecified amount "to give some encouragement in those foreign plantations for the breeding up of hopeful youths both at the grammar school and college, for the public service of the country in future times." He specified that five hundred pounds be given to New England for "upholding and promoting the kingdom of Lord Jesus Christ in those distant parts of the earth." [36] Nothing was done about the bequest until the death of Hopkins's widow in 1699, at which time litigation began that soon was reduced to a rivalry between Harvard and the newly established Collegiate School of Connecticut for the money. Harvard commissioned one Henry Newman of the class of 1687 to look after its interests in the estate.[37] Not until 1712 was a decision reached in the Chancery Court of England whereby the money, with accumulated interest, went to Harvard.[38]

Some philanthropists made more specific statements of the ways in which they desired their money to be applied. For example, the Reverend Theophilus Gale, a noted English philosopher, philologist and theologian associated with Oxford and in his later years with the dissenting academy at Newington Green, in 1678 bequeathed his entire library of some nine hundred volumes to Harvard College with the intention of supporting his religious opinions. He felt that Harvard, as the college of Puritan dissenters, could best fulfill his purposes.[39] Another man who hoped his philanthropy would perpetuate a personal interest was Thomas Brattle, a successful merchant and one of colonial New England's most accomplished astronomers and mathematicians, who corresponded with Sir Isaac Newton. In 1713 Brattle bequeathed two hundred pounds toward the support of a master of arts student "and especially of such an one as is best skilled in ye Mathematicks and shall by all proper

methods endeavor the improvement thereof . . . and making observations and communicating them to ye Learned abroad, as in
some measure I have done." [40] The bequest eventually went to
the support of the Hollis Professor of Mathematics and Natural and
Experimental Philosophy, a disposition by the college which undoubtedly would have pleased Brattle.

While the importance of sustaining higher education in the colonies was declared to be the leading motive behind many of the
benefactions Harvard received in its first century, an occasional
donation suggested that there might be others of a more personal
nature. In this category must be placed the bequest of Robert
Keayne, who used philanthropy as a means of assuaging his con-
science and vindicating himself before a critical society.

Born in London in 1595, Keayne came to Boston at the age of
forty and immediately established a prosperous business selling im-
ported goods from the mother country. His success was so marked
that in 1639 the General Court charged him with taking an inordi-
nately high rate of profit and consequently violating the Calvinistic
conception of a just price. Called to task before the court, Keayne
"did, with tears, acknowledge and bewail his covetous and corrupt
heart." [41] The court fined him, and he narrowly escaped excom-
munication at the hands of the church. Although he did not die
until 1656, he never forgot his censure and public disgrace.

The fifty-thousand-word will of Robert Keayne is an early example of a rich American struggling with the problem of the proper
uses of wealth. He made it the occasion of both a defense of his
conduct as a merchant and the means of devoting his considerable
fortune to good works. Keayne's motives were twofold. He was anxious to demonstrate to his critics that he was not a covetous merchant but rather a public-spirited individual who understood the
duties implicit in the possession of wealth. Secondly, with an eye to
his salvation, he desired to perform a final good work. Although
at one point in his will Keayne acknowledged that God alone would
determine his fate, he later spoke of being judged "according to
the works that I have done in this life according as they have beene
good or evill in the sight of God." [42] He believed the support of
Harvard to be a work of the proper sort.

Keayne made his bequest of several hundred pounds to the college with extreme care. He specified that the money should not be

put into buildings and repairs, "for that I thinke the Country should doe & looke after," but rather constitute an endowment for the use of "poore and hopefull schollrs whose parents are not comfortably able to maintain them there for theire dyett & learning." Having said this, Keayne confessed his ignorance of educational matters and turned to those who did for the management of his bequest: "Therefore because I have little insight in the true ordering of schollrs & other things thereto belonging in a Collidge way & so possibly dispose of my gift where there is lesse neede & that it may doe more good . . . I am willing to referr it to the President Ffeofees & Overseers that are intrusted with the care & ordering of the Collidge & Schollrs . . . what they shall together judge to be the best & most needfullest way of imploying of it amongst the Schollrs. . . ." [43]

Such wisdom in philanthropic practice, more than the good work itself, was greeted later by a historian of Harvard in a way that would have satisfied Keayne's hopes for vindication. In 1848 Samuel A. Eliot remarked that "the approbation of posterity should be bestowed on such wise self-renunciation, as an offset for the rebukes which Capt. Keyne [*sic*] endured from the church, and the penalties he paid in the Court . . . for making too much profit on his merchandise." [44]

The proportion of merchants among the men who gave substantial amounts to Harvard in this period was strikingly high.[45] Keayne, of course, was a merchant, and so were Henry Webb, Joseph Cogan, and numerous other donors listed in the college records. Four generations of Browns, a merchant family of Salem, were major benefactors of Harvard.[46] In 1654, out of twenty-five persons who donated for repair of the college, only four were not primarily involved in business and commerce.[47] In England, on the other hand, merchants lagged a poor fifth in support of higher education behind the professional classes, clergy, nobility, and upper gentry.[48] The predominance of merchant giving in the New World reflected, first, the fact that it was men of this occupation who were making the most money in colonial society. With relatively full pockets, groups of merchants like the lumber dealers of Portsmouth could afford the luxury of philanthropy. Many members of the clergy and the magistracy were rich mainly in ideals and determination. In the second place, the domination of early New England society, especially in the early years, by the dictatorship of the holy and regenerate [49] to the exclusion of the merchants [50] influenced giving habits. Support of higher education offered the merchants an opportunity to assert the social importance to which they felt entitled by their economic position.

Colonists were not wholly responsible for the philanthropic support of Harvard in its first century. After the success of *New England's First Fruits,* England was regarded as a prime source of potential benefactions. Up to 1712, gifts and bequests from England constituted 31 percent of the total income Harvard received from philanthropy.[51] This percentage subsequently rose because in 1719 Thomas Hollis, a London merchant, made the first of his donations, which at the time of his death in 1731 amounted to more than five thousand pounds.

The amount of Hollis's philanthropy was unprecedented in Harvard's experience and remained its largest single benefaction until well into the nineteenth century. Through the power of his philanthropy, Hollis attempted to effect a major change in college policy. The ensuing clash between philanthropist and college officials was the first of its kind in the history of American higher education. While accepting his money, Harvard defied Hollis's wishes to liberalize its religious policies, but the Englishman was successful in making one inroad on the traditional classical curriculum.

The interest of Thomas Hollis in Harvard began when he was named a trustee to the will of his uncle, Robert Throner, who in 1690 bequeathed five hundred pounds to the college.[52] In 1710 Hollis notified Henry Newman, who was working to secure the Hopkins bequest, that Harvard was the object of a bequest in his own will. It was not Newman, however, but Benjamin Colman who played the leading role in wedding the philanthropist and the college in a fruitful if not always idyllic marriage. Colman was one of the colonies' leading intellects of widely recognized liberal tastes. He spent four years in England at the turn of the century and formed an acquaintance with Hollis's father. Colman and the younger Hollis struck up a correspondence in 1718 after the former had returned to the colonies and taken the pastorate of Boston's Brattle Street Church. From this post Colman rose to leadership of the more liberal wing of New England Congregationalism.[53] His extensive correspondence with Hollis convinced the Englishman that Harvard would receive preferred benefactions in a liberal spirit. For Hollis, a Baptist concerned that Congregational Harvard might discriminate in the application of his money, such an assurance was a prerequisite for philanthropy.

In 1719 Hollis began to dispense a portion of his bounty. In that year he sent the first of numerous gifts of books and several hundred pounds for student scholarships.[54] His gifts in the next two years totaled more than a thousand pounds. In thanking him for these gifts both Harvard's president, John Leverett, and Colman observed that the college lacked a divinity professor and invited him to endow one. Hollis was surprised by the deficiency and agreed to the proposal, stipulating that an annual salary of forty pounds be paid to the professor from the income of the money he had already given. On February 14, 1721, Hollis took the initiative in executing formal "Orders" for the establishment of a professorship of divinity, the first endowed chair of any kind created in the British colonies. The issuance of Hollis's "Orders" launched the controversy between college and philanthropist.

Although Hollis was a devout Baptist, he inherited a family tradition of benevolence without regard to sectarian bounds. A remarkable expression of his liberal views occurred in a letter written in relation to the Harvard library: "If there happen to be some books not quite Orthodox, in search after truth with an honest design dont be afraid of them, a publick library ought to be furnished if they can, with Con as well as Pro—that students may read, try, Judg—see for themselves and believe upon argument and just reasonings of the Scriptures—thus saith Aristotle, thus saith Calvin."[55] Hollis's philanthropic creed followed the Pauline doctrine of the stewardship of wealth. "After forty years' diligent application to mercantile business," he wrote Colman, "my God . . . has mercifully succeeded my endeavours, and with my increase inclined my heart to a proportional distribution."[56] In 1720 he wrote to Colman, "I love them that show, by their works, that they love Jesus Christ. Charity is the grace, which now adorns and prepares for glory."[57] With his gift to Harvard, Hollis hoped to encourage a movement in the direction of religious liberalism. He felt, and Colman encouraged him to feel, that the dissenting institution in Massachusetts Bay would respond to his gifts in a spirit of toleration more like his own than any other college or university of the day.

Although Harvard first proposed the idea of a professorship of divinity, the philanthropist took the initiative in drawing up the conditions under which the professor would hold his office. Hollis carefully refrained from stipulating what the religious beliefs of the professor should be, thereby opening the chair to men of various faiths. His purpose was not to impose a Baptist on Harvard as a professor of divinity but to avoid preventing a Baptist from ever holding the chair. In a section of the "Orders" pertaining to the holders of student scholarships, Hollis emphasized *"that none be refused on account of his belief and practice of adult baptism,* if he be sober and religiously inclined." [58] Furtherance of the Christian religion rather than of a particular sect was the end Hollis sought to obtain through his philanthropy. In keeping with his habit of active interest in the management and results of his gifts, Hollis's "Orders" made clear his desire to approve personally the professor and students the college would select to receive his money. Further, he reserved the right to make changes in the terms of the gift. Harvard was unaccustomed to dealing with such a strong-minded philanthropist.

Dissension within New England Congregationalism between a liberal and an orthodox wing shaped the reaction of Harvard's administration to the Hollis benefaction. Thomas and William Brattle, Colman, and President Leverett, who led the liberals, were willing to relax the narrow sectarianism of the orthodox Puritans and permit intellectual intercourse with Anglicans as well as certain variations in church practice. [59] Personal ambitions and enmities within the Harvard community made the religious controversy more complex. Increase and Cotton Mather, staunch bastions of orthodoxy, were displeased with their treatment at the hands of the college. In 1701 Increase resigned from the presidency in disgust, being unable to cope with the liberal influences in the college, and seven years later Harvard passed over his son for its president in favor of the liberal Leverett.

At the time of the Hollis gift the Corporation, composed of the president and the faculty, was predominantly liberal, while the nonacademic magistrates and ministers on the Board of Overseers held orthodox convictions. As might be expected, the Corporation responded to Hollis's "Orders" in the same liberal spirit in which the benefaction was made. The only material amendment it proposed was: "As to the Professor's being in communion with a particular church, we judge it highly fitting; and, as to the limitation, we leave it to [Hollis]." [60] The Corporation did not specify any test of religion for the professorship. It proceeded to elect Edward Wigglesworth as the first Professor of Divinity and forwarded his name to Hollis for approval.

Although the Corporation had acted in the spirit of the benefaction, by the charter of 1650 both the foundation of the professorship and the election of an incumbent required the assent of the Board of Overseers. These bastions of the Congregational way, as traditionally practiced in New England, regarded infant baptism as an important article of their faith. A gift by a proponent of adult baptism such as Hollis was suspicious enough, and the control the philanthropist desired to maintain over the professorship seemed intolerable. Consequently, the Overseers discarded the original "Orders," drafted an entirely new set of conditions governing the use of the benefaction, and forwarded them to Hollis for approval. The Englishman worked over the new draft with several London associates and the "Rules and Orders Proposed Relating to a Divinity Professor in Harvard College in New England," which was completed August 22, 1721, became the establishing document.

Its first article, taken from the Overseers' draft, provided that the professor be a communicant with either the Congregational, Presbyterian, or Baptist denominations. Apparently this was a sop the Overseers threw to the philanthropist, but they relied on another device to thwart his wishes. The final article of the document read: "That it be recommended to the electors [of the professor], that at every choice they prefer a man of solid learning in divinity, of sound and orthodox principles; one who is well gifted to teach; of sober and pious life and of a grave conversation." [61]

The key words of the final article were "sound and orthodox principles." Hollis intended them to have a permissive and flexible meaning within the bounds of the current Protestant denominations. His idea was to exclude "radical" religious views only. The Overseers, however, interpreted "sound and orthodox principles" as meaning traditional New England Congregationalism to the exclusion of any other faith.[62] Perhaps sensing that this would happen, Hollis appended a "Form" to the "Rules and Orders" according to which the candidate for the professorship at his inauguration was to "declare it as his belief, that the Bible is the only and most perfect rule of faith and practice; and that he promise to explain and open the Scriptures to his pupils with integrity and faithfulness, according to the best light that God shall give him." [63] This broad affirmation would not have excluded any Christian of that day.

Early in 1722 the Overseers met to consider the second Hollis draft. The terms of the benefaction bore on such important matters as the nature of religious instruction at Harvard and provoked a heated debate. One of the participants was the diarist Samuel Sewall, who protested the first article permitting the professor to be a Presbyterian or Baptist as well as a Congregationalist: "I objected against it, as chusing rather to lose the Donation than to Accept it. In the afternoon, I finally said, One great end for which the first Planters came over into New England, was to fly from the Cross in Baptisme." Sewall explained that "the Qualifications of the Divinity Professor, is to me, a Bribe to give my Sentence in Disparagement of Infant Baptisme: and I will endeavour to shake my hands from holding it." [64] Rather than allow a philanthropist to control college policy, Sewall would refuse the gift. But with the money already in hand, outright rejection was painful, and the Overseers chose instead to circumvent the donor's intentions.

Harvard's Board of Overseers altered Hollis's draft in such a way as to make "sound and orthodox principles" a test which would be required of the professor.[65] They then arranged the examination of the first candidate, still Edward Wigglesworth, to establish a precedent that would define the faith of the incumbent. This was, in fact, orthodox Congregationalism. In this fashion the exponents of orthodox New England Congregationalism placed their particular construction on the requirements for soundness and orthodoxy of principle and thereby sought to fix permanently the doctrinal beliefs to which the Hollis Professor of Divinity must subscribe. In so doing, they provided against the possibility that a Baptist and, indeed, anyone but a high Calvinist would ever expound theology to the students at Harvard.

Thomas Hollis was never fully apprised of the extent to which the spirit of his gift was distorted by its recipients, but that he suspected something of the sort was evident in a letter to Benjamin Colman in response to a request for his portrait for the college: "*I doubt not but that they are pleased with my moneys;* but I have some reason to think, that some among you will not be well pleased to see the shade of a Baptist hung there, unless you get a previous order to admit it, and forbidding any indecency to it; which, if they do, I shall be grieved; as I have been already." [66]

The controversy between Thomas Hollis and Harvard College over the establishment of a divinity professorship raised at an early date the problem of what relationship should exist between a philanthropist and a college. Should the donor's desires be the sole criterion used in administering a contribution? Or is the college justified in altering the philanthropist's terms if it feels that by so doing it can better serve the purposes of higher education? The answer depends on whether one believes the donor or the college officer is better qualified to interpret the needs of the institution. In the case of the first Hollis benefactions, Harvard's administrators believed that they, and not the philanthropist, had the best interests of higher education in New England at heart.

In spite of the unhappy circumstances surrounding the creation of Harvard's first endowed professorship, Thomas Hollis continued to support the college. His subsequent attempts to use philanthropy to innovate in higher education were more successful. The establishment of the Hollis Professorship of Mathematics and Natural and Experimental Philosophy in 1727 was an important breakthrough for science in the classical curriculum of colonial Harvard. It was also one of the first attempts by a philanthropist to use his donation in a creative rather than a sustaining fashion.

Hollis's plans for his second professorship were long in the making, and incurred the ridicule of some fellow Londoners. He wrote Colman in 1726: "Though jeered and sneered at by many, I leave the issue to the Lord, for whose sake I perform these offices and services, and hope I shall be enabled to continue firm and finish this affair which I call a good work." [67]

A gift of more than a thousand pounds in the same year provided the endowment for the professorship. At the same time, perhaps as a result of the unfortunate circumstances of his earlier benefaction, Hollis had five English men of science draw detailed plans for the new chair. As accepted by the college, the "Rules and Orders" required the professor to teach "Pneumaticks, Hydrostaticks, Mechanicks, Staticks, Opticks" together with "Geometry . . . Proportions, the Principles of Algebra, Conick Sections, Plane and Spherical Trigonometry . . . Mensurations, Planes and Solids." In his care also was put the instruction of "the Motions of the Heavenly Bodies according to the different hypotheses of Ptolemy, Tycho Brahe, and Copernicus." [68] Hollis himself provided much of the equipment for instruction and experimentation in these fields.

Hollis placed the Professor of Mathematics and Natural and Experimental Philosophy under full control of Harvard's officials, providing only that he was not to be dismissed "except for some just and valuable cause." The establishing document contained no stipulation that the professor's principles be sound and orthodox. The only section touching religion was a provision requiring him to "declare himself to be of the Protestant reformed religion, as it is now professed and practiced by the churches in New England, commonly distinguished by the name of Congregational, Presbyterian, or Baptist." [69] The acceptance without difficulty of this provision by the college Overseers suggests that in their eyes such matters in a professor of science were not as crucial as in a professor of religion. But some of the old difficulty reappeared in the appointment of a man to fill the professorship.

Isaac Greenwood of the Harvard Class of 1721 at first gained the approval of Hollis after they had met in England. But lapses in Greenwood's character, including defaulting on his debts, caused Hollis to have second thoughts concerning his fitness for the post. Consequently he indicated to the Harvard officials his interest in another man, who was a Baptist. Immediately the Corporation wrote back, requesting Hollis not to nominate a man of that religion—it wished to avoid a recurrence of difficulty with the Overseers. Hollis took the statement as a personal affront. Heatedly he replied that the man he had in mind was a liberal like himself and added: "What has the dispute of baptism to do to enter into one Professorship or the other. But where persons are prejudiced, no good thing can come out of Nazareth." [70] Rather than risk having Hollis recommend a Baptist, the college quickly approved Greenwood for the position.

After his inauguration on February 13, 1728, Greenwood served for only a few years before being dismissed for intemperance. His successor, the younger John Winthrop, held the chair for more than forty years and was one of the colonies' most distinguished men of science. In 1738 the Overseers debated and defeated a proposal to apply a test of religious principles to Professor Winthrop, thus belatedly recognizing the spirit of Hollis's benefactions.[71]

The Hollis Professors of Mathematics and Natural and Experimental Philosophy did much to lessen the hold of Aristotelian authoritarianism on American science and to replace it with techniques of empirical observation, mathematical evidence, and tentative hypotheses.[72] In this case philanthropy took a leading role in clearing away belief in supernatural agencies for such phenomena as earthquakes and encouraging naturalistic explanations.

The Hollis-Harvard controversy revealed that the willingness of college authorities to accept innovations determined the creative role that philanthropy might play in higher education. A college can refuse the donation, accept it and the conditions under which it is given, or take the philanthropist's money but not his ideas. Harvard followed the last policy in the case of Hollis's divinity professorship and frustrated his hopes for religious liberalization. But the idea of extending Harvard's curriculum with the creation of a professorship in science was accepted because the college officials were convinced of the validity and value of scientific study of natural phenomena.

Private philanthropy in this period was not the only source of revenue available to Harvard.[73] Student fees accounted for a small income. The General Court of Massachusetts Bay made the all-important initial appropriation of four hundred pounds, without which it might never have occurred to John Harvard to support a college. Through the first century of Harvard's history most of the revenue from the state was appropriated specifically for the president's salary. Precise amounts of private and state support are debatable. To 1726, according to one authority, Massachusetts gave £3,693 sterling and £4,602 in the colony's currency to the college. Over the same ninety years private philanthropy accounted for £13,103 sterling and £6,748 in local currency.[74] For a shorter period, 1636 to 1686, another source puts the colony's contribution at £550 sterling and £2,870 in colonial currency and private support at £5,091 sterling and £4,604 in local currency.[75] The latest study of colonial Harvard's economics before 1712 shows that individual gifts and bequests, voluntary subscriptions under government auspices, and income from privately donated endowment together surpassed public aid and tuition as a source of income.[76]

Clearly a major burden of launching higher education at Harvard fell on private philanthropy. That it was able to meet the challenge was a tribute to both colonists and residents of the mother country who appreciated the importance of higher learning in the New World. Although philanthropy to Harvard tended to be of the traditional rather than the innovating variety, it accomplished much in just establishing an institution in a wilderness and sustaining it through lean years. With the notable exception of Thomas Hollis, most of Harvard's early benefactors regarded the fact that a college existed as more significant than what kind of training it dispensed. Their idea was to duplicate Oxford and Cambridge in the New World, leaving modification and adaption to later philanthropists and educators. Usually the first donations Harvard received were made without condition—simply "to the college"—and could be applied freely to the crucial necessities, buildings, faculty salaries, and books. This creation of the framework of higher education was a genuine achievement. Of even greater importance in the long run was the beginning of the tradition of supporting America's colleges with voluntary contributions.

Chapter II

Colleges in the Colonies

While the colonists inherited from the mother country the habit and methods of philanthropy to higher education, in one respect their unique situation in the New World occasioned a departure from English precedents. Two universities, complexes of many colleges, dominated the higher learning in England. For centuries Oxford and Cambridge absorbed practically the entire output of collegiate philanthropy.[1] Although Harvard existed alone for almost six decades, it did not monopolize colonial higher education. By the time Thomas Hollis established his professorships, the College of William and Mary (founded in 1693) in Virginia and the Collegiate School of Connecticut (1701, later Yale) were already offering alternatives to the institution in Massachusetts Bay. In the four decades after the Hollis benefactions six other institutions were founded: the College of New Jersey (1746, later Princeton), King's College (1754, later Columbia), the College of Philadelphia (1754, later the University of Pennsylvania), the College of Rhode Island (1764, later Brown), Queen's College (1766, later Rutgers), and Dartmouth College (1769). The size of the continent, religious differences, rivalries among the colonies, and a willingness on the part of philanthropists to back new ventures fixed on America a system of higher education with the characteristics of diffusion and diversity.

The search for revenue was the highest barrier standing between the nascent colonial colleges and permanency. As Bishop Berkeley, himself a major benefactor of Yale, wrote to Samuel Johnson when King's College was being planned: "Colleges from small beginnings grow great by subsequent bequests and benefactions. A small matter will suffice to set one going. And when this is once well done, there is no doubt it will go on and thrive." [2]

State financial support was a major factor in the beginnings of only William and Mary. The government helped Harvard and Yale to some extent and King's to a lesser degree, but contributed virtually nothing to the other colleges.[3] Even those colleges fortunate enough to receive state aid welcomed the life-giving flow of private philanthropy. For those that were not so fortunate it was essential. To keep gifts flowing both at home and in England required the determined efforts of college officials and friends. The Collegiate School of Connecticut was fortunate in having such friends, who attracted to it the interest of a Londoner rich with the spoils of India, Elihu Yale.

One of the most important of the Collegiate School's philanthropic "middle men" was Jeremiah Dummer, a native of Massachusetts Bay who received a Harvard degree in 1699 and eleven years later became the English agent for the colony of his birth. He also served Connecticut in a similar capacity.[4] In 1711 James Pierpont of the struggling Collegiate School wrote to Dummer appealing for financial help. Using his connections with "men of Learning & Estate," [5] Dummer was able to collect a library of some eight hundred volumes, which arrived in installments beginning in 1714. Among the contributors were Sir Isaac Newton, Sir Richard Steele, who gave a complete set of the *Tatler* and the *Spectator*, and Elihu Yale. Dummer himself paid for more than a hundred volumes.[6] He was not satisfied with his effort, however, complaining that he had "almost as many benefactors as books." [7] Yet his philanthropy and that of his English acquaintances gave the Collegiate School one of the best libraries in the New World.

Dummer had much higher hopes with regard to Yale's benefactions than several hundred pounds' worth of books. In response to Pierpont's plea, Dummer wrote that a likely prospect for a major gift or bequest was the fabulously wealthy Yale, who had told him that he intended to bestow a charity on some college at Oxford. The gift would be more appropriate if Yale directed it to the colonies, Dummer felt, "seeing he is a New England and I think a Connecticut man." [8] Pressure in the form of letters and personal interviews should be applied to the old man, Dummer suggested.

Although Yale was not "a Connecticut man" as Dummer thought, he was a New Englander, born in Boston in 1649. But his father, disgruntled with the authoritarian and exclusive Puritan government, took his family back to England when Elihu was only a few years old. In his twenties Yale went to India to make his fortune and succeeded extraordinarily well. He rose to the governorship of the East India Company's Fort St. George in Madras and returned to England about the turn of the century. [9] Yale's estate was huge; he made a wedding gift of twenty thousand pounds to his daughter. [10]

The process of convincing Yale to dispense some of his bounty on the Collegiate School of Connecticut went on slowly and unsuccessfully until early 1718, when Cotton Mather lent his support. Since Mather was a graduate of Harvard, the son of its late president, Increase Mather, and both an overseer and a fellow, his action on behalf of the Connecticut institution was highly unusual. A clue to Mather's behavior lies in wounded pride and the same controversy between liberal and orthodox Congregationalists at Harvard that influenced the reception of the Hollis benefactions. A man of immense learning, Mather was peeved at being passed over in the election of his father's successor. When the presidency went to the liberal John Leverett, Mather's resentment deepened. Disgusted with both his personal treatment at Harvard and its growing inclination to a more liberal brand of Congregationalism, he turned his interest and influence elsewhere. [11]

Mather was well known in England from his numerous publications and in 1713 received a membership in the Royal Society. Yale was elected to the society four years later. As a consequence, Mather's letter of January 14, 1718 to Yale carried considerable weight. After reminding Yale of his colonial birth, Mather expounded the philosophy that "the chief good that we have in our estates lies in the good we do with them." Swallowing his pride in the interests of obtaining a donation, Mather next argued that the few points of difference between the Anglican and dissenting churches in the colonies should be no obstacle to Yale's philanthropy. Climaxing his appeal in a manner well calculated to interest a man who had lost his only son, Mather wrote: "Sir, though you have your felicities in your family, which I pray God continue and multiply, yet certainly, if what is forming at New Haven might wear the name of YALE COLLEGE it would be better than *a name of sons and daughters*. And your munificence might easily obtain for you such a commemoration and perpetuation of your valuable name, which would indeed be much better than an Egyptian pyramid." [12] Mather added that Dummer, "a tender, prudent, active, and useful patron of the infant College at Connecticut," would call on Yale shortly in an attempt to secure the benefaction.

Dummer's visit proved a necessity because, as a member of the Church of England, Yale had serious doubts about the propriety of aiding a dissenting institution. After their interview Dummer reported that "when we had discourst that point freely, he appears convinc't that the business of good men is to spread religion and learning among mankind, without being too fondly attach't to particular Tenets about which the World never was, nor ever will be, agreed." [13] Dummer's skill as a fund-raiser obtained results. Shortly before the commencement of 1718 the college officials received word that a shipment of goods from Yale for the benefit of their institution had left London. Expectations were high. Yet when the goods were converted to cash the Collegiate School realized only £562, hardly a sacrifice for their donor.

In the expectation that the first shipment was an earnest of more to come, the officials of the Collegiate School quickly conferred on their institution the name of "Yale." [14] Mather predicted that the gift was only "sensible proof" that Yale had taken the college under his patronage and added that "what he does now is very little in proportion to what he will do, when he finds, by the name of it, that it may claim an adoption with him." [15] But effusive letters of thanks and continued proddings by Dummer failed to produce more than a few small shipments of goods and a full-length painting of the philanthropist.[16] Apparently Dummer's success in liberalizing Yale's point of view was ephemeral, because in his declining years he drew closer to the Anglican-oriented Society for the Propagation of the Gospel in Foreign Parts and shunned the dissenters in the colonies. In a rough draft of his will Yale put "Connecticote College" down for five hundred pounds. The use of this name, instead of his own, suggested Yale's trepidations about being known as a benefactor of a dissenting college.[17]

In contrast to Harvard's greatest colonial benefactor, Thomas Hollis, Elihu Yale took slight interest in the objects of his philanthropy. He attempted nothing creative with his gifts, and his primary motive in giving seems to have been escape from bothersome appeals of Dummer and the colonial letter-writers. But Yale's benefaction came at a critical time in the history of the Collegiate School, which had been torn by rivalries within the colony into branches functioning in various communities. The money from England, given to the officials at New Haven, helped fix its location permanently. The unconditional nature of Yale's gift permitted his beneficiary to apply the money to essential purposes: the building of a hall for the students and faculty. Still, the cost of architectural flourishes and the coat of cerulean paint applied to the structure might have been better devoted to scholarships, salaries, or teaching apparatus.[18] In view of what he might have given, Yale earned his immortality cheaply, but his gift remained the second largest individual donation to Yale College for more than a century.

Yale's greatest benefactor in the colonial period was the Anglican prelate and philosopher George Berkeley. His support of the college in the early 1730's arose from personal disappointments in founding a college of his own and through the influence of another philanthropic middle man, the American clergyman and educator Samuel Johnson.[19] A decade before coming to the colonies in 1729, Berkeley had conceived a plan to found a college for Englishmen and natives on the Island of Bermuda. He collected subscriptions and the promise of a munificent royal grant. The American trip was intended to pave the way for his college, but several factors, including the discovery that Bermuda was not centrally located in the colonies and the failure of the royal grant to materialize, wrecked Berkeley's plans.[20]

From his residence in Rhode Island, Berkeley wrote to Johnson in March, 1730, asking him if the library at Yale would accept the writings of the Anglican divines Hooker and Chillingworth.[21] Johnson apparently replied affirmatively, because Berkeley left a small gift of books for Yale before returning to England in 1731 to break the news to his supporters of the Bermuda project's failure. However, many of those who had backed Berkeley joined with him in transferring their enthusiasm to Yale and permitted their gifts to go to that institution, especially on learning that it "breeds the best clergymen and most learned of any college in America." [22] As a consequence Berkeley decided to make two handsome presents to the college. The first was the deed to his farm in Rhode Island, worth several thousand pounds. The importance of Johnson's influence in securing this donation was evident in the statement of Berkeley to Johnson shortly before the gift that he would help Yale "the more as you were once a member of it, and have still an influence there." [23] As sent to Johnson, the deed stipulated that income from the farm be used for the support of graduate students called "scholars of the house." The donor stipulated that recipients were to be chosen competitively after a two-hour examination in Greek and Latin. [24]

On receiving word of the Berkeley gift, Benjamin Colman—whose liberalism, as manifested in the Hollis controversy at Harvard, did not extend to Anglicans—wrote frantically to Rector Elisha Williams of Yale. Colman warned him to refuse the donation if it was "clogged with any Conditions that directly or indirectly tend to the Introduction of Episcopacy, and consequently to the Subversion of the true Intent and Foundation of your College." [25] Berkeley's gift was not clogged with sectarian conditions; instead its declared purpose was the support of higher education in general in the New World. Yale accepted it, although not without misgivings, [26] and the recipients of the Berkeley Scholarships have, through the years, proved among the ablest of the college's graduates. [27]

Further evidence of Berkeley's esteem for higher education in the colonies came in 1733, when he sent Yale more than nine hundred volumes for its library. Berkeley clearly stated his desires and intentions to Johnson: "Being desirous so far as in me lies to promote sound learning and true religion in your part of the world [and to] . . . shed a copious light in that remote wilderness." [28] Enlightening the books were, and probably the finest collection to come to the colonies at one time.

According to the diary of Ezra Stiles, president of Yale at a later date, Berkeley directed his philanthropy toward New Haven because Johnson persuaded him to believe the college would soon become Anglican and would embrace his Idealist philosophy. [29] Nevertheless, considerable evidence points to different intentions on Berkeley's part. On receiving "agreeable specimens of learning" from Yale, he wrote to its president that "the daily increase of learning and religion in your seminary of Yale College give me very sensible pleasure, and an ample recompense for my poor endeavors to further those good ends." [30] The advancement of learning and religion in general was the end Berkeley sought to secure with his philanthropy. Years after the gifts, Johnson wrote to Yale's President Thomas Clap protesting the requirement that all students in New Haven attend the Congregational chapel. After presenting arguments why this violated the rights of Anglicans and others, Johnson added: "And ought not the catholic design of the principal benefactors also in strict justice to be regarded, who, in the sense of the English law, are to be reckoned among the founders? . . . What Mr. Yale's views were, I had not the opportunity of knowing. . . . But I was knowing to Bp. Berkeley's which were, that his great Donation should be equally for a common benefit, without respect to parties. For I was, myself the principal, I may say in effect the only person in procuring that Donation, and with those generous, catholic, and charitable views . . . to which I was prompted by the sincere desire that it should be for a common benefit, when I could have easily procured it appropriated to the [Anglican] Church." [31] The letter testified both to Berkeley's liberal designs and to Johnson's key role in bringing his bounty to the aid of Yale.

Few colonial colleges had such skillful, determined, and influential friends as Dummer and Johnson, and they turned to new devices for stimulating philanthropy. One of the favorites was selling the location of the college to the highest bidder. After calculating the economic worth of a college and its prestige value, communities were quick to make handsome offers to secure it. Part of the reason Yale College settled in New Haven was the donation that community offered. In the early 1750's the founders of the College of New Jersey confidently set one thousand pounds, ten acres of cleared land, and two hundred acres of woodland as their asking price for locating their institution. New Brunswick and Princeton were the finalists in the competition, with the latter finally getting the college on the strength of a subscription of £1,700. [32] A decade later, when another institution was proposed, New Brunswick recouped its losses by offering enough to obtain Queen's College. [33] The well-endowed Dartmouth College stimulated a widespread competition among communities in several colonies when it proposed to move from Lebanon, Connecticut. New Hampshire's generous land grant on the Connecticut River won the prize. The heated competition between Newport and Providence for the College of Rhode Island produced more than four thousand pounds in subscriptions for the institution, which ultimately was located in the latter community.[34] The Brown family, well-to-do merchants whose name later became more closely associated with the college, were among the most determined to obtain its location in Providence. They personally subscribed £760 and argued that "building the college here will be the means of bringing great quantities of money into the place, and thereby greatly increasing the value of all estates to which this town is a market." Another reason the Browns advanced was that the location of a college in Providence would promote "the weight and influence of this northern part of the Colony in the scale of government in all times to come."[35] In such cases philanthropic support of a college was divorced from idealistic assumptions about the value of higher education. But officials of chronically destitute colleges were willing to receive funds regardless of the motives for giving them, and selling the location proved lucrative indeed.

In their efforts to interest philanthropists, and especially to induce one big donor to give enough to drive the wolf of poverty permanently from the college campus, founders and officers of the colonial institutions taxed their imaginations to the extreme. As James Manning, the young president of the Baptist-sponsored College of Rhode Island, wrote in 1770: "It would be happy for us if we could find in England a family of Hollises to patronize our college; but I fear the Baptists are not to expect such an instance of public spirit in their favor, although I have heretofore indulged in such hopes, and am yet unwilling to give them up."[36] In the hope of bringing a philanthropist like Hollis to the aid of his college, Manning in the early 1770's investigated the possibilities of using honorary degrees as an inducement to prospective philanthropists. That such an honor might be useful was evident from the experience of Yale College, where a donor had asked for and received an honorary degree in return for a contribution of books. In this case, the M.D., which he received, was styled by Yale wits as signifying *Multum Donavit* (he gave much).[37]

From a correspondent in England, President Manning received a list of no less than seventeen prospects for degrees, including three Anglicans, six Baptists, and eight of no affiliation. One was described as "an old, rich, learned man, that can leave £100 to the college." [38] Manning expressed some worry that if the degrees were granted without determining whether the subjects desired them, the college might suffer more harm than good. His correspondent sagely replied that it was better policy to grant the degrees without previously informing the recipient because "for my own part, I would not have given you a single farthing, or so much as a thanks . . . if I had it not in my power with the utmost truth to say, 'I neither sought it, nor bought it, nor thought for a moment about it.'" [39] The degrees were conferred at the commencements of 1773 and 1774 but, with the growth of ill feeling between the colonies and mother country, did not produce the hoped-for benefactions. [40]

The founders of the College of Rhode Island, anticipating the need for private philanthropy, had included in the original charter of the institution a clause providing that "the greatest & most distinguished Benefactor" would have the honor of naming the college, presumably after himself. [41] After the failure to raise money with honorary degrees, and even after the Revolution, Manning used the charter provision in an appeal to a wealthy English Baptist: "Cambridge College was so fortunate as to attract the attention of a Hollis, New Haven of a Yale, and New Hampshire of a Dartmouth, who have given their names to these seats of learning. We should think ourselves no less happy in the patronage of a *Llewelyn. Llewelyn College* appears well when written, and sounds no less agreeably when spoken. Nor do I know a name which would please me better to hear extolled on our public anniversaries as the founder of the Institution. . . . I know your philanthropy and principles of liberty would not suffer you to object that we are now independent of the British Empire. . . ." [42] Despite Manning's perceptive final thrust that "it is the ardent wish of the human mind to establish permanent fame," Thomas Llewelyn could not respond, had he been so inclined, since his death occurred before the proposition reached England.

While letters from the colonies to the mother country were occasionally effective, especially when seconded by the efforts of agents such as Jeremiah Dummer, college officers felt that carefully planned fund-raising missions would be even more profitable. They had the example of Harvard's campaign in the early 1640's to follow. Even more stimulating was the history of British support of the College of William and Mary. As early as 1619 Sir Edwin Sandys, treasurer of the Virginia Company, obtained a grant of ten thousand acres for the establishment of a university at Henrico to train both Indian and English youth.[43] On the recommendation of James I, £1,500 and assorted books were subscribed in English parishes. The venture was about to be opened in 1622 when a disastrous Indian massacre put an end to the plans, and the money was placed in the hands of trustees. In 1660 the idea of a college was revived and subscriptions taken in the colony. Finally in 1688 a few English merchants subscribed £2,500 for higher education in the Virginia colony. The Reverend James Blair, a Scot and a Harvard graduate, went to England for a charter and additional funds. He encountered some opposition from the English attorney-general who, when told that Virginians needed a college to save their souls, retorted, "Damn your souls! Make tobacco!"[44] In other quarters Blair found a more receptive audience, and he returned to the colony with a royal endowment of twenty thousand acres, two thousand pounds from Virginia quitrents, revenues from a tax of a penny per pound on tobacco exported from Maryland and Virginia, and the proceeds of the office of surveyor-general.[45] For its part the colonial assembly first contributed the export duty on "wild catt skin" and other furs, later adding other tax revenues and appropriations.[46] Founded in 1693, the College of William and Mary was by far the richest, although hardly the largest, of the colonial colleges. In later years state and private benefactions continued to flow from England. On the eve of the Revolution its annual income from endowment was several thousand pounds, probably more than that of the eight other institutions combined.[47]

The good fortune of William and Mary whetted the appetites of later colonial colleges for English philanthropy. All except Queen's College joined in attempts to milk the mother country, and this Dutch Reformed institution sought aid in Holland. The marked success of the missions to England was based in large part on the condition of the English economy, which was such that it could afford extensive philanthropy far more easily than could the colonies. In addition, many Englishmen were concerned with doing their share in helping bring civilization and Christianity to the New World and regarded higher education as an ideal instrument.[48]

In 1753 Gilbert Tennent and Samuel Davies sailed for England on the first major fund-raising mission of the College of New Jersey. Tennent, a leading evangelistic Presbyterian, was the son of the founder of the Log College at Neshaminy, which later became the College of New Jersey. His connections with the English revivalist George Whitefield started the campaign in a promising fashion. Davies was also an evangelist and later president of the college. The two solicitors used the English coffee houses to make contacts with influential clergymen and to present the case for their college. As with Harvard's Weld-Peter mission over a century before, Davies and Tennent sensed the need for promotional literature, and *A General Account of the Rise and State of the College, Lately Established in the Province of New Jersey* (1754) joined *New England's First Fruits* as one of the earliest fund-raising tracts for higher education. "It is hoped," wrote Davies and Tennent, "that the Pious and Benevolent in *Great-Britain,* into whose Hands these Papers may fall, will extend their generous Aids, in the Prosecution and Completion of so excellent and useful a Design." [49] Entire congregations as well as individuals responded to the appeal. Late in 1754 Davies and Tennent returned to the colonies with more than three thousand pounds. Since the money was given without conditions, it could be devoted to essentials: a building to house the college—the famed Nassau Hall—and a residence for its president.[50] A good start toward a library was made shortly afterwards with the receipt of a 450-volume collection from New Jersey's governor, Jonathan Belcher.[51]

So important was philanthropy to the existence of the colonial colleges that its solicitation was usually entrusted to high officers in the institution. So much the better if they were known abroad. Such was the case with the College of Philadelphia, which in 1762 sent its provost, William Smith, to England for money. Smith had the essential English contacts. He was a Scot by birth and had been abroad twice in the 1750's, each time arousing interest in the college. His mission beginning in 1762 made an encouraging start with a contribution of five hundred pounds from Thomas Penn, but a cloud soon darkened Smith's prospects in the person of James

Jay, who was representing King's College on a similar mission. In this situation Smith discerned "a strange clashing of interests and applications, and the common friends of both Colleges were afraid that both schemes might be defeated by this method of doing business, and that the public would be disgusted with such frequent applications, and so close upon the heels of each other."[52]

Smith and Jay realized they would have to either work in separate areas or combine their efforts. They elected to join forces, and on August 12, 1763 obtained a "royal brief" entitling them to solicit in England. The brief was in the form of an appeal calling for an endowment of six thousand pounds for each institution.[53] After a remarkably thorough canvass, this was almost exactly what each college received: £5,936 10s 6d.[54] George III gave four hundred pounds to King's but only half that amount to the College of Philadelphia, which he felt the Penn family amply supported. While the royal brief was read in church parishes throughout England, Smith and Jay buttonholed the wealthy for additional donations. Discouraged at one point, Smith wrote that prospective donors were "so harassed with an infinity of appeals" that they sometimes had to be visited twenty times before a gift was actually secured.[55] Determination paid off, however, because the solicitors returned in 1764, Smith with £8,700 for Philadelphia and Jay with £7,500 for King's.[56] The combined returns of their mission represented the largest single philanthropic windfall received by the colonial colleges.

Occasionally in the history of philanthropy a case can be found in which money was solicited for one purpose but applied to another. The first major case of this kind in the history of American higher education occurred in the English fund-raising mission of Moor's Charity School of Lebanon, Connecticut.

This institution was begun informally in 1754 for teaching American Indians. It expanded under the direction of Eleazar Wheelock, and in its second decade prepared for a mission abroad in search of funds. In searching for the right representative, Wheelock had the advice of the evangelist Whitefield, who wrote: "Had I a converted Indian scholar that could preach and pray in English, something might be done to purpose."[57] This advice proved Whitefield a keen student of the English mind. Almost from the first contact with the inhabitants of the New World wilderness there had arisen in England a great clamor to civilize and Christianize the "savages." [58] In the seventeenth century considerable funds had been collected for the Society for the Propagation of the Gospel in New England, which backed the work of "apostle" John Eliot and other missionary-educators among the Indians.[59] Eleazar Wheelock realized that in Samson Occom, a Mohegan graduate of his school, he had an ideal agent. Occom could speak fluent English and deliver impassioned sermons, and even in the dress of white men he retained an impressive Indian appearance. Here, indeed, was one of New England's first fruits.[60]

In 1766, in the company of Nathaniel Whitaker, Occom arrived in England. The appearance of a devout English-speaking Indian in London caused a major sensation. When he took the pulpit to appeal for money to educate and convert his brethren in the wilderness, English pockets opened wide. More than three thousand pounds was collected in the first eight months. The King contributed two hundred pounds, and highly placed nobles like William, Earl of Dartmouth, made substantial donations. Yet most of the gifts were small ones from people anxious to give their mite toward Christianizing the heathen. When Occom and Whitaker returned to the colonies, they left the impressive sum of £12,026 in the hands of English trustees. After expenses some eleven thousand pounds remained.[61] This money, raised largely by an Indian and given with expectation of its being used to teach the rudiments of Christianity and a few basic educational skills to the Indians, built Dartmouth College.

Even before he dispatched Occom and Whitaker to England, a series of adversities with his Indian students had convinced Wheelock that it would be well to take a few English youths into his program. These young men could be trained as missionaries to the Indians. In 1768, when the fund-raisers returned, the number of English approximately equaled the number of Indians in the school. The following year there were twice as many whites, and in 1770 only three out of twenty-one were Indian.[62] By the time Wheelock established his institution in New Hampshire in the early 1770's, Moor's Charity School had become a college for colonial youths.[63] To be sure, the Indian school continued, but as a feeble preparatory institution for the college. Only two Indians graduated during Wheelock's regime. Even the idea of training white missionaries to the Indians lost ground rapidly to that of producing lawyers,

clergymen, and teachers.[64] Samson Occom declared that this use
of the money he had raised was a "fraudulent diversion of the
fund." [65] The trustees in England became suspicious of Wheelock's
use of the money and repeatedly warned him that educating and
converting Indians, not building a college for whites, was the donors' intent.[66]

The task of hewing a community and a college from the New
Hampshire wilderness was expensive, and by 1774 the trustees informed Wheelock that his account was overdrawn. The English
benefactions had not turned many "heathen" into Samson Occoms,
but they had added another college to the growing roster in the
colonies. As for Wheelock, a dogged, selfless worker who himself
gave more than £1,500 to his institution,[67] the misrepresentation
that resulted from his application of philanthropy was almost unconscious. He never plotted to trick the English, but his belief that
whites were better teachers of Indians than Indians themselves
pushed him further and further into the college enterprise. Still,
Wheelock's failure to advise the trustees of his change in plans
and his stubborn insistence that the funds were serving the purposes of their donors was a violation of the principles of fund-raising
ethics.

Even in the years in which one mission followed another to the
mother country, philanthropy was also sought closer to home. The
College of New Jersey's John Witherspoon proved one of the most
effective fund-raisers. He assumed the college's presidency in 1768,
when its finances were nearly hopeless. The proceeds of the Davies-
Tennent mission had been spent or lost in unwise investment.
Witherspoon realized that his college must have money or perish,
and he spent the better part of this year touring the colonies in
search of philanthropists. His success was remarkable. From 1770
to 1774 he raised more than seven thousand pounds, which was
more than sufficient to get the college out of the red.[68] An example
of Witherspoon's ingenuity and talent was his *Address to the Inhabitants of Jamaica and Other West-India Islands in Behalf of
the College of New-Jersey* of 1772, in which he attempted to encourage the islanders to direct their sons and their philanthropy
toward his college. President Witherspoon pointed out how over-
worked the college's limited faculty was, especially the president,
who "is obliged to teach Divinity and Moral philosophy as well as

Chronology, History and Rhetoric, besides the superintendance and government of the whole." Continuing the personal touch, Witherspoon declared that "the short lives of the former Presidents have been by many attributed to their excessive labours, which it is hoped will be an argument with the humane and generous to lend their help in promoting so noble a design." [69] The follow-up campaign to the islands failed when Witherspoon's agent became ill and died in Barbados. [70] But using similar arguments, Witherspoon squeezed funds from Americans.

Several colleges turned to the Southern colonies. First on the scene was Hezekiah Smith of the College of Rhode Island, an institution that had to pioneer in seeking philanthropic aid because of its lack of state support. In the winter of 1769–70, working mainly in the larger cities, Smith collected several hundred pounds. The notations on his list of prospective donors tell the story of many a charitable campaign: "no money," "doubtful" "probable," "call again," "out of town," and "go thy way for this time." [71] The proceeds of Smith's trip were spent immediately by his hard-pressed college. In 1771 the College of Philadelphia collected a thousand pounds in colonial currency from South Carolina, but found that plans for a college in Charleston, for which contributions were being solicited, hurt its appeal. [72] When the College of New Jersey received word that a thousand pounds in produce had been collected for it in Georgia, a ship was promptly dispatched to claim the goods. [73]

Despite the success of missions abroad and in distant parts of the colonies, a large proportion of the philanthropic support of the colleges came from their immediate locales. As we have seen, selling the location of a college was one form of local support. So were the subscription lists that were circulated in support of the institutions at Providence, New Brunswick, Princeton, and Philadelphia. It was considered desirable to have one's name appear on the lists of college patrons, thereby identifying the donor as a pillar of his community. [74] In cases where the college represented a particular set of religious beliefs, such as those of the New Light Presbyterians at the College of New Jersey or the Baptists at Rhode Island, men of means subscribing to these views were expected to provide financial support.

The feeling of sectarian responsibility prompted one of the largest gifts from an individual to a colonial college. Several lotteries had raised more than five thousand pounds for a college in New York City, when in 1755 Trinity Church agreed to give a valuable farm property on Manhattan Island on the condition that the college's president be a member of the Church of England and that its services be in the Anglican liturgy.[75] Although the grant also stipulated that no student would be excluded on account of his religion, Presbyterians led by William Livingston heatedly protested the sectarian nature of the proposed college. As a result it was decided that the proceeds from the lotteries, which had been staged without an Anglican college specifically in mind, should not go in entirety to King's College.[76] This incensed New York Anglicans, including Joseph Murray, a prominent and wealthy lawyer and a trustee of Trinity Church. Identifying himself with the new college and desiring to make up to it what had been lost from the lottery proceeds, Murray bequeathed it his residuary estate. This generous donation, consisting of real estate and a library, was valued at the time of his death in 1757 at seven to eight thousand pounds in New York currency.[77]

Some of the philanthropy to the colonial colleges was conservative in that it sought to sustain the traditional pattern of sectarian instruction in divinity. Unable to forget a philanthropic controversy of earlier years, Daniel Henchman gave Harvard £250 in 1747 to support the Hollis Professor of Divinity but only "so long as he shall be a member in full communion with some Congregational or Presbyterian Church, and shall profess and teach the principles of the Christian religion, according to the well-known confessions of faith, drawn up by a synod of the churches in New England." [78] On the failure of either condition, the money was to support a poor scholar.

In his donation to Harvard three years later, Paul Dudley demonstrated how philanthropy could be used to defend the old order. Dudley was the son of the unpopular governor of Massachusetts Bay, Joseph Dudley, and a strict Congregationalist. He pursued a political career, eventually attaining the position of chief justice in the Bay. Dudley and his father inevitably clashed with the liberal, independent elements in Harvard's Corporation during the Leverett administration. On one occasion they almost caused the Corporation to resign by siding with a student who had sued his

Harvard tutor for refusing to grant him a degree.[79] In making a bequest to the college of more than a hundred pounds, Dudley took extreme precautions to insure its support of orthodoxy. His will stipulated that the money was to support a series of four lectures to be delivered annually in four consecutive years and continued as long as the funds lasted. The intent of the discourses Dudley himself proclaimed to be the explanation and proof of the validity of Congregational polity "as the same hath been practised in New England, from the first beginning of It and so continued at this day." [80] Rather than trust this weighty task to immature hands, Dudley declared that the lecturer must be "at Least Forty years of Age." In an attempt to protect his alma mater from dangerous ideas, Dudley declared the third lecture was intended for "detecting and convicting and exposing the Idolatry of the Romish Church, their Tyranny, Usurpations, damnable Heresies, Fatal Errors, abominable Superstitions, and other crying Wickednesses." [81] The Dudleian Lectures, given annually until well into the nineteenth century, were designed by their donor to keep Harvard treading the old paths of New England faith.

While most colonial philanthropists sought to preserve and strengthen traditional patterns, a few looked in new directions. An instance of the creative force of American philanthropy to higher education appeared in the role it played in transforming theologically oriented colleges into universities offering professional training in many phases of the liberal arts and sciences. In the case of Harvard this process of transformation required many decades, but its beginnings can be traced well back into the colonial period. While with one of his professorships Thomas Hollis strengthened the program of instruction in divinity, with the other he encouraged the practice and teaching of experimental science. Toward the end of the colonial period other benefactions came to Harvard that either established or led to the establishment at a later date of professorships in a host of new fields.

When he died in 1764, Thomas Hancock, a Boston merchant with one of the largest fortunes in the colonies, bequeathed a thousand pounds for the support of someone "to profess and teach the Oriental Languages, especially the Hebrew," at Harvard.[82] Unlike Thomas Hollis, Hancock left it to the Corporation to draw up rules and orders for the professorship. In 1765 Stephen Sewall was installed as Hancock Professor of the Hebrew and Other Oriental Languages. This was the first instance in which an American endowed a professorial chair.

Ezekiel Hersey, a physician of Hingham, Massachusetts, died in 1770, leaving a thousand pounds toward "the support of a Professorship of Anatomy and Physic, and for that use only." [83] The college voted to invest the money until it accumulated interest or the generosity of others provided sufficient funds for the appointment of a professor. In 1782 James Warren was chosen Hersey Professor of Anatomy and Surgery, while Benjamin Waterhouse received an appointment as Professor of the Theory and Practice of Physic. [84]

The will of Nicholas Boylston provided a stimulus to instruction in letters with a 1771 bequest of £1,500 for the foundation of "a Professorship of Rhetoric and Oratory." Funds had accumulated sufficiently to permit the appointment of John Quincy Adams as the first Boylston Professor in 1804. [85] In 1779 a former chief justice of the Superior Court of New Hampshire bequeathed £100 to Harvard "to be laid out and improved in purchasing such books as may be thought most useful in the study of the civil, statute, and common law of England. . . ." [86] In such donations as these there were the seeds of a university.

Colonial philanthropy also acted creatively when it opened college doors to minority groups. The College of Rhode Island received a gift from a Jewish merchant of Charleston and promptly voted "that the children of Jews be admitted into this Institution, and entirely enjoy the freedom of their own religion without any constraint or imposition whatever." [87]

Sometimes private giving was designed to promote new ideas. This was the motivation of Thomas Hollis, a great-nephew of Harvard's earlier benefactor. Hollis dedicated his life to preserving and extending the English heritage of personal freedom. Colonial liberty was one of his concerns, and in 1758 he began sending books to Harvard to further this cause. Ultimately the Harvard library owed at least five thousand titles to Hollis's generosity. Most of the books pertained to the development of free institutions and free thought in England. The Hollis gifts made Harvard a foremost depository of tracts expressing eighteenth-century liberalism, a distinction it retains today. [88]

The efforts of Benjamin Franklin and the philanthropy of a score of Philadelphia's prominent citizens constituted the boldest attempt to effect a change in the curriculum of a colonial college. In 1749 Franklin published his *Proposals Relating to the Education of Youth in Pennsylvania,* which conceived of an institution in which the traditional college diet of Latin and Greek would be varied to suit the requirements of particular careers. Prospective merchants, for example, might dispense with the classical languages and instead learn French, German, and Spanish.[89] Franklin even suggested that while the student studied natural history, "might not a little gardening, planting, grafting, inoculating, Etc., be taught and practiced. . . ."[90] The English language, history, geography, surveying, and even the history of commerce were emphasized in this curriculum, the first attempt to adapt higher education to the circumstances of life in the New World.

Franklin distributed his *Proposals* to well-to-do Philadelphians and recorded in his *Autobiography* that "as soon as I could suppose their minds a little prepared by the perusal of it, I set on foot a subscription for opening and supporting an academy."[91] The results must have satisfied his expectations; twenty-four men formed a board of trustees and pledged eight hundred pounds annually for five years to start the academy.[92] The motives of the trustees in making their contributions lacked some of Franklin's idealism. Among the reasons they advanced for the academy, later known as the College of Philadelphia, were the saving of expense in sending their sons elsewhere and the opportunity to "draw numbers of students from neighboring Provinces, who must spend considerable Sums yearly among us."[93] The new departures in curriculum were apparently of little interest to the trustees, apart from Franklin.

The institution opened in 1751 but with a constitution in which the trustees watered down Franklin's innovations and partially restored the classical curriculum to its traditional preeminence.[94] Why risk an innovation, the trustees reasoned, when a traditional college would serve their purposes as well? With the inauguration of William Smith as provost in 1754, the trend away from Franklin's ideas continued. Although the College of Philadelphia was the only colonial college not controlled in large part by a church, Smith, himself a clergyman, returned the study of the divines and classic authors to the top of the academic ladder.[95] Franklin was incensed at the turn of events in the institution he had proposed and for which he had raised considerable funds.[96] Nevertheless, the wealthy, worldly Philadelphians who backed the college helped make it more secular, more attuned to the Enlightenment, and bolder in introducing fields such as medicine and chemistry than the other colonial colleges.

The achievement of philanthropy to the colonial colleges lay not so much in the departures it pioneered as in the base for later expansion it helped create and sustain. Many gifts were made without conditions, simply for the propagation of learning and religion. Colleges used the funds for essentials: buildings, books, salaries for professors, and scholarships for students. At a time of hand-to-mouth existence for most colleges, the receipts of private generosity went to meet current expenses or, more often, to pay past debts. Large endowments were rare, and only occasionally did a donor add a new subject to the curriculum or a new professorship to the faculty. By present standards the donations were small, but so were the colleges. More important than size was the fact that higher education and its philanthropic support were planted as ideas and actualities in American soil.

Chapter III

The College Boom

As president of the College of New Jersey since 1768, John Witherspoon was well aware how many times the struggling colonial colleges had knocked on England's door and been rewarded with philanthropy. But then a revolution changed England's relationship from mother to competitor. While on a fund-raising trip abroad in 1779. Witherspoon learned how tightly the hostilities had closed English purses. Frustrated in England and with his college sinking into debt, he turned to John Jay and Benjamin Franklin, who were in Paris as United States commissioners. Witherspoon wondered whether continental nations, especially France, would be receptive to fund-raising missions for American higher education. Franklin's reply was negative; he added that "the very request would be disgraceful to us, and hurt the credit of responsibility we wish to maintain in Europe by representing the United States as too poor to provide for the education of their own children." [1] Witherspoon was reminded that in philanthropic support of higher education as in politics, Americans were obliged to face the challenges and responsibilities of independence.

With aid from abroad unlikely and the nine existing colleges in complete or partial disruption as a result of the war, the future of higher education in the new American nation was uncertain. Friends and officers of the colleges looked anxiously toward their fellow citizens, wondering if they would be equal to the task of taking up the slack left by the withdrawal of England from the field of educational philanthropy.

It was not long before the fears of 1780 were eased, and then replaced with new ones. When John Witherspoon died in 1794 there were fifteen new colleges. Twenty-five more were in existence before 1830, and in the next three decades 133 were established. Moreover, these 173 new colleges before the Civil War include only permanent institutions. Adding to them those that closed after brief periods of existence, the number of antebellum foundings approached a thousand.[2] These educational ventures, many of which flattered themselves with the designation "college," developed as a part of the process of expansion toward the frontier. They sprang up in the Maine woods, along the hardwood ridges of the upper South, in the oak openings of Illinois and Wisconsin, and on the rolling grasslands west of the Mississippi. In many places the transformation from wilderness to college was only a matter of months. Of such proportions was the college boom that Absalom Peters's prediction of 1851 was already a reality when made: "It is therefore placed beyond all doubt, that our country, in the whole extent of it, is to be a land of Colleges."[3] By 1860, Ohio had more institutions of higher learning than the German Empire. Quality was another matter.

Given the large number of colleges and the relative scarcity of money in the young country, a struggle for existence was inevitable. The fittest in this competition were the institutions that were successful at raising money. In this situation philanthropy assumed crucial importance in the selection of survivors. For the colleges that received a constant flow of donations there was permanence and growth; those founded by men whose zeal exceeded their cash assets usually had short lives. Of course, voluntary private giving was not the only source of income. Receipts from tuition payments, including money raised by selling term and perpetual scholarships, helped to fill college treasuries. State and municipal appropriations in money and land and state-approved lotteries sometimes bolstered voluntary support. But only a few favored institutions experienced the public largesse. In many states policy dictated the support of only a single college out of several dozen. Yet all of them were free to seek benefactions, all of them did, and their future depended on their success.

Of great importance in attracting gifts was the assurance established in the Dartmouth College Case (1819) that private institutions would remain private. In holding Dartmouth College to be an eleemosynary corporation endowed by private individuals for specified purposes, the Supreme Court declared that one great inducement to such gifts was "the conviction felt by the giver, that the disposition he makes of them is immutable." "It is probable," continued Chief Justice John Marshall, who wrote the decision, "that no man ever was, and that no man ever will be, the founder of a college, believing at the same time that an act of incorporation constitutes no security for the institution. . . . All such gifts are made in the pleasing, perhaps delusive hope, that the charity will flow forever in the channel which the givers have marked out for it." [4] Had the law of the land not given such assurance to donors and potential donors, gifts making possible the college boom might in considerable part have been withheld. At the same time the Dartmouth College decision opened the way for an overexpansion of weak colleges.

Most of the colleges founded between the Revolution and the Civil War had similar financial histories. The founders and faculty were usually clergymen of a particular denomination who circulated a subscription list for the means with which to build their college. The lay members of the region in which the college was established were expected to give whatever they could spare. On the fringes of settlement this was never much and frequently consisted of donations in land, produce, or labor. As the main college hall rose, agents of the institution returned to the fund-raising circuit. In many cases they solicited in the older seaboard regions where donations tended to be larger, but they learned the slips between a written pledge and money in the college treasury. Depressions and business adversity could cause a subscriber to retract his offer, and litigation to recover it was long and expensive.

The fact that a college was "church-related" or "denominational" did not assure it a steady source of income. The various organized churches and their education societies were not foundations with independent assets, and like the colleges they relied on philanthropy. At best they could provide a college with publicity and the opportunity to make its plea before congregations with some degree of sympathy on sectarian grounds. Only rarely did a denomination make a direct appropriation to a college, and even this money had to be raised among its members. Typically, the small denominational college struggled on the edge of existence for several decades. After a subscription it might feel temporarily secure, but soon an urgent need for funds would reappear. Again and again the college begged for aid until even its friends sickened at the sight of a subscription list and the sound of old arguments. Yet towns were anxious to have a college for economic reasons, and the threat of moving to a new location often squeezed out a few more dollars.

Finally, the typical college faced a crisis. It either had to attain a sound financial status or close. The successful colleges found a single wealthy benefactor, obtained money abroad, collected a large subscription, or were taken under the patronage of state or city. This windfall pushed the struggling institution out of purgatory into permanence.

Colleges founded in the East had the benefit of locating near a society capable of relatively generous benefactions. But in many cases it was the united efforts of a host of small contributors that launched a college in their community. The first college to be added to the nine holdovers from colonial days was Washington College in Chestertown, Maryland. In 1780 William Smith, who had already served the College of Philadelphia as president and expert fund-raiser, was dismissed from that institution. He arrived in Chestertown, assumed the leadership of a country academy, and in two years raised enough money to convert it into a college. In one five-month period Smith collected fourteen thousand dollars, including a donation from George Washington. Only in 1784, after philanthropy had launched it, did the state of Maryland begin making a small annual appropriation for Washington College.[5]

Many of the early foundings in New England and New York subsequently received benefactions from a single individual or family that enabled them to achieve permanence. In the case of Middlebury College in Vermont the stalwart was Gamaliel Painter, an old settler with extensive real estate holdings in the region. In 1797 Painter led a subscription drive that netted four thousand dollars and enabled the college to open three years later. Middlebury gave repeatedly to its college over the next two decades, but a combination of the financial depression of 1819 and the refusal of Vermont to furnish aid resulted in a twenty thousand dollar debt. Salvation finally came in the form of Painter's thirteen thousand dollar legacy.[6]

Bowdoin College, Brunswick, Maine, received extensive land grants from the state before opening in 1792. Its name had been selected, however, in the hope of attracting the attention of a family of wealthy Boston merchants and statesmen. The elder James Bowdoin died in 1790, and his son and namesake inherited the estate. The first indication of interest the younger Bowdoin showed in the college was a contribution of a thousand acres of land and a thousand dollars in 1795. When Bowdoin died childless in 1811 he made the college his residuary legatee. The institution received thirty-three thousand dollars, including books, real estate, a collection of minerals, and works of art.[7]

Williams College and Amherst College arose within a few miles of each other in western Massachusetts and in their early years competed for the limited local philanthropy. But the large-scale donations of Massachusetts manufacturers stabilized the colleges as permanent institutions.

Williams was the older. It received a charter in 1793; the name came from Ephraim Williams, who four decades previously made a bequest that ultimately went to the college.[8] Williams crept into the nineteenth century with an income of a few small donations, tuition fees, and several small appropriations from the state. In 1815 the college announced its intention of quitting Williamstown and locating elsewhere. The door was thus thrown open to "bids" from other communities. Six towns in Hampshire and Berkshire Counties entered the competition with offers of up to thirteen thousand dollars, but Williams delayed in accepting. Again in 1819 the board of trustees placed the location of their college on sale. This time the town of Amherst made a determined effort to capture the prize, launching an ambitious subscription drive for fifty thousand dollars. Canvassing the small towns of western Massachusetts, the representatives of Amherst's "Charity Fund," as it was known, were remarkably successful. In less than a year they raised thirty-seven thousand dollars from 274 individuals for most of whom philanthropy of any amount was a sacrifice.[9] The larger communities of the eastern part of the state ignored the drive. But fifty thousand dollars was needed, and nine of Amherst's citizens pledged themselves to cover the deficit.[10]

While the town of Amherst was collecting its fund, the Massachusetts legislature decided that Williams College should remain in Williamstown. In gratitude, Williamstown raised $18,186 for its college.[11] The citizens of Amherst were disappointed but saw their hopes realized in 1821 when Amherst College opened. Since the Charity Fund was restricted to endowment, current expenses and the cost of buildings had to be met with further campaigns in 1822 and 1823, which produced subscriptions as low as a few cents annually for several years. The college began a four-year campaign in 1841 and raised one hundred thousand dollars, but it severely taxed the generosity of the surrounding region.[12] College officials searched hopefully for the patronage of one of Massachusetts's wealthy industrialists.

Amherst looked in the right direction when it named Samuel Williston to its board of trustees in 1841. Williston was a native of Easthampton, Massachusetts whose father had been among the farmers who contributed what little they could spare to Amherst's Charity Fund. When he was appointed to Amherst's board, Williston was amassing a considerable fortune from the manufacture of buttons. His first gift to the college was made in 1845, when he endowed a professorship of rhetoric and oratory. Donations for chairs of natural theology, Greek, and Hebrew followed. Williston gave Amherst $150,000 before his death in 1874 and elicited from the college's first historian the tribute that "Amherst *is* his foster-child. He is her foster-father. She owes to him her preservation, her very life." [13]

Williston, had help, however. At the time of his gifts Amherst also received generous donations from David Sears and Samuel A. Hitchcock, both Boston merchants. Hitchcock's philanthropy amounted to $175,000 and was devoted in large part to scholarships.[14] Beginning in 1861 the college received the first contribution of William Johnson Walker, a Charlestown, Massachusetts, physician with investments in railroads and manufacturing. Walker graduated from Harvard and five years before his death in 1860 offered his alma mater $130,000 for improving the medical school. Harvard welcomed the money but balked at the conditions he attached to it: an entirely new faculty was to be appointed, acceptable to him! When Harvard refused the gift, Walker changed his will in favor of Amherst, Tufts, Williams, and the Massachusetts

Institute of Technology. Altogether, Walker's philanthropy to American higher education amounted to more than $1,000,000, of which Amherst received two hundred thousand dollars.[15] With the exception of two minor state grants, the story of Amherst is one of philanthropy, in small amounts and large, erecting a college.

Amos Lawrence was the counterpart of Amherst's Samuel Williston in the history of Williams College. A leader in the early development of New England's textile industry, Lawrence retained enough of the old Puritan piety to formulate a remarkable philanthropic philosophy. On January 1, 1829 he began to keep a small book for recording his philanthropies. In his eyes they were investments in salvation. Included with his gifts for 1844 was a frank confession of the philanthropic motive: "The *more I give,* the more *I have; I do most devoutly and heartily pray to God,* that I may be faithful in the use of the good things *entrusted to me,* and that I may at last be received among the *faithful stewards,* with the *'well done'* promised; and thus secure what is *beyond price* compared with any thing Earthly; (that Heaven we all hope for.)"[16]

In Lawrence's benefactions to Williams, personal friendship with its president, Mark Hopkins, joined the doctrine of stewardship as an impelling force. The first contact of the men was on the occasion of Hopkins's presentation of the Lowell Lectures in Boston. Lawrence, a Unitarian, approved of the catholicity of Hopkins's views and in January, 1844 sent his son to the president's hotel room with the news that he wished to bestow five thousand dollars on Williams. Other gifts for faculty salaries, a library, land, a telescope, and student aid followed. Lawrence's philanthropy added about eighty thousand dollars to Williams's resources, removed its burden of debt, and helped stabilize it as a permanent institution.[17]

President Hopkins, aware from the first of a good thing, took pains to cultivate the philanthropist's interest. In numerous letters the men expressed their mutual admiration. On August 1, 1846, Hopkins wrote to Lawrence that "the more I think of it, the more I see the importance of the great principle of *stewardship.* It is as you said, *everything.*"[18] On his part Lawrence cherished the esteem of Hopkins and gave his money as much to the president as to the college.[19] To Amos Adams Lawrence, his father's devotion to Williams seemed so irrational that on June 25, 1846 he protested the gifts to an unseen institution and the flattery of the Hopkins family. To this criticism Amos Lawrence responded emotionally in typical fashion: "I am especially desirous *to do my work* while I can and *not doubt,* and cavil by the way as some of my wisest friends do [to the end] . . . that their proper work will be left undone and the dirt and filth *that ought to be washed off, will be on them, when summoned to the bar of God."* [20] The spiritual cleansing to which Amos Lawrence subjected himself resulted in the dispensation of some seven hundred thousand dollars, of which Williams College received a substantial share.

Without the large-scale giving of Americans who capitalized on the nation's expanding economy in making fortunes, few Eastern colleges could have survived the trying years between the Revolution and the Civil War. Some men of wealth applied their money to surviving colonial colleges and had the satisfaction of seeing the institutions take their names. Henry Rutgers earned the honor comparatively cheaply with the gift of five thousand dollars and a bell.[21] Nicholas Brown, Jr. continued the tradition of his family by supporting the College of Rhode Island, which took his name in 1804. His donations amounted ultimately to $160,000.[22]

Large individual donors were also prominent among the new foundings. A gift of a thousand pounds from Benjamin Franklin launched a college in 1787 in Lancaster, Pennsylvania, known today as Franklin and Marshall College.[23] Waterville College in Waterville, Maine was contemplating closing after more than four decades of existence in 1864 when the philanthropy of Gardner Colby rescued it; the grateful college then adopted his name.[24] About the same time the gifts of Benjamin E. Bates enabled Bates College to open in Lewiston, Maine.[25] A gift of land from Charles Tufts and a total of five hundred thousand dollars from William J. Walker and Sylvanus Packard saw Tufts College, Medford, Massachusetts, through crucial years after its opening in 1855.[26]

New York Baptists scraped to support the Hamilton Literary and Theological Institute, founded in 1819. When it changed its name to Madison University in 1846, William Colgate, a soap and toiletries manufacturer of New York City, had given over half its resources. Colgate's sons continued their father's habits of generosity, and in 1890 the institution was renamed Colgate University.[27]

The $150,000 donation of Isaac Rich, a Boston fish mogul, stabilized the finances of Wesleyan University in Middletown, Connecticut. In addition, he persuaded Daniel Drew, not noted for generosity, to give a like amount to Wesleyan. Rich left his entire estate of a million and a half dollars to help in the establishment of Boston University.[28]

Occasionally a member of the academic community accumulated enough money to make a substantial benefaction. Eliphalet Nott, president of Union College in Schenectady, New York from 1804 until 1866, suffered the embarrassment of a legislative inquiry into the college's finances, which he had mixed with his own. Three years later, in 1854, after the investigation had cleared him, Nott turned over to Union an endowment fund of six hundred thousand dollars, which he had made from the invention of a stove and careful investment, for professorships and scholarships.[29]

With large donations in their treasuries, some Eastern colleges attained the financial security necessary for permanence and development. These examples, representative rather than exhaustive, suggest the importance of philanthropy to the American pattern of higher education as it was taking shape.

The college boom was not confined to the East. Dedicated clergymen carried it across the Appalachians and eventually to the Pacific. They thought of colleges as a means of giving impetus to the "home missionary" movement for extending the message of their denomination into the heathen West. What better way of keeping lit the torch of religion and civilization in the wilderness than institutions of higher learning? Consequently, young men made solemn resolves to go West and found colleges. Orations were delivered by the hundred from cornerstones or bare plots. Enthusiasm, however, was no substitute for cash in the field of higher education. Plans rich in zeal but poor in means usually did not materialize.

Speaking in Lexington, Kentucky in 1840, President Robert Davidson of Transylvania University observed that if instruction alone were involved in running a college, student fees might suffice for its maintenance. However, the need for buildings, a library, and apparatus justified an endowment. To raise one was the problem, and Davidson realized that a demand for higher education had to be created in the locality of a college if it was to receive community support.[30] In the West the sequence of demand for a college, local benefactions, and philanthropy from the East or from England was repeated in village after village. Davidson's own college, Transylvania, was the first to be founded west of the mountains in what was then Kentucky County, Virginia. When it relocated in Lexington in 1789, Transylvania began to receive generous support from that community in donations of land and subscriptions. Local aid was climaxed in 1823 when Colonel James Morrison bequeathed twenty thousand dollars for a professorship and made the college his residual legatee, from which it realized fifty thousand.[31] In 1795 Transylvania also made a profitable canvass of the East. The ten thousand dollars raised included contributions from George Washington and John Adams.[32] Although Transylvania subsequently received some city and state appropriations, voluntary giving saw it through its early history.

The devotion of the pioneer settlers to higher education appeared in the subscription lists of a host of western colleges. Like the early supporters of Harvard, they regarded a college as an important agency of civilization and were willing to sacrifice to see one founded in their communities. From a more materialistic viewpoint, townspeople appreciated the economic value of a college which, like a canal or railroad, would bring business to their community. Philander Chase, the founder of several colleges, termed his discovery that philanthropy decreased in direct proportion to the distance of a college, "human nature exposed." He found the attitude of distant Ohioans to be, as he phrased it: "Place the [college] near my residence, or in the vicinity of my property, or near the town or village that I inhabit, and I will give, *liberally give*, but otherwise not a cent from my pocket shall you have." [33]

At Granville, Ohio, the Baptists collected a few thousand dollars for a college, which opened in 1831. With the hard-earned money a building was erected, but fire consumed it. Unwilling to lose their college so easily, the citizens of Granville scraped together another $2,800 and rebuilt the hall. But debts mounted, and in the mid-1840's it was proposed to relocate the college where money came easier. Again Granville dug into its pockets and raised enough to keep the college. The long-hoped-for major benefaction finally came in 1854 in a ten thousand dollar donation from an Ohio farmer, William S. Denison. Along with a sixty-five thousand dollar subscription collected among Ohio Baptists, the Denison benefaction guaranteed the permanence of Denison University at Granville.[34]

Occasionally the constant demands of a college for money became so burdensome as to occasion protest. Among the Baptists of North Carolina, Wake Forest College conducted a continual, intensive fund-raising campaign. After a dozen years of being asked by college agents to demonstrate their "loyalty," one newspaper editor exclaimed in exasperation: "It is *College, College, College,* forever! Will the cry of *College* never cease?" Yes, the agent assured him, when the institution was adequately endowed.[35]

In the case of many colleges, the response from people of small means was encouraging. For instance, when Western Reserve University began its existence at Hudson, Ohio in 1826, the farmers in the area pledged support in kind or in labor if cash was scarce. One man took the responsibility for bringing stone for the buildings from a quarry ten miles away; the job required the work of an entire winter. A farmer's wife promised fifty dollars annually from her butter and egg money and bore this sacrifice for ten years.[36] Grass-roots philanthropy such as this saw many a struggling Western college through crucial early years.

Some pioneers built substantial fortunes in the West as the nineteenth century unrolled. Colleges that could attract their patronage were frequently relieved of the agony of existence on a shoestring budget. In 1850 a group of Methodists laid plans for a college in Chicago. Orrington Lunt, a native of Maine who had moved to Chicago in 1842 and made a fortune in wheat, immediately contributed five thousand dollars. Lunt's gifts continued, and others demonstrated a degree of generosity that permitted President Clarke Titus Hinman to raise $64,000 in 1853, his first year of association with Northwestern.[37] This was a good start, indeed. In Indianapolis, donations of land and money from Ovid Butler, a local lawyer, permitted the 1855 opening of a substantial institution. The college, later renamed in Butler's honor, was also fortunate in having the services of John O'Kane. As an agent, O'Kane worked eighteen months in 1850 and 1851, visited sixty-six Indiana churches, made three hundred speeches and turned $75,200 over to the college.[38]

Sometimes a college had to wait decades before a large donation came its way. Indiana Asbury University struggled for over forty years after its opening in 1838 before receiving a windfall from Washington Charles DePauw, a native of Indiana who made millions in banking. DePauw and his family gave six hundred thousand dollars and their name to the college, assuring it status as a major center of higher learning.[39]

The relatively wealthy society of the Eastern seaboard was the mecca of fund-raisers of the Western colleges. But the old reliable argument of giving to support a college in the donor's locality was useless there. New methods of persuasion had to be found. One of the most frequently used was that Easterners had a responsibility in continuing the American "mission" of renovating the world. Colleges, it was argued, were the ideal vehicle for the spread of "progress" into the West. American greatness and American morality depended on the establishment of Western colleges.[40]

Their eyes lifted by the screams of the eagle, Easterners were made to look beyond the needs of their own region. Another tack that stimulators of philanthropy took was to make clear the danger the East faced if irresponsible radicalisms were permitted to take root in the West for want of sound colleges. Without Eastern benevolence the West would tend to barbarism and lower the whole character of the republic. "The East cannot save itself without saving the West. Selfishness is suicide," one plea stated.[41] Social unity and order, as well as higher education, should be a motive for philanthropy.

Another argument that succeeded in drawing money from Eastern pockets emphasized the fact that the Eastern colleges had received foreign philanthropy: "Harvard and Yale, Bowdoin and Nassau, went abroad for aid. The strong then helped the weak. And by their timely and efficient sympathy, our colleges lived through their periods of feebleness, and have been enabled to accomplish their glorious work."[42] The obvious conclusion was that the Western colleges were related to the East as the colonial institutions had been to England.

Continually, agents for the new colleges reminded their audiences of their responsibilities. Before groups in which denominational loyalty was strong, a plea to extend sectarian influence was effective in raising money. Protestant denominations were worried about the expansion of the Jesuits in the West; one orator alleged that they threatened "to subvert the principles of the Reformation, and to crush the spirit of liberty." The battle must be sustained. "We must build College against College." [43] The competition among Protestant sects also stimulated giving. Eastern members were encouraged to associate themselves through philanthropy with the institutions that struggled to uphold their denomination's influence across the mountains. The denominational colleges were looked to as training grounds for ministers and centers of religious revivals. On the other hand, too strong an emphasis on the sectarianism of a college might discourage contributions from nonaffiliates. The agent had to choose his appeal carefully.

Sometimes Easterners donated without solicitation, as was the case with the New England women who organized as Kenyon Circles of Industry to use their sewing needles on behalf of Kenyon College in Ohio. [44] But more commonly the president of a college toured the East in search of funds. The first president of Illinois College, founded in 1835, was Edward Beecher, formerly associated with the Park Street Church, Boston. Beecher's prominence and the fact that the college's founders were New England Congregationalists known as the "Yale Band" provided a basis on which to solicit in the East. Subscription lists were circulated, ten thousand dollars raised, and considerably more promised on one campaign, but the crash of 1837 and subsequent depression nullified most of the pledges. [45]

The initial duty of Edwin Baldwin, a popular New York minister who had been appointed president of Wabash College, Indiana, in 1835, was to tour New England and New York. Speaking from the pulpits of scores of churches, Baldwin raised $28,757 in money and books for his college. [46] President Charles Coffin proved a good provider for Greenville (later Tusculum) College in Tennessee when, before 1805, he gathered fourteen thousand dollars on several tours to New England. [47]

Western Reserve had agents in the East almost continually after its founding in 1826. Charles B. Storrs first served the college as an Eastern agent and collected numerous donations, many of which were in the form of Western land held by New England speculators. Later Storrs assumed the presidency, but his duties as fundraiser continued. In 1830, immediately following his appointment, he was back in New York City raising $23,000, including a ten thousand dollar endowment from Arthur Tappan. [48] Some college presidents agreed with Stephen Olin of Randolph-Macon and Wesleyan, who wrote to his wife in 1847 that "this is the least agreeable of all my functions—the begging part, I mean." [49] But somehow philanthropy had to be stimulated if there were to be college presidents at all.

In 1843, the year of the organization of the Society for the Promotion of Collegiate and Theological Education at the West, Western colleges were in serious financial difficulty. The society represented a departure in efforts to tap the sources of Eastern benevolence. The decision of four Western colleges to establish the society was prompted by recent adversity they had experienced in raising funds in the East. The depression that began in 1837 and slowed the national economy until well into the 1840's also retarded philanthropy. Even more significantly, it caused people who had previously pledged gifts to colleges to retract their offers. Another factor in the slackening receipts from philanthropy was the colleges' competitive fund-raising campaigns. Then, too, money was aked for "wildcat colleges" of dubious status if existent at all. "Good men," a fund-raiser explained, "were becoming weary of the uncertainties of Western Institutions, and of the exhaustless multiplicity of their demands." [50] The situation demanded a more efficient approach to prospective Eastern benefactors.

The Society for the Promotion of Collegiate and Theological Education at the West took shape in Cincinnati in 1843 as the result of a joint agreement on the part of Illinois College, Marietta College, Wabash College and Lane Theological Seminary to conduct a united fund-raising campaign.[51] In its organization and conduct Congregationalists and Presbyterians joined forces. The plan called for each institution to send an agent to the East. The society, directed by an Eastern board, would give each agent an area in which to solicit, rotating them for maximum effectiveness. As explained by Theron Baldwin, the long-time corresponding secretary of the society and a member of the Yale Band, the idea of the organization was to simplify the machinery of benevolence while making it more economical.[52] The pastors of Eastern churches played a crucial role in the campaigns. They served as permanent voluntary agents and opened their pulpits for addresses when paid agents of the society made their annual calls. In addition, prominent Eastern clergymen and educators, including Mark Hopkins, Henry Ward

Beecher, and Noah Porter, delivered speeches on behalf of the society that were printed and widely distributed.

Receipts from the society's campaigns were placed in a common fund and distributed annually according to a pre-established ratio. The money was given for current expenses only. Member colleges were expected to solicit locally for benefactions to pay their debts and create endowments. When a college had achieved financial health, it was replaced on the society's lists by a needy institution. By 1874, when it lost its identity in a merger with another organization, the society had aided eighteen colleges from Ohio to California with a total of $1,036,026.[53]

The achievement of the Society for the Promotion of Collegiate and Theological Education at the West was to select promising institutions and to nourish them through embarrassing times to permanence. Reports from the member colleges testify to the society's importance: Illinois College declared that its receipts "saved this College from extinction, and placed it in a position of great promise of lasting usefulness." Wabash testified that its share of the proceeds "has been the salvation of the College; for, without this assistance, the Faculty could not have been sustained, nor the Institution carried through the period of its greatest embarrassments." [54]

In everything it did the society sought to check rather than promote the college boom. Its written statements deplored the tendency to undue multiplication of Western colleges, and its power to reject applicants for aid provided an opportunity to discourage colleges in a tangible manner.[55] Moreover, a college that did not have the society's sanction found itself at a marked disadvantage in attempting to raise funds independently in the East. Before a college was added to the society's list of recipients a careful investigation, including a visit to the campus, was conducted.[56] In the hands of the society, philanthropy exercised a selective power on the field of Western higher education.

Most of the contributions collected by independent college agents and those working with the society were small. But occasionally a large donation flowed from an Eastern philanthropist to a Western college. Amos Adams Lawrence, the son of the textile king who contributed to Williams College, became interested in Wisconsin when he acquired five thousand acres of land in the Fox

River Valley. With scant respect for a distant landlord, squatters moved onto the property. Lawrence responded not with coercion but with a proposal to found a college "not only for improving the tone of morals and the standard of education in that vicinity, but also of conferring a lasting benefit on a portion of our countrymen who most need it." [57] Specifically, he offered ten thousand dollars if an equal amount could be raised in Wisconsin. Lawrence was an Episcopalian, but he realized the widespread unpopularity of that church and consequently vested control of the college with the Methodists. His wisdom was demonstrated when six thousand local Methodists under the leadership of William Harkness Sampson subscribed eleven thousand dollars to match the initial gift. [58] In still another matter Lawrence sacrificed his own desires to the conditions that prevailed in Wisconsin. He intended the college to be located on his own lands near De Pere, but men on the scene found a superior location on the Fox River and were permitted to build Lawrence University in the town of Appleton. [59]

Massachusetts proved to be the richest mine of philanthropy to Western colleges. In 1871 William Carleton, a Charlestown lamp manufacturer, gave fifty thousand dollars and his name to a tiny college in Northfield, Minnesota that Congregationalists had opened immediately after the Civil War. This amount exceeded any single previous donation to a college in the West. [60] And Samuel Williston, the generous friend of Amherst, extended his philanthropy westward to Marietta and Grinnell. [61]

In the late 1830's the benefactions of Arthur Tappan, a native of Massachusetts who made a fortune importing dry goods in New York City, saved Oberlin College from extinction. From its foundation in 1833, Oberlin held precariously to existence with the help of small Eastern donations. In 1835 John Jay Shipherd started on a final do-or-die mission as agent of the college. Casting about for a persuasive argument, he hit upon the idea of capitalizing on Oberlin's adamant antislavery position. Shipherd's plan was first to recruit the abolitionist leaders Asa Mahan, John Morgan, and Charles G. Finney for the college's faculty. Then he would confidently approach wealthy New York abolitionists, especially the Tappan brothers, Arthur and Lewis, with requests for aid. The plan worked to perfection. Lane Theological Seminary lost abolitionist support when it forbade free discussion of the slavery question on

campus. Oberlin promptly voted to permit this freedom and even
to admit Negroes as students.[62] The proposed additions were
made to the faculty, and the expected patronage followed quickly.
In a moment of optimism Arthur Tappan promised Finney his entire income of a hundred thousand dollars a year minus the amount
necessary to support his family.[63] In fact, Tappan provided seventeen thousand in gifts and loans by the end of 1835, with promises of more to come. A group of New Yorkers agreed to support
eight professorships with a stipend to each of six hundred dollars
annually.[64]

Oberlin boomed, but its financial troubles were not over. The
crash of 1837 dampened the enthusiasm and compromised the ability of Oberlin's Eastern friends to pay their pledges or make new
donations. Even Arthur Tappan was prostrated. In addition, Oberlin's blatant abolitionism alienated Easterners with less radical
views on the subject of slavery. At the beginning of 1839 Oberlin
again faced extinction.

The only alternative was to seek funds in England, which in
1833 had emancipated her slaves and expressed considerable sympathy with American abolitionists. On May 20, 1839, John Keep
and William Dawes started for England, subscription books in
hand. Like Dartmouth's agents in the 1760's, Oberlin's representatives had a cause well calculated to open English purses. Then it
had been the Indian to whom the blessings of religion must be
extended; now the Negro needed to be freed. Portraying Oberlin
as the American center of the antislavery movement, Keep and
Dawes collected thirty thousand dollars and in 1840 returned tri-
umphantly to Ohio.[65] Once again English philanthropy proved to
be the salvation of an American college.

Sectarian loyalty was another basis on which American colleges
could appeal for aid in England. In 1790 Georgetown University
in Washington, D.C. found some support among English Catholics,[66] but in 1823 Philander Chase struck a far richer vein when
he appealed to Anglicans to patronize an Episcopal college in Ohio.
He had the good fortune to become friends with influential members of the English nobility, especially Lord Kenyon and Lord
Gambier. But Chase had fund-raising talent of his own, as he
demonstrated in a letter to a wealthy English widow: "Amidst our
wild woods, where so lately were heard only the war-whoop of the

savage and the howlings of the forest wolf, will be sung the sweet songs of Zion, mellowed by the controlling power of the pealing organ." [67] This appeal netted several hundred pounds, and when Chase returned to Ohio in 1824 he brought with him more than $25,000 for Kenyon College.[68]

Private voluntary giving made possible the boom in colleges that took place in the eight decades after Independence. Because individuals, communities, and congregations were willing to support colleges throughout the country, American higher education acquired its present diffusion and diversity. In contrast to the Old World, where a few university centers held a monopoly of higher learning, few Americans of 1860 had to travel more than a hundred miles to find a college. Such a wealth of colleges implemented democracy.

On the debit side was the point James Bryce made on his visit in the 1880's, that the American passion for college founding leads "to the establishment of new colleges where none are needed, and where money would be better spent in improving those which exist." [69] To some extent this was true, but philanthropy had a way of weeding out from a horde of institutions those that merited survival. Writing in 1876, a college president observed: "If a college attracts to itself patronage and endowment, it has a right to live; if it does not, it will die. The law of natural selection applies to colleges as well as to the animal and vegetable world . . ." [70]

The question then came to what criteria would be used to judge fitness. If the answer was solely the ability to raise funds higher education would be the loser, since attracting philanthropy was not its *raison d'être*. The philanthropists, however, usually selected as recipients those colleges they believed to be most worthy of help as educational institutions. The selection, in turn, depended on what purpose a donor felt higher education should serve. On this point new ideas arose that challenged the traditional religion-oriented college even as it was undergoing nationwide extension.

Chapter IV

Toward a Practical Higher Education

At the same time that colleges and universities were springing up at practically every crossroads, a reorientation of their purpose gradually took place under the impact of demands for a more practical higher education. The desires of some nineteenth-century Americans that higher education dispense training with greater relevance to the problems of an expanding economy revealed itself in large-scale philanthropy supporting a redefinition of the traditional college curriculum. With the force of big money behind them, scientific, technological, and commercial instruction chipped substantial niches in the standard course of study.

Classical educators formerly regarded any interest in learning a specific vocational or professional skill as evidence of narrowness, if not of crass materialism. They expected the classical curriculum to discipline the various faculties of the mind in general. Practical education for making a living should properly come *after* college. Gentlemen, not engineers or businessmen, were thought to be the rightful product of four college years. But the exigencies of nation-building and the characteristic utilitarianism of Americans could not leave the classical colleges untouched. On every hand came the boast that Americans of the nineteenth century lived in a "new era," the highest stage yet on the ladder of progress. Were the classical colleges to go along for the ride? Many Americans answered negatively and asserted that higher education must also pass the test of utility. Indeed, many believed that colleges had a special responsibility to spearhead the nation's advance. In view of this, the logic, theology, and Latin traditionally dispensed in institutions of higher learning seemed sadly irrelevant. Instruction in these subjects seemed unlikely to produce a Fulton, a Morse, or an Edison. At the various world's fairs beginning in 1851, Americans had further reason to question the effectiveness of their colleges. The clear revelation in the exhibits of the superiority of European industrial products and design came as a shock.[1]

The pressure for change toward the practical that philanthropy applied to higher education during the nineteenth century depended also on the emergence of a new elite in American society. In roughly the first generation after Independence, entrepreneurs, financiers, and industrialists encroached on the stronghold of social and economic preeminence that classically trained "gentlemen" formerly dominated.[2] Increasingly the men of means were businessmen who built railroads, extended commercial networks, and directed the operation of factories. The confidence and self-esteem of this new elite distinguished it from the merchants and traders of colonial America. Practical men of affairs in that period aspired to the gentility of the clergyman, the lawyer, and the man of letters. But the businessman of the "new era" ceased trying to emulate aristocracy. Instead of complying with the old standards of social worth, they advanced new ones based on ability in practical affairs and financial success. And instead of patronizing the classical colleges run by and for the old elite, many nineteenth-century entrepreneurs sought to transform existing institutions or to found new ones that would be more responsive to current demands as *they* defined them. The great fortunes of the members of the new elite gave them the opportunity, through philanthropy, to implement their novel educational ideas.

A striking similarity existed in the careers and attitudes of the major benefactors of practical higher education. Their common experience in the world of business and industry impressed upon them the need for technical talent. They were well aware that the graduates coming from the campuses of the classical colleges were totally unprepared to meet the problems involved in building a bridge, operating a bank, or designing a machine. With few exceptions these businessmen-philanthropists were not college graduates.[3] Most of them had not needed the traditional curriculum to make a success in their professions and consequently had little desire to perpetuate what they considered a sterile tradition. Their vital education had come instead from participation in the world of affairs, and they were proud of it. But most shared the belief that they had learned the hard way. The Americans who patronized practical education did so in the belief that they themselves could have profited from a few years of intensive training at the beginning of their own careers. Their benefactions sought to correct a defect they perceived in the preparation America offered its young men and women by reorienting higher education in a utilitarian direction.

Scientific and technical training on the college level was not an American innovation. When technical institutes began to appear in the United States the Old World had already made extensive progress in this field. The names of Pestalozzi, Fellenberg, and Birkbeck, as well as institutions such as the École Polytechnique and the École Centrale des Arts et Manufactures in Paris and the Royal Institute of Great Britain were widely known in America.[4] To be sure, science, taught under the catch-all terms of "natural philosophy" and "natural history," was nothing new to the American college scene. It had been an important part of the classical curriculum and had received the benefactions of Thomas Hollis and other philanthropists in the colonial period.[5] But the classical orientation of scientific study precluded instruction in applied science or the training of engineers. However, there were a few attempts to alter the colonial curriculum. Benjamin Franklin was one of the first to question the efficacy of classical education in the New World setting. His *Proposals* of 1749, which began the movement for the College of Philadelphia, recognized that while Greek and Latin were suited for prospective clergymen, the study of geography, practical chemistry, the history of commerce, and English were far better equipment for the would-be man of affairs to take from his college years. But Franklin had little money to back his ideas, and he found his arguments ineffective in loosening the hold of tradition on the colonial colleges. What scientific instruction they offered was taught to train the mind and to reveal the glory of God's creation.

In the early nineteenth century a new note sounded in benefactions for science. In 1805 Harvard received thirty thousand dollars from 150 citizens of Boston to establish a professorship of natural history and a botanical garden. The Overseers expressed thanks for this promotion of a branch of learning that was calculated, they felt, not only "to give rational entertainment, but to promote the valuable interests of our country."[6] New ideas were stirring. Even more revealing were the conditions which Benjamin Thompson (Count Rumford), an American by birth who moved to England and gained widespread recognition as a physicist, placed on a bequest for Harvard. In 1816 he left a one thousand dollar annuity for a professorship, the holder of which was required to teach "the utility of the physical and mathematical sciences for the improvement of the useful arts, and for the extension of the industry, prosperity, happiness, and well being of society."[7] In 1835 Benjamin Bussey of Roxbury, Massachusetts signed a will bequeathing Harvard a two hundred-acre farm and other property worth about four hundred thousand dollars. The will stipulated that the farm must be used to establish "a course of instruction in practical agriculture . . . and in such other branches of natural science as may tend to promote a knowledge of practical agriculture."[8]

In the 1820's the first attempts to offer a scientific and technical education instead of the time-honored program received the contributions of interested businessmen and industrialists of the communities in which they were founded. In 1823 the Gardiner Lyceum in Gardiner, Maine, was opened with the purpose of instructing farmers and mechanics in the scientific principles of their profession. Courses were offered in chemistry, surveying, architecture, carpentry, and agriculture, with emphasis on applying theory to problems of everyday life. In his inaugural address the first president, young Benjamin Hale, made a statement of educational philosophy in regard to the Lyceum's students: "It is not sufficient for them, as for the general scholar, to be taught the general laws of chemistry; they must be instructed particularly in the chemistry of agriculture and the arts. It is not sufficient for them to be able to repeat and to demonstrate a few of the general laws of mechanics; they must be taught the application of the laws. They must be made acquainted with machines."[9] A large part of the support for this ideal, which was directly contrary to the objects and methods of classical education, came from Robert H. Gardiner, a local landholder interested in scientific farming. He gave 434 acres of land fronting on the Kennebec River as well as cash, but the lyceum closed after a decade.[10]

Other early efforts at reorienting education were more successful. In 1825 the Maryland Institute for the Promotion of the Mechanic Arts opened in Baltimore with the financial backing of a group of citizens who linked the prosperity of their city with the degree of training its technicians received.[11] At about the same time the appropriately named Franklin Institute began instruction for Philadelphians.

The careers of the three men most prominent in the Franklin Institute's early financial history suggest the source and the motives for support of pioneer ventures in technical education. James Ronaldson, the first president of the institute, was a typefounder and a leader in Philadelphia's cotton-textile industry. The second president and a founder of the institute was Samuel V. Merrick, whose career had included experience in manufacturing heavy machinery and service as chief engineer in the construction of Philadelphia's gas works and as first president of the Pennsylvania Central Railroad Company. Another founder, William H. Keating, was an expert in mineralogy and mining. Men like Ronaldson, Merrick, and Keating knew first-hand the importance of applied science to their vocations and were willing to back the training of skilled technicians with philanthropy.[12]

The benefactions of an heir of the Dutch patroons of the Hudson Valley gave the United States the honor of awarding the first degrees in civil engineering in an English-speaking nation.[13] Rensselaer School (later Rensselaer Polytechnic Institute) in Troy, New York, also offered America's first courses in higher agricultural education. The life of Stephen Van Rensselaer was unlike that of many of the benefactors of scientific and technical education; he had the benefit of a college education begun at Princeton and finished at Harvard. With more than a thousand farms in his giant estate, Van Rensselaer had, if anyone did, the right to call himself a gentleman. Yet, like men who made their fortunes in business and industry, Van Rensselaer was sensitive to the needs of a society concerned with material progress. The responsibility of his holdings in land impressed on him the need for the application of science to agriculture in the interests of more efficient production. In 1823 he patronized a geological and agricultural survey of central New York under the eminent zoologist and geologist Amos Eaton. Even earlier, Van Rensselaer's interest in engineering led him to propose a canal to connect the Hudson River and the Great Lakes. As chairman of the Erie Canal Commission he had every opportunity to become familiar with the technical requirements of such an undertaking and undoubtedly was frustrated at the shortage of competent engineers, surveyors, and mechanics to perform the work.[14]

As a result of his own experiences, Van Rensselaer was disposed to accept a suggestion by Eaton in 1824 that he patronize a small institution devoted to practical science. A letter of November 5, 1824, which the patroon signed, outlined the school's aim: "I have established a school at the north end of Troy, in Rensselaer county . . . for the purpose of instructing persons . . . in the *application of science to the common purposes of life.* My principal object is to qualify teachers for instructing the sons and daughters of farmers and mechanics . . . in the application of experimental chemistry, philosophy and natural history, to agriculture, domestic economy, the arts and manufactures. . . . I am inclined to believe that competent instructors may be produced in the school at Troy, who will be highly useful to the community in the diffusion of a very useful kind of knowledge, with its application to the business of living." [15]

The choice of Eaton as director of the school was fortunate, for he worked harmoniously with the philanthropist to build Rensselaer Polytechnic Institute into a college that within a few decades claimed the majority of the country's naturalists and engineers as its graduates.[16] After a few years, agricultural courses dropped out of the curriculum as civil engineering received increased attention. The methods of teaching as well as the curriculum marked an innovation in American higher education. Laboratory experiments and field work received primary emphasis and lectures, many of which were delivered by the students themselves, had only a supplementary function. The academic atmosphere was one of mutual investigation by students and teachers in practical subjects rather than the acquisition of gentlemanly accoutrements.[17]

Van Rensselaer intended to support his school for only three years and hoped that the public would then relieve him of the burden. He was disappointed in this expectation, however, and was obliged to continue his benefactions, which by 1832 amounted to about $25,000, besides the distribution of a number of scholarships. After 1851 the state of New York came to the aid of the institute with occasional appropriations, but they were small compared to the amount donated by alumni, trustees, and citizens of Troy.[18]

For two decades after its founding, Rensselaer and the military academy at West Point were the only institutions in the United States where higher training in applied science and technology could be obtained. Late in the 1840's, however, several of America's oldest institutions made places in their courses of study for practical scientific education. In each case philanthropy figured prominently in supporting the innovation.

At Harvard the pursuit of science, in the "pure" or classical sense, continued to be held in high esteem. In 1820 a voluntary subscription financed the establishment of a professorship of mineralogy and geology, and in 1842 the Fisher Professorship of Natural History and the Perkins Professorship of Mathematics were named in honor of their donors. The Rumford Professorship and Lectureship on the Application of Science to the Useful Arts of 1816 revealed the existence of a new purpose for scientific study on the part of both Count Rumford and the Harvard officials who accepted the bequest. The same idea—that scientific education in the colleges should serve society—was given eloquent expression in 1846 in the inaugural address of Harvard's president, Edward Everett. He anticipated the need for a twofold expansion of Harvard's science curriculum. A program of graduate study was one necessity and the other, "a school of theoretical and practical science, for the purpose especially of teaching its application to the arts of life, and of furnishing a supply of skillful engineers and of persons well qualified to explore and bring to light the inexhaustible natural treasures of the country, and to guide its vast industrial energies in their rapid development." [19] Shortly afterward several members of the faculty submitted to the Harvard Corporation a plan for a school of advanced instruction in literature and applied science. The college even established a "School of Instruction in Theoretical and Practical Science," but it existed only on paper.[20] In order to transform the idea into reality the expense barrier had to be surmounted. In this case Harvard was fortunate in attracting the attention of a philanthropist to whom the ideas for a scientific school outlined in Everett's inaugural had strong appeal.

Abbott Lawrence, a member of a family that had already demonstrated its proclivity for philanthropy, was born in Groton, Massachusetts and educated there at the district school and academy. In 1808 he became the apprentice of his brother, Amos Adams Lawrence, who was the proprietor of a Boston warehouse. The brothers formed a prosperous partnership and expanded their activities in 1845 into cotton and woolen textile manufacturing in Lawrence, Massachusetts.[21] In 1847 Harvard's treasurer, Samuel A. Eliot, and President Everett brought to Abbott Lawrence's attention the faculty plan for advanced literary and scientific instruction. Lawrence warmed to the scientific part of the proposal.

On June 7 he addressed to Eliot a long and thoughtful letter offering fifty thousand dollars for a school of applied science. He pointed out that the existing system of higher education in America was well suited to train theologians, doctors, and lawyers. "But where can we send those who intend to devote themselves to the practical applications of science? How educate our engineers, our miners, machinists, and mechanics?" His close involvement in the economic transformation of New England put him in an ideal position to recognize that "the application of science to the useful arts has changed, in the last half-century, the condition and relations of the world." He cited the contributions of the German chemist Justus Liebig to agriculture as a case in point. But he realized painfully that America had been "somewhat neglectful in the cultivation and encouragement of the scientific portion of our national economy." [22]

Lawrence's letter proposed a school for men who had already completed their college education and intended to become engineers, chemists, or "men of science" in general. The areas in which instruction should be given, he stated, were engineering, mining and metallurgy, and the invention and manufacture of machinery, in that order. Assuming that Harvard's Rumford Professor, Eben W. Horsford, would teach chemistry, Lawrence called for the creation of professorships in engineering and geology as the nucleus of the school. He concluded by offering his donation "to be appropriated as I have indicated in the foregoing remarks." [23]

The failure of Harvard to comply with all the philanthropist's requests and Lawrence's own changes in the plans resulted in large

part from the presence in America of the eminent Swiss zoologist,
Louis Agassiz. Agassiz arrived in October, 1846 and took the country by storm with a combination of scholarly attainment and the
ability to entrance popular audiences. Harvard was extremely desirous of securing the services of so distinguished a European scientist, and several friends suggested to Abbott Lawrence the possibility that his gift might induce Agassiz to accept a professorship.
That was precisely what happened. On October 3, 1847, Agassiz
accepted the professorship of zoology and geology created for
him by the Harvard Corporation with the Lawrence benefaction.[24]

Agassiz was hardly the man to teach the practical science Lawrence had originally contemplated. The Swiss naturalist's knowledge of geology was most acute in the field of glaciation and had
nothing to do with mining and metallurgy. His interest in collecting
fish and other specimens for studies in comparative zoology
similarly had little relevance to practical matters. But he was a
prestige scientist whom Harvard and Lawrence found irresistible.
When in 1850 a building was completed for the Lawrence Scientific
School, as it was named at commencement in 1848, Agassiz moved
in with his collections of specimens. Lawrence evidently approved
this modification of his plans; in 1849 he guaranteed payment
of Agassiz's salary for five years. In 1853 Lawrence again promised
payment for the scientist's services, although he refused to establish
a permanent zoological museum.[25]

Although the magnetism of Louis Agassiz swayed Lawrence
from his intention to establish a school of applied science in which
the study of geology would aid mining, the philanthropist's plans
for engineering instruction bore fruit. In 1849 Henry L. Eustis, formerly a professor at the United States Military Academy, came to
Harvard as professor of engineering in the Lawrence Scientific
School. By 1855 the institution was offering, according to the annual report, "thorough practical instruction" in chemistry and engineering. Apparently pleased with what his benefactions had accomplished, Lawrence bequeathed the school a second fifty thousand dollars, which it received on his death in 1855.[26] But Lawrence's heirs were dissatisfied with the failure of the Lawrence Scientific School to produce competent technicians and engineers. The
pressure they created by 1870 caused Harvard's new president,
Charles William Eliot, to make overtures to the young and flour-

ishing Massachusetts Institute of Technology for a consolidation, but Eliot's proposal was rebuffed.[27]

What Abbott Lawrence was to Harvard, Abiel Chandler and Sylvanus Thayer were to the college in Hanover, N.H. In 1851 Dartmouth received a completely unsolicited bequest of fifty thousand dollars from Chandler, a Boston businessman. The donor's will stipulated that the money be applied to the instruction of "the practical or useful arts of life composed chiefly in the branches of mechanics and civil engineering, the invention and manufacture of machinery . . . together with bookkeeping and such other branches of knowledge as may best qualify young persons for the duties and employments of active life. . . ."[28] Completely taken aback, Dartmouth's president, Nathan Lord, hesitated to accept the bequest for fear of the possible effect on his college's traditional academic standards. Moreover, neither he nor his faculty had any idea how the new subjects were to be taught. But for any college in the mid-nineteenth century fifty thousand dollars was not to be lightly regarded. Lord carefully explained that he was expanding and changing the substance of the present system, and in 1852 Dartmouth opened the Chandler School of Science and the Arts.[29]

Philanthropy made possible another step in the same direction when Sylvanus Thayer gave Dartmouth forty thousand dollars in 1867 and shortly afterward added thirty thousand for a graduate school of civil engineering. Like most of the philanthropists of scientific and technological education in the nineteenth century, Thayer gave to strengthen the profession in which he made his money. After graduating from Dartmouth in 1807, Thayer joined the faculty of the United States Military Academy and began a distinguished career as an engineer. He studied in Europe and on his return shaped the academy into America's foremost engineering center. At Dartmouth the Thayer School of Civil Engineering opened in 1871.[30]

The change that took place in the educational ideas of President Lord was one result of the philanthropy for applied science that Dartmouth received. Like most of the traditional college presidents, Lord was a clergyman and a firm believer in the merits of a classical higher education. In 1828, just beginning his presidency, Lord asserted that Dartmouth would hold fast to the time-honored moorings. *His* college was not to be "designed for individuals who were

to engage in mercantile, mechanical or agricultural operations." [31]
But later, reflecting on four decades in which the Chandler and
Thayer benefactions along with federal land-grant money for agricultural education wrought great changes in Dartmouth, Lord
displayed a different attitude. He wrote of the "necessity now becoming constantly more evident of a higher education in the 'practical and useful arts of life.'" Those engaging in professional pur-
suits had declined not only in number but in what Lord referred
to as "the general estimation." A new elite of manufacturers, industrialists, businessmen, and scientific farmers had replaced them
in the American social hierarchy. President Lord had doubts about
the consequences of this transformation, but he realized that it
was "a law no more to be overcome than that of gravity." Consequently, cooperation and direction of the new order on the part of
educators seemed a better policy than resistance.[32] Faced with the
rise of a new and wealthy elite, men like Nathan Lord either had
to adapt to new demands or forfeit their college's share of the philanthropy earmarked for a practical higher education. President
Lord chose to put Dartmouth on the side of the newer and more
lucrative ideas. Philanthropy had been a crucial factor in his intellectual about-face.

   At Yale, as at Harvard, the college took the first steps in loosening
the hold of the classical curriculum, but a philanthropist's dollars
brought the new ideas to fruition. In August, 1846, at the same
time Harvard was making plans for its scientific school, the Yale
Corporation resolved that two new professorships be established.
John P. Norton was to be professor of agricultural chemistry and
vegetable and animal physiology, and Benjamin Silliman, Jr., professor of practical chemistry. Silliman was to teach "the application
of chemistry, and the kindred sciences to the manufacturing arts,
to exploration of the resources of the country and to other practical
uses." [33] In 1852 the Corporation appointed William A. Norton professor of civil engineering, and three years later it designated George
J. Brush as professor of metallurgy. But the Yale Scientific School,
as the combined chemical and engineering program was called
after 1854, struggled against the burden of inadequate financial
resources. The Yale Corporation, when creating the professorships,
had assured their incumbents that the college was too poor to pay
even their salaries, much less support a school. Silliman, Brush, and

the two Nortons were left to their own devices in the matter of finance, and by 1857 it was apparent that the venture was in danger of collapse.[34] They had only to look northward to Providence, where President Francis Wayland was abortively attempting to reorient Brown's classical curriculum in a practical direction, to see that chances of success were slight without philanthropic support of the business community. The problem was to locate a man of wealth who would back the new trend.

With this goal in mind, Yale undertook an intensive publicity campaign. In 1856 Yale's well-known geologist and mineralogist, James Dwight Dana, addressed the alumni on the need of endowment for the Scientific School if it were to meet the demands of mid-century America. Dana softened the implied blow to the traditional curriculum with the assertion that the school's program so blended the classical with the practical that the student would graduate "not shaped only for a single narrow channel of life, but with cultivated intellect and broad views of the world . . ."[35] The Yale faculty sought to encourage philanthropy with a reassuring declaration: "During its whole existence, Yale College has shown itself a safe and prudent trustee of all funds committed to its keeping; and no better guarantee can be desired than its history furnishes for the faithful appropriations of all funds which the future may place at its disposal. The names of Governor Yale, and Bishop Berkeley, of Clark, Munson, Perkins, and many others, are inseparable and honorably connected with her history, and are destined to live forever in grateful remembrance."[36]

Daniel Coit Gilman, a young scientist who had previously taught at the Lawrence Scientific School and later became the first president of The Johns Hopkins University, also campaigned on behalf of Yale. His approach was well calculated to open the pockets of industrialists and businessmen. He began with the assertion that America was quickly learning that "for a long and successful competition with the manufactures of Europe the same union must be established . . . which exists abroad, between Applied and Theoretical Science." His conclusion clinched the argument for progress-minded men of affairs: "It is a characteristic of our citizens to do upon a liberal scale whatever is attempted. Our colleges, our popular schools, our public libraries, our observatories have often received munificent endowments. In the present condition of our country, it is not less important that a Scientific School of the highest order should receive a corresponding degree of sympathy and support. Anything less than a liberal provision for its wants, would but half accomplish the task that is to be performed. Large investment, on the other hand, will re-act most efficiently on the welfare of the land." [37] Had Gilman desired, he could have cited as an example of the utility of scientific schools the analyses John P. Norton made in 1848 on crude and vulcanized rubber for a hopeful industrialist named Charles Goodyear.[38]

One of the New Haven residents who heard the cries for aid issuing from Yale's floundering Scientific School was Joseph Earl Sheffield. Born in Connecticut, Sheffield had quit school at the age of fourteen to go South and make a fortune in cotton. In 1835 he returned to New Haven and began building railroads and canals.[39] One of Sheffield's daughters married John A. Porter, who in 1852 succeeded John P. Norton as director of the Yale venture. This connection prompted Sheffield to give five thousand dollars to the Scientific School in 1853, and three years later he added an equal amount. Shortly after his initial gifts Sheffield offered about one hundred thousand dollars for a building and equipment for the school and for an endowment for its professorships. In recognition of his philanthropy the Yale Corporation in 1861 attached Sheffield's name to the institution. In later years Sheffield's benefactions continued, permitting the institution to expand. In 1864 the Sheffield Scientific School became the land-grant college of Connecticut under the Morrill Act of 1862, a development that greatly pleased the philanthropist. At Sheffield's death in 1882 Yale received more than five hundred thousand dollars, bringing his total contributions in the name of applied science to an unprecedented $1,100,000.[40]

Sheffield's motives were simple and clear: "I take special pleasure in promoting here the study of physical, natural and mathematical sciences with reference to their practical applications." [41] His relations with Yale approached the ideal in educational philanthropy, according to the statement of the Sheffield Scientific School's governing board in the year of his death: "His whole conduct in connection with the institution was governed entirely by a disinterested zeal in behalf of higher education, which is rare even among those who have made great contributions to advance it, and by a clear sighted judgment, often entirely unknown to men even of great cultivation, which recognized the fact that schools of learning can only be successfully managed by those who know what learning is." [42] Joseph Sheffield provides one of the best examples of a nineteenth-century businessman-philanthropist who had made his own way to success and in the process realized that traditional higher education was totally unsuited for training young men to meet the new demands in the world of affairs they would encounter outside the campus.

Philanthropy was vital to the transformation of a number of other institutions. Lafayette College, for example, was a struggling Presbyterian institution with a purely classical curriculum until the 1860's, when it received the benefactions of Ario Pardee. Thereafter it enjoyed a rebirth as a leading center of applied science and engineering. Pardee's training was like that of most of the philanthropists of practical higher education. "My education," he said, "was limited to what I learned at my father's fireside and the ordinary district school; though, fortunately I had for a time the advantage of an excellent teacher in the Reverend Moses Hunter, a Presbyterian clergyman who . . . taught our district school two winters. I was then fifteen years old, and his teaching about finished my school education, though I was an industrious worker at my books at home." [43] Pardee learned engineering as a rodman for surveyors, and he subsequently extended his interests to include iron and coal operations. His contribution of three hundred thousand dollars for a science building was more than all of Lafayette's other buildings were worth. For those colleges like Lafayette that would embrace the utilitarian trend in higher education, the result was frequently financial salvation.

Although applied science led the way, commerce and business administration soon followed in receiving the support of practical-minded philanthropists, enabling these subjects to enter the college curriculum. In most respects the motives for giving were similar, but the supporters of higher training in business had the added incentive of establishing it as a profession worthy of learning, teaching, and respect.

On March 1, 1881, the trustees of the University of Pennsylvania received a communication from a Philadelphia manufacturer of zinc, nickel, and iron named Joseph Wharton. He pointed out that numerous technical and scientific schools had been established as the result of "the general conviction that college education did little toward fitting for the actual duties of life any but those who purpose to become lawyers, doctors, or clergymen. . . ."[44] Then he observed that unfortunately there was no comparable training for a commercial career, and he proposed to found at Pennsylvania a "School of Finance and Economy." The hundred thousand dollars Wharton offered to fulfill his proposal tempted the trustees into immediate acceptance. The Wharton School of Finance and Commerce, the first of its kind in the United States, later received five hundred thousand dollars more from its founder.[45]

At the root of Wharton's decision to support practical higher education was his dislike of the traditional college curriculum as a preparation for future businessmen. In an address of 1890 entitled "Is a College Education Advantageous to a Business Man?", he said that "a very small proportion of the successful business men of this country have been college graduates, and a very small proportion of the college graduates successful business men."[46] Wharton's own career was a case in point. His formal education ended at sixteen, when he began to work on a farm. Later he entered a Philadelphia countinghouse and learned the principles of bookkeeping and business administration.[47] This background encouraged in him a scornful attitude toward classical higher education. In his 1890 address he declared: "It will scarcely be disputed that college life offers great temptations and opportunities for the formation of superficial light-weight characters, having shallow accomplishments but lacking in grip and hold upon real things. . . . Our college system is liable to breed distaste, if not disability, for that close grapple with sordid earth-born cares which beset every man's path, and which must be conquered."[48] It occurred to Wharton that the solution was to reorient higher education toward the practical, and he was willing to apply his wealth to this purpose.

Wharton's ideas did not stop at simply desiring collegiate instruction in business subjects. He wanted particular views to be taught, especially the necessity of a protective tariff for American industry. Wharton was a leading spokesman for manufacturers' organizations opposing free trade. He advocated protection before Congress and in numerous tracts and addresses, and his philanthropy was consistent with these convictions. In his 1881 letter to the trustees of the University of Pennsylvania, Wharton included a section bearing the heading "General Tendency of Instruction." In it he demanded that, among other things, the Wharton School must teach its students "the necessity for each nation to care for its own, and to maintain by all suitable means its industrial and financial independence." He firmly added that "no apologetic or merely defensive style of instruction must be tolerated upon this point, but the right and duty of national self-protection must be firmly asserted and demonstrated." [49] He was apparently satisfied in later years that the school had complied with these demands, but he maintained his attack on "the sneers and sophistries of pedants" opposing protectionism in other colleges. He found it remarkable that American manufacturers continued philanthropic support of these institutions. [50]

Philanthropy also accounted for the inception of higher business education at other colleges. John D. Rockefeller's millions backed the College of Commerce and Administration that opened at the University of Chicago in 1898, and two years later a group of New York City businessmen donated both their instructional ability and their financial resources in establishing a School of Commerce, Accounts, and Finance at New York University. [51] The Amos Tuck School of Business Administration at Dartmouth was established in 1900 as a result of the benefactions of Edward Tuck in memory of his father. Both Tucks were Dartmouth graduates, and the son made his money in banking and investment. He established the school for college students "who desire to engage in affairs rather than enter the professions." [52] At Harvard the graduate program in business administration, which began in 1908, received five million dollars from the banker-industrialist George F. Baker. This windfall enabled it to move into quarters of its own and assume national importance in its field. [53] The philanthropy of Wharton, Tuck, Baker, and the others spearheaded an extension in the scope of higher education in the American college and university with the aim of developing men capable of giving skilled practical leadership to America's business and industrial concerns.

Some benefactors of practical higher education in the nineteenth century were not content to make their donations to colleges that already existed. In many cases these philanthropists felt that only in their own institutions could their educational ideas be given complete and unopposed implementation. Stephen Van

Rensselaer was the first American to use his wealth to found an institution dispensing what he conceived to be a more useful sort of training than was found in the classical colleges. Not until 1859 did the doors of the next major undertaking open as the result of the benefactions of a remarkable New Yorker named Peter Cooper.

Unlike Van Rensselaer, but in the pattern of most philanthropists who supported the practical in higher education, Cooper was self-made financially and educated without the benefit of college. As a traveling salesman, retail grocer, glue-factory proprietor and, ultimately, ironworks and telegraph magnate, Cooper amassed well over a million dollars. He also became acquainted with the needs of the American working public.[54] His philosophy of philanthropy was summarized in the statement: "While I have always recognized that the object of business is to make money in an honorable manner, I have endeavored to remember that the object of life is to do good." [55]

Cooper first formed about 1828 the idea of establishing an institution for the practical education of youth. The stimulus was a friend's account of the work of the École Polytechnique in Paris. Cooper learned that young Frenchmen lived on crusts of bread and underwent a variety of hardships just to study there. Then, recalling his own experience, he admitted: "[H]ow glad I would have been, if I could have found such an institution in my youth in [New York City], with its doors open to give instruction at night, the only time that I could command for study. And I then reflected at the fact that there must be a great many young men in this country, situated as I was, who thirsted for the knowledge they could not reach, and would gladly avail themselves of opportunities which they had no money to procure." [56] Benjamin Franklin had approximately the same idea in 1749 but could only spare ten dollars for the College of Philadelphia then in the process of organization. To his disappointment, Franklin saw the college turn away from his ideals of an institution offering Philadelphia's youth cheap and practical instruction. Money enabled Cooper to establish the kind of educational institution he wanted.

At an initial expense of more than six hundred thousand dollars, Cooper built the school of his dreams in downtown New York City. In 1859 he turned the Cooper Union over to a board of trustees "to be forever devoted to the advancement of science and art, in their application to the varied and useful purposes of life." [57] It opened on November 2 of the same year with a diversified program including night courses in applied science and industrial arts as well as political and social science, a library and reading room, a school of useful arts for women, and public lectures on general subjects. All the services of Cooper Union were free of charge and open to all regardless of race, color, or religious faith. No longer was higher education the exclusive province of gentlemen. Cooper Union offered a five-year course of study leading to degrees in various technical sciences. To be sure there were scoffers at Cooper and his radical ideas about higher education. George Templeton Strong, for example, wrote in 1856 that "Cooper is very well meaning but very silly for a self-made millionaire. All his conceptions of his future university . . . are amorphous, preposterous and impractical. Unless he has wise counsel, and consents to follow it, he will produce nothing but $500,000 worth of folly." [58] The New York public did not agree with Strong's reservations, and persons of all ages swamped the union, filling its courses to capacity in the first day of registration. As training began for over a thousand students in a variety of practical subjects, Peter Cooper had the satisfaction of seeing his dream become a reality.

In the years following the opening of his union, Cooper continued to support it with money and constant interest. His ultimate objective embodied the ideas and spirit of the Enlightenment and was akin to that of classical education: the production of a superior human being. Man, using reason and living in a democratic society, had the chance to realize his full potentialities. The sole impediment was ignorance. With educational opportunities man could live the moral life God intended for him. Although Cooper put the love of man before that of science and industry, he was convinced that the proper means for helping men to more satisfying lives lay in a practical rather than a classical curriculum. It was this motive that stimulated him to make one of the most creative applications of philanthropy to American higher education. Before his death in 1883 he gave more than one and a half million dollars to the Cooper Union, and bequests in his will and gifts from his family brought the ultimate total to well over two million. [59]

The founding of Cooper Union was a spur to other Americans with money and a belief in practical higher education. The numerous "institutes" that resulted were for the most part the creations of men with similar backgrounds and values. The typical founder, like Peter Cooper, was educated through village schools, apprenticeship, and experience in the world of business and industry. One trait common to all of them was a dissatisfaction with existing schools and colleges. Their purpose in founding technical institutions was to provide the type of education needed in a society whose forte was economic expansion and technological advancement. In their own business experience, the businessmen-philanthropists found that higher education did not supply either the skilled technicians or the inventive scientists with an eye to the application of their discoveries required by industrial progress.

Immediately following the Civil War, several new schools of technology opened in the country's scattered industrial complexes. New England industrialists had long desired an institution in their region where research in the applied sciences could be pursued and skilled technicians trained. The Lawrence Scientific School at Harvard was a partial disappointment in this respect, and as early as 1846 William Barton Rogers prepared plans for a polytechnic institute. He took the lead in 1861 in securing a charter for the institution known today as the Massachusetts Institute of Technology. But the charter required the proposed school to accumulate a fund of a hundred thousand dollars within a year before it would be confirmed. As the allotted time expired and an extension neared its deadline, Rogers was still short of the required amount. At the last moment in 1863 a donation of sixty thousand dollars arrived from William J. Walker, a wealthy physician who had already given to several liberal-arts colleges in New England. M.I.T. also obtained a share of the state's land-grant money under the Morrill Act of 1862, but it was philanthropy that sustained the school, which opened in 1865, in its precarious early years.[60]

A bright future lay ahead. Between 1912 and 1920 M.I.T. received almost twenty million dollars from the Rochester, New York camera manufacturer, George Eastman. President Richard C. Maclaurin openly solicited Eastman's philanthropy with flattering comments about his Rochester plant and the proposal that he aid M.I.T. in a major building program.[61] Even more persuasive from Eastman's point of view were a number of valuable technicians in the Eastman Kodak Company who had received their training at the institution.[62] The large-scale giving of Eastman and others launched M.I.T. on its great career in the twentieth century as a pioneer in new areas of technology that proved of vital importance to national industry and defense.

Pennsylvania's mineral-rich Lehigh Valley was the site of another post-Civil War foundation. The valley already had three small and struggling institutions, but Asa Packer felt it needed another deriving its spirit and purpose from science and technology rather than from classical models. Packer himself owed nothing to classical higher education. After a limited education in the local schools of Groton, Connecticut, he had launched enterprises involving canals, coal, and railroads. As he conceived Lehigh University, it would be a "polytechnic college" teaching civil, mechanical, and mining engineering and making use of the splendid opportunities the industrialized Lehigh Valley presented for field work. Packer began his benefactions to Lehigh with a half million dollars and 115 acres of land in South Bethlehem, Pennsylvania. The men he placed in control of the institution, which opened in 1865, were entrepreneurs with coal, railroad, and iron interests in the valley. But while Packer approved of the dominance of engineering in Lehigh's curriculum, in 1878 he blocked an attempt of some alumni to exclude the liberal arts completely. Before his death in 1879 and through his will, Packer increased his support of Lehigh to more than two million dollars, but he steadfastly refused to let the institution adopt his name.[63]

In most cases, philanthropic support of practical higher education reflected the vocational interests of the donor. Invention and engineering were family traditions with Edwin A. Stevens. His father, John Stevens, was a pioneer in the application of steam power to watercraft, and builder of the first steam-driven engine and train in America. The son invented an improved plow and, with his brother, the first iron-clad warship. Stevens's father hoped that part of the family fortune could be applied to the establishment of a college-level technical institute. Edwin determined to respect these hopes, but unlike Peter Cooper he had little personal interest in shaping an institution during his lifetime.

Stevens's will, dated 1867, bequeathed $650,000 to found an institution in Hoboken, New Jersey, but did not lay specific plans for its curriculum and purpose. After his death the following year

the executors decided that, in view of Stevens's interests, technological education would be an appropriate use of the bequest and
secured the services of Henry Morton as the first president. This
proved a fortunate choice, because Morton created at the Stevens
Institute of Technology one of the nation's finest programs in mechanical engineering. The decision of the executors and the en-
ergy of President Morton made a success of the indiscriminate
variety of philanthropy that Edwin Stevens practiced.[64]

The conviction that a new age of industrial development demanded new forms of higher education with an emphasis on applied science motivated Leonard Case to donate more than two
million dollars to found and sustain the Case School of Applied
Science in Cleveland, Ohio. A quiet and scholarly Yale graduate
whose father made a fortune in banking and real estate, Case's
career differed from that of the usual nineteenth-century donor to
practical education. But unlike Edwin Stevens, Case gave considerable thought to the problem of disposing his fortune. In 1880,
when the Case School was incorporated, the trustees had before
them the philanthropist's specific instructions in regard to curriculum and course of study.[65]

The first technical institutions served as guides for those established in later years. Worcester Polytechnic Institute, which the
philanthropy of Massachusetts manufacturers had begun in 1865,
furnished both the model and the first president for Rose Polytechnic Institute of Terre Haute, Indiana, which opened in 1883.

Chauncey Rose had received only village-school education when
he left his birthplace in Connecticut to follow the advice of Horace
Greeley. He went as far west as Terre Haute and established himself as a contractor and merchant. Like so many of his contempo-
raries, he found in the spreading network of railroads the way to
wealth. Rose began his philanthropy with several gifts to a small
Presbyterian college in Indiana but was dissatisfied with its traditional program.[66] As early as 1874 he determined to found a technical institute. Admittedly unequipped to plan a college, Rose dispatched two agents to make a survey of existing institutions offering practical instruction. The program at Worcester appealed to
him as did its president, Charles O. Thompson, who soon was on his
way to Indiana. Before he came, however, Rose sent him on a tour
of European technical institutes to collect information and ideas.

After almost a decade of planning and the expenditure of five hundred thousand dollars, Rose Polytechnic Institute received its first students. They could choose as a four-year course of study either mechanical, electrical, or civil engineering combined with architecture or chemistry.[67]

Time and again the founders of institutes for practical higher education listed as a prime motive their personal experiences as young men in a society that provided no facilities for learning useful skills. Charles Pratt was one of a family of ten born on a Massachusetts farm. He clerked in a Boston grocery, served as a machinist's apprentice, and entered a New York paint and oil firm. As an old man reflecting on his life, Pratt declared: "In my early youth I had to struggle, as most young men do, for a living. At first I worked on a farm, but finally learned a trade and then at about 19 years of age went into commercial business. Twenty or more years ago when I began to have a family ready for school, I felt the need of a place for their education, which led me to become connected with the school to which they went—the Adelphi Academy. My connection . . . with . . . that institution . . . and my interest in the young, led me to feel, as soon as my business promised a competency, that I would try and do something for young people situated as I had been." [68]

Pratt's business, crude-oil refining, soon attained the desired "competency" and was absorbed in 1874 in the Standard Oil Company, in which Pratt became a leading executive. But the amassing of wealth did not gratify him. "The greatest humbug in this world," he told a friend, "is the idea that the mere possession of money can make any man happy. I never got any satisfaction out of mine until I began to do good with it." [69]

The example of Peter Cooper admittedly guided Pratt in his efforts to perform good works. It seemed to Pratt that Cooper Union, with its utilitarian emphasis, had done more for New York than any classical college. Consequently the act of incorporation of the Pratt Institute, dated May 19, 1887, defined its curriculum as "such branches of useful and practical knowledge as are not now generally taught in the public and private schools [of New York]." [70] Pratt's basic desire was to help young New Yorkers help themselves through the study of architecture, mechanical drawing, decorating, bookkeeping, stenography, and similar skills. His disappointment was great when only twelve students presented themselves for the opening of classes in 1887, but within a year the enrollment was more than a thousand. Both young people wanting to learn a mechanical or artistic trade and individuals already engaged in such vocations in search of further training were welcome. Pratt was careful to provide his institute with adequate endowment as well as plant and equipment. At the time of his death in 1891, Pratt had donated more than three million dollars toward higher technical education.[71]

Other major cities in the East soon found their equivalents of Peter Cooper and Charles Pratt. In 1900 Andrew Carnegie made a gift of two million dollars to his adopted city, Pittsburgh, for a technical school. Opened in 1905, it quickly developed a college program and, as the Carnegie Institute of Technology, became a leader in the teaching and advanced study of metallurgy while expanding its program to include the humanities and fine arts. Carnegie supported its work directly with five million dollars more and the Carnegie Corporation appropriated four times that amount.[72]

In Philadelphia it was the three million dollars of the banker Anthony J. Drexel that enabled the Drexel Institute to open in 1891 with departments of art, science and technology, domestic economy, and business as well as programs of evening classes, public lectures, and exhibits. Drexel's purpose was similar to Peter Cooper's: the provision of an opportunity for anyone who desired it to obtain training in the skills required for success in an industrial age.[73]

The remarks of Chauncey M. Depew at the inaugural ceremonies of the Drexel Institute in 1891 summarized much of the philosophy of higher technical education that motivated men like Anthony Drexel. Depew pointed out that the "culture" the classical colleges sought to impart had become "the veneer of the quack, and finally the decoration of the dude." He continued: "[I]t was not culture, either in its lofty significance or in its degraded use, which the times required. They needed the practical training of youth for the new and sterner realities which science and invention had created. The old education simply trained the mind. The new trains the mind, the muscles, and the senses. The old education gave the intellect a vast mass of information useful in the library and useless in the shop."[74] In the face of new demands, Depew accused the classical college of retreating to a hostile defense of its conservative curriculum and methods. He recognized that a few colleges had scientific departments but applauded the technical institutes as being more in step with the times and of more value to society and country.

On the West Coast a self-made entrepreneur named James Lick bequeathed $540,000 to found a mechanical-arts school. Although the bequest was made in the 1870's, the will, which included a $700,000 bequest for an observatory, was contested, and the California School of Mechanical Arts did not open in San Francisco until 1896. It offered two-year courses in manual training and in the technical skills of ten industrial occupations. Lick's institution later combined with the Wilmerding School of Industrial Arts, also the result of one man's philanthropy, to form one of the West's centers of higher industrial education.[75] Farther south in Pasadena, Amos G. Throop donated two hundred thousand dollars in 1891 for the creation of a polytechnic institution offering training on both secondary and collegiate levels. In 1903 Arthur H. Fleming, a Canadian-born lumber magnate, became a member of the board of Throop Polytechnic Institute and began a series of contributions that transformed it into California Institute of Technology. Fleming's five million dollars enabled Cal Tech to attract outstanding scientists who won world renown for the institution as a research and training center in the physical sciences and their applications.[76]

A technical institute for Chicago resulted from a combination of the money of Philip D. Armour and the ideas of Frank W. Gunsaulus. Armour, typically, received only a village-school education and then turned to the world of business. After a try at mining on the West Coast and the wholesale grocery business in Milwaukee, Armour joined his brothers in a meat-packing company in Chicago. When Frank W. Gunsaulus came to Chicago in 1887 as pastor of the Plymouth Congregational Church, Armour was worth millions and had already begun to give portions of his wealth to philanthropic ventures.

Gunsaulus, who numbered Armour among his congregation, was convinced of the importance of technological education for American greatness and as a means of building character in youth. He put these ideas into his sermons. In one in particular, entitled "If I

had a Million Dollars," Gunsaulus declared that if he were a millionaire his wealth would found a technical institute. A millionaire
was in his audience this particular Sunday. Armour is said to have
approached Gunsaulus after the sermon and asked, "Young man,
do you believe what you just preached?" The pastor assured him
that he did, whereupon Armour declared, "I will give you a million dollars, if you will give me five years of your life." [77] What
Armour had in mind was for Gunsaulus to direct a technical institute in Chicago that he would found and support.

Armour had several reasons for desiring to undertake a philanthropic venture in practical education. He realized, for one thing,
that his public reputation could stand improvement. The execra-
ble working conditions in the Chicago stockyards and the equally
bad living conditions in the "stockyard district" were gradually
becoming matters of public knowledge and concern. The intensity
of these feelings in the late 1880's and early 1890's did not equal
that of the following decade, but in 1891, two years before the
Armour Institute of Technology opened, a Senate investigating
committee disclosed unflattering facts about the meat-packing
giants' treatment of cattlemen, small competitors, and customers.[78]
Armour could not have failed to appreciate the beneficial effects
of a large expenditure of money in the public interest on his reputation and that of his company. A technical institute also appealed
to Armour as the source of valuable industrial improvements. His
company, the first to recognize the desirability of coupling science
and meat packing, established a research department in 1885.[79]

Together Armour and Gunsaulus planned the institute. Correspondence was exchanged with previous founders, including Pratt
and Drexel, and in 1892 the philanthropist and the minister visited
their schools as well as the Cooper Union. Armour sank about two
million dollars in plant and endowment, and the institute opened
in 1893. At first he envisioned the school as serving the needs of
economically underprivileged men and women who sought vocational training or a practically oriented high-school education. But
even before it opened he agreed to expand its program to include
work in engineering at the college level. Within the first decade
President Gunsaulus and his faculty dropped most of the work
that did not contribute directly to a student's progress through high
school and college toward a bachelor of science degree in engi-

neering. After the death of his father in 1901, J. Ogden Armour presented seven and a half million dollars to the school, which subsequently became the Illinois Institute of Technology, for a new campus and buildings. Behind this gift too was the persuasive influence of Frank W. Gunsaulus.[80]

Private philanthropy was not the only means by which practical higher education advanced in the United States. The federal government gave impetus to the movement with the Morrill Act of 1862, which created the land-grant colleges. The descriptive title of this measure was "an act donating Public Lands to the Several States and Territories which may provide Colleges for the Benefit of Agriculture and Mechanic Arts," [81] and the state universities, many of which received land-grant money, usually defined higher education in a utilitarian fashion. In fact, considerably prior to the Morrill Act it was a state institution, the University of Virginia, that pioneered under Thomas Jefferson's leadership in reorienting its curriculum in a practical direction.[82] Several colleges also undertook the addition of courses in applied science and technology without the aid of donations for that specific purpose. But philanthropy provided the major impetus for the shift toward the practical in higher education.

The nineteenth century in no sense ended with a "victory" of practical over classical education. What took place in the years after Stephen Van Rensselaer founded the first major scientifically oriented college in the United States was a reorientation, not a revolution. The humanities, theology, and social studies remained in the college curriculum and continued to receive some philanthropic support, but they were obliged to make extensive room for the strong young newcomers, applied science, commerce, and technology. Daniel Coit Gilman expressed the spirit of compromise and acceptance he hoped was emerging: "Heretofore, the complaint has been that the classics were the only means of liberal education. Henceforward science will offer its aids to intellectual culture in organized schools. Both classes of institutions will flourish side by side, and each will be strong in the other's strength. The Creator and his laws, man and his development, or, in other words, science and history, alike offer abundant discipline for the mind, and appropriate preparation for the active work of life." [83] Most American colleges entered the new century with this ideal, but frequently the attraction of philanthropists to the practical threatened to disrupt the balance Gilman saw between the liberal arts and the applied sciences. Although entrepreneurs like Armour avoided it, there was danger also in the tendency of some bene-factors to regard the scientific schools or departments they sup-ported as research laboratories producing information and person-nel. But philanthropists of the nineteenth century attached few conditions either in letter or spirit to their donations other than that they should be used to promote a certain kind of training. Occa-sionally a Joseph Wharton would insist that the protective tariff be championed in his school, but the primary motive in giving was to extend to America's future businessmen, engineers, and in-ventors the benefits of a formal practical education that the do-nors themselves had missed.

The emergence of a practical curriculum was an innovation of great significance for colleges and universities. The efforts of nu-merous philanthropists, combined in some cases with the ideas of others, worked creatively to produce a profound change in Ameri-can higher education with broad economic, technological, and so-cial repercussions. In his 1883 inaugural address at Rose Polytech-nic Institute, President Charles O. Thompson declared: "The day has forever passed when the old idea that the study of Latin, Greek and the humanities is the only education. The definition of an edu-cated man will bear still more expansion, but it has broadened rapidly, during the last quarter century." [84] The philanthropy of men like Chauncey Rose was a prime force in this reorientation to-ward the secular and the utilitarian. Accustomed to leadership in their own professions, the businessmen-philanthropists refused to follow the lead of the old-time colleges in defining the means and ends of higher education.

Chapter V

Women on the Campus

Once the halls of a college were raised, two questions remained: what would be taught and to whom? Philanthropy helped answer the first question with its support of practical additions to the curriculum; it was even more influential in determining to whom the college would open its doors. The extension of college-level instruction to women, which began slowly in the nineteenth century and reached a climax in the twenty years following the Civil War, was a strikingly creative achievement of American generosity. The foundation of colleges bearing the names of Vassar, Smith, Wellesley, and Bryn Mawr resulted from large donations by single individuals. Numerous other independent women's colleges as well as coeducational and coordinate institutions drank deeply at the life-giving fountain of private wealth.

Women's higher education in its beginning did not have the general acceptance that colleges for men enjoyed.[1] Recognition of the need for higher training of men was widespread in the colonies. Precedents existed in England and on the Continent. The question facing the early Americans was not *if* young men should be educated in colleges but *how* this was to be brought about. With women the "if" came first.

The inclusion of women in the college and university community was an American innovation. In the 1830's collegiate coeducation began at Oberlin, and Mary Lyon was trudging New England's hills in the search for funds for the opening of Mount Holyoke. The idea of Vassar was conceived in the mid-1850's and in 1865 it opened as a bona fide college. Smith and Wellesley followed ten years later. Development outside the United States was slower. In England, Queen's College and Bedford College, actually secondary schools, were begun in 1848 and 1849 to train young ladies for the vocation of governess and to prepare them for bona fide colleges. No real attempt at women's higher education existed until the opening in 1872 of Girton College as a part of Cambridge University. Seven years later Oxford took under its care two colleges for women, Lady Margaret Hall and Somerville Hall.[2] Elsewhere in Europe the higher education of women was slower in developing. In France women were not excluded from the existing institutions by law, but no woman entered until 1868, and then it was an American girl seeking medical training. Uppsala and Lund in Sweden opened their doors to women in 1870. In Italy the date was 1876, in Germany and Russia 1878, and in Belgium 1880. In the Far East, where a woman's position was traditionally subservient, the inception of her higher education was still later.[3]

Several factors contributed to make American soil the most fertile for the growth of women's higher education.[4] The acceptance in America of eighteenth-century ideas of natural rights, the rationality of all human beings, and humanitarianism spread from the political to the social sphere and gave women a new importance. Quakerism likewise insisted on equality of the sexes. While the process of civilizing a wilderness continent retarded the development of some higher aspects of culture, it demanded from women equal sharing of hardships and won increased respect for their abilities as individuals. It was hardly an accident that the first coeducational colleges developed in Ohio. The increasing demand for capable teachers occasioned by the development of the public school system and the attraction of men to more lucrative vocations also pointed to a need for women's colleges. As molders of youth the female contribution to an enlightened citizenry was understood and appreciated. Finally, the heady social ideas of Jacksonian democracy emphasized the universal right of opportunity, which was construed in some quarters to include women.

Important as the American context was to women's higher education, achievements would have been sparse without philanthropic support. Many Americans, including professional educators, ridiculed collegiate instruction for women and suggested a host of reasons for its irrelevancy and failure. Even the dedicated efforts of enthusiastic champions of the cause were in large part powerless to break new paths against the conservative inclination of public opinion. But dollars behind new ideas meant achievement. With a single act a philanthropist could accomplish what a college or a state legislature might have required generations to do. An individual was far more likely to adopt a new idea than a board of trustees or a whole nation. If that individual happened to be rich, philanthropy offered him a tool for translating his idea into an institution.

The female academies or seminaries that preceded the first women's colleges [5] marked a transitional stage in which the idea of higher education for women grew and the practice of supporting it with private donations was established. The first attempts were entirely dependent on philanthropy. The Abbott Female Academy of Andover, Massachusetts (1829) and the Wheaton Female Seminary of Norton (1835) received sizable gifts and bequests from Sarah Abbott and Laban M. Wheaton respectively.[6] Other schools were obliged to live a hand-to-mouth existence on a diet of small contributions. In 1842 the Augusta Female Seminary of Staunton, Virginia was founded on the strength of a few dozen gifts of less than one hundred dollars.[7] Methodists scraped together nine thousand dollars to open the Georgia Female College in 1839 and $37,000 for Tuskegee Female College, which began instruction in 1856.[8] Illinois Methodists, not to be outdone by their Southern coreligionists, launched Illinois Conference Female Academy in 1846 and saw it through an early history in which the debt collector was only a step behind the harassed college officers. Fortunately for the Illinois Academy they enlisted the services of Colin D. James, who performed the seemingly impossible task of raising thirty thousand dollars from a money-poor frontier community to fund the debt. Attesting to James's skill as a fund-raiser was the story later told his son: "Your father was the greatest money raiser I ever knew. I subscribed $100 when that was all I could hope to clear in that year from my labor." [9]

Another extraordinary fund-raiser was the diminutive Mary Lyon, founder of Mount Holyoke Seminary in South Hadley, Massachusetts. Born in 1797, she taught in several New England schools for girls before determining in 1834 to establish her own. Her first problem was money, and she knew there were two distinct ways to raise it: "First, to interest one, two, or a few wealthy men to do the whole; second, to interest the whole New England community, beginning with the country population, and in time receiving the aid and cooperation of the more wealthy in our cities."[10] Inspired by Amherst's success in getting funds "not from the rich, but from liberal Christians in common life,"[11] she chose the second method of securing philanthropy. Selling the location of the school, a traditional recourse of founders, brought eight thousand dollars from South Hadley. Next she began a canvass of New England with the goal of twenty thousand dollars. The economic depression of the late 1830's was in progress and her prospects were not bright. Moreover, she faced traditional opposition to women's education in such forms as the refusal of the Boston *Recorder* to publish articles on the proposed school unless they were paid for as regular newspaper advertising.[12] But Miss Lyon was determined. "Let ladies come forward," she exhorted, "and plead our cause with their husbands their fathers, and their brothers, and the work will be done."[13] Through the bitter winter of 1836–37 she traveled alone over the hill farms of western Massachusetts, pleading, arguing, begging for money and sometimes, in her zeal, refusing to take her foot off the wheel of a wagon until a farmer promised to give at least a portion of his crop to the seminary then under construction in South Hadley.

So persuasive was Mary Lyon that few could escape giving at least a few dollars. One man gave what he could, then came to South Hadley and built with his own hands. Miss Lyon eventually collected $27,000 from one thousand subscribers living in ninety separate communities. The amounts contributed varied from six cents to a thousand dollars, and on their strength Mount Holyoke Seminary opened its doors to eighty girls on November 8, 1837.[14] In order to furnish the students' rooms Mary Lyon asked individual towns to "sponsor" a room by providing feather bedding, pillows, and sheets.[15] In the depressed years of the late 1830's these materials were often easier to come by than cash. When the seminary made the transition from fireplaces to steam heat, students and faculty wrote hundreds of letters in an effort to raise funds. In the winter of 1867–68 the "steam money" trickled in by small amounts until eventually $5,450 was collected.[16]

Elmira Female College had the benefit of a wealthy philanthropist's frendship. But the relationship of Simeon Benjamin and the college had liabilities as well as advantages. Benjamin amassed a fortune during and after the War of 1812 from a dry-goods business on Long Island and in New York City. In 1835 he moved to the small community of Elmira, New York and increased his fortune through real-estate operations. In the 1850's a group of civic leaders in Albany broached a plan for a women's college, and Simeon Benjamin's offer of financial aid fixed its location in Elmira.

Benjamin hoped that Elmira's citizens would support the institution, but they entertained the expectation that *he* would furnish the needed funds. Benjamin realized that if there was to be a college he must carry the lion's share of the financial responsibility. His gifts of more than fifty thousand dollars enabled Elmira Female College to open in 1855 to 150 young ladies, but the philanthropist's stipulation that the money was for endowment instead of current expenses was not suited to Elmira's needs. In 1861 he put a clause in his will providing $25,000 to the college, but on the condition that its trustees amend the charter to vest control in the Presbyterian Church's Synod of Geneva, in which he was a pillar and benefactor. He hoped that church affiliation would put Elmira on a sound financial basis. His communication to the trustees on the matter pointedly reminded them that he was "the largest subscriber towards the founding of the Institution." [17] In this situation, the trustees had little choice but to comply with the wishes of the philanthropist. Elmira became allied with the highly conservative Presbyterian Synod of Geneva, a fact which tended to discourage financial support from other sources. [18]

The philanthropic history of American higher education was marked by the transition in the middle decades of the nineteenth century from the subscription and small-gift era to the period of donations of six and seven figures. The expanding economy placed large fortunes in many hands, and women's colleges were among the first recipients of the large-scale philanthropy that such wealth made possible. Vassar College, for example, received $1,250,000 from a single family.

Matthew Vassar left England in 1796 and settled with his family in Poughkeepsie, New York. Dropping out of school at fourteen, he went into the brewery business and was highly successful. His fortune made, Vassar visited England in 1845 and toured a hospital that a distant relative, Thomas Guy, had given the people of London. This example of benevolence inspired Vassar to do something similar for Poughkeepsie.[19]

For a decade after his return to America, Vassar could not decide on a beneficiary for his philanthropic impulse. But his niece, Lydia Booth, who conducted the Cottage Hill Seminary for girls in Poughkeepsie, attracted her uncle's attention to the field of women's education. When in 1855 Milo P. Jewett bought Cottage Hill Seminary, Vassar found someone with ideas and vision far beyond his niece's. Jewett was a Vermont-born and Dartmouth-trained educator who in 1839 had founded the Judson Female Institute in Marion, Alabama. When he moved to Poughkeepsie and met Vassar, he took the opportunity to tell the wealthy brewer about his plans for "a college for young women which shall be to them what Yale and Harvard are to young men." [20] Realizing that in Vassar's fortune was the means to implement his ideas, Jewett appealed to his desire to serve mankind, his local pride, his Christian faith, and his interest as a childless man in perpetuating his name. Together Jewett and Vassar planned a college.

The result of the coming together of a man with ideas and a man with money was a historic meeting held in Poughkeepsie on February 26, 1861 of the trustees of the proposed Vassar Female College. Rising at the head of the table with a tin box at his side, Vassar first told the board of the gospel of wealth: "It having pleased God that I should have no descendents to inherit my property, it has long been my desire after suitably providing for those of my kindred who have claims on me, to make such a disposition of my means as should best honor God and benefit my fellowmen." [21] He declared it his intention to establish a complete women's college, giving as his motive his belief "that woman, having received from her Creator the same intellectual constitution as man, has the same right as man to intellectual culture and development." Vassar went on to say that he hoped future mothers and teachers would derive benefit from what he believed was the world's first fully endowed institution for women's higher education. The only conditions Vassar put upon his gift were that Vassar Female College should not be a finishing school but rather a fully equipped college teaching a curriculum similar to that taught in the best men's colleges, and that "all sectarian influences should be carefully excluded; but the training of our students should never be intrusted to the skeptical, the irreligious, or the immoral." [22] Concluding his address, Vassar handed over the tin box which contained four hundred thousand dollars, principally in railroad stock and bonds.

Before his death in 1868 Matthew Vassar added another four hundred thousand dollars to his original donation, and the family later gave still more. Philanthropy of such magnitude was unheard of previously in the history of American higher education. Harvard, for instance, in the first six decades of the nineteenth century did not receive a single donation of more than a hundred thousand dollars.

In his relations with the college he had founded, Vassar revealed considerable wisdom. Recognizing his own lack of experience in matters of higher education, he surrounded himself with a board of skilled trustees and permitted them autonomy.[23] In the years from 1861 to 1865, when the college was under construction, he corresponded with the best minds in American higher education, including Edward L. Youmans, Henry Barnard, Samuel F. B. Morse, and Augustus W. Cowles, president of Elmira Female College. Vassar sent Jewett, his first president, to Europe in 1862 to study the practices of the foremost colleges and universities in England and on the Continent. The fact that Vassar had begun the disposal of his fortune during his lifetime allowed him to supervise the dispensation of funds. He felt his business background equipped him to manage the college's endowment, but he left academic matters to professional educators, asking only that they be well trained.

The resignation of President Jewett in 1864, before the college opened, provided an illustration of Vassar's conception of the role of the educational philanthropist. Impatient over delays in opening the college and thwarted in some pet educational schemes, Jewett wrote a heated letter criticizing Vassar as childish and fickle. Inadvertently a copy reached the philanthropist. Deeply hurt, he recommended to the board of trustees that they ask for Jewett's resignation, but emphasized that it be done only with the good of the college in mind, not his personal affront.[24]

In contrast to Mount Holyoke Seminary, which had to beg for

room furnishings, Vassar Female College opened for the fall term in 1865 with sumptuous accommodations for 350 women. The faculty numbered among its members noted teachers and scholars, including Maria Mitchell, the astronomer. The expenses of the undertaking had greatly exceeded Vassar's original estimates, but he cheerfully increased his original gifts. The college became for him "the favorite child of my age, and to see it in the full career of success and usefulness will be the crowning pleasure of my life." [25] When his health permitted he visited the campus daily to enjoy the enthusiasm of students and faculty. Once he received a letter in his college office from a graduate warning that "a college foundation which is laid in beer will never prosper." A student overheard Vassar exclaim, "Well, it was good beer, wasn't it?" [26] On Founders Day in 1866, when the girls of the college paid him the unexpected tribute of an outdoor pageant, he remarked that "this one day more than repays me for all I have done." [27]

Writing in *Harper's Monthly* in 1876, Anna C. Brackett contended that higher education for women was better concentrated in one institution than scattered among many. Now that Vassar College was off to a good start, she argued, philanthropy should be directed toward it rather than to new foundings. [28] But wealthy Americans, many of whom had made their own fortunes, did not like to follow another's lead. If they were going to spend hundreds of thousands of dollars on a college, they wanted it to be theirs, not the product of someone else's philanthropy. They also had different ideas as to what a college should do and where it should be situated. Moreover, the demand for women's higher education far exceeded the capacity of any one institution.

The profits from a company closely associated with opening the American West founded the next major women's college. Henry Wells made his fortune in the operation of the American and Wells Fargo Express Company. Early in his life Wells resolved to found a college. As a youth he had been greatly impressed with the institution for orphans that the philanthropy of Stephen Girard had erected. Recalling how he felt on seeing it for the first time, he wrote: "Standing there alone, I thought I would rather be Girard, as he was thus represented, than the President of the United States, or the ruler of any of the great nations of the world." [29] Unlike many philanthropists, Wells's idea of founding a college wasn't an afterthought to success but a leading motive to attain it. Founded in 1868 in Aurora, New York, Wells Seminary for the Higher Education of Young Women (later Wells College) received about two hundred thousand dollars from its founder.[30]

The year 1875 was a banner one in the history of women's collegiate education. In that year both Smith College and Wellesley College first opened to students. Philanthropy was wholly responsible for both institutions.

Fourteen years before, Sophia Smith, a timid, deaf spinster of Hatfield, Massachusetts, unexpectedly inherited a fortune of several hundred thousand dollars from her brother. Dismayed at this windfall she turned to her pastor, young John Morton Greene. At first Greene refused to advise her, fearing involvement in a lawsuit, but Miss Smith wept and confessed: "I did not want this money; it is none of my seeking; but it has come to me and I must dispose of it, and you must help me." [31] Reluctantly Greene agreed to see her through the process of bestowing her money on a worthy cause. Among the first suggestions he offered was a women's college, having himself long been convinced of the importance of higher education for women. Miss Smith welcomed the suggestion, saying, "I wish I could have enjoyed the advantages of such a college when I was a girl; it would have made my life far richer and happier than it has been." [32] Greene provided her with the facts of Vassar's founding, Thomas Wentworth Higginson's essay "Ought Women to Learn the Alphabet?" and a paper by Henry Thomas Buckle entitled "The Influence of Women on the Progress of Knowledge." [33]

Greene corresponded with the presidents of Harvard, Yale, and Williams about the possibility of starting a women's college in connection with their institutions, but these educators dismissed it as "foolish," "hazardous," and even "wicked." [34] He next tried to interest Miss Smith in giving her money to Amherst, even arranging a tea for her with its president, but Miss Smith had a curious antipathy toward Amherst. Neither could she be interested in supporting Mount Holyoke.

Miss Smith's first wills were in favor of an academy in Hatfield and an institution for deaf-mutes. In 1868, however, a deaf-mute institution was endowed by a Northampton man, and Greene, Pro-

fessor W. S. Tyler of Amherst College, and George Hubbard, a
neighbor and friend, persuaded Miss Smith to reconsider her will.
Knowing her coolness toward existing colleges, Greene drew up a
"Plan for a Woman's College" for her consideration.[35] Its ideas,
even its exact wording, went into Miss Smith's final will, dated
March 8, 1870, which stipulated that "Smith College" be founded
"to furnish for my own sex means and facilities for education equal
to those which are afforded now in our Colleges to young men."
The will, as Greene had written it, continued with a fuller statement of intent: "It is my opinion that by the higher and more
thorough Christian education of women, what are called their
'wrongs' will be redressed, their wages adjusted, their weight of
influence in reforming the evils of society will be greatly increased, as teachers, as writers, as mothers, as members of society,
their power for good will be incalculably enlarged." The will, according to the principle which she undoubtedly shared with Greene
that "all education should be for the glory of God," asked that the
Scriptures be systematically read and studied at her college as part
of a well-rounded liberal arts program. She stipulated that if Northampton was to be the seat of the college it must raise $25,000, a
condition its citizens promptly met. Only half the bequest, which
ultimately amounted to $393,107, was to finance the building of
the physical plant; the other half must be put into an endowment
fund for faculty and equipment. The will concluded with the
declaration that "I would have the education suited to the mental
and physical wants of women. It is not my design to render my
sex any less feminine but to develop as fully as may be the powers
of womanhood." [36] Miss Smith died on June 12, 1870; the trustees
organized the following year; and in 1875 Smith College admitted
a class of fourteen girls.

Although colleges like Vassar and Smith started with large donations, they soon found themselves in financial difficulty. The bulk
of the founding sum was used to meet initial expenses of building
and equipment, and there was a discouraging lack of contributions
from persons other than the founders. In fact, the very magnitude
of the founding donation frequently checked the subsequent philanthropic flow that had kept Mount Holyoke alive. Americans could
not be persuaded that colleges so handsomely founded could be
poor within a few years, and the image of a struggling college was

of vast importance in successful fund-raising. In 1872 Greene undertook a six-months' campaign for Smith College. The proceeds were absolutely nothing.[37] After its initial contribution to secure the location of the college, Northampton turned its back. Even the young Amherst professor whom the Smith trustees sought as president demurred at first because he regarded the endowment insufficient.[38] Vassar had a similar experience in 1864 when John Howard Raymond declined the presidency, protesting in a letter to Matthew Vassar that "the munificent sum consecrated by you, sir, three years ago to this sacred cause should, to so large an extent, have been absorbed in mere material provisions, compelling us to begin the ungracious work of retrenchment and enforced economy just as we reach the vital part—the men and women who are to infuse their spirit into its life, and to put upon the College for all time the impress of their heart and brain—in other words, compelling us after the old fashion *to pinch and starve the College at its heart.*"[39] Vassar was fortunate in that its philanthropist was still alive and willing to supplement his original gift, but Smith's source of funds ceased with the single bequest, and as late as 1876 the only additional donation the college had received were a clock and a bell.[40]

A father's grief, a desire to serve God, and the possession of a million dollars were responsible for the foundation of Wellesley College. Henry F. Durant, who steadfastly refused to give his name to the college because he saw in it a monument not to himself but to God, graduated from Harvard in 1842 and entered the legal profession. Born Henry Welles Smith, he adopted the name "Durant" in order to distinguish himself from eleven other lawyers named Smith practicing in Boston. Durant's career as a lawyer was meteoric. He expanded his business ventures and soon had a vast fortune at his disposal. With his career well launched, he married his cousin, Pauline Cazenove Fowle, a frail and deeply religious young woman. One of his aspirations was to leave his son, Henry Fowle Durant, Jr., a material springboard to greatness, and to fulfill this plan he purchased property on Lake Waban in the town of Wellesley, about twelve miles west of Boston. Tragedy struck in 1863, however, when the boy died at the age of eight. Completely shaken, Durant renounced the legal profession and with his wife's help turned to evangelical religion. He even burned his law library because he found it to conflict with his faith.[41]

With his son and heir dead, Durant sought an object on which to bestow his wealth that would be at the same time a memorial to his son and a tribute to the glory of God. His first thoughts were for a school for boys and an orphanage. But remembering the influence on his own childhood of women teachers and recalling his experience since 1867 as a trustee of Mount Holyoke Seminary, which was turning away hundreds of qualified girls each year, he finally settled on a women's college. In 1870 Wellesley College received a charter, and the following year Mrs. Durant placed a Bible in the cornerstone of the main building bearing the inscription: "This building is humbly dedicated to our Heavenly Father with the hope and prayer that He may always be first in everything in this institution; that His word may be faithfully taught here; and that He will use it as a means of leading precious souls to the Lord Jesus Christ." [42] On September 8, 1875, in an extremely religious atmosphere, Wellesley opened to 314 students.

It is impossible to say exactly how much Durant expended on the college during its building and its early years, since he paid the bills from his own pocket as they came in. [43] In view of Vassar's expenditures, Durant's must have approached a million dollars. But Durant felt too much personal responsibility for it to be content with merely providing its revenue. He hovered over every detail of Wellesley College. One student wrote home that "he rules the college, from the amount of Latin we shall read to the kind of meat we shall have for dinner; he even went out into the kitchen the other day and told the cook not to waste so much butter in making the hash, for I heard him myself." [44] Wellesley's president, Mount Holyoke-trained Ada L. Howard, was little more than a figurehead, as the philanthropist assumed the right to dictate college policy in regard to curriculum, faculty, and student conduct. Durant held the reins tightly, even in the face of faculty and student protest, until his death seven years after the founding. But occasionally he was obliged to give ground. At one point he ordered Wellesley's second president, Alice Freeman, to inquire into the religious beliefs of certain students and attend to those who did not attain the degree of holiness he deemed desirable. The strong-willed Miss Freeman absolutely refused, and Durant gave up his demand. [45] Also to Durant's credit was his determination that the curriculum embrace fresh subjects, including original experimentation in the sciences.

Wellesley experienced the same difficulties as Vassar and Smith in obtaining philanthropic support from sources other than the founder. Alice Freeman, now Mrs. Palmer, was disappointed, according to her husband, because "the public could not be brought at once to the support of Wellesley. Few gifts came from outside the circle of Mr. Durant's friends, though within that circle there were generous and discriminating givers." [46] This was an accurate appraisal. Professor Eben N. Horsford of Harvard gave $120,000 for the library and Isaac D. Farnsworth of Boston contributed one hundred thousand dollars toward an art building, but both men were inspired to give from friendship for Durant rather than dedication to women's higher education. The first major outside donation came in 1884 when Valeria G. Stone, wife of a Malden, Massachusetts, merchant and a generous benefactor of numerous educational institutions, left Wellesley $110,000 for the construction of a residence hall in her name. [47] A financial crisis was averted in the 1890's only through the development of the alumnae association as a major fund-raising organ.

Bryn Mawr was the last of the major independent women's colleges founded before the turn of the century. The philanthropist responsible for it was Joseph W. Taylor, a Quaker who shared his religion's insistence on the ministerial equality of the sexes and extended it to the field of education. Haverford College had existed for Quaker men since 1833, and Taylor's service on its board of managers suggested to him the need for a sister institution. The opening of The Johns Hopkins University, also the work of a wealthy Quaker, in 1876 gave Taylor additional impetus to devote the money he had made in the tannery business in Ohio to establishing an institution offering a similarly high quality of instruction to women. Contact with the Johns Hopkins trustees, especially Francis T. King, strengthened his purpose while providing concrete suggestions. [48]

In 1877 Taylor made Bryn Mawr the major beneficiary of his will, but in the four years of life that remained to him he worked, as had Matthew Vassar, in behalf of his college. Like Vassar, Taylor appointed a board of trustees—many of whom served Johns Hopkins in a similar capacity—and left to them the task of organizing the college. But the philanthropist closely supervised the construction of the physical plant, writing and traveling to Smith, Wellesley, and Mount Holyoke for ideas and advice.[49]

Taylor's will, by which Bryn Mawr received about eight hundred thousand dollars, contained several specific conditions that proved embarrassing to the faculty and trustees. The college was to be controlled by Quakers and must "endeavor to instill into the minds and hearts of the students, the doctrines of the New Testament as accepted by Friends, and taught by Fox, Penn . . . and Braithwaite . . . and which I believe to be the same in substance as taught by early Christians."[50] Although girls of all sects might be admitted, they had to agree to be taught according to Quaker principles. Soon after its opening in 1885, Bryn Mawr was straining at the bounds of its founder's denominationalism and rapidly becoming a leading center of collegiate and postgraduate study for women. This had also been one of Taylor's wishes, and President James E. Rhoads used the philanthropist's desire for top-quality education as a means to circumvent his religious stipulations. Rhoads declared that a sufficient number of students and teachers of Quaker faith could not be found to equip a college of the standards desired by the founder. Consequently, assuming that high standards superseded sectarian loyalty in the founder's mind, the latter was relaxed.[51]

While accepting this reading, legal advisers warned that the board of trustees must remain Quaker for fear that Taylor's will would be broken. However, a Pennsylvania law requiring every incorporated institution to be controlled by a "board of directors" came to the college's aid. Since Taylor's will had required only "trustees" to be Quaker, Bryn Mawr's officers promptly appointed "directors" of diverse faiths to conduct the college. If the philanthropist's specific demands were violated, the college felt justified in pursuing the goal of quality.[52]

Like her sister colleges, Bryn Mawr required more funds than the founder had provided and discovered that they were difficult to raise. In 1893, for example, $140,000 was needed for a new building, but public generosity offered only thirty thousand dollars in response to the pleas of Martha Carey Thomas, the dean. Miss Thomas fared better in 1902, when as president she raised $250,000, but deficits remained that only the Rockefeller bounty erased.[53]

The spectacular acts of philanthropy that started Vassar, Smith,

Wellesley, and Bryn Mawr received most of the attention as higher education for women began, but they were not alone. A bequest that topped them all was that of John Simmons, a Bostonian who made millions in the men's clothing business. In 1870 he bequeathed property that eventually realized $1,400,000 to establish Simmons Female College. Desiring to repay the class of women that provided the seamstresses who made his fortune possible, Simmons asked that his college be dedicated to enabling its students to achieve independence in a vocation such as teaching, music, drawing, designing, and telegraphy.[54] In the South the philanthropy of James L. Coker, John F. Goucher, and Agnes Scott was instrumental in the development of three independent women's colleges bearing their names.[55]

In the twentieth century, although increasingly more philanthropy went to existing institutions, the founding of women's colleges continued. Mrs. Indiana Fletcher Williams's half a million dollars and eight-thousand-acre plantation enabled Sweet Briar College to open in 1906 in Virginia. Sarah Lawrence College in Bronxville, New York and Scripps College in Claremont, California, opening in the 1920's, were products of the extensive philanthropy of single persons, William Van Duzer Lawrence and Ellen Browning Scripps. In the case of Sarah Lawrence, philanthropy made it possible to put John Dewey's theories of progressive education into practice.

The close association of an ambitious college president, Clarence P. McClelland, and a corporation president, James E. MacMurray, transformed Illinois Women's College from a struggling denominational institution into one of the Middle West's foremost centers of higher learning for women. MacMurray's donations, which began in the 1920's, totaled close to five million dollars in 1943, the year of his death. In 1930 President McClelland proposed that the name of the college be changed to MacMurray College for Women. Of this he wrote: "Needless to say, I had made no suggestion in advance to Mr. MacMurray as to what might be expected of him in the way of additional financial aid if the College were named for him. And to tell the truth, I was not at all sure that the change in name would mean further gifts from him but of course I had great hopes."[56] McClelland's expectations were fully gratified,

since after the renaming of the college MacMurray gave it the
bulk of his total contribution as well as his constant attention.[57]

Independent colleges were not the only places where women appeared on the campus. A few colleges began with or accepted
coeducation. Women participated in the experiment in the Ohio
wilderness known as Oberlin College from its beginning in 1834.
Although philanthropy to Oberlin was directed to the college as
a whole, those who gave were aware that their money went to
support the higher education of women as well as men.[58] The
same was true in the case of William Mills, who in 1852 gave twenty
thousand dollars and twenty acres of land to help found Antioch
College in Yellow Spring, Ohio, but subsequent philanthropy was
not forthcoming to back the liberal ideas of its first president, Horace Mann, and the college floundered for years.[59]

The most dramatic use of philanthropy in inaugurating coeducation occurred at Cornell University. Andrew D. White, the first
president, favored women's higher education, but in view of the
conservative nature of the New York legislature he did not press
the matter when drafting Cornell's charter.[60] Ezra Cornell was
also generally in favor of admitting girls to the university he did
so much to create. At the inauguration ceremonies held at Ithaca
on October 7, 1868, a few references were made about the hope
of including women. Afterward Henry W. Sage, millionaire lumber baron of Ithaca, New York, approached President White and
said: "I believe you are right in regard to admitting women, but
you are evidently carrying as many innovations just now as public
opinion will bear; when you are ready to move in the matter, let
me know." [61] Sage's devotion to women's higher education arose
more from sentimentality than from a desire to provide girls with
practical training. He declared that "every grace and virtue which
adorn her nature . . . every element of usefulness and helpful-
ness . . . may be increased without limit by education and culture. . . ." [62]

In Cornell's case the college acted before the philanthropist, because in 1870 it admitted a single woman student, but the icy
hills of Ithaca that she was forced to climb from town, as there
was no residence for her on the campus, forced her to withdraw.[63]
Then Sage moved. President White had expected his proposal at
the inauguration to refer to a fellowship or at most a professorship

for women. To his amazement, Sage offered to build an entire residence college and on May 15, 1873, groundbreaking ceremonies were held for the Sage College for Women. It was completed at a cost of $267,000, and opened in 1874 as part of Cornell. The *Christian Union* praised Sage as a man who "matches his dollars with ideas" and noted that his example proved that "commerical pursuits need not narrow the intellect nor harden the heart." [64]

Cornell's officers had been favorable to women's higher education before Henry Sage made his donation, but in the case of the University of Rochester philanthropy forced the door that the trustees were bracing in an effort to keep women out. In 1899, under considerable public pressure, Rochester's trustees grudgingly agreed to admit women if one hundred thousand dollars could be raised in a year to finance the innovation. They felt certain that so large a sum could not be collected, and their assumption proved correct as the women of the community had but forty thousand dollars after more than a year of campaigning. Faced with more pressure, the officers consented to take fifty thousand dollars if it was in their hands before their meeting on September 16, 1900. On the morning of the crucial meeting eight thousand dollars was still lacking. At this point the ardent feminist Susan B. Anthony took matters into her own hands and begged pledges for the needed amount. She rushed to the hall where the trustees were meeting and laid the subscriptions on the table. The surprised board carefully scrutinized the pledges and ruled that one for two thousand dollars was insufficiently guaranteed. Furious, Miss Anthony put up her own life insurance for this amount. The trustees had no alternative but to accept the fifty thousand dollars and the women students. [65]

Philanthropy was also the tool used to secure coeducation in medicine at The Johns Hopkins University. Although Johns Hopkins by no means pioneered in admitting women to the study of medicine, [66] the acceptance of women at this "model" university was a major blow to the sex barrier and attracted widespread notice. While a school of medicine had been part of the original plans of Johns Hopkins, lack of funds had delayed its opening. By 1890 there was considerable displeasure in Baltimore over the failure to inaugurate medical training, and Martha Carey Thomas, the daughter of a Hopkins trustee, holder of a Ph.D. from Zurich and later president of Bryn Mawr, saw an opportunity to advance the higher educational possibilities of her sex. With several friends, including the wealthy daughter of the president of the Baltimore and Ohio Railroad, Mary Garrett, Miss Thomas organized the Women's Fund Committee. Its purpose was to raise enough money to enable Johns Hopkins to establish a medical school but to offer it only on the condition that women be admitted on equal standing with men.[67]

The Women's Fund Committee had branches in many of the major cities in the East and included among its members the First Lady, Mrs. Benjamin Harrison. Late in 1890 the drive had accumulated one hundred thousand dollars, of which Mary Garrett contributed almost half, and the committee offered it to the Johns Hopkins trustees. On October 20, 1890, the trustees accepted the gift and the conditions on which it was offered.[68] They did not, however, feel it was sufficient to establish a first-rate medical school. "It would be a noble act," said President Daniel Coit Gilman, "if the women of this country should complete the endowment which they have so successfully initiated." [69] He suggested five hundred thousand dollars as a goal. The committee went back to work, but funds were slow in accumulating. Impatient with the delay, Mary Garrett offered in 1892 to complete the needed five hundred thousand dollars herself. More than three hundred thousand dollars was required, bringing her total contribution to the fund to $354,764.[70]

In the letter accompanying her gift, Miss Garrett, besides requiring women to be admitted, laid down qualifications for admission to the school that all students would have to meet. This action aroused the trustees and faculty. The qualifications were extraordinarily high; William Osler told a colleague on the medical faculty, William Welch, that "it is luck that we get in as professors; we could never enter as students." [71] More seriously, the principle of university autonomy was involved. President Gilman made clear that a philanthropist must not usurp the prerogative of the university in determining on what conditions students may be admitted, discharged, and graduated.[72] Mary Garrett hastened to assure the officers that she had no intention of assuming their role, and the School of Medicine opened in 1893 with seventeen students, three of whom were women.

Something of a compromise between the independent women's college and coeducation was the coordinate college for women, which maintained a degree of separateness while existing on the campus of a men's institution. Here, too, philanthropy played a crucial role in founding and supporting the colleges. Radcliffe College began in 1879 as the Society for the Collegiate Instruction of Women on the strength of a subscription fund of fifteen thousand dollars. Elizabeth Cary Agassiz, wife of the noted Harvard scientist, took a leading part in raising the money. She knew the financial resources of Harvard were devoted to educating men and could not be diverted into the women's "annex." Consequently, Radcliffe's friends sought to raise an endowment of one hundred thousand dollars. Their success led to a new charter in 1894 confirming Radcliffe's coordinate status with Harvard.[73]

The establishment of Sophie Newcomb College in connection with Tulane University in New Orleans resulted from the benefactions of a single woman, Mrs. Josephine Louise Newcomb. After the death of her daughter in 1870, Mrs. Newcomb resolved to "enshrine her memory in a manner best fitted to render useful and enduring benefit to humanity."[74] When President William P. Johnston of Tulane and others proposed to her the establishment of a coordinate college for women, she accepted and in 1886 placed a hundred thousand dollars in the hands of Tulane's trustees. The letter of donation gave them a free hand with the money, specifying only that the education be confined to white girls and that the dates of her daughter's birth and death be remembered in the services of the college chapel.[75] Through additional gifts and Mrs. Newcomb's will Sophie Newcomb College received more than three and a half million dollars, the largest amount given to women's education by a single donor to that time.

Jackson College at Tufts, Pembroke at Brown and Flora Stone Mather at Western Reserve all traced their origins to philanthropy, but Barnard College, rising in the shadow of Columbia, outdistanced them all in benefactions. Like Harvard in its relation to Radcliffe, Columbia made it clear that a sister institution must fend for itself in matters of finance. Barnard's beginnings in 1889 were small: a five-thousand-dollar donation and a brownstone house at 343 Madison Avenue, New York City, from J. Pierpont Morgan. The great need of the college was an uptown location near Columbia's Morningside Heights campus, but New York real estate prices posed a great obstacle. In 1903, despair turned to joy at Barnard when Elizabeth Milbank Anderson, the heiress of a fortune made in a

New York grocery business, bought three uptown blocks at a cost of a million dollars and presented them to the college. Earlier, gifts bearing the names Brikerhoff, Fiske, and Rockefeller had financed the purchase of a smaller uptown lot and the erection of several buildings. In support of Barnard in the twentieth century, Mrs. Anderson raised the total of her benefactions to about three million dollars and Margaret Olivia Slocum Sage (Mrs. Russell Sage), the foremost woman philanthropist of her time, gave eight hundred thousand as part of a program for higher education of far wider scope. Two million dollars came from old and lonely Horace W. Carpentier, who said he had not a friend in the world "except that dog there"—to which the alert Barnard treasurer, George A. Plimpton, replied, "I will be your friend, General Carpentier." [76]

The higher education of women gained momentum during the nineteenth century to become an accepted national institution in the twentieth largely as a result of philanthropy. When Mary Lyon launched Mount Holyoke the pattern of many small donations from numerous contributors prevailed, but the early history of Mount Holyoke was not duplicated in most of the later foundings. Vassar, Smith, Wellesley, and Bryn Mawr, among others, all began as the philanthropic creations of single individuals and found it difficult to raise money from the general public. The relationship of the college and its founder varied. The autonomy that Matthew Vassar awarded the trustees and faculty, combined with his intense interest in his college's welfare, provided an ideal medium for growth and development. Less fortunate was the domineering attitude Henry Durant took in regard to Wellesley.

With creativity as a criterion, the support of college training for women marked one of American philanthropy's greatest achievements. Dollars honed the cutting edge of a new idea. The first colleges that resulted were not copies of an Old World achievement but American innovations. Yet, while some philanthropists thought for themselves, credit must also go to the Jewetts, Greenes, and Johnstons, who had the ideas that directed the generosity of the Vassars, Smiths, and Newcombs. Both the idea and the money were essential in giving women the opportunity of higher education.

Chapter VI

Great Gifts for New Universities

It is well known that the traditionalism of American colleges in the post-Civil War years provoked counterforces that led to major conflicts. Out of the conflicts developed what began to be known as "the new education." Whereas the traditional college emphasized religious and moral values, mental discipline, and the making of gentlemen, "the new education" set store on vocational training and public service, the advancement of knowledge through original investigation, the importance of management or administration, and, with less force, the reassertion of the claims of literary culture. The relation between these values and their institutionalization has been documented with insight and learning by Lawrence Ross Veysey.[1]

The modern American university resulted from this educational upsurge. But it could not have issued from the conflict between tradition and innovation alone. Philanthropy played an indispensable role. Of the several contributions of philanthropy to American life in the later nineteenth century, none was more important than this.

With a few notable exceptions, the colleges before the Civil War owed their existence and development to private support. In terms of academic standards these colleges varied greatly. As late as 1874 Andrew D. White held that sectarian and private giving had failed to develop in the West a single academic institution that, in faculty, library, laboratory, or observatory, could claim to be of third rank even by American standards.² On the other hand, private giving had provided at Harvard and Yale some of the ingredients of a university both in the European sense and in what was to be the American conception. These ingredients included the Lawrence Scientific School, the Bussey Institution and the observatory at Cambridge and the Sheffield Scientific School and the Trumbull Gallery at New Haven. Interestingly, all these additions were the result of philanthropy. At both Harvard and Yale endowment had enabled some scholars and scientists to make important contributions to knowledge, and this was true to a lesser extent at a few other places.

Yet even these achievements did not constitute the modern university, since the main emphasis was on undergraduate instruction in limited fields. The first essential to the new institutions that took shape after the Civil War was, of course, the university idea itself. Americans interested in higher education in the middle of the nineteenth century were, to be sure, familiar with Cambridge, Oxford, Paris, and the famous universities of Germany. Long before the Civil War, far-seeing scholars at Harvard, on coming home from advanced study abroad, wanted to introduce the newer fields of knowledge, to develop a faculty of outstanding scholars, a great library, adequate laboratories, and sufficient freedom from long hours of classroom teaching for sustained research. The progenitors of New York University likewise appreciated these essentials for a true university and saw, further, the need for integrating full-fledged professional schools into the projected institution. Also in New York Samuel Ruggles, a leading citizen and a dedicated trustee of Columbia College, urged as early as 1854 the remaking of the college into a true university worthy of the growing metropolis. In discussing, in 1866, this and other proposals made over the past decades for creating a "magnificent institution," Frederick A. P. Barnard, president of Columbia, noted that while the resources of the college were more than sufficient for undergraduate work, boldness and imagination were imperative if Columbia was to rise to the "great mission" of deepening and broadening knowledge, in short, of becoming a true university.³ And across the Alleghenies Henry Tappan, head of the publicly supported University of Michigan, understood the difference between American and European institutions of higher learning and tried courageously to make Michigan into an authentic university. Yet if a dozen or so seats of learning bore the name "university" at the end of the Civil War and if educational leaders were exploring the true dimensions of the concept, no institution had yet developed sufficiently beyond the collegiate stage to be properly classed with Paris, Leipzig, Berlin, and Göttingen.

Despite such beginnings, the growth of the idea of a university in an American milieu was not easy. Germany provided the pattern for most Americans who were eager to transform colleges into institutions for increasing knowledge in all fields in an atmosphere of free inquiry and for offering advanced training in the professions.[4] But it was clear that many conditions made any mere copying impossible. The preparatory schools on which the universities of the Old World depended—gymnasiums, lycées, and the English public schools—carried students well beyond the point at which even the best American academies and high schools stopped. This meant that the college must meet academic needs provided overseas by secondary schools. Moreover the American college, in the spirit of the European preparatory schools, conceived of education as a disciplinary process rather than as an intellectual adventure and a quest for new knowledge and understanding, the distinctive emphasis of the great universities of Europe. The American college was also dominated, unlike the German university, by the classics and mathematics. When the natural sciences were given a place this was done with condescension and in a peripheral way, as the Lawrence and the Sheffield scientific schools bore witness. Except at Rensselaer and—in aspiration rather than in actuality— in the newer state universities, the program of study seemed to some educators and to many laymen unrelated to the changing social and economic needs of an America on its way to industrialization. At the same time the most outspoken champions and philanthropic supporters of "practical" higher education often conceived of these not in the spirit of a university dedicated to the increase of knowledge but rather as providing a narrow training for scientific farming, engineering, and mining. Finally, there was no consensus among those in favor of the "reform" of higher education on the question of whether the democratic ideal was feasible on an advanced academic level. Many assumed that only a few gifted minds properly trained could profit from such higher studies as a university offered. It was generally admitted, however, that such an elite was by no means exclusively identified with the favored classes.

Even a partial understanding of the university idea in an American context was not enough for actualizing the institution itself. It was equally necessary to have leaders capable of transforming the idea into reality. The achievement would have been impossible without such men as Charles W. Eliot, Andrew D. White, Daniel Coit Gilman, James B. Angell, William Rainey Harper, and G. Stanley Hall. To be sure, none of these men had at the outset anything like a blueprint for a university. Except for G. Stanley Hall, none of them wanted to duplicate the German university, and several were fairly critical of it. Undergraduate study was important in the administrations of all these men except Hall and Gilman. As administrators each of them, on some occasion, failed in a test of true academic freedom. In the eyes of European university scholars, all, or almost all, made concessions to utilitarianism and democracy that put their institutions below the level of their Old World counterparts. Yet whatever their shortcomings and compromises, the leadership of these men was indispensable for university building in America.

But the idea and the leaders were only two of the elements necessary for the emergence of universities. Financial support on a vaster scale than American colleges had ever known was needed to build great libraries and adequate laboratories and to attract and maintain outstanding scholars and creative scientists capable of advancing knowledge and of training investigators and teachers imbued with the university spirit. Only two sources for such outlays were at hand. One was the legislatures, hiterto unable or unwilling to do the job. The other was private wealth, together with the readiness of those having it to give generously during their lives or at their deaths to permit such leaders as Charles W. Eliot of Harvard and Seth Low of Columbia to change colleges into universities and Gilman, White, and Harper to establish new universities.

In the 1860's and again in the 1880's much of the country experienced extraordinary economic growth, which resulted in a great increase in wealth and the rise of spectacular fortunes. Even after taking into account the great destruction of property values in the Civil War (often hidden by currency inflation), the total wealth of the country in 1880 was estimated at thirty billion dollars as against sixteen billion in 1860. The part played by the rising elite of wealth was crucial in enabling educational leaders to realize the growing conception of a true university.

Necessary though voluntary giving had been in founding and keeping alive the antebellum colleges and in enabling two or three to take steps toward becoming universities, what was given from the new wealth of the 1860's and the following decades overshadowed in magnitude all earlier gifts to higher education. For example, Columbia's income from endowment in 1864–65 was $93,361; in 1900–1 it was $1,215,358. Or consider that a single gift, five hundred thousand dollars, which established one of the new universities, matched the total endowment of *all* colleges at the opening of the nineteenth century. Another gift that endowed a new university, $3,500,000, was larger than the total benefactions Harvard had received in 250 years. Such lavish gifts for founding universities were the most striking examples of philanthropy's contributions to the shaping of the modern American university.

The bold decision to build an entirely new university was generally avoided by public institutions. It was still uncertain whether state institutions could win enough public support to realize the aims also cherished by the founders of the new universities: equality of educational opportunity (particularly in the case of Cornell and Stanford), a practical and utilitarian program (also with Cornell and Stanford in the lead), and original contributions to knowledge in all fields (which distinguished Hopkins, Clark, and Chicago). In any case, it took a great deal longer to convince entire legislatures than single philanthropists. As it turned out, Cornell and Hopkins served as models for many of the newer state institutions.

The simpler and more conventional procedure of building universities was to help the established colleges remake themselves. Persuasive arguments were offered by the older institutions. A new institution, it was pointed out, would duplicate the costly library, laboratory, and faculty of an existing one, especially if the enterprise was planned in the same geographical area. One prospective founder of a university resisted such arguments from the spokesmen of at least three nearby institutions. Another was discouraged on the ground that whatever he might do would militate against the success of the recently established state university which, in any case, could take care of all those seeking higher education for decades to come. Moreover, prominent educational leaders shared the view expressed in 1866 by President Barnard of Columbia that universities could not spring like Minerva from Jupiter's head, but rather must "grow by gradual accretion continued through a long series of years." [5] The example of Harvard and the European universities was cited in support of this contention.

Yet within a generation new foundations at Ithaca and Baltimore belied Barnard's argument and before his death the promising beginnings of Chicago, Stanford, and Clark further weakened it. What factors influenced the donors and how did the idea become actuality?

It is, of course, one thing to have wealth and another to give it for public purposes. Not every man of large means did so despite the precedents in the pre-Civil War period of the Lawrences, Rensselaers, Girards, and Tappans. [6] In an effort to publicize such early gifts to education and to encourage others of means to follow the example, Henry Barnard had included, in the years following 1856, laudatory sketches of donors in his *American Journal of Education*. These biographies emphasized the bearing of such donations on public well-being and on the immortality of the donor's name. [7] Such considerations as well as those of institutional prestige no doubt played a part in the decisions of men of wealth to provide the older colleges with the means for becoming universities. Similar desires influenced the men of great wealth who, having founded universities, continued to help them develop.

Among the many motives of such men was the desire to show that just as they had been able to create great fortunes, so they could build great universities. Many also felt that gifts to older colleges would be less effective in meeting the demands of a new age than institutions committed from the start to the university idea as the founders conceived it or as they came to conceive it under the tutelage of educational leaders.

Relations with and attitudes toward family were also influential personal factors for founders. The lack of close family connections, particularly of sons to perpetuate the family name, was important in some cases. Johns Hopkins and Paul Tulane never married and perpetuated their names in the institutions they founded. Jonas Clark and his wife had no offspring, a fact of major significance in his decision to found a university. The only child of the Stanfords, a gifted and bookish lad who was the idol of his parents, died at the age of sixteen. Stanford admitted that one reason for establishing a university in his son's memory and with his name was that it seemed in part to fill the vacuum in his wife's life. Such consideration for her also led him to provide, in case he died first, that his wife's surrogate interest in the university be sustained by making her, in effect, the sole trustee. Ezra Cornell had children but believed that they would be better off if they inherited only a "competency," as the phrase was. It was with genuine reluctance that he consented to have his name attached to the university. Rockefeller's wealth was so vast and increased so phenomenally that he could enlarge his philanthropies without affecting the large legacies he planned for his children. Whether because he had sons to carry on the family name or whether from modesty, he firmly refused to have the university he helped establish at Chicago named for him.

The example of friends also affected the decisions of the men who made possible the new universities. When, in his later years, Johns Hopkins gave increasing thought to the disposition of his fortune, he seems to have been struck by a friend's remark that two things were sure always to live: a university, for there would always be youth to train, and a hospital, since there would always be suffering to relieve. More important were the talks he had with the renowned international banker, George Peabody, who like himself had made the beginnings of his fortune in Baltimore and was unmarried. Peabody told Hopkins of his own decision to name trustees to administer his fortune for the well-being of mankind, including the education of youth.[8] Stanford knew Ezra Cornell and was impressed by what he was doing at Ithaca. Again, in his own California days, Jonas Clark was acquainted with Stanford and eyed with interest the founding of the institution at Palo Alto. And the men of means who gave generously to Cornell were friends of the founder whose example markedly influenced them.

But family considerations and the example of friends were often of less weight in the decision to found a university than other factors. As self-made men the founders were not college graduates.

Except for Stanford, who attended an academy, none had more than common schooling. Although all believed staunchly in self-help, all of them wanted to enable other young men to have educational opportunities they themselves had not enjoyed. As men of affairs, however, they believed that existing institutions failed to give young people the equipment needed for successful achievement in business, agriculture, and the sciences.[9] At the opening of Cornell its founder thus expressed the hope that the foundation had been laid for an institution "which shall combine practical with liberal education, which shall fit the youth of our country for the professions, the farms, the mines, the manufactories, for the investigations of science, and for mastering all the practical questions of life with success and honor."[10] Clark's idea was to give young men an education that would fit them for "good citizenship and their work in life."[11] The Stanfords had in mind an institution which would "qualify students for personal success and direct usefulness in life" as well as instilling in their minds "an appreciation of the blessings of this Government, a reverence for its institutions, and a love for God and humanity."[12]

Johns Hopkins, the donor of the largest sum in the 1870's and 1880's for founding a new university, had no clear idea of what a modern university involved. He had shown no particular interest in higher education, either through reading or visiting colleges. With wisdom that matched his generosity he used the simplest phrases to express his wishes, and he did not embarrass the trustees he named to administer the bequest with detailed specifications. The only stipulations Hopkins made were that buildings should not be paid for from capital funds and that the trustees should keep the Baltimore and Ohio stock, that formed the greater part of the endowment, and guard the railroad against political influences. In addition, he asked for scholarships for young men from Maryland, Virginia, and North Carolina. This seemed to some of the trustees an indication that the founder had in mind an institution geared to local and regional needs, one, presumably, of collegiate standing. But the wording of the will and the associated letter of gift was sufficiently general to enable the majority of trustees, with the guidance of the president they chose, to build an institution national in scope and unique in the emphasis given to independent research on the part of a distinguished faculty.

Liberal support of graduate education and the subsidizing of such learned periodicals as the *American Journal of Philology,* the *American Journal of Mathematics,* and *Studies in Political Science* also received emphasis. Thus in using the single word "university," in unfolding no specific plan, and in not establishing the university while he was still living, Hopkins gave maximum freedom to those better equipped than he to build a great and distinctive institution. Conflicts between the founder and those who had to clarify the idea and implement the intention were thus avoided, and the contribution of the philanthropist was limited to providing the financial means to a general end.[13]

The role of no two founders was alike, yet all had one thing in common with Hopkins: none of them envisioned, at least initially, the essentials of a true university. Cornell had founded a free library in Ithaca and had become increasingly interested in promoting opportunities for youth to acquire knowledge and skills in agriculture and mechanics. He thought to set on its feet a stillborn agricultural college in the nearby village of Ovid by a substantial gift conditional on the legislature's assurance of part of the returns from the Morrill Act land grant. But this one-time Quaker and versatile entrepreneur had the capacity for understanding what was involved in a great university. Under the tutelage of Andrew D. White, in effect a cofounder, Cornell came to appreciate the conception of an institution that would embrace all fields of knowledge—literary culture and social science as well as natural science and its applications—and that would be nonsectarian, coeducational, and of high intellectual caliber. And Cornell ingeniously provided material means beyond his first generous gift.[14]

Like Cornell, the Stanfords at first had in mind an institution dedicated to training for the useful vocations, and also emphasizing the development of character and citizenship. And like Cornell, though in lesser degree, they had the capacity to enlarge their original idea and, in the case of Mrs. Stanford, the surviving founder, to make great sacrifices for the institution they had established.[15]

On the other hand, Jonas Clark could not come to grips with the basic problems in the making of a modern university and was unable fully to understand and appreciate the concept. To be sure, he initially conceived of an institution combining college and university, sensed the importance of a library, and favored the advancement of knowledge through research. Under the prodding of the president and trustees he chose, Clark agreed to give the university priority at the start. But he chafed at their reluctance to establish, on inadequate funds, an undergraduate program that he himself came to regard as more important than research and the training of scholars, if he had not always done so.

John D. Rockefeller was unique in his understanding of the university idea. Deeply interested in education and generous in helping Baptist schools, colleges and seminaries, Rockefeller was not entirely unresponsive when his former Cleveland pastor, Dr. August Strong, president of the Rochester Theological Seminary, presented to him in 1885 the idea of a great institution of advanced standing in New York, under Baptist control. Strong conceived of it with an initial endowment of the unheard-of sum of twenty million dollars, capable of supporting outstanding professors in all fields at high salaries and a large number of well-subsidized graduate students. The whole would be dedicated to the enhancement of the Baptist faith and the enrichment of American civilization.[17] But the oil magnate insisted on assurance of a genuine need for and interest in any institution he supported. This had to be demonstrated in the gifts of others.

With his deep concern for his church, Rockefeller had centered his attention on the Morgan Park Theological Seminary near Chicago, for whose faculty, especially Thomas W. Goodspeed and William Rainey Harper, he had great respect. When the old University of Chicago, a feeble school connected with the seminary, closed its doors in 1886, Rockefeller was urged to establish a new University of Chicago to meet the needs of the rapidly growing city and of Middle Western Baptists. The movement gained strength when the American Baptist Education Society, under its new secretary, Frederick T. Gates, a clergyman of great business astuteness and organizing talent, presented the claims of Chicago in strong terms to Rockefeller and when, further, it seemed clear that local businessmen were prepared to help in establishing a new university. The proposal was to begin with a strong college that in time might become a great university, comparable to the one August Strong envisioned for New York. Rockefeller approved of this procedure and offered to give six hundred thousand dollars on the condition that Middle Western Baptists and Chicago businessmen give four hundred thousand.

Above all, Rockefeller was eager to have Harper, former professor of Hebrew at Morgan Park and currently a highly valued member of the Yale faculty, as head of the new institution. Harper was nationally known for his success in Chautauqua and for enlisting clergymen in Hebrew correspondence courses. He shared Strong's idea of a great university, though he would tie it less tightly to the orthodox wing of the Baptist church. However, he was unwilling to leave Yale to become the head of merely another college. It was largely his insistence that a university be established from the very start that persuaded Rockefeller to go beyond his initial conditional gift of six hundred thousand dollars and to make possible through gifts in the millions, both conditional and unconditional, the almost overnight establishment of a great university in Chicago under Harper's leadership. With evidence of success in the undertaking at hand, Rockefeller generously helped meet the never-ending calls for additional funds needed for a university of the first rank. Part of his willingness to help stemmed from the tact President Harper used in approaching his greatest patron.[18] Rockefeller continued to give despite widespread criticism throughout the country, especially in Populist stongholds. His enemies claimed that he was creating a university to improve his reputation and to further the monopolistic views he would expect his professors to teach.

At each new university the conditions, size, and effectiveness of giving varied, but it was only too quickly apparent that in no instance was the endowment adequate for realizing the purposes of the founders and directors. The largest outright gift was the $3,500,000 of Johns Hopkins to the projected university in Baltimore. This was supplemented by an identical amount for a hospital to be related to the university medical school. Since none of the capital fund of the university was to be spent for buildings, Johns Hopkins started with an annual income that enabled President Daniel Coit Gilman to select both great and promising scholars and to enable them to give time and energy to original investigation. Outstanding graduate students were attracted by the faculty and the liberal fellowships. Gilman's charming personality and persuasive arguments won the support of most of the citizens of

Baltimore, who previously had favored a conventional college for the area. The whole educational world was startled by the success of Gilman and the trustees in launching a great university and, for the time, the only one in America to subordinate undergraduate teaching to research and training specialized scholars. Presently young men with Hopkins doctorates were themselves developing graduate work in other universities, and the vogue of seeking advanced training in Germany weakened. President Eliot, at the twenty-fifth anniversary of Gilman's inauguration, testified that the "graduate school of Harvard University, started feebly in 1870 and 1871, did not thrive until the example of Johns Hopkins forced our faculty to put their strength into the development of our instruction for graduates." [19]

Yet all this was done on what proved to be an inadequate and precarious financial base. In 1887 the dividends of the Baltimore and Ohio stock that Hopkins obliged the trustees to keep failed altogether. It looked as if the doors of the university would have to close. But Baltimore businessmen rallied to raise an emergency fund of $108,700. In 1896, when the railroad stock was again imperiled, the business community rallied a second time, and the legislature appropriated fifty thousand dollars a year for two years. By 1902 gifts from Baltimoreans had exceeded the original endowment of the university. [20]

At the very time that the Hopkins was undergoing its financial crisis, Leland and Jane Stanford were taking steps to found in California a university that was reported to be endowed with the total family estate, estimated at the vast sum of twenty million dollars. Admirers of the Stanfords and friends of higher education at home and abroad hailed the announcement as an act of unparalleled generosity. But Stanford's numerous enemies spared no invective in denouncing him for egotistically enshrining the memory of his son in an institution that California, in view of the slender enrollment at the struggling state university, did not need. Much was also made of the fabulous treasure, all "ill-gotten," the railroad magnate was pouring into his son's educational monument.

The new California institution only appeared to be the richest educational enterprise in the world. Actually, when it finally opened in 1891, it possessed only the campus with the first of the handsome Romanesque quadrangles and three unproductive but extensive tracts of land. Aware that bequests often failed to be managed in a way to realize the donor's intention and convinced that he could best handle his own fortune, Stanford merely assured David Starr Jordan, whom he had chosen as president, that he could have all he needed. When Stanford died in 1893 his wife was his sole heir, and the charter had already given the surviving spouse complete control of the university. Mrs. Stanford was determined to realize her husband's purpose, which she fully shared, of making the infant institution into a "university of high grade." But the depression that was just breaking dealt a hard blow to the Southern Pacific stock that, with shares of subsidiary corporations, made up the bulk of the estate aside from the great tracts of almost worthless land. Worse, it looked as if the estate was in debt some eight million dollars. Until the will could be probated the university was without funds for operating costs. Mrs. Stanford's advisers urged her to close the doors until the estate was settled, but with a determined courage she refused to follow the advice. The court permitted her ten thousand dollars a month and ruled that she might regard the faculty as her personal servants. Despite every economy, including a twelve percent pay cut and frequent postponement in paying what was due, it seemed impossible to carry on. At one point Mrs. Stanford went to London with her jewels, her only personal assets, valued at half a million dollars, hoping to sell them at Queen Victoria's Jubilee. But the market was dull and she brought most of the treasure back. To make matters still worse, the United States government in 1894 filed a contingent claim for fifteen million dollars against the estate, a claim that if recognized meant complete financial ruin and a blot on her husband's honor. After exasperating delays Mrs. Stanford went to Washington and personally persuaded President Cleveland to expedite the procedure. In the end the Supreme Court gave a decision in her favor.[21]

But new problems appeared. Mrs. Stanford had considerable trouble with the Southern Pacific and her husband's former railroad partners. In 1899 she gave the railroad properties to the university, but the returns were never enough for its ever-expanding needs and rising costs. Since the impression still prevailed that the university was incomparably rich, gifts from new donors were slow in coming. But they did come. Decades later, when California's fantastic population growth skyrocketed the value of the land, which Stanford had stipulated was not to be alienated, the university at last seemed to have won out in its long struggle with poverty.[22]

As for the institution established by Jonas Clark at Worcester, it did not fulfill his hopes during his lifetime, nor did it realize the expectations he permitted G. Stanley Hall to entertain when he accepted the presidency. One reason was Clark's personality. Like Stanford, he insisted on keeping in his own hands the greater part of his estate. Who, he asked, was better equipped to manage it? Although he familiarized himself with colleges and universities and achieved respectable self-culture, his reticence and failure to communicate with his trustees and President Hall concerning his actual purposes and plans for the financial support of the institution led to endless grief. It was generally supposed that his fortune ranged from eight to twenty million dollars, yet Clark failed to let those in charge of the university know. The university opened with a plant and with the six hundred thousand dollars the founder conferred on the board of trustees, the income of which was utterly inadequate to maintain the small but distinguished faculty that Hall had assembled.

For the first three years Clark partly made up the difference between endowment income and expenditures. But although he himself had approved the spending plans, he came to feel they were far too great. After this time he gave nothing at all. Since the income from endowment and fees was much too small to permit Hall to keep his promises to the faculty—in fact, he had to cut staff and salaries—discontent throve. Nor could Hall explain matters to the faculty. He felt he must "cover" for Clark in the hope that the founder might still resume his support or at least provide generously in his will for the university. The result was that when President Harper appeared in Worcester with offers of much higher salaries than Clark could give, most of the faculty migrated to Chicago. Hall was heartbroken. He understood the position of those who left, though he regarded Harper's raid as somewhat reprehensible. But he gallantly picked up the pieces and carried on in the hope that the founder might still enable the university to fulfill the high purposes for which it was established. Such was not the case. When Clark died in 1900, his estate was much smaller than anyone had anticipated. The bulk of it went to endow an undergraduate college, which apparently was what Clark had always wanted most. Thanks to Hall's reputation as a father of modern psychology and child study, the university continued to maintain advanced studies in these and in a few other fields and to remain, during Hall's lifetime, a distinguished if small institution. But it did not attract enough gifts from well-to-do citizens of Worcester to become the great graduate center Hall had set his heart on, with the initial encouragement of the founder.[23]

The relationship of Ezra Cornell to the institution he made possible was happier, if by no means an altogether smooth one. A "tough-minded idealist," Cornell had great foresight, practicality, and selfless devotion to the democracy of the intellect. At first minded to make a gift to a half-built agricultural college and to secure for it part of New York's share of the public lands provided by the Morrill Act, Cornell was won over by the argument of Andrew D. White, his colleague in the legislature, that the total share of public lands ought to go to one outstanding institution. Cornell made his first gift of half a million dollars in Western Union stock and a site for a university on the condition that the state allocate all its share of the land scrip to the new institution.

Cornell used his political skill to secure legislative approval of the plan, a victory of no mean character in view of the determined opposition of some twenty sectarian colleges and of two nominally existing institutions founded to give the kind of practical education outlined in the Morrill Act. Then, rather than have New York's nine million acres sold for a song in a glutted market, Cornell, after failing to persuade the trustees of the new university to buy the land scrip and keep it until prices rose, himself bought some of the land, supervised its location in Wisconsin's pineries, and resisted pressure from President White and most of the trustees to sell it to meet operating costs. The vitriolic denunciations that had been showered on him in church-college circles, the press, and the legislature itself during the battle in Albany were now resumed. Cornell was charged with making a new fortune for himself by buying and manipulating the land scrip. It took a legislative investigation to set the record straight. In the end, Cornell's stubborn determination to keep the land until the market rose netted the university five million dollars; had the scrip been sold initially, the endowment from the sale could not have run above six hundred thousand. Cornell also aided in laying out the campus, supervising the buildings, and meeting from his own often slender purse the salaries of faculty when current income was inadequate. He purchased for the museum the Jewett collection of fossils and for the library Charles Anthon's seven thousand volumes of classical literature and, at a cost of a thousand dollars, Piranesi's rare *Antiquities of Rome*.[24]

More than all this, Cornell opened his mind to new ideas; he knew, furthermore, how to mold them into his own educational objectives. He supported White's pathbreaking innovations, the liberalizing of the arts curriculum by recognizing the importance of such subjects as literature, the social sciences, and architecture and by giving students greater freedom to choose their courses. He stood with White for a nonsectarian institution and suffered the wrath of the churchmen. He also supported White's plans for coeducation and for scientific research. To a degree even greater than White he set store on the utilitarian values of educational training, an emphasis he was convinced need not weaken traditional cultural values and programs. At times White was impatient and even vexed with Cornell's penchant for such "practical" schemes as giving the ill-fated vocational training idea another chance and for connecting his beloved Ithaca with costly railroad facilities. But he fully appreciated the mind, character, and generosity of Cornell and worked more harmoniously with him than any other president was able to do with the founders who took an active part in building the new universities.[25]

Cornell's friends and business associates helped to enlarge and strengthen the institution at Ithaca. In 1869, when the outlook was dim, John McGraw made possible the building of needed lecture halls and the scientific museum. John Sibley established the engineering college along new and fruitful lines. Henry W. Sage, in addition to taking over the supervision of the land-grant pineries after Cornell's death and devoting himself as chairman of the board of trustees to the financial interests of the university for more than a quarter of a century, gave a chapel for nondenominational worship, endowed a school of philosophy, and built a dormitory that made possible the striking innovation of coeducation at the university level. In all, Sage's gifts totaled well over a million dollars. Others, including White himself, enriched the library.[26]

One misfortune cast a shadow over the philanthropic largess that made Cornell what it came to be. Inheriting the fortune of her father, John McGraw, Jennie McGraw Fiske provided in her will for a gift of two million dollars, chiefly to be used for a great library. The charter of the university had stipulated that its assets should be limited to three million dollars, the value of Harvard's endowment at the time of Cornell's incorporation, but its assets had already edged above this figure. Jennie McGraw's husband challenged the will. After much litigation the university lost its appeal to the Supreme Court of the United States. Too late, the legislature changed the charter provision limiting the assets to three million. Sage, to make up in part for the blow for which in refusing to accept a compromise he was partly at fault, gave six hundred thousand dollars for a library. But the great opportunity to make Cornell's the outstanding university library of the country was, to White's persisting regret, lost.[27]

In view of the rough seas Cornell and White faced in launching their university and guiding it during the early years, their achievement was unique. Among their accomplishments were the combination of public and private support, alumni representation on the governing board, the inclusion of both the older and newer disciplines, and recognition of the value of research, coeducation, and nonsectarianism. To be sure, during White's long absence in foreign service Cornell experienced setbacks, but thanks to the part Sage played in choosing Jacob Gould Schurman as the new president the university again established a position of leadership among the nation's institutions of higher learning.

In contrast to Cornell's efforts for his university, John D. Rockefeller maintained a detached, if friendly, interest in the University of Chicago while expanding the magnitude of his giving. His continued generosity, often made conditional on other gifts, enabled President Harper and the trustees to augment the university's resources. These included the contributions that Marshall Field added to his first gift of land for the campus; the gift of Martin Ryerson, a devoted trustee, which made possible the physical laboratory in which Albert Michelson helped to revolutionize knowledge of the universe; Charles T. Yerkes's gift of a great telescope and observatory; the half million dollars from the estate of William B. Ogden for the Ogden Graduate School of Science; and a series of benefactions which established twenty-nine distinguished professorships named for the donors. Chicago rallied to the university and this, together with the thirty-five million dollars the founder gave before 1910, provided a means by which Harper shaped its character—a combination of urbanity and respect for religion—and, in an incredibly short time, guided it to greatness.[28]

Johns Hopkins, Cornell, Chicago, Clark, and Stanford, although the most influential of the new universities born of philanthropy, did not exhaust the impulse. The story of Vanderbilt University is interesting, partly because Cornelius Vanderbilt, the richest man in the years immediately after the Civil War, was contemptuous of both higher education and philanthropy. Under ordinary circumstances he would, as a nonchurchman, have refused to listen to the needs of Central University which Holland McTyerie, a bishop of the Southern branch of the Methodist Episcopal Church, had established in Nashville in 1872 to give a better training to ministers and, hopefully, to become a great university. But Vanderbilt's second wife, a Mobile lady and a devout Methodist, together with her pastor, Charles F. Deems, persuaded him to make what was for him an unprecedented gift of half a million dollars to save the languishing institution and, through its influence, to strengthen intersectional ties. Accustomed as he was to managing his own affairs in a dictatorial way, Vanderbilt specified that Bishop McTyerie should, as head of the institution, be vested with complete power. Pleased when the trustees renamed the institution for him in 1873, Vanderbilt contributed another sum equal to his original gift. He made no effort to interfere with the university. His example and the persuasive efforts of Bishop McTyerie and his successors interested sons, grandsons, and other members of the family to give, by the end of World War II, approximately ten million dollars.[29] Vanderbilt University found other benefactors, too, notably Anna Russell Cole, the wife of a Nashville railroad magnate,[30] and the Carnegie and Rockefeller foundations. In time it achieved the university status of which Bishop McTyerie had dreamed.

Paul Tulane, a self-made man of New Jersey background, made

his fortune in New Orleans in dry-goods enterprises and in real estate. During the Civil War his sympathies were with the Confederacy, and he wanted to help the white youth of New Orleans in getting a useful education. A bachelor who had been liberal with his gifts to needy individuals and institutions, Tulane decided in 1882 to transfer his New Orleans real estate to a board of trustees in the interest of "such a course of intellectual development as shall be useful and of solid worth, and not be merely ornamental or superficial." His initial gift, valued at more than three hundred thousand dollars, was followed by others that altogether totaled more than a million dollars. He planned to give even more, but he died in New Jersey without a will and the residue fell to nieces and nephews. The trustees Tulane named were unusually free to decide on ways seemingly best fitted to realize the donor's general aim. Rather than build an institution to rival the impoverished University of Louisiana, it was decided to absorb it. The state surrendered its claims and ceased its meager support.[31] Thanks to later gifts, including that of Mrs. Josephine Louise Newcomb for a women's college,[32] the institution, renamed Tulane, developed into one of true university rank rivaling Vanderbilt as a leader in Southern higher education.

In the case of Trinity College, a Methodist institution in North Carolina, a university resulted from the gradual growth of interest of one family. In 1892 Benjamin Newton Duke, whose fortune rested on tobacco, railroads, cotton manufacturing, and power development, decided to give up his plan of building an orphanage in Durham, North Carolina and to strengthen enfeebled Trinity College on condition that it move to his home town. Although Duke's concern for his religion was evident not only in what he did for the college but also in the aid given for the rehabilitation of rural churches and for a preachers' pension fund, he was also deeply interested in the improvement of the community and state in which he made his money and in using it as a stimulus for self-help. Between 1898 and 1925 his gifts to Trinity approximated two million dollars. Moreover, his example influenced his brother, James Buchanan ("Buck") Duke, to create, in 1924 and 1925, an endowment fund of approximately a hundred million dollars, designated largely for transforming the college into Duke University.[33]

The Duke Endowment did not lack critics, however. Ernest

Seeman, a former manager of the Duke University Press, asserted that the institution's chemistry department and medical school were merely branches of private industry. He also charged the Duke trustees with suppressing liberal opinion by attempting to muzzle professors. Seeman complained that Dr. Edmond Soper, dean of the school of religion, was forced to resign because of his pacifist activities. Dean Justin Miller of the law school opposed a demand by the fund's trustees that he prevent professors from aiding the New Deal, and had to leave Duke. Seeman said John P. Troxell, professor of economics and business administration, was forced from his job because of his pro-worker course on labor, and Leslie Craven, professor of law, resigned after his courses in public utilities drew criticism from trustees. Another critic, Ben Dixon Mac-Neill, said Duke University was designed to placate public opinion while the main purpose of the Duke Endowment was to preserve the family tobacco and electric power empires. "Buck" Duke's arrogant admission of the last charge suggests that idealistic devotion to the higher learning was not a major part of his philanthropic motivation.[34]

The conception of the stewardship of wealth, evident in some degree in Duke's benefactions, was even more strongly apparent in what another Southern millionaire did in the transformation of a Methodist college into a leading university. Asa Candler was a Georgian who had been prevented by his family situation from attending college and medical school, on which he had set his heart. He entered the drug-store trade instead and developed a phenomenally successful business in making and distributing Coca-Cola. A devout Methodist, he believed that God had blessed him beyond his just deserts by giving him "such a measure of this world's goods as to constitute a sacred trust" to be administered "with conscientious fidelity with reference to His divine will."[35]

Deeply interested in Christian education, Candler developed a special concern for Emory College, a small, church-supported liberal-arts school near Atlanta. He took his first step in 1914 in response to the decision of Vanderbilt University to accept from the Carnegie Foundation for the Advancement of Teaching a million dollars, conditional on secular control, to bolster its faltering medical school. Since it appeared that Vanderbilt University was thus swerving away from its denominational moorings, the Methodists decided to establish two church-controlled institutions. With the cooperation of the Atlanta business community and the church, Candler played a major role in transforming Emory College into Emory University. His initial gift of a million dollars toward an endowment was the largest gift a Southerner had made for Southern education. It was followed by other benefactions, mounting in all to eight million dollars. Candler also served as a devoted trustee of the new institution,[36] and other members of the family also supported the university generously. Candler's son, Howard, a graduate of the old Emory and a staunch advocate of free enterprise in business and freedom in higher education, gave the university thirteen million dollars before he died in 1957. The Candler support attracted other gifts, including foundation grants.[37]

The doctrine of the stewardship of wealth inspired others besides Methodists to make possible the founding of new universities. In 1888 John B. Stetson, who had made a fortune in the family hat business, became interested in a Baptist academy at his winter home in Deland, Florida. He had long been generous in aiding Baptist institutions, and he began making liberal gifts in money and buildings to the academy, which renamed itself John B. Stetson University. On his death in 1906, however, Stetson left his entire estate of five million dollars not to his namesake, but to his family.[38]

Religious motives played a leading part in the decision of a Roman Catholic businessman in Omaha in 1874 to found an institution of collegiate grade. But Edward Creighton died before he carried his intention into action. His widow, inheriting his fortune and purpose, did not live long enough to carry out the plan either, but her will provided for the allocation of an estate of a hundred thousand dollars to trustees, and in due course Creighton University opened its doors under Jesuit auspices. A younger brother, John, supported the university with gifts estimated at more than a million dollars. Thanks to the generosity of the Creightons and to other well-to-do Nebraska Catholics the university developed professional schools, and though never adequately endowed it played an increasingly important part in the community.[39]

Leading clergymen took the initiative and bore the burden of establishing a better-known and stronger Catholic institution of higher learning in the nation's capital. Since in the 1880's Catholics still had no true university of their own, a group of leading bishops promoted a plan for raising the intellectual level of the church in America by establishing a new university, national in scope and dedicated solely to advanced studies. When the ecclesiastical way was clear, the organizing committee was in a position to solicit support from well-to-do Catholics.

It interested Mary Gwendoline Caldwell, a wealthy New York heiress, who, on November 13, 1884, announced her intention of giving three hundred thousand dollars for an institution for the higher education of the clergy. The donor specified that the School of Philosophy and Theology was to be under the control of a committee of bishops, that it was never to fall under the sway of a religious order, that it was to be open only to ecclesiastics who had completed elementary courses in theology and philosophy, and that other faculties might be added to form the Catholic University of America. In turn she was to be regarded as the founder of the institution. Her philanthropy was rewarded with a papal medal.[40]

Other donors fell into line. Eugene Kelley, a multimillionaire businessman and banker, endowed a chair of ecclesiastical history and served as treasurer and financial consultant, for which he received the papal honor of Chamberlain of the Cape and Sword. Other wealthy laymen, including the Drexel sisters of Philadelphia, the Misses Andrews of Baltimore, Myles O'Connor of San José, and M. P. O'Brien of New Orleans, endowed chairs and made other gifts.

However, Bishop Keane, the rector, was optimistic in informing Cardinal Gibbons ten months before Catholic University opened that "sufficiency of funds is now secured for all needs." The university did not have all that was needed to realize the high hopes for building a great institution of advanced studies. And unfortunately the treasurer, Thomas Waggaman, a highly respected businessman, used university funds for speculation, with the result that by the autumn of 1904 only a third of the endowment was available. After much litigation the institution collected $360,000 of the nine hunred thousand dollars entrusted to Waggaman, but the affair left a scar that contributed to the slow pace with which gifts came. Miss Caldwell, now Marquise des Monstries Merinville, even threatened to have the charter revoked.[41]

Secular as well as religious factors were responsible for new

foundings. William Marsh Rice, a Yankee who migrated to Texas
before the Civil War, made a fortune of eight million dollars in
Houston as a wholesale grocer and importer and through investments in railways and land. Although twice married, Rice had no
children. He left Houston during the Civil War because of his
Unionist sympathies. When he revisited it in 1891 he developed
a plan for an educational institution to be established after his
death. Meantime he made several gifts to a foundation he had set
up and provided that it should be the chief beneficiary of his
estate.

His death in New York in 1900, some years after that of his
second wife, was clouded with mystery. A sensational disclosure
at last revealed that he had been murdered by his butler, acting
for his lawyer, who had forged a new will. In 1912, however, the
Rice Institute was at last opened with a notable academic festival
graced by world renowned scholars and scientists whose published
papers in three elegant volumes augured well for the standards of
the new institution. Thanks to the generous endowment and the
decision of the trustees to emphasize quality rather than size, the
new institution, later to become William Marsh Rice University,
was an impressive testimony to fruitful philanthropy almost frustrated by a murderous conspiracy.[42]

The twentieth century's record in the founding of new universities by a single donor was not limited to Rice. Another Texan
contributed a far greater sum to higher education with quite a
different outcome. Hugh Roy Cullen dropped out of school at the
age of twelve, worked in a candy factory, at sixteen went into the
cotton buying business, and subsequently moved into wildcat oil
enterprises. By 1930 he was fabulously rich, with a fortune estimated at two hundred million dollars.

In 1937, just three years after Houston Junior College announced
its intention of becoming a university and accepted a gift of a 110-
acre tract, Cullen made his first gift: $350,000 for a liberal-arts
building in memory of his only son, who had been recently killed
by a collapsing oil derrick. Cullen successively built laboratories,
dormitories, lecture halls, and developed the campus of the rapidly
growing institution, which interested him, he insisted, because
it was committed to being an institution for working men and

women. In all, Cullen poured more than twenty-six million dollars into the University of Houston.

Unfortunately, only a small part of this great sum went for endowment. By 1957 the university was facing a deficit and Cullen started a campaign for a Living Endowment Association to encourage Houston citizens to add to the university's endowment, which was only a bit more than three million dollars. But Cullen died before the campaign had really begun, and troubles continued. Houston's story shows that wisdom and foresight in planning and leadership were as necessary in university building as big money.[43]

Single donors played the leading role in three other twentieth-century establishments. George E. Merrick, beginning in 1912, developed Coral Gables, near Miami, into a famous resort. He also originated and made possible by promotion and by his own gifts totaling five million dollars the establishment of the University of Miami in 1925.[44]

Quite different in his role was William Volker, a penniless German immigrant who established a dry-goods business in Kansas City in 1882 and by 1906 was a millionaire. His quiet, anonymous gifts to hundreds of needy individuals and charitable organizations interested in human rehabilitation as well as in relief prepared him for supporting after 1930 the newly founded University of Kansas City. Volker began by offering the promoters an anonymous gift of a hundred thousand dollars to buy a site for a campus. He later gave for operating expenses, buildings, books, and student aid in the conviction that it was important to help young working people continue their education in evening classes. In 1944 an unrestricted gift brought Volker's donations well over the two-million-dollar mark.[45]

Fairleigh Dickinson's more modest gift for higher education in the New Jersey suburban precincts of New York City led to the mushroom growth of a largely tuition-supported, coeducational, nonsectarian institution emphasizing services to industry and to a rapidly growing student population that found it impossible or inconvenient to take advantage of existing educational facilities.[46]

While single donors built most of the new universities, the conviction of a group of men and women of the need of channeling a larger share of Jewish philanthropy into higher education resulted in the establishment in 1948 of Brandeis University. Along with Rice, it was one of the few foundings to achieve distinction soon after its inception. An ingenious plan of "foster alumni" secured annual pledges of a hundred dollars to be used for the operating expenses of the university, which expressed the desire of Jews to make "a corporate contribution to higher education in the tradition of the great secular universities that have stemmed from denominational generosity." Contributions for buildings, professorships, scholarships, and library, while perpetuating the names of donors, did not overshadow the collective character of the support Brandeis received.[47]

The gifts from businessmen who founded and strengthened institutions of higher learning brought to the fore the whole matter of academic freedom. In the last decades of the nineteenth century and in the years thereafter, two theories, developed by radicals and liberals, won considerable acceptance. These have been designated by the leading historians of academic freedom as the conspiratorial theory and the mutual incompatibility theory.[48] The one held that conservative businessmen endowed universities and colleges in order to insure the teaching of orthodox economic and social ideas. The other assumed the existence of a basic and irreconcilable conflict between the academic and the business mind, with the former insisting on unhampered search for truth and the latter on the right of a founder to manage an institution he had established or supported in the manner he controlled his own business. The record does not support either theory, at least in any simplistic sense. Nevertheless, evidence points to occasional interference with freedom of teaching and discussion, just as it also indicates that "Populistic" convictions led some of the state universities to purge their faculties of conservative or orthodox economists.

There were examples of interference with tenure on the part of founders themselves. In the case of Jonas Clark, the single example did not involve a conflict in economic or social views. Disagreeing with the head of the chemistry department over details of equipment, Clark demanded the professor's dismissal. "I had to ask it and the board to approve it, which we did with the greatest reluctance," G. Stanley Hall confessed.[49]

If no conflicts of fundamental views were involved in this instance,

such was not the case at Stanford, despite Mrs. Stanford's statement that the religious, social, and economic ideas and the private
lives of faculty were of no concern to her. H. H. Powers, a much-
liked political scientist, in 1898 offended Mrs. Stanford, a devout
Christian, by his remarks on religion during an address. Although
President David Starr Jordan tried to persuade "the mother of the
University" that Powers should be kept because of his value to the
institution, he bowed to her imperious will.[50]

More significant was the case of Edward A. Ross, professor of
economics and sociology at Stanford. In a university founded by
a leading capitalist, Ross had the temerity to defend publicly Eugene V. Debs, a socialist regarded by those sharing the prevailing
views of the business community as a dangerous man. Ross also
supported William Jennings Bryan in the campaign of 1896, an
act which led Mrs. Stanford to forbid the faculty from taking any
public part in political activities. He also advocated the municipal
ownership of utilities and criticized unrestricted immigration of
Chinese coolies despite the fact that the railroads Stanford and his
associates built had used such labor. "When I take up a newspaper
. . . and read the utterances of Professor Ross . . . ," Mrs. Stanford wrote to President Jordan, "and realize that a professor of the
Leland Stanford Junior University, who should prize the opportunities given him to distinguish himself among his students in the
high and noble manner of his life and teachings before them, thus
steps aside, and out of his sphere, to associate himself with the political demagogues of this city, exciting their evil passions, drawing
distinctions between man and man, all laborers and equal in the
sight of God, and literally plays into the hands of the lowest and
vilest elements of socialism, it brings tears to my eyes. I must confess
I am weary of Professor Ross, and I think he ought not be retained at
Stanford University." [51] Although the president was vested with the
power to appoint and dismiss members of the faculty, Mrs. Stanford
was, in accordance with the charter, acting in place of the trustees
and thus could exercise complete power. Jordan tried to convince
her that dismissal would not be justified in view of Ross's scholarship, judicious classroom instruction, and admirable personal life,
but Mrs. Stanford stood her ground. Ross had to go. For protesting
against this violation of academic freedom and as a result of his

refusal to apologize in public, Professor George Howard was also dismissed. Other professors resigned in protest.

Jordan understood and valued the principle of academic freedom and knew that restriction on it lowered the prestige of Stanford among scholars everywhere. Thus one of the significant aspects of the affair was his pathetic effort to justify the dismissal on the grounds that, after all, Ross was not the man for the place, that Ross had, as Mrs. Stanford insisted, jeopardized the political neutrality of the university (despite the fact that fifty members of the faculty had come out strongly for McKinley in 1896 without incurring any rebuke). Jordan, lacking the strength to defend academic freedom against the bias and strong will of Mrs. Stanford, rationalized his position on the ground that the institution might face financial ruin if she was defied.[52]

But Jordan was not alone in his inability to stand out against interference with teaching staff by a powerful patron. After the death of Ezra Cornell, whose own religious views were hardly orthodox and who, with Andrew D. White, had insisted on the freedom of the university from sectarian pressure, a case arose which tested the devotion of the institution at Ithaca to academic freedom. Felix Adler, founder of the Ethical Culture Society, had been appointed to the faculty on the nomination of Joseph Seligman, who paid his salary. In part at the insistence of Henry W. Sage, chairman of the board of trustees and a generous donor who wanted to make Cornell into a more explicitly Christian institution, Adler was dropped because of his religious liberalism and the presumable damage it did to the image of the university as a nonsectarian institution. The trustees, however, vindicated their action on the ground that gifts for endowed professorships could be accepted only if the choice of the incumbent was left to them, a procedure which, while academically sound, was invoked *ex post facto*. Sage's discontent with W. C. Russel, who was both a professor and vice president, was related in part to Russel's religious liberalism and was one factor in his dismissal while White was on leave as minister to Germany.

An even more clear-cut case of violation of academic freedom occurred in 1886, when Professor Henry C. Adams was asked to fill in at a moment's notice for a speaker who was unable to appear for an appointed discussion of the strike of the employees of the

Gould railroads. The newspaper distortion of the pro-labor speech led Sage to demand Adams's dismissal. "This man must go," Sage told President White. "He is undermining the very foundation of society." White reluctantly decided that he had no alternative but to bow to Sage's demand.[53] Sage consistently opposed faculty participation in educational policy-making and, jealous of the power he conscientiously felt he was using as a philanthropist and businessman in the best interests of the university, was often at loggerheads with President White and was largely responsible for the resignation of his successor, Charles Kendall Adams.[54]

John D. Rockefeller, probably from lack of interest, refrained from taking part in the appointment or dismissal of professors at the university he founded. And President William Rainey Harper firmly declared that "no donor of money to a university . . . has any right before God or man, to interfere with the teaching." Yet I. A. Hourwich, after taking part in a Populist convention, was dismissed in 1894. And Edward W. Bemis, a well-trained economist, publicly championed antimonopoly views the following year and went on to criticize the policies of railroads seeking special privileges. President Harper, much annoyed, proposed that Bemis, during the rest of his association with the university, "exercise very great care in public utterances about the questions that are agitating the minds of the people." Bemis soon received his dismissal and felt it was punishment for his views; Harper insisted the reason was incompetence. Behind Harper's stand may have been his obsession with the idea of a great university and his desire to stay in the good graces of his patrons, without whose generous financial support it would be impossible to realize his dream.[55]

These instances do not, of course, warrant the conclusion that large gifts jeopardized academic freedom. In fact, in at least one instance, the much publicized John Spencer Bassett case at Trinity College, the trustees followed the lead of Benjamin Duke, the most generous benefactor of the institution, in refusing to truckle to a great deal of public pressure for the dismissal of a highly competent scholar whose thoughtful comment on racial relations had offended public opinion.[56] However, the weight of the evidence in similar cases, together with the several examples of the violation of freedom of teaching for those holding conservative economic views by those in control of state institutions during the high tide of Populism, suggests that a full understanding of academic freedom had not yet formed in the minds of either well-to-do benefactors, administrators, and trustees of private institutions or those who controlled the state institutions.

On the constructive side, the great gifts enlarged the freedom of activity of educational experts who shared with the philanthropists joint leadership in building privately supported universities. One of the trustees of The Johns Hopkins University, mindful of the scope that the bequest of the founder gave his colleagues and the president they chose, commented on this freedom in a conversation with Andrew D. White: "We at least have this in our favor; we can follow out our own conceptions and convictions of what is best; we have no need of obeying the injunctions of any legislature, the beliefs of any religious body, or the clamors of any press; we are free to do what we really believe best, as slowly and in such manner as we see fit." [57] Except insofar as unanticipated financial problems imposed obstacles, this was relatively true for Johns Hopkins. It was less true in the case of the other new universities, none of which had sufficient assets to permit anything like complete freedom even when, as at Cornell, the founder's special ideas of what the university should be presented relatively few hurdles for the expert leadership. Even when these allowances have been made, however, philanthropy created great new centers of higher learning and stimulated the transformation of older private institutions into true universities.

Chapter VII

From Friends

The gifts and bequests of men and women who had never studied in the colleges or universities they favored were generally smaller than those of alumni and founders. Nevertheless such gifts and bequests made significant contributions to the transformation of Harvard, Yale, Princeton, Columbia, and New York University, to cite obvious examples, into celebrated centers of learning. In some cases, institutions known as universities but important chiefly in their own community became nationally respected by reason of the generosity of a donor who had little or no previous association with the beneficiary. And hundreds of colleges survived or became more useful as the result of gifts from those who were merely friends. The reasons for the benefactors' choice and the impact of their gifts and bequests make an important chapter in the story of philanthropy's role in shaping American higher education.

Alumni might be expected, for reasons of sentiment, to give to their alma mater without special appeals,[1] but such could hardly be the case for those who had never developed collegiate loyalty in ivy-clad halls. Though it became necessary for educational leadership to give a good deal of attention to potential donors among the alumni, until the First World War it usually sufficed to state the needs of an institution in general terms to an anonymous public in the hope of striking a responsive and lucrative chord.

Just as gifts were almost entirely responsible for such distinction as Harvard, Yale, Columbia, and the College of New Jersey enjoyed at the end of the Civil War, so philanthropy was to play the major role in the transformation of these colonial-era schools, which had some of the attributes of the modern university, into internationally respected institutions truly worthy of the name. Gifts to each in the later decades of the nineteenth century and in the early years of the twentieth owed something to the rivalry between them. Emulation, particularly of the example set by such new universities as Johns Hopkins, Cornell, and Chicago, also stimulated gifts and bequests. So did local pride. But giving was largely related to the attitudes and activities of presidents, trustees, alumni, and members of the faculty in their role as fund-seekers and to friends and donors hitherto unconnected with the institution. In each of the older Atlantic seaboard colleges the contributions of these parties to the making of a distinguished university differed considerably.

Before being chosen president of Harvard in 1869, Charles W. Eliot had called attention in much-discussed articles in the *Atlantic Monthly* to the expanding and changing needs of higher education and had outlined in general terms what, in his view, needed to be done. His inaugural address spelled out these needs in reference to Harvard. The speech gave considerable attention to philanthropy, past and prospective.[2]

Forgetting at least one notable exception,[3] Eliot expressed pride in what he termed the fact that through its long history Harvard had guarded gifts so carefully that no one could point to a single example of malfeasance or betrayal of the donor's intention. He did, to be sure, note that while the university accepted gifts and kept these in a special fund if the donor so stipulated, a single mistake in the management of such an isolated fund might be disastrous. For this reason wisdom suggested the advantages of not restricting too narrowly the uses to which a gift might be put and of allowing it to be managed within the main stream of the institution's resources. Although Harvard had only lately received gifts enabling it to establish the Museum of Comparative Zoology and to found the Museum of American Archaeology and Ethnology, Eliot stressed the point that except for the observatory no agency in the university was sufficiently endowed to permit investigators to devote full time for research. He went on to say that, thanks largely to gifts of the last fifteen years, funds were at hand to enable worthy students, however poor, to enjoy Harvard's advantages. But he made it equally clear that much more money was needed if all the poor but able young men who wanted to study at Harvard were to be enabled to do so. "The future will take care of itself," Eliot continued with an eye on future alumni, "for it is to be expected that the men who in this generation had the benefit of these funds, and who succeeded in after life, will pay manifold to their successors in need the debt which they owe, not to the College, but to benefactors whom they cannot even thank, save in heaven." [4]

Boston had long nourished Harvard, and the new industrial wealth flowed more freely than ever before in response to Eliot's program for developing a distinguished faculty of creative scholars, graduate study, well-supported professional schools, and other facilities needed to make Harvard a great university. Eliot held that in general it was a mistake for the president of a large university to ask directly for money unless it had been previously intimated that such a request would be welcome: he should rather have his plans so clearly shaped that these would appeal to a man who might be interested. In discussing Harvard benefactors he noted that gifts for three dormitories, put up early in his administration, and a home for the law school came without any solicitation from him or from any other officer of the university. [5] On occasion he pointed out to industrialists that a needed laboratory might well yield new knowledge highly useful to their businesses. For the most part, however, Eliot emphasized Harvard's contributions to public service, making clear what was wanted and why it was needed. Gifts flowed in, with the result that endowment funds tripled between 1869 and 1878 and tripled again in the next twenty years. During the crucial period between 1869 and 1889 gifts for current use increased nearly 150-fold, growing from the insignificant sum of $829 to $124,266. And by 1909, when Eliot retired, the sum of gifts for current purposes was double the 1889 amount. [6] Only rarely, it seems, did the president refuse gifts. But on one occasion he did turn down an offer of a bell tower, made contingent on the restoration of compulsory chapel.

Eliot's successor, Abbott Lawrence Lowell, an inheritor of wealth and social position and a scholar in law and government, saw the endowment increase from $22,117,599 in 1909 to $128,520,519 on his retirement in 1933. In addition, gifts for current use ran to many millions. In augmenting both kinds of resources Lowell's personality and educational leadership played an important part. Like Eliot, he believed that an essential part of Harvard's tradition was openness to change. Lowell proved very effective in educating Harvard's potential donors in the reasons why changes were needed. This is evident, for example, in the telling support he gave to Professor Frank W. Taussig and other members of the economics department when they met with indifference and opposition in projecting a plan for a graduate school of business administration.

To take another example, he believed, as Eliot had, that student housing ought to be provided without reference to religious affiliation—Jewish students should not congregate in particular dormitories—and further that housing ought to cut across the differences in the social backgrounds of students. To realize these goals Lowell set about the task of building the new freshmen dormitories. Later he called attention to the need for developing corporate living units, or "houses," in which undergraduates might meet faculty and with which they might feel a special sense of identity. To avoid the opposition that had wrecked a similar proposal at Princeton, Lowell consulted with and won over student leaders. He spoke persuasively to alumni and friends of the advantages of such a system of student life and interest, and thanks to Edward Harkness, a Yale man whose alma mater had at the time of his proposal been unable to agree to accept a gift for a similar plan, President Lowell's plan was realized.[7]

Although Lowell insisted that he had no talent for soliciting funds and believed that gifts would come if genuine and pressing needs were made apparent, on at least one occasion he proved a highly effective solicitor. Lowell was eager to have Mrs. Russell Sage contribute toward one of the new freshmen dormitories, but she had never shown any interest in Harvard. Her previous philanthropy had been in the sphere of women's education and social welfare. Moreover, her closest adviser suggested that Harvard's own graduates and the Boston business community might be expected to provide for the college. Lowell's arguments in letters and in visits to Mrs. Sage included the idea that a freshman dormitory would promote social democracy in student life, a value, he reminded her, she had always believed in. When the gift proved inadequate to cover the cost, which was greater than had been anticipated, Lowell, by additional persuasive letters and personal visits, induced Mrs. Sage to increase her gift to cover the whole cost of the dormitory.[8]

Also important for the growth of the university and for improvement in the quality of its programs was Lowell's own quiet, generally anonymous example of giving. According to his biographer, these gifts reached unknown millions. In so giving he was less influenced by a desire to see quick results associated with his own name than by a faith in imponderables and by a firm commitment to the stewardship of wealth.[9]

At the same time Lowell was discriminating in his attitude toward proffered gifts. Thus he refused Albert Pillsbury's offer of $25,000 for a counterattack on the growing tendency of women to curtail domestic interests in order to play a larger role in professional and public life. (Yale, Columbia, and Princeton likewise refused Pillsbury's offer.) Again, Lowell would have none of a large sum offered to promote the controversial and untested claims of the eugenicists. And, in an effort to avoid needless duplication of equipment and instruction in the field of engineering, he did all he could to have the largest gift in Harvard's history channeled to a sister school.[10]

By 1900 Harvard's capital assets had grown to thirteen million dollars while Yale's had reached only five million. Some years later, when Yale turned to John D. Rockefeller for support, the oil magnate asked for an explanation of the striking difference between the resources of the two institutions. The secretary of the university replied that the first and main cause was the attitude of Noah Porter, president between 1871 and 1886.[11] A conservative not only in theology but in wanting to keep Yale to its old moorings, Porter refused to solicit funds and opposed the movement, which had some faculty support, to remake Yale into a university in which the college was to be a subordinate, rather than a dominating, unit. The situation at Yale began to change when Timothy Dwight became president in 1886. He tried to carry out the ideas he had set forth in 1870 when, as a professor in the Divinity School, he had been a spokesman for a group that favored greater emphasis on creative scholarship and scientific investigation. As president, Dwight secured a legislative act authorizing the title "Yale University." He bolstered the several constituent schools and pointed to the need for buildings and increased funds. Graduate studies, authorized as early as 1860, were at last put on an organized footing; the library was enriched; and scholarship and original investigation were increasingly emphasized. If Dwight himself did not solicit funds for these larger ends, he made the needs known and set an example by turning his salary back into the treasury and by giving more than a hundred thousand dollars besides.[12]

Under Dwight's successor, Arthur T. Hadley, an economist and the first lay president (1899–1921), Yale developed into a great national university. While this was in part "the natural fruition of time," Hadley did much to attract philanthropic support for the library, laboratories, and graduate and professional study. He did this without minimizing the traditional Yale spirit of liberal culture, teamwork, and the development of character among undergraduates.[13]

The situation at Columbia in the 1870's and 1880's differed in many ways from that in New Haven. President Frederick A. P. Barnard and Professor John W. Burgess, who organized a graduate faculty of political science in 1880, pointed the way toward the transformation from college to university.[14] In Barnard's time the first substantial gifts from both alumni and nonalumni friends began to augment Columbia's resources.

The promising beginnings of a new day at Columbia were more largely realized under the administration of Seth Low, a wealthy political reformer with telling contacts in the business world. At Low's inauguration in 1890 Harvard's President Eliot forcefully pointed out that much larger funds were imperative: "It is simply impossible to carry on a great university in this expensive city with any such meager resources as those which Columbia now possesses. She must have manifold more."[15] The significance of the figures Eliot presented on the resources of Harvard and Columbia was not lost. Convinced that donors would be more likely to give to an institution with distinguished scholars, Low brought in such men as John Bassett Moore and Henry Fairfield Osborn. His administrative skill, which impressed well-to-do leaders in industry and finance, was reflected in the development of the University Council, in the closer relation with the recently founded Teachers College and Barnard College, and in the new tie with the College of Physicians and Surgeons, which the Vanderbilts began to patronize.

Low was also chiefly responsible for the decision to move the campus to Morningside Heights, strengthening in the process the financial resources of Columbia through the lucrative rents the old campus in the heart of the city brought to the treasury. Of the three million dollars needed for the move uptown, Low himself subscribed a third of the three percent bonds and persuaded others to take the rest. At times his zest for donations ran ahead of what was considered proper academic procedure, as when he had to be dissuaded from taking a gift for a professorship of music made contingent on the donor's naming the incumbent. To crown his work, Low gave a million dollars for a library, named for his father. Impressive in style, if badly designed for its function, the Low Library nevertheless set a new standard in America for a facility indispensable to a true university.[16] Low's associates in administration, especially Grace Dodge, secretary of Teachers College, and Dr. James W. McLane, president of the College of Physicians and Surgeons, proved to be effective in attracting much-needed support from such families as the Dodges, Macys, Thompsons, Milbanks, and Vanderbilts.[17]

Columbia's next president, Nicholas Murray Butler, who before his inauguration in 1903 worked closely with Low, proved to be an even more successful fund-raiser. Determined to make Columbia "a national and international powerhouse of scholarship and service," Butler publicized his university as no American educator had ever done, with the possible exception of Harvard's Eliot. During the first ten years of his administration, sixteen million dollars in gifts and bequests augmented Columbia's resources; twenty million more was added between 1911 and 1921. During his long presidency Butler may have raised as much as a hundred million dollars. His annual reports and academic addresses pointed to the university's needs and these invitations, set forth as opportunities for enabling Columbia to perform public services, were supplemented by personal contacts in the consequential metropolitan world.[18] And of long-run importance, not only for Columbia but for all higher education, was Butler's leadership in opposing measures to tax bequests and gifts.[19]

Columbia's neighbor, the College of New Jersey, took halting steps during the administration of James McCosh (1869–88) toward broadening a traditional liberal-arts program and encouraging scholarship through providing several promising graduates with fellowships for overseas study. McCosh, in opposing all suggestions for renaming the college "Princeton University," represented the great majority of the alumni. In 1885, however, he announced that he would no longer stand against the change. Concerned lest alumni who cherished the college they remembered might curtail their gifts, the trustees did not adopt the new name until 1896. During the presidency of McCosh's successor, Francis Patton (1888–1902), some steps were taken toward introducing an engineering and a liberal-arts graduate program and in replacing retiring professors of clerical background with scholars who had pursued advanced study in their specialized fields. But Princeton remained primarily an undergraduate institution with an emphasis on training gentlemen in liberal culture.[20]

In 1902, when Woodrow Wilson became president, Princeton's productive resources totaled less than four million dollars and annual deficits were met by emergency gifts from alumni and friends. The new president asked for funds for a preceptorial system of undergraduate teaching, a school of science, buildings, faculty salary increases, and a graduate school—twelve million dollars in all.[21] This was a staggering sum for Princeton to raise. Wilson wrote letters to philanthropists but found it hard to confront prospective donors personally without feeling himself to be a beggar. Nor could he and his wife bring themselves to entertain men of wealth in the hope of inducing them to give. Wilson's vigorous academic program, however, stimulated contributions.

Of significance for philanthropy, higher education, and politics was student and alumni opposition to Wilson's determination to develop student houses in place of the aristocratic eating clubs. In effect, Wilson believed that graduate students should not be isolated but should live with undergraduates in the proposed new quadrangle "colleges" on which he had set his heart in the interest of democratic student relationships. A bitter quarrel developed on this point between Wilson and the witty and urbane Andrew D. West, professor of classics and dean of Princeton's Graduate School. West received from William Cooper Procter, a former student and well-to-do manufacturer of soap, an offer of half a million dollars, contingent on its being matched, for a separate graduate school. The faculty and trustees were divided on the matter, but Wilson, committed to a deeply held principle, refused to compromise. Nor would Dean West make any concession. In the course of the conflict the president severely criticized some of the methods by which great fortunes had been built in America and moved toward the more liberal political and economic position he was to take as governor of New Jersey and candidate for the presidency of the United States. Meanwhile the majority of the trustees, unwilling to turn down the gift, overruled Wilson. Princeton, as a result, developed a small and, in the eyes of Wilson's partisans, esoteric graduate school.[22]

Trustees as well as presidents were responsible for much of the philanthropic support that made it possible for the older colleges to become distinguished universities. Indirectly, the reputations of the trustees of Harvard, Yale, Columbia, and Princeton as leading bankers and businessmen encouraged gifts by providing donors with assurance of careful handling of their money. Trustees also often made direct gifts for pressing needs and contributed to specific programs. A few examples may suggest the range of contributions. Two of Columbia's trustees, neither a Columbia graduate, proved especially generous. John Stewart Kennedy provided the means for building Hamilton Hall and, in founding the New York School of Philanthropy, established a pioneer professional training center that in time became Columbia's distinguished School of Social Work.[23] Another trustee, A. Barton Hepburn of the Chase National Bank, in 1916 contributed $150,000 without publicity for a chair in business administration, the nucleus of the new School of Business. Skillfully, Hepburn used his influence in breaking down indifference toward the venture, which many, even in the business community, felt was unnecessary. He also got from Emerson MacMillan the means for building a home for the new school.[24] Or, to take a recent example of trustee philanthropy, Henry Krumb, a former mining executive, set aside for Columbia a large share of an estate totaling several million dollars with the specification that $500,000 of it should be used to endow a chair of mining engineering.[25] Across 120th Street, such trustees of Teachers College as the Dodges and the Macys not only provided buildings but met innumerable needs, including annual budget deficiencies.[26]

At Harvard, members of the Corporation and the Board of Overseers made an immeasurable contribution to the greatness of the university. The point may be illustrated by citing a few examples: the fireproof building that Nathaniel Thayer provided for the safekeeping of Asa Gray's famous herbarium; the help given by Perkins, Wadsworth, Byrnes, and others in raising large sums at the end of World War I for art, chemistry, business training, and salary increases; Thomas Lamont's contribution to the drive that netted more than fourteen million dollars, together with his gift of the unique undergraduate library and his bequest of five million dollars; the path that Bishop William Lawrence opened in 1923 for George F. Baker's gift of five million dollars for the new quarters of the Graduate School of Business Administration.[27]

Members of the faculty as well as presidents and trustees helped to augment the resources of Ivy League institutions. Sometimes a gifted teacher interested a student who, later on, gave substantially to his alma mater. Thus Harvard's great teacher of Greek, Evangelinus Sophocles, aroused in William F. Milton of the class of 1851 a respect for the life of the mind that in time resulted in a gift of a million and a half dollars for research. Professor Nathaniel S. Shaler, an outstanding geologist and a captivating teacher, was chiefly responsible for Harvard's receipt in 1903 from Gordon Mac-Kay of the largest bequest it had ever received.[28] The devotion of Kuno Francke, a humanist, to his subject enlisted gifts from Adolphus Busch and other German-Americans for America's first museum of Germanic culture. It was also at Harvard that Professor Crawford Toy and Professor David Gordon pioneered in Semitic researches that led Jacob Schiff of Kuhn Loeb and Company to give the Semitic Museum and to finance fruitful explorations of the site of Samari.[29] Without the zest for art history that Charles Eliot Norton stimulated it is unlikely that Harvard would have received the gift from William Hayes Fogg and his wife that was the beginning of a great collection and a distinguished center for art history and museum training.[30] The pioneer work in social ethics that Professor Francis Greenwood Peabody developed at Harvard led Alfred Tredway White, a New York philanthropist and an early leader in tenement reform, to ask Peabody in 1903 if something could not be done to help undergraduates appreciate the opportunities and obligations for social service. Shortly thereafter he gave Harvard $50,000, a third of the cost of the new Emerson Hall, with the proviso that space be reserved for exhibits and instruction in social ethics. This stimulated the organization, three years later, of the Department of Social Ethics.

At Columbia, Professor E. R. A. Seligman of the well-known banking family opened his own purse and persuaded friends and relatives to contribute to the making of a great university.[31] To the same institution John W. Burgess, who did so much to build the renowned faculty of political science, left a large bequest, as did Professor William Shepherd, a pioneer student of European expansion.

At Yale the theological faculty, shortly after the Civil War, raised the money to rebuild the Divinity School. In a new field that challenged orthodox religion Professor Othniel C. Marsh, an authority on vertebrate fossils, persuaded his kinsman George Peabody, the Baltimore-London banker, to give $150,000 for the Museum of Natural History and Science. Professor Edward Salisbury, a great Oriental scholar, gave Yale his library and other gifts. This included the priceless DeSacy Arabian manuscripts, a mine exploited by William Dwight Whitney and others, who made Yale a center of this field of scholarship.[32]

Although alumni, both as individuals and in their corporate capacity, proved to be increasingly important donors, the gifts and bequests of men and women having no direct connections with a college or university were major factors in helping colleges attain university status and in strengthening existing universities. Even without comprehensive statistics, it is possible to come to some judgment concerning the criticism, often heard in the late nineteenth and early twentieth centuries, that these gifts on the whole went for less important needs and often involved, especially in the case of buildings and new projects, burdens the recipient could carry only at the expense of the most essential purposes of a university.[33]

In some instances, examples of which have been cited in connection with early Cornell and Johns Hopkins, donors were moved to give to an institution with which they had had no association because of the example or influence of a friend. In others the important factor was the advice or influence of an alumnus who served as the attorney of a wealthy man or woman. In most instances, however, the factors that led to a decision to give were related to a donor's own thwarted aspirations. Thus Sheldon Clark, a farmer whose penurious grandfather kept him from going to college, developed the habit of frequenting nearby Yale to learn what he could from professors and students. He returned to live frugally at his farm with the determination to be remembered as a patron of learning. The president and professors at Yale entertained him and encouraged his interest. The result was the Clark scholarships, which in due course proved of genuine value in helping Yale develop graduate studies.[34]

Abraham K. Wright, who had wanted to attend Princeton but could not afford to do so, bequeathed the university the residue of an estate valued at two and a half million which he had built up in the coal business.[35] Still another example was a gift to Yale by a woman of $125,000 to found a chair of equity jurisprudence in memory of her brother, who had not received the college education he had wanted but who nevertheless had become a well-known lawyer.[36]

No doubt pride in a local institution influenced the decision of many donors to give to a college or university with which they had no association as a student. This was true of many of the businessmen who contributed to the development of the University of Chicago, and it seems to have also influenced the decision of Walter P. Murphy, head of the Standard Railway Equipment Company, in giving almost seven million dollars to Northwestern University for an engineering school (the Northwestern Technological Institute) together with housing for it and for the Departments of Physics and Chemistry in the College of Liberal Arts. When Murphy, who once said that his early ambition to make money had been replaced by one to use it wisely, died in 1942, his will left the residue of his estate, approximately twenty-five million dollars, for the further development of the institute. As he had wished, an experimental plan of technical training, in cooperation with industry, led to similar programs in other institutions.[37] Other examples include John Hardin's $1,250,000 bequest to Baylor University in 1936, the largest gift in the history of this Baptist institution in Texas.[38]

It is not unlikely that a desire, conscious or unconscious, to be identified with a prestigious institution influenced some self-made men to give to such universities as Harvard, Yale, and Princeton. The handsome gifts George Peabody made to Harvard and Yale for natural history museums in 1866 heralded much more to come.[39]

In the post-Civil War years Harvard was able to build three much-needed dormitories, Thayer, Matthews, and Weld Halls, thanks to the generosity of friends—not alumni. Speaking many years later of these gifts, President Eliot testified that each had been "of great value to the University, and . . . likely to be serviceable through many generations." [40] In 1876 the legacy of the eccentric bachelor, Price Greenleaf, who had never forgotten his uncle's division of those without worldly goods into "the Lord's poor, the Devil's poor, and the poor devils," established an $800,000 endowment for freshmen who would otherwise have been unable to attend the college. Both Eliot and Lowell felt that the ways in which Jacob Schiff, the Jewish immigrant who became a New York banker, made his gifts to the university for Semitic studies testified to his imagination, grace, and good sense.

The Fogg Art Museum, the gift of a widow of a collector and patron, seemed to some a mere "mouse-trap" better suited for "a tomb for an excessively secret undergraduate society" than for a repository of art. It was indeed poorly adapted even for the limited teaching purposes for which it was intended, but it nevertheless marked the beginning of one of the world's great museums, in terms of both its collections and its program in training teachers and curators of art. The wide range of gifts from non-Harvard men was also illustrated by Edward Mallinckrodt, son of a German immigrant and trained in chemistry at the University of Berlin. This "ammonia king," prompted by the belief that chemistry held more potential benefits for mankind than any other science, felt that by aiding Harvard in establishing a greatly needed laboratory he might help all American laboratories approach the higher standards of those in Europe. [41]

Of all gifts from non-Harvard men, that of Gordon McKay, a self-trained and fabulously successful engineer and inventor, opened wider opportunities and presented more problems than any other donation of the modern era. McKay's will, probated on his death in 1903, established a trust whose income was ultimately to accrue to Harvard for the establishment of professorships, scholarships, and other facilities bearing his name. All funds, the will stipulated, must be allotted in the interest of furthering the applied sciences, especially mechanical engineering, in an environment of general culture and broad intellectual outlook. But President Lowell felt it was unwise to duplicate facilities already at hand in the neighboring Massachusetts Institute of Technology, which was in financial difficulty. He proposed a cooperative arrangement by which much of the McKay bequest, at an estimated twenty million dollars the largest Harvard had ever received, might be allocated to M.I.T. and thus serve the donor's intention more efficiently. Professor Nathaniel S. Shaler, who had much to do with McKay's plans, opposed the so-called "merger," as did many alumni of both institutions. In 1917 the Massachusetts Supreme Court gave the opinion that the agreement did not accord with the provisions in McKay's will, however advantageous it promised to be; the donor had specified that if Harvard did not accept the bequest within a given period of time it was to be used for establishing a new institution bearing the McKay name. Harvard quickly took the money and developed its own engineering school.[42]

Columbia, like Harvard and Yale, benefitted from the generosity of men of wealth unconnected with the university. Jacob Schiff, for example, aided it in funding its debt, helped the move to Morningside Heights, established a loan fund for students and a fellowship in political science, and contributed to professorships in social legislation and social ethics. Schiff also responded generously to Mrs. Annie Nathan Meyer's effort to establish a college for women at Columbia, serving as treasurer in the campaign effort. He even expedited details as mundane as the purchase and proper ordering of kitchen equipment for Barnard's first dormitory. In 1915 Schiff supplemented his many gifts with half a million dollars for Barnard's student center.

Princeton's chief gifts came from her own alumni, but non-Princeton men also strengthened the university. Paul Guenther, founder of the Onyx Hosiery Mills, bequeathed a large part of an eight million dollar estate to Princeton's trustees to be administered as they saw fit.[43] Henry Clay Frick, whose schooling was limited to thirty months in an academy and in Otterbein University [later Otterbein College] in Ohio and whose great zest for art collecting exceeded all his nonbusiness interests, began to give to Princeton in the first year of Wilson's administration when he provided for needed land and a gymnasium. In 1916, in lending $100,000 to the university to enable it to protect certain rights, Frick helped it to realize a net profit of $225,000 from a transaction with the Chase

National Bank. Before his death in 1918, his gifts totaled over $358,000. His will left to Princeton almost a third of the residue of his estate.[44]

Another major figure in the industrial world, Harvey S. Firestone, whose five sons went to Princeton, contributed one million dollars to the long and difficult campaign for six million for a greatly needed library. The undertaking enlisted 1,250 donors, but the Firestone million was much greater than the next largest single contribution.[45]

The Institute for Advanced Study in Princeton, not part of the university, received the gift of a Trenton merchant, Louis Bamberger, and his sister, providing facilities and stimulus for basic research in the sciences and humanities.[46] Such philanthropy to centers for specialized study was common in the twentieth century and aided in giving prominence to the research function of higher education.

Charles Butler heads the list of business and professional men who contributed to making New York University a great institution. A leading lawyer with large interests in western railroads, real estate, insurance, and banking, Butler devoted more than sixty years to the service of New York University, rescuing it on more than one occasion from a financial crisis. His generous gift in 1890 was in memory of his brother, founder of the university's law school, and of his son, a member of the class of 1853.[47]

Philanthropists sometimes chose to distribute gifts to more than one institution. Such a man was Daniel Fayerweather. As a poor, young Yankee peddler, he had been kindly received and encouraged by professors at the University of Virginia at Charlottesville, who aroused his interest in the sort of education he had missed. Before his death in 1890 Fayerweather had become the leading leather merchant in the country. Without solicitation or encouragement and with no indication of wanting his name perpetuated, he drew up a will that left all but a small part of his estate of five million dollars to higher education. Having specified twenty colleges and universities as beneficiaries, he was reminded by a confidant of a New York state law against bequeathing more than half of an estate to charitable purposes. Consequently he specified in a codicil that the schools were to receive two million dollars and that most of the remainder was to go to trustees for allocation as they saw fit—also, by understanding, to higher education. Fayerweather's widow and nieces contested the will and only after long and costly litigation did the designated institutions receive their share.[48]

In giving to two favored institutions while he was still living, Henry Phipps, a former president of Carnegie Steel, was wiser than Fayerweather. In 1908 he gave five hundred thousand dollars to Johns Hopkins to establish a psychiatric clinic and six years later backed this pioneer venture with a million dollars. In 1926 Phipps and his wife, having earlier founded the Phipps Institute for tuberculosis control at the University of Pennsylvania, added five hundred thousand dollars to its funds.[49] Other examples of giving to more than one institution include James Sheridan, who in 1931 left a million dollars to Yale, the same amount to Harvard, and half a million to the Massachusetts Institute of Technology. Henry W. Putnam, whose fortune was made from manufacturing barbed wire and hardware, left almost two million dollars each to Harvard, Yale, and Princeton.[50]

A bequest unique in the years elapsing between the death of the philanthropist and the time the colleges received the money was that of Alexander Gardiner Mercer. A versatile man, Mercer served, after his graduation from the College of New Jersey in 1837, as a lawyer, a professor of belles-lettres, and rector of Trinity Church in Boston. On the side, and unknown to his friends, he amassed a considerable fortune. When he died in 1882 his will was found to contain bequests totaling more than a million dollars to various institutions ranging in size from Kenyon and Bowdoin to Yale and Penn. The money was to provide scholarships for graduates of public secondary schools. But the estate was soon involved in complicated legal snarls that delayed payment of the bequests year after year. Not until 1939 was the act of philanthropy finally completed.[51]

One of the first women to give large sums to a university not admitting her own sex was Mrs. Robert Stuart. Daughter of a successful New York merchant and widow of a wealthy sugar refiner and art patron, she was most frequently remembered for her refusal to support the Metropolitan Museum unless it closed its exhibition halls on Sundays. This Presbyterian lady gave Princeton $150,000 in 1883 to put the department of philosophy on "a working basis." She subsequently contributed buildings, scholarships, and three hundred thousand dollars for the affiliated Princeton

Theological Seminary.[52] Another woman donor to Princeton was Mrs. Mary Winthrop. Her pastor interested her in its scholarship fund, and she contributed to it in her later years and bequeathed a million dollars.[53] Devotion to the interests of their husbands explained Mrs. Sophia Williston's gift of $275,000 to the Harvard Graduate School of Business Administration and Mrs. Mary McBurney Gardner's contribution of $250,000 for a chair in oceanic history in memory of her husband, a leader in the Navy League.[54]

Although several women made generous gifts to universities,[55] two are outstanding as donors. Long before her death in 1919 Mrs. Margaret Olivia Slocum Sage, widow of Russell Sage, had included educational institutions in her varied philanthropies. On inheriting something more than $63,000,000 when her parsimonious husband died in 1906, Mrs. Sage helped missionary enterprises, hospitals, and the Young Men's and Young Women's Christian Associations, and established the Russell Sage Foundation for improving living standards in the United States. She also contributed generously to Harvard, Yale, Princeton, and other universities and gave a million dollars to the Emma Willard School, of which she was a graduate, a gift that resulted in the founding of Russell Sage College in 1918. Mrs. Sage's will named eighteen institutions of higher learning as beneficiaries.[56]

Whereas Mrs. Sage took an active part during her life in educational philanthropy, this seems not to have been true of Mrs. Hetty Sylvia Howard Green Wilks, daughter of Hetty Green, the world's most famous woman financier and one of its wealthiest women. On her death in 1957 Mrs. Wilks allocated seventy million dollars to sixty-nine institutions of higher learning. Several received a flat sum of two million dollars (Columbia, Harvard, Johns Hopkins, New York University, M.I.T., the University of Vermont, Middlebury, and Stevens Institute of Technology). Yale and Fordham got a million dollars each; Vassar, half a million.[57]

A consideration of the transformation of a small and inconspicuous liberal arts college into a national university which, in terms of endowment, ranked fifth in the nation by the 1930's may illustrate the interactions between the leadership of an established undergraduate institution, a rich donor, the foundations, and friends in the community. The case in point is the University of Rochester. During the presidency of David Jayne Hill (1888–1895), Rochester, a liberal-arts college with an affiliated Baptist seminary, began to move toward modernization. The curriculum was liberalized, work in the natural sciences was strengthened, freedom of discussion of controversial subjects, especially evolution, was proclaimed, interest of alumni was aroused through a new athletic program, work for the master's degree was begun, extension lectures were inaugurated, and the endowment was increased.

Yet in 1900, when Dr. Rush Rhees, a professor of New Testament from the Newton Theological Institution, was inaugurated as president, the university's faculty consisted of seventeen members, the student enrollment was 187, and the annual disbursement was only $45,000. The institution was barely known outside of Rochester.[58] Rhees was gifted with unusual talents for administration, though scholarly and judicious in temperament. Moving by slow, orderly steps, he planned and executed a program that made Rochester a true university. Reserved and even austere, he was nevertheless effective in discussion and quickly showed an ability to carry through whatever he started.[59]

When Rhees came to Rochester, its leading citizen, George Eastman, who had already made a fortune in the photographic industry, displayed no particular interest in education. He was one of the self-made men who deprecated formal education as impractical and useless, and he especially disdained the higher education of women, his ideal being the old-fashioned type represented by his beloved mother. As the work of the Eastman Kodak Company came to depend increasingly on well-trained chemists, however, Eastman recognized the value of skilled specialists and the role of higher education in training them. President Rhees noted this development as well as Eastman's broadening interest in music, art, and community affairs.[60] Even more important was Rhees's appreciation of Eastman's dislike of pressure to contribute to worthy causes.

Only once did Rhees directly ask Eastman to do something for the university. That was in 1904, when it was obvious that the university needed a new science building. The shy, hesitant approach Rhees made to Eastman seemed the right one, for he obtained a substantial contribution. Eastman added, however, that it was the last gift he would make.

"You need not be told," Rhees wrote the reluctant donor, "that such confidence is the strongest possible challenge to me to so use your liberal gift that you will be continually satisfied with having made it. We are making final plans. As they are put in shape I shall hope to talk them over with you. It goes without saying that I shall eagerly welcome your suggestions concerning any feature of them that you care to speak of. The prospect that this business will bring me into closer fellowship with you so far as your time permits is for me personally very attractive." Rhees ended by thanking Eastman for what he had done and "for the way you have done it." [61]

Meanwhile, Eastman began to enlist the interest of other well-to-do men, particularly George B. Selden, who was profiting from an automobile patent.[62] It is also worth noting that, four years after his initial gift, Eastman refused to accept an honorary degree on the score that he "did not care for that sort of thing" and that, besides, he had always felt that degrees should be conferred only on professional men. But he added that he had got more satisfaction out of the offer than he would have had from the degree itself.[63]

Eastman's first great gift to Rochester came in 1912 when the university was involved in a million-dollar endowment campaign. "This is to confirm our recent conversation," Eastman wrote to President Rhees, "in which I stated that I would duplicate any amounts, up to a total of five hundred thousand dollars, which the Trustees of the University can raise during the present calendar year, for the purpose of increasing the endowment fund of the University." [64] Rhees's graceful and warm expressions of appreciation for the half-million that followed ended: "Inasmuch as words are entirely incapable of expressing my sentiment with reference to the share you have had in creating this magnificent new endowment for the University, I shall not attempt to say what is in my mind, but will only say that such an expression of regard and confidence will make it one of the strongest ambitions of my life to accomplish for the University and through it for the city such increase of power for good as will yield you satisfaction in the part you have played so generously at this time." [65] This was a man speaking Eastman's own language.

The University of Rochester really came onto the national educational map in 1919 with the establishment of the Eastman School of Music and Theater. This was indeed an outstanding innovation in American academic life. What distinguished it, apart from the high professional standards in the performing arts, was the success it enjoyed in identifying itself with the community. Eastman insisted that musical concerts be such as to lead a popular audience to appreciation and enjoyment, rather than to discourage interest. Though there was some resistance on the part of the professional musical directors,[66] the school made a genuine place for itself in the city.

The next year something happened that brought still more national attention to the university. Dr. Abraham Flexner of the General Education Board, having failed to strengthen the clinical and research facilities of the medical schools in New York City, persuaded his associates that conditions could be bettered by setting a standard upstate. Flexner was impressed by the leadership of President Rhees, by the distinctive success of the Eastman Dental Clinic for Rochester's children, and by Eastman's own growing interest in the university. At dinner at the house of President Rhees, Flexner indicated the Rockefeller interest in medical education in Rochester and opened the door to a generous response on the part of Eastman. The Kodak manufacturer, remarking that in recent years he had given $31,000,000 (largely to the Massachusetts Institute of Technology), wanted to know what the new medical school would cost. Flexner estimated from eight to ten millions. Eastman replied that he had consulted his financial adviser and that he could spare $2,500,000. When Flexner inquired where the rest was to come from, Eastman said simply from Mr. Rockefeller's fund, of course. Flexner said that in such an event "it would be our school, not yours; it must be yours." When Eastman repeated that $2,500,-000 was the best he could do, Flexner indicated that there was no hurry; Eastman could sell more Kodaks.[67]

Three days later Eastman sent a telegram to Flexner asking him to come to Rochester again. On further thought, he could spare three and a half million dollars. Flexner made the same objection as before.

A few weeks later Eastman invited Flexner to lunch. He would make one more offer, then he never wanted to see Flexner's face again. Expressing regret, Flexner asked what the offer was. It was five million dollars, including the dental clinic, valued at one million dollars, all conditional on a matching five million dollars from the General Education Board. Though he had no authorization, Flexner quickly risked an affirmative reply. "Beware, with one gift we have finished," he warned, "but you have just begun." Eastman protested that he was mistaken, but admitted Flexner was the best salesman he had ever known.[68] Later he remarked to an associate that Flexner was "the worst highwayman that ever flitted in and out of Rochester. He put up a job on me and cleaned me out of a thundering lot of my hard-earned savings." [69] Eastman wrote Rockefeller, however, that he considered him the foremost philanthropist of the age, that he had long admired the vision with which he had distributed his great wealth, and that it was a pleasure to be associated with him in this new community service.[70]

Eastman took great pleasure in planning and supervising the buildings of the new medical school. He induced the daughters of a deceased partner, Henry Strong, to give a million dollars for a hospital in memory of their parents.[71] The medical school quickly took its place as one of the leading institutions of the country, combining high standards of teaching with research and discovery. It also stimulated new standards and levels of achievement in the rest of the university.

Meanwhile Dr. Rhees had planned a new campus for the university and proposed at a dinner meeting for the citizens of Rochester a campaign for ten million dollars to make this dream come true. The task seemed stupendous, but large gifts came in, the chief being one of $2,500,000 from Eastman, with the General Education Board contributing $1,750,000 and the alumni $1,800,000. Before the end of the year, 1924, Eastman announced another gift, this time six million dollars, one-half for the Eastman School of Music, a quarter to the School of Medicine and Dentistry, and a quarter for the College for Women. The last item was surprising in view of Eastman's long indifference and even hostility toward the education of women.[72]

Having long given on a magnificent scale to the Massachusetts Institute of Technology and in smaller sums to Hampton and Tuskegee, it was not unnatural for Eastman, still unmarried, in making his will in 1924 to assign the bulk of his wealth in equal proportions to these institutions and to the University of Rochester. Before his death in 1932 he changed his will to favor Rochester. All in all, the university received, during his life and at his death, more than forty million dollars. Thanks to this generosity, Rochester jumped from a relatively minor liberal-arts college to an institution internationally known for its music and medicine and fully competent by American university standards in many other fields. In the making of privately supported universities, the achievement was one of the most striking.

What Eastman did for Rochester, Walter Brookings in some part did for Washington University. A foundation of pre-Civil war vintage in St. Louis, the university had a reputation for solid scholarship but lacked national distinction. In 1896, when he was but forty-six years old and had accumulated a fortune of several millions, Brookings decided to devote the rest of his life to self-improvement (he had developed an interest in art and literature) and to public service. Being a bachelor, his fortune was free from family claims. As president of the University Corporation he helped the institution acquire a new site and buildings and interested others, including his partner, Samuel Cupples, head of a distributing firm, in giving to endowment. Brookings was responsible for raising fifteen million dollars for transforming the university's mediocre medical school into a center that competent authority declared, within three years of the renewal, to be second to none.[73]

The story of philanthropic support of small liberal-arts colleges, as distinct from universities or colleges like Trinity and Emory that gifts converted into universities, is so long and complex that it cannot even be outlined adequately in the scope of this discussion. It would certainly include the gift of 150 acres valued at $250,000 that William W. Corcoran, the real estate speculator and art collector, made to the Columbian University in the nation's capital;[74] the two million dollars Mrs. Valeria Stone, widow of a Malden, Massachusetts drygoods merchant, gave to colleges between the death of her husband in 1880 and her own death three years later;[75] and the role of A. Barton Hepburn, New York banker and railway expert, in helping Middlebury College, at which he had studied for a year in his youth, lift itself from a weak to a strong institution through conditional gifts.[76]

An even more striking case of the rehabilitation of a faltering college through dedicated philanthropy was the Baptist-related University of Lewisburg in Pennsylvania. For sixty years this struggling institution received the devotion and gifts of William A. Bucknell, whose fortune was made in public utilities and investment in Philadelphia. Bucknell, who continued his early habit of giving away a tenth of his earnings—he contributed a half million to Baptist missions—gave more than $150,000 to the institution that took his name in 1887, just three years before his death.[77]

And any outline would have to take into account Andrew Carnegie's decision to help not the Ivy League institutions but small "fresh water" colleges, as he called them, particularly through conditional giving for libraries and laboratories. In all, Carnegie gave approximately twenty million dollars to the small colleges, which he believed were more likely to raise the intelligence of the masses than Harvard, Yale, and Princeton.[78]

Impressive in magnitude though this aspect of his philanthropy was, Carnegie was not the most influential or significant donor to small colleges. The honor belongs rather to Daniel K. Pearsons. Forced by poverty to leave Dartmouth after a year of study during which he existed on a dollar a week, Pearsons received in 1841, after a short course, a degree at the Vermont Medical College. Subsequently he peddled a school physiology text and lectured on the human body, bought woodland in Michigan, made money as a land-selling agent of the Illinois Central Railroad, and multiplied his assets through Chicago real estate and bank stocks. He lived frugally, saving on clothes, never going to sports events or, except once to his regret, the theater.

His attention was drawn to the principal object of his philanthropy by someone's remark on the uselessness of the small, struggling colleges that had sprung up in the West. In 1890, at the age of 70, Pearsons decided to devote the rest of his life to giving wisely to small colleges in the West and South. He did this, with the full approval and advice of his childless wife, in the conviction that the small, Christian college was the best training ground for the men and women who he felt would exert the largest influence on the nation's future. Such institutions, Pearsons believed, kindled and nurtured the light of liberty, religion, and learning. He offered colleges gifts only after he was convinced that they were strategically located, had enough strength to remain viable, and could count on the generosity and loyalty of a clearly defined constituency.

When he offered hard-pressed Beloit College a hundred thousand dollars on the condition that it raise four hundred thousand in what seemed an impossibly short time, he set the pattern for his subsequent giving to almost forty colleges in the West and South. Many of these gifts stimulated other men of means to give; all of them broadened the giving constituency. Eccentric and caustic in his criticisms, yet a reverent and realistic idealist, Pearsons was honored and loved by those who knew him. "You cannot say anything too good of Pearsons," Carnegie remarked. In speaking of the forms and conditions of his charity, the steel magnate observed that "it is the best line of benevolence in America." And to Pearsons himself Carnegie paid the significant compliment: "You have taught us all how to do it." [79]

Gifts to privately supported institutions attracted more donors and larger gifts than did those maintained by states and municipalities. Yet it was clear that no legislature or city council ever provided enough funds to enable publicly supported institutions to give sufficient educational services. For various reasons—local pride and a sense of responsibility to public interest, or the influence of regents or administrators—a few well-to-do men began fairly early to make gifts to state institutions. The tendency became more marked in the later decades of the nineteenth century, and the precedent thus set continued in the twentieth.

One of the earliest examples of this kind of philanthropy was the money Dr. William Terrell, a Virginian who received his medical education in Philadelphia, gave in 1853 to establish an agricultural professorship at the University of Georgia. The donation of twenty thousand dollars was attached to the salary of the professor of chemistry in the College of Arts and Sciences, and though for a time it was held by a New Yorker who edited *The Southern Cultivator* it seems to have had little effect on the agricultural practices of the state.[80] On the other hand, in the 1880's the initiative of Sam Inman, expressed in a gift of five thousand dollars and the collection of $75,000 from Atlanta citizens, secured a state appropriation that built the Georgia Institute of Technology.[81] This interdependence of private and public support was also evidenced somewhat later when the Georgia legislature appropriated $25,000 for the State Normal Building Fund on condition that $25,000 be raised privately. The requirement was met thanks to the efforts of James Smith, Harry Hodgon of the Empire State Chemical Company of Athens, students and faculty, and George Foster Peabody, a New York banker deeply interested in Georgia.[82]

There are innumerable other examples of voluntary contributions to nineteenth-century state-supported institutions, such as the contributions of the citizens of Bloomington toward rebuilding Indiana University's campus after fires in 1854 and 1883 and a campaign for thirty thousand dollars for a woman's building in 1901, which proved so successful that fifty thousand dollars was raised, to be supplemented by an equal sum from John D. Rockefeller.[83] In the early 1890's, at a time when it was much needed, William B. Spooner of Boston gave a library building with a 100,000-book capacity to the University of Kansas. Several state institutions received gifts for scholarships; a generous example was the endowment of $150,000 Charles B. Gregory gave to the University of Missouri.[84]

Special interests also governed many gifts; thus J. C. Penney, the chain store magnate, gave Missouri a gift totaling $725,000 in value. It included a herd of prize cattle for breeding, research, and educational purposes.[85] Another notable special-interest benefaction was the million and a half dollars Clarence Mackay, a socialite educated in European Catholic institutions, gave to the University of Nevada's School of Mines. This had been founded by his father, an Irish miner who made a fortune of seventy million dollars by exploiting the Comstock Lode and other properties.[86]

The role of philanthropy in another small and poorly supported institution, the University of Vermont, has special interest. Its first great president, James Marsh, "father of New England Transcendentalism," resigned just before the first fund-raising campaign began.[87] One of his distinguished successors, James B. Angell, cultivated relations with townsmen and farmers by addressing county fairs and schools. He found it hard, however, to convince the people, even after the Morrill Land Grant Act established agricultural and mechanical training, that the university could do very much for them. He did, nevertheless, succeed through great efforts in getting eighty thousand dollars in pledges from well-known men. Fear that these might not be redeemed was the main factor for his prolonged hesitancy in accepting an invitation to become president of the University of Michigan.[88] Though an exceptional alumnus was in a position to do something for the university and occasionally did, the institution, with inadequate support from a poor state, maintained only with difficulty its high standards in a traditional curriculum. Hope came in the battle against poverty in 1929 with the windfall bequest of more than two million dollars from James B. Wilbur, a Chicago banker and summer resident of the Green Mountain State. Wilbur unfortunately made the gift (it was for scholarships primarily for Vermont boys) on condition that attendance at the university be limited to 1,000 students annually, to be increased at the rate of 250 for each addition of 100,000 to the state's population beginning with the 1920 census. As the university was pressed for funds and Vermont boys needed help, the gift was accepted with an understanding that the conditions need not apply literally. By 1929, after thousands of Vermonters had received aid from the Wilbur fund, the whole bequest was challenged on the ground that the university had disregarded the philanthropist's stipulations on size of enrollment. It seemed as if it would be allocated to the Library of Congress, which Wilbur had named as an alternative recipient, but in the end the courts ruled that Vermont could keep the money.[89]

The tradition of private giving to the University of Michigan was established relatively early in part because of the active efforts of President Angell and others to attract gifts and in part because of the relatively small number of privately supported colleges in the state. Many of the early gifts were of small monetary value but they helped to create a custom. The first fifty years saw relatively few alumni gifts: donations came largely from friends who viewed the university with pride. Between 1817, the date of the founding, and 1931, the grand total of private donations was $32,834,562. Of this the alumni gave twice as much as the general public. In 1939, when the total assets of the university were estimated at seventy-five million dollars, voluntary giving accounted for thirty-eight million, the nonalumni share being approximately fifteen million dollars. During the decade 1931 to 1939, however, alumni contributed only $3,775,000 of eighteen million dollars received from philanthropy.[90]

Of the conspicuous nonalumni donors, Horace and Mary Rackham were outstanding for the range, originality, and magnitude of their gifts. Although Rackham's own education had ended with high school and night study of law, he prospered materially. Borrowing on a four-acre truck farm, he subscribed for fifty shares of stock of the Ford Motor Company, the incorporation papers of which he had drawn up. The money was all he ever put into the company, but it earned him a fortune of sixteen million dollars. The Rackhams' benefactions included a fund for loans and gifts for deserving students, support for overseas archaeological investigations (which resulted in major discoveries in Egypt and elsewhere), research on human physical and psychological maladjustments, sociological inquiries into industrial conditions at Flint, and a great center for graduate study at the university itself. The Rackham philanthropy, both in terms of the flexibility of the grants and the constructive purposes to which it was put, was of great benefit to Michigan and, indeed, one of the major contributions of private giving to American higher education in the twentieth century.[91]

Like other state universities, Illinois had generous friends. None gave a more surprising gift than George A. Miller, professor of mathematics, who despite unorthodox graduate training—he took a nonresident Ph.D. at the University of Cumberland—contributed first-rate papers in group theory. Miller's salary never topped six thousand dollars a year, but he built a million-dollar estate, presumably by lucky investments in the stock market. In 1951, Miller, without immediate living relatives, left his estate to Illinois for "the educational purposes of the University." The bequest has been used to bring to Champaign-Urbana eminent visiting professors and to support the *Illinois Journal of Mathematics,* a needed and useful channel for reporting research in the field.[92]

The University of California fared better than most state universities, whether by reason of the number of great fortunes in the state, remoteness from Eastern prestige institutions that might otherwise have attracted donors, the early policy of academic leadership in emphasizing the importance of giving to a publicly supported institution, or pride in its future. In any case, well-to-do Californians began to favor the university soon after the first discouraging years.

One of the earliest large benefactions was that of Edward Tomins, a regent who, impressed by the importance of trade relations with the Far East, established a professorship of Oriental languages. A. K. P. Harmon, a "forty-niner," gave a gymnasium. Michael Reese, a San Francisco banker, enlarged the library by gifts and bequests that enabled it to spend $150,000 for books without touching the capital fund itself. The rich collections of the Pacific Coast historian, Hubert H. Bancroft, came to the university partly because he donated one hundred thousand dollars toward the $250,-000 purchase price. California's pioneer jurist, Serranus Clinton Hastings, who as California's first Chief Justice skillfully administered the transition from Spanish to American law, made a fortune by investments and professional practice. He gave one hundred thousand dollars to endow the university-affiliated Hastings College of Law, one of the most important educational institutions of the state. Other pioneers also interested themselves in the university. Darius Mills, at the suggestion of a friend on the Board of Regents, established a professorship of intellectual and moral philosophy, to which George Howison was named, and later built Stiles Hall.[93]

Of special importance was the observatory and its powerful telescope that James Lick, who had made a fortune through venturesome land purchases, provided for by setting aside $700,000 before his death in 1876.[94] But of all California's early benefactors, Mrs. Phoebe Hearst was the most outstanding. Her generous giving began in 1891 with the establishment of scholarships for young women. She built Hearst Hall, a social center for women, and the Hearst Memorial Mining Building; provided funds for the ethnological museum, to which she gave her own collections; supported funds for books and lectureships; built the Greek theater; and as a regent encouraged others to open their purses.[95]

With such precedents and with the continued growth and prosperity of and pride in the state and the university, giving became fashionable. In the 1920's gifts reached the impressive figure of sixteen million dollars. These included the International House given by John D. Rockefeller, Jr., A. P. Giannini's million dollar endowment of the Foundation of Agricultural Economics, and the Edwin F. Searles benefactions of substantially the same figure. Other gifts included the Kearney bequest fund of more than $1,000,-000 and the George William Hopper endowment totaling a similar amount.[96]

Municipal colleges and universities drew even less private philanthropy than state universities; the assumption in each case was that public support lessened or removed altogether any responsibility for giving either from graduates or from well-to-do citizens of the community. But there were some exceptions. At his death in

1858 Charles McMicken, a Cincinnati bachelor of limited schooling, left most of his property, estimated at one and a half million dollars and acquired through land buying, to found a college for men and one for women. Since much of the property was in Louisiana and since the laws of that state did not allow municipal corporations, in this case the City of Cincinnati, to hold funds in trust, there was insufficient residue to carry out the full wishes of the donor. Nevertheless a start was made and the University of Cincinnati, chiefly supported by municipal grants, gradually gained stature. In 1930 Annie Sinton Taft, whose family had long supported Cincinnati's cultural institutions, established a fund of two million dollars in memory of her husband, Charles Phelps Taft, to assist, maintain, and endow the study and teaching of the humanities in the College of Liberal Arts and the Graduate School of the University of Cincinnati. The motive of this generous gift was related to the special interest of her husband and herself in humanistic culture, and it proved a source of strength for the purpose it was established.[97]

In 1924 Louis D. Brandeis, Justice of the United States Supreme Court, began to make the municipal university in his home city, Louisville, an outstanding institution and a creative force in the community. This he did in part with carefully planned gifts. The development, under his stimulus, of special collections on topics of local, national, and international concern and on cultural achievements and issues enriched the library of the university. Understandably, the law school was also the object of Brandeis's special concern. The university received as a bequest a quarter of his estate, estimated, before taxes, at a value approximating three million dollars.[98] Although other municipal universities and colleges received some support from friends in the community,[99] none had such a singularly forceful and constructive friend as the University of Louisville.

Some commentators held that in terms of the capacity of men of great wealth to give to higher education, the number that did so was relatively small.[100] On the whole, however, foreign observers [101] and Americans themselves felt that philanthropic giving to colleges and universities was unprecedented. It is certainly true that such giving as there was by nonalumni depended, before the great "drives" of the years after World War I, not on organized efforts but on whatever influence general statements by educational leaders about needs, together with trustees and alumni, might happen to have on people of wealth who themselves had no collegiate background.

Many with some general inclination to do something for philanthropy were uncertain how to proceed. When several patrons of the Hanover Bank in New York asked for advice as to needy and meritorious institutions, it developed a Department of Philanthropy that gave advice on request and built up a library of materials on the subject. The collection, augmented by records of miscarriages of philanthropic intentions that Alvin West collected, guided many in making decisions as to what to give, to whom, and how.[102] Apart from this service, the chief organized effort to encourage wise giving to educational institutions on the part of friends was the decision of *Who's Who in America* in the 1930's to list annual awards to donors to educational institutions, selected with reference to the size of the gift in relation to the assets of the beneficiary, to the news interest in the gift, and to its possible effect on other prospective donors.[103]

Although most Americans, when they gave any thought to the matter, seem to have taken satisfaction and pride in the impact of gifts and bequests on colleges and institutions, others viewed such philanthropy critically. A writer in *The Nation* in 1869 (probably E. L. Godkin, the editor) contended that self-made men did not have sufficient first-hand knowledge to give wisely and constructively to colleges and universities.[104] The early history of some of the institutions that owed their existence to a single donor lent some credence to his caveat.[105] While admitting that the public was as yet insufficiently appreciative of the value of higher education to support it adequately through taxation, the writer called attention to the danger that great gifts might result in a feeling on the part of the public that it was unnecessary to make the effort and sacrifice to enlarge and improve higher education at the taxpayer's expense. The slow but growing support of the state universities was largely to disprove this fear.

Critics also felt that dependence on private philanthropy jeopardized academic freedom. In terms of direct interference this proved to be the exception rather than the rule. Even so, some liberals agreed with a contention of the British economist, J. A. Hobson, in 1905. Trustees and administrators eager to attract the philanthropy of potential givers, he wrote, might unconsciously if not consciously have taken care to make "safe" appointments in such controversial fields as the social sciences.[106] At the same time academic criticism of the economic and social order was by no means unknown. Nor is it possible to make a conclusive evaluation of a related criticism—that educational leaders, in soliciting funds from private donors, took on unduly the characteristics of businessmen and that the institutions over which they presided assumed the characteristics of a business civilization.[107]

It is also hard to assess the evidence offered in support of another criticism of the role and influence of individual donors of large gifts —that they too frequently supported functions of colleges and universities that were not truly educational. Bryce, writing in 1887, reported that the criticism of educational philanthropy he heard most frequently concerned the predominance of special and restricted giving for buildings, scholarships, and endowed chairs at the expense of general endowment. In 1930, Abraham Flexner expanded the criticism to include many gifts for so-called practical and vocational programs, for "research" that merely compiled unanalyzed data, and for costly but dubious innovations that drained funds from more basic needs. American generosity, Flexner argued, was not directed or controlled by intelligent purpose. Admitting the delicacy of refusing a gift for some object that might prove a drain, Flexner nevertheless indicted educational leaders for failing to enlighten givers, for accepting gifts they could not in fact afford to take. "It is a thousand pities that of this vast total so much has been applied to poor and unworthy purposes," for what President Wilson called "side-shows." "No American University president of recent years," Flexner continued, "has fearlessly hewed to the line, accepting money for general and important purposes—the central disciplines, the accepted and necessary professions—and refusing to accept special gifts which almost invariably make the university poorer and weaker, rather than richer and better. For almost every activity once undertaken grows, and as it grows, needs further support. The asset of today becomes a liability tomorrow." Flexner realized the difficulty of attracting gifts for general salary increases and for what he called basic educational programs as opposed to spurious ones of an ad hoc, vocational nature.[108]

In contrast to this indictment was the contention that such donors as Eastman and Duke poured their money into conventional institutions rather than boldly experimenting along new lines. The desire to establish institutions like the Ivy League schools, this critic continued, was evidence of the proneness of the Rotarian mind to want for his community something obviously "bigger and better." [109]

It was all these criticisms that spurred the movement to emphasize the importance of a mass base of unrestricted giving to meet rising costs and unexpected needs and contingencies. The most obvious sources to supplement or supplant large individual gifts from friends of colleges and universities were alumni, foundations, and corporations.

Chapter VIII

In the Name of the Negro

Like women, Negroes had to overcome traditional ideas about the scope and purpose of higher education before they were able to carve a place for themselves in America's colleges and universities. In each case philanthropy was primarily responsible for opening college doors. The achievement of philanthropy in regard to the American Negro commands special attention in view of the obstacles raised by his social situation and his relatively low economic status. The result of the latter was that nearly all the philanthropic support of his higher education had to come from Northern whites. This difference in race between the philanthropist and the object of his benefaction posed serious problems in regard to the kind of education that the Negro would receive.

Before the Civil War only a few token attempts were made to provide higher education for the Negro, and these were confined to the free states.[1] Concern over his welfare was restricted, for the most part, to efforts at abolishing slavery. But after emancipation the emotional excitement generated by the condition of the slave was transferred to a preoccupation with "uplifting" the freedman and extending to him the same opportunities for self-improvement other citizens enjoyed. Providing education for Negroes seemed the right way to implement these plans. What better way was there to prepare him for intelligent citizenship? Higher education assumed special importance, as suggested by John C. Calhoun's statement that "if a Negro could be found who could parse Greek or explain Euclid, I should be constrained to think he had human possibilities." [2] Others, sure that Negroes had the same intellectual capacity as whites, felt their successful training in colleges would constitute positive proof. Friends of the Negro saw in philanthropy a way to translate ideals into actuality.

The situation that existed in 1865 posed an immense challenge to Americans with philanthropic intentions. There were about four million former slaves in the country, and only a tiny fraction of them were literate. In the areas of heaviest Negro concentration not even a primary school system existed. Moreover the Negro was unable and the white Southerner unwilling to create and support for people of color educational opportunities similar to those others enjoyed. If anything was to be done Northern philanthropists and the federal government would have to take the responsibility.

As an individual the Northerner with a desire to help educate the freedman found himself helpless. There were no colleges to which he could send contributions, and Southern resistance coupled with Negro poverty precluded the possibility of their arising. Organizations were clearly needed that could first create the objects of Northern benefactions and then channel dimes and dollars to them.

The major religious faiths quickly formed philanthropic agencies to channel northern dollars toward the Negro. Even before the war was over one such agency, the American Missionary Association, established an institution at Fortress Monroe, Virginia that soon became the Hampton Institute. Drawing a large portion of its funds from the Congregational Church, the A.M.A. was instrumental in the founding before 1870 of a series of institutions that would come to dominate Negro higher education: Howard University in Washington, D.C., Fisk University in Nashville, Atlanta University in Atlanta, and Talladega College in Talladega, Alabama. [3] The philanthropy was on a large scale; the A.M.A. distributed more than a hundred thousand dollars to Negro colleges in 1888. [4] Small contributions in thousands of Northern churches formed the bulk of its philanthropic resources, but occasionally the association served as the intermediary for a major philanthropist such as Seymour Straight of Ohio, who in 1869 made possible the founding of Straight College in New Orleans.

The Freedmen's Aid Society of the Methodist Church had the

broad purpose of the relief, evangelization, and education of former slaves. Through the good offices of this association the money of the Claflin family of Boston was applied to the founding of Claflin University in South Carolina, the Meharry brothers to the Meharry Medical College in Tennessee, and Mrs. Philander Smith of Oak Park, Illinois, to Philander Smith College in Little Rock, Arkansas.[5] The largest contributor to the Methodist organization was Elijah H. Gammon, a minister in northern Illinois, who gave a half million dollars for the establishment and support of Gammon Theological Seminary in Atlanta, Georgia.[6] In its first decade of existence, to 1876, the Freedmen's Aid Society contributed more than $650,000 to Negro schools on all levels, and by 1888 the figure reached $2,000,000.[7] The American Baptist Home Mission Society also took an active part in founding institutions of higher learning for Negroes. In the late 1860's it supported Roger Williams University at Memphis, Virginia, Union University at Richmond, and Shaw University at Raleigh.[8] In the case of Leland University in Baker, Louisiana, the Baptists received about $165,000 from Holbrook Chamberlain of Brooklyn, New York.[9] Spelman College, a women's institution in Atlanta, Georgia, benefited in a similar manner from the philanthropy of John D. Rockefeller, who gave the college the name of his wife's family.[10] Other denominations served Negro higher education in similar ways.[11]

In 1865 Congress established the Freedmen's Bureau to "cooperate with private benevolent associations in aid of the freedman."[12] Its functions were soon extended to include education. Most of the colleges founded by the denominational associations also received support from the Freedmen's Bureau. In many cases the government simply subsidized the work of the various private agencies. So important was the Freedmen's Bureau that when it closed operations in the summer of 1872 Negro education faced a major crisis. Only through increased efforts on their own behalf and on the part of the religious groups were the struggling Negro colleges able to survive.

Fisk University, which opened in Nashville in 1866, was one of the institutions supported by the American Missionary Association. It began as a primary and normal school with intentions of living up to its "university" designation in time. Fisk took its name and thirty thousand dollars from General Clinton Bowen Fisk, head of the Freedmen's Bureau's western branch. The institution was scarcely launched when its treasurer, George L. White, realized that failure was certain unless it attracted the attention of philanthropists. Besides having charge of Fisk's finances, White also served as vocal music teacher. It had been his practice to take groups of students on singing tours in the vicinity of Nashville, and in 1871 it occurred to him that music might be the way to the hearts and purses of Northerners. He staked what remained in the school's treasury on a tour through the North and left Nashville on October 6, 1871. At first the eleven members of the troupe had scant success and barely made their expenses. Nonetheless they persisted, moving to New York and Boston and adopting the attractive name "Jubilee Singers." Success followed. For the first time the group collected more than a thousand dollars at a single concert in Boston, and three months after leaving Nashville they returned with twenty thousand.[13]

A typical program of the Fisk Jubilee Singers mixed Negro spirituals with speeches concerning the work of the university. The haunting melodies of songs such as "Swing Low, Sweet Chariot" and "Nobody Knows the Trouble I've Seen" captivated Northern audiences. When "John Brown's Body" was rendered the assembly frequently leaped to its feet and cheered wildly. The concerts closed with a pointed reminder in the form of a song entitled "What Shall the Harvest Be?"[14]

George White was quick to follow up his successes. Another Northern tour raised another twenty thousand dollars, and in 1873 the Jubilee Singers made the first of their trips to Europe. As in colonial times, England proved a generous benefactor of higher education in America. The English were led to believe that Fisk graduates would carry the message of Western civilization and Christianity to Africa, although in fact this seldom occurred. After performing in England before Queen Victoria, the singers gave concerts before royal audiences in Germany and the Netherlands. The demand for concerts everywhere was overwhelming, and with the proceeds of the various tours at home and abroad Fisk University was able to finance the construction of Jubilee Hall, accommodating more than four hundred students. The institution's resourcefulness in stimulating philanthropy assured it a major place in Negro higher education.[15]

Fisk's success inspired the Hampton Normal and Agricultural Institute to undertake a similar singing tour. The members of Hampton's troupe brought their schoolbooks and gave five hundred concerts in eighteen states and Canada. While the singers raised something, Hampton was fortunate in having as its president an expert fund-raiser. Samuel Chapman Armstrong was born to missionary parents in the Hawaiian Islands, graduated from Williams in 1862, and embarked on a military career. After the war he took charge of the federal government's educational program for freedmen in Virginia and developed Hampton as a center where Negroes could learn vocational skills and the art of teaching. Later a true college program was undertaken. During Armstrong's association with the institute it was plagued by a chronic shortage of funds. He repeatedly toured the North, making as many as three speeches a day. Even in Boston, which he described as a place "where for every dollar even the richest are able to give there are ten chances to put it to good use and twenty demands for it from one source or another," [16] he was successful in raising money. After 1878 he faced the necessity of raising fifty thousand to eighty thousand dollars each year just to keep the institute functioning. For two decades he supplemented the government's appropriation with an equal amount received from philanthropists. Over the years Armstrong observed the North tiring of repeated Southern demands for philanthropy, yet he knew there was no other source of income for his institution.[17]

Another channel through which Northern dollars flowed to Negro colleges in the South was the philanthropic foundation. The first American foundation in the educational field dated from 1867 as the result of a $1,000,000 gift from George Peabody, an international merchant and financier. A second million followed two years later. The philanthropist placed his money in the hands of white trustees from the North and the South with the stipulation that it be used for improving education among the poorer classes of the South without regard to race.[18] While most of the money went to white primary and normal schools, Negro teacher's colleges received a few grants. The greatest significance of the Peabody Education Fund was as a model in educational philanthropy for subsequent benefactions.[19] In 1914 the Peabody Fund dissolved after having disbursed more than three million dollars. In the final disposition of its resources $350,000 went to the John F. Slater Fund, which had been established in 1882 as the first philanthropic foundation devoted exclusively to Negro education.

John F. Slater was a Rhode Islander who became rich in the manufacture of textiles. His reason for giving a million dollars to Negro education in 1882 stemmed from his conviction that schooling was essential if the ex-slave was to become a responsible citizen.[20] Slater appointed an eminent board to administer his gift and gave them a free hand. It was his belief that their collective wisdom and experience acquired from direction of the fund would be a far better guide to policy than anything a single philanthropist could propose in advance. Slater was concerned, however, that his money be distributed "in no partisan, sectional, or sectarian spirit" and that it should promote rather than discourage self-help on the part of the Negroes in the South.[21] In its first years of operation the Slater Fund benefited institutions of higher learning as well as public school systems. After receiving the $350,000 from the Peabody Fund in 1914, it was equipped to play for several decades a major role in the development of Negro higher education.

Other philanthropists followed the example of Peabody and Slater. In 1888 the American Missionary Association announced the receipt of $1,000,894 from a native of Connecticut who had made a fortune as a merchant in Augusta, Georgia. The Daniel Hand Educational Fund for Colored People was to be administered by the A.M.A. Hand made no restrictions in the deed of trust, and the association was able to advance its work on all educational levels.[22] The Hand Fund, along with the Negro Rural School Fund, which a Philadelphia Quakeress named Anna T. Jeanes established in 1907, was not directly concerned with higher learning.[23] Their significance lay in freeing the existing colleges for development as true institutions of higher learning instead of serving as preparatory schools.

The establishment in 1902 of John D. Rockefeller's General Education Board was a major event in the history of American philanthropy.[24] No other agency, public or private, exerted a comparable force in shaping Negro higher education. At the prompting of his son John Jr., Rockefeller created the Board with a gift of a million dollars. Ultimately his gifts totaled over $129,000,000. "The object of this Board," declared the initial gift-bearing letter, "is to promote education in the United States of America without distinction of sex, race, or creed." [25] But its immediate attention was to be focused on the South. By 1918, Negro colleges had received $1,141,282 from the General Education Board, but this only hinted at what was to come. [26]

The various means by which the early Negro colleges received financial support had in common their near-total dependence on the philanthropy of Northern whites. [27] But there were also liabilities inherent in a situation in which control, or at least direction, of the institutions rested in noncolored and non-Southern hands. All too frequently philanthropic support of Negro higher education stemmed from zeal and pity rather than from a careful appraisal of needs and circumstances. Many of the early schools, which their supporters chose to call colleges, had students with at best a primary education. Nevertheless, many of the idealistic white benefactors and faculty members were determined to teach a classical college curriculum even on a dirt floor and to scarcely literate students. The competitive spirit among the sectarian societies caused much overlapping of educational facilities with a resultant lowering of quality. [28] Distorted claims were made, and in some cases solicitations were conducted for nonexistent colleges. Institutions that had sprung up in the first bloom of philanthropic concern for the Negro withered when the enthusiasm and support declined.

Zealous Northern philanthropy had clearly undertaken too much too soon. The General Education Board recognized in 1915 that "the number of institutions now struggling for existence is out of all relation to the number of qualified teachers and students . . . , the financial resources available . . . , and the service to be performed." What had resulted from the early philanthropy, the board contended, was a rash of inferior institutions that called themselves colleges but offered in all but a few cases a level of training far below college standards. It was imperative "that under existing conditions only a few efficient colleges for Negroes can or ought to be maintained." [29] The board directed its disbursements with an eye to this need.

The delicate social situation that existed in the South in regard to the Negro posed another pitfall for Northern philanthropy. Southern whites were suspicious of the attempts of Northerners to give higher education to Negroes. In 1890 Jabez Lamar Monroe Curry, a Southerner and administrator of several educational foundations concerned with the South, commented that the education Northern dollars bought for the Negro was "unsettling, demoralizing, pandered to a wild frenzy for schooling as a quick method of reversing social and political conditions." [30] More forthright was Senator James K. Vardaman of Mississippi: "What the North is sending South is not money but dynamite. This education is ruining our Negroes. They're demanding equality." [31]

In spite of such outbursts, the fact was that early Northern philanthropy directed toward the Negro colleges frequently operated in a conservative fashion from the standpoint of Southern whites. Looking back on the decades following the Civil War, Carter G. Woodson, a Negro scholar, contended that the educational system in which the white man picked up the bills and laid down the academic law served only to re-enslave the Negro. Instead of elevating the Negro and fostering pride in his racial heritage, Woodson declared that white-supported education impressed on the Negro a feeling of racial inferiority. In short, the Negro "has been trained to think what is desired of him." [32] Woodson's charge had particular applicability to the philanthropic foundations. The agents selected to administer the Peabody Fund, first Barnas Sears and in 1892 Jabez L. M. Curry, followed the principle of cooperating with Southern opinion. This meant that segregation was maintained, vocational training promoted, a policy of inequity established in allocation of funds to white and colored schools, and control of the institutions kept out of Negro hands. [33]

In its early years the General Education Board followed a similar policy of respecting the feelings of Southern whites. This its leaders deemed essential for the success of any program of Negro education. [34] Wallace Buttrick, long a head of the board, believed that cooperation with Southern whites meant excluding Negroes from administrative positions in the foundation. Even such notable figures in Negro education as Booker T. Washington were not invited to serve. Buttrick hesitated to support any bold innovation in behalf of the Negro for fear of alienating Southern opinion. Grants were made to agricultural and vocational training, more in keeping with the Southern idea of the Negro's "place" than liberal arts and professional instruction. A recent student of the work of the General Education Board and other philanthropic foundations has gone so far as to charge that their conservatism permitted Southern whites to fix the Negro more firmly in the role of second-class citizen.[35] This was in some degree true, but it was *not* the deliberate aim of the philanthropists and their agents, who instead sought to improve the Negroes' lot. A more liberal stance by Northern donors, while benefiting a few Negroes during their college years, would have so aroused the Southern white as to defeat the purpose of the long-range effort.

But even given the fact of white support, some degree of Negro control was possible, as Booker T. Washington demonstrated at the Tuskegee Normal and Industrial Institute. Founded in 1881, Tuskegee was dedicated to training Negroes of both sexes in vocational skills such as metalworking, tailoring, and agriculture. Instead of sharpening the Negro's desire for white collar jobs, Washington stressed the dignity of all honest labor. He was always careful not to tread on the delicate ground of white supremacy.[36] For his pains Washington was rewarded with abundant philanthropy as well as the right to direct the institution he had founded so long as he did so in accord with the expectations of his white benefactors. Tuskegee began with an annual state appropriation of two thousand dollars. When Washington died in 1915 the institute had an endowment of two million dollars and a yearly income of several hundred thousand. At a time when the competition among Negro colleges for Northern philanthropy was so great that Washington could report seeing no less than six agents in the office of a wealthy businessman at the same time,[37] this was astonishing success. John D. Rockefeller, Andrew Carnegie, Collis P. Huntington, and J. Pierpont Morgan were among those Tuskegee listed as its friends and benefactors. Washington even persuaded Southern whites to make a few contributions.

While Booker T. Washington solved the problem of obtaining white philanthropy for a colored college under nominal colored direction, he really begged the question by offering a variety of training compatible with the Southern white's ideas of the Negro's "place." Criticism of Washington on this point came from W. E. Burghart DuBois, a graduate of both Fisk and Harvard. Vocational training, he contended, served only to make the Negro a more efficient common laborer. It did not confer on the student the badge of respectability that many hoped would be the result of higher education. He called on his race to cast off the psychology of the slave and to produce its own cultural and professional leaders.[38] If the Negro colleges were to follow this advice, they would have to seek financial resources among Negroes or else find white benefactors who shared DuBois's ideals.

After World War I philanthropy faced a serious challenge in the low quality of Negro higher education. A comprehensive survey of existing facilities made in 1915 and 1916 revealed that of all the alleged "colleges" only Howard University, Fisk University, and Meharry Medical College deserved that designation. Of the 12,726 students attending the "colleges," 10,089 were at elementary and secondary levels. Financial resources were universally scarce.[39] In this situation organized philanthropy and the colleges themselves had a real opportunity to reconstruct higher learning for Negroes. One immediate aim was a reduction in the number of "colleges," with some dropping back to secondary schools and others emerging as full-fledged universities. Another goal was the federation of several institutions with higher standards than could be achieved separately. Finally, it was hoped that agricultural and vocational curricula would give way to those emphasizing the professions and liberal arts. Each of these objectives bore witness to the change that was occurring in the opinions of many Americans in regard to the capabilities and rights of Negroes. Philanthropy provided the instrument for the institutionalization of ideals.

With the bounty of the Rockefellers filling its coffers, the General Education Board was in a position to exert the greatest influence on Negro higher education. Consequently, a statement it issued in 1919 assumed considerable importance: "It is not universally recognized that the Negro needs wise and well trained leaders of his own race. It is . . . highly important that Negro physicians, Negro lawyers, Negro clergymen, and Negro business men should enjoy the advantage of academic training." [40] This marked a departure from the board's earlier emphasis on vocational and agricultural education and the associated conviction that the white man should provide leadership for the Negro.

As a means of implementing its new philanthropic philosophy, the board selected certain institutions to receive its funds with the idea of grooming them for a leading role in Negro higher learning. Fisk University in Nashville had used the income from its Jubilee

Singers to maintain a precarious existence. Beginning in 1920 the General Education Board poured more than five million dollars into Fisk, with the result that it emerged as an outstanding academic center.[41] Although Howard University in Washington, D.C. was government supported, the board used its gifts to prod Congress to action and to establish a comprehensive program of medical and liberal-arts training on the graduate level. But the outstanding achievement of the General Education Board in the field of Negro medical education was the support and development of the Meharry Medical College in Nashville. Meharry took its name from five white brothers of Indiana who responded with twenty thousand dollars to the appeal for a medical school made by the Methodist Freedmen's Aid Society immediately after the Civil War. When support of the school strained the church group, it appealed to other philanthropic organizations. The General Education Board responded with gifts that by 1960 totaled $8,673,700. In the late 1930's, in the face of the deterioration of Meharry's program, the board used philanthropy as a means of securing the appointment of a new president and faculty. These white appointees raised the caliber of the instruction, but the move had the unfortunate effect of compromising the internal freedom of the institution.[42]

Having recognized the necessity of the improvement in quality and reduction in quantity of Negro colleges, the General Education Board determined to promote the consolidation of institutions in one locale. When it was beginning to support Fisk, the General Education Board tried unsuccessfully to unite it with Meharry. The suspicion of the trustees involved overcame even the tempting offer of a $1,500,000 plant for Meharry directly across the street from Fisk. In New Orleans and Atlanta, however, philanthropy was more successful in overcoming the colleges' reluctance to submerge their identities in a central unit. Dillard University in New Orleans resulted from the affiliation of Straight University, New Orleans University, and the Flint-Goodridge Hospital. The General Education Board, with assistance from the Rosenwald Fund,[43] the American Missionary Association, and the Methodist Episcopal Church, purchased the site for Dillard and bore the initial expenses. The formal opening in 1935 marked a new era for the higher education of Negroes in Louisiana.[44]

As early as the 1880's the trustees of the Slater Fund had been aware of a lack of unity among Negro institutions in Atlanta, Georgia. In 1895 they denied further aid to Clark and Atlanta Universities because of their refusal to coordinate industrial training, but no consolidation was obtained. However, after World War I the philanthropic foundations, with their immense and desperately needed resources, held a whip hand over Negro education, and the result was different.[45] At the time it contemplated consolidation, the General Education Board was already supporting Spelman College for women and Morehouse College for men, both in Atlanta. Grants of a million and a half dollars to these colleges in 1927 and 1928 smoothed over any objection they might raise to the plan. But Atlanta University balked at the board's idea that it should become solely a graduate and professional institution. On the other hand, the heavy debt under which Atlanta labored made the prospect of a large-scale philanthropy from Rockefeller enticing. The board applied additional pressure by offering to build a library for the colleges only if it would be used jointly. This, in effect, enlisted the other colleges against Atlanta. Finally, in 1929 Atlanta agreed to negotiations, which resulted in the Atlanta University Affiliation. Spelman and Morehouse would offer undergraduate training while Atlanta would become a postgraduate institution. Subsequently, Clark University and Morris Brown College joined the affiliation.[46] With the addition of the Gammon Theological Seminary, the Atlanta group acquired the means for advanced nondenominational theological and missionary training.[47]

Its desires gratified and a new board of trustees in control of the university, the General Education Board made good its promises to Atlanta—$1,500,000 for new buildings, $1,700,000 for endowment, and $1,000,000 for the joint library. The gifts were not, however, universally acclaimed. Carter G. Woodson drew the distinction between the natural evolution of a Negro university and the forced construction of one with Northern dollars. It was possible, Woodson observed, to "go almost anywhere and build a three million dollar plant, place in charge a white man to do what you want accomplished, and in a short while . . . secure or have trained to order the men necessary to make a university."[48] In Woodson's opinion such rapid development entailed grave liabilities. The administrators and faculty of such hothouse institutions would be out of contact with the needs of the students. What were required, Woodson con-

cluded, were Negro universities staffed and managed by Negroes.
Such leaders were rare, but he felt confident that in time they
would emerge and stand ready to provide the kind of direction
best suited to the higher education of their race. According to
Woodson, the General Education Board was rushing the process
of university development in the same way the zealous church organizations had attempted to create "colleges" in the aftermath
of the Civil War.

Critics of foundation philanthropy to Negro colleges like Woodson did not give sufficient credit to the careful study that preceded
the gifts nor to the way in which intelligent giving corrected many
of the unfortunate results of the earlier philanthropy. But lingering
behind the foundation giving was the trustee philosophy: education
for the Negro but *by* the white man. In an effort to escape this
paternalism, some Negro colleges endeavored to secure their own
philanthropy and received foundation gifts in a spirit of independence. Talladega College in Alabama was established in 1867
by the American Missionary Association. In 1917 only 57 of 628
students were in the college department. During the 1920's Talladega was able to raise funds for new buildings and to improve its
standards. This manifestation of self-help attracted the attention
of the General Education Board, which in 1928 pledged a half
million dollars for endowment on the condtion that the college raise
another half million. Talladega fulfilled the requirement and in
1932 numbered about half of its 441 students as college grade. It
also maintained its autonomy.[49]

Biddle University in Charlotte, North Carolina, was one of the
few Negro colleges in the nineteenth century to have a Negro president. In 1907 this policy was continued with the appointment of
Henry L. McCrorey. The college prospered for a few years but in
1921 found itself on the brink of financial failure. At this time
President McCrorey was fortunate to meet a wealthy citizen of
Pittsburgh, Mrs. Johnson C. Smith, and to interest her in the college. The result was benefactions of more than seven hundred thousand dollars, which saved Biddle and renamed it the Johnson C.
Smith University.[50] It also profited from the 1924 announcement
of James B. Duke, a Charlotte tobacco magnate, that it would receive four percent of the annual income of a $40,000,000 trust
fund.[51] The Duke benefaction was especially noteworthy in that

it marked the first major gift to Negro higher education from a Southern white.

After World War I, Hampton and Tuskegee continued to attract the largest share of philanthropic donations given to Negro colleges, and they maintained their policy of Negro control. In September, 1924 the institutions launched a joint campaign for an endowment of five million dollars. The General Education Board offered one million conditional on the raising of an equal amount by the recipients. A Committee of the Hampton-Tuskegee Endowment Fund was organized with headquarters in New York City and a membership composed of financial and business leaders. The John Price Jones Company, a professional fund-raising organization, helped in the campaign. Negroes contributed several hundred thousand dollars, but it was the large gifts of white donors that made the campaign a success. Edward S. Harkness gave $250,000 and Senator T. Coleman du Pont matched this figure. John D. Rockefeller, Jr., made a donation of one million dollars entirely apart from the General Education Board's contribution of the same amount. The money came to Hampton and Tuskegee without condition in regard to policy or program, and the maintenance of their traditionally practical curriculum was entirely voluntary.

The largest contributor to the Hampton-Tuskegee campaign was George Eastman, the Rochester camera millionaire. Eastman was one of many Northern businessmen whom Booker T. Washington had interested in the work carried on at Tuskegee. In 1913 Eastman wrote to Julius Rosenwald, "I have a very high opinion of Dr. Washington and the work he is doing and it has always been a pleasure to help it along." [52] From early in the twentieth century his gifts totaled more than four million dollars. Yet there was in Eastman's attitude a suggestion that he had no intention of using his philanthropy to extend equal opportunities to Negroes. In making his two-million-dollar gift to the Hampton-Tuskegee campaign, Eastman accepted the belief that industrial, not liberal arts, higher education was the best way to make the Negroes "useful citizens" and to brush the Negro "problem" under the rug. In spite of such attitudes on the part of their benefactors, Hampton and Tuskegee accepted the money gracefully, maintained their autonomy, and emerged from the campaign by far the wealthiest of the Negro colleges. [53]

As with other institutions, the Depression reduced philanthropic gifts to the Negro colleges while at the same time lessening the value of endowment secured previously. Many of the foundations had extensive stock holdings that declined in value with the falling market. The General Education Board was obliged to return to a policy of making annual grants for current expenses instead of supporting growth and improvement. The result for the colleges was curtailment of the tremendous expansion of the previous decades.[54]

Since 1938 philanthropy has not made the revolutionary changes in Negro higher education that characterized the previous decades. In the earlier period the needs of Negro colleges were unique. The problem of philanthropy was to create a system of bona fide higher education from the indiscriminate mass of lower-grade institutions that chose to call themselves colleges and even universities. But by the late 1930's sustained large-scale philanthropy had remedied many of the shortcomings resulting from earlier giving and had established genuine centers of higher learning. A definite, if somewhat unhealthy, maturity had been reached. The needs of the Negro colleges more nearly paralleled those of other colleges. As a consequence, philanthropy has turned to less revolutionary but equally important developments: the support of scholarship programs, improvement in the training and pay of faculty, the creation of new departments and the strengthening of older ones, and provision of better buildings and equipment.

The foundations, which had done so much to make Negro higher education a reality, continued to be an important source of funds during and after World War II. But Negro higher education was rapidly becoming too big a business for even the richest of the foundations to support. Moreover, many of the foundations that had been of great service to the development of Negro education began to close out their operations. Rockefeller's General Education Board which had given so generously to Negro higher learning in the past, was considering closing out its philanthropic activities.[55] The Rosenwald Fund brought its operations to a close in 1948, and the resources of the Slater and Jeanes Funds, which had merged in the Southern Education Foundation, were declining. The Baptist Home Mission Society, which had at one time exerted great influence on Negro education, watched its financial resources approach the vanishing point. The horde of veterans who flooded the campuses immediately following the end of World War II increased the urgency of the situation.[56] In attempting to meet the financial crisis, the Negro colleges were handicapped by the composition of their student bodies. Since most students came from lower economic groups, tuition could not be raised to increasingly higher levels, as happened in the white colleges.[57] As it had so often been in the past, philanthropy appeared to be the only means available to solve the financial difficulties of Negro higher education.[58]

In January, 1943, Frederick Douglas Patterson, the president of Tuskegee Institute, addressed a letter to the presidents of other private Negro colleges. Patterson was deeply troubled over Negro education's bleak prospects for financial support. He proposed that the colleges unite in a joint fund-raising campaign—an educational community chest in the name of the Negro. The General Education Board and the Rosenwald Fund agreed to underwrite a portion of the expenses of the first campaign. In 1944 twenty-seven private, accredited Negro colleges (later the number rose to thirty-three and finally stabilized at thirty-two) launched the initial campaign of the United Negro College Fund. It was a pioneer effort in joint campaigning by educational institutions in America and subsequently had many imitators.[59] In addition, the fund represented a philanthropic declaration of independence by which Negroes made clear that the direction and application of the funds, if not their contribution, would be in colored hands.[60] Shortly after its fifteenth campaign the fund reached an important milestone when the amount it had raised for its member institutions surpassed the $41,000,000 the General Education had dispensed to Negro higher education over the years.[61]

The United Negro College Fund organized for its first campaign with a board of directors composed of all the college presidents and sixteen outside members. It also brought to its support in advisory capacities many men and women prominent in finance, education, and the professions.[62] Headquarters were established in New York City and campaigns conducted in 120 communities. The initial campaign was a striking success. Whereas in 1943, the last year before the joint effort, the member colleges had separately raised a total of three hundred thousand dollars, the fund in 1944 col-

lected $765,000. About seventy-five percent of the donors had not
previously given to Negro education. Except for a slight drop in
income during 1946, the fund gradually increased its harvest, reach-
ing $1,210,000 in 1950 and surpassing $2,000,000 for the first time
in 1960. New York City usually contributed twenty-five to thirty
percent of the total. The aim of the fund was to raise approximately
ten percent of the current expenses of the member colleges, a sum
that often meant the difference between efficient operation and a
deficit.[63]

The emphasis of the campaign appeal shifted somewhat over
the years. During World War II the United Negro College Fund
emphasized the Negro contribution to the war effort. At a meeting
in May, 1945, for instance, General Mark Clark lauded the Negro
troops and urged support for the fund's drive so that returning
veterans might have an opportunity for higher education. At the
same time a message was read from Sergeant Jerry Davis, the first
Negro to win the Legion of Merit, in which he said that he had
fought so that he would later be able to study.[64] With the opening
of the Cold War emphasis was placed on the importance of the race
problem in shaping the world's image of America. In 1947 the fund
warned that "Americans who would demonstrate practical democracy to the world must teach hope by helping to release our own
minority groups from despair." [65] Throughout the campaigns it
was emphasized that the private Negro colleges furnished a liberal-
arts education and produced leaders in medicine, teaching, nurs-
ing, social work, and law. The old idea of confining Negro education to agricultural and vocational training was clearly a thing of
the past.

The three major sources of contributions to the fund in its first
decade were individuals, corporations, and foundations, in that order. While donations from individuals and foundations had long
been part of the philanthropic history of Negro higher education,
corporation giving was something new. American business, in fact,
stepped in to fill the gaps left in college financing caused by the
slackening of other forms of philanthropic interest. In 1955 more
than 1,000 corporations large and small gave more than $450,000
to the fund, and a substantial part of the $264,000 credited to
foundations came from special corporate boards.[66] Much of the
corporation philanthropy was directed toward research in areas of

particular relevance to the products of the company. At Tuskegee, for example, the George Washington Carver Foundation had been established by the famous chemist in 1940 to continue his investigations and preserve his museum. Much of the work of the Carver Foundation after the war was financed by corporations. Swift and Company supported the use of the mung bean as poultry food; the Abbott Laboratories, fermentation chemistry; the Upjohn Company, the synthesis of drugs; and the Parker Pen Company, the development of inks.[67]

In addition to the regular yearly drives to raise funds for current expenses, the United Negro College Fund in 1951 began a five-year campaign for endowment and capital improvements. To give the campaign a flying start, John D. Rockefeller, Jr. in March of 1951, made an unconditional contribution of five million dollars saying: "Because I believe so profoundly in the importance to the nation at large of these constituent colleges, because I realize how greatly the fund now sought is needed and how inadequate even so substantial a sum of money will be to meet present needs, I count it a privilege to make this gift." [68] The Carnegie Corporation departed from its policy of not contributing to public fund-raising drives and gave a half million dollars to the campaign.[69] Business corporations were willing supporters, and so was the General Education Board itself in a gesture of acknowledgment that the United Negro College Fund had assumed leadership in the philanthropic field of Negro higher education. In 1956, when the campaign terminated, $17,500,000 had been obtained.[70] With the success of the fund the destiny of Negro higher learning was finally in colored hands.

The creation of Negro higher education was an example of the way in which philanthropic dollars and new ideas worked together to produce innovation. As in the case of the education of women, philanthropy implemented democracy by enlarging the opportunities of social groups previously excluded from the campus. For the Negro a college education opened an avenue to success and respectability, but it was especially significant as an opportunity for him to demonstrate that his capabilities, and consequently his rights, were no different than those of other Americans.

Chapter IX

For Alma Mater

While the philanthropy of men and women who had no personal ties other than as friends of their beneficiaries was of vital importance in shaping the development of colleges and universities, alumni had even better reason to give generously. As individuals they had traditionally supported their alma maters, usually for designated purposes. After 1918 organized alumni support gained momentum. The efforts of particular graduating classes and of the overall alumni organization provided the means by which private institutions could count on a dependable annual income.

Before World War I, alumni giving was, with some notable exceptions, on a relatively small scale. Efforts of older institutions in the nineteenth century to raise greatly needed funds from alumni met with varying results. The College of New Jersey, in an effort to "renew" itself in the 1830's, almost reached its goal of one hundred thousand dollars and thereby in effect "saved" the college—and this despite the fact that the largest single gift was five thousand dollars. On the other hand, when the Rutgers faculty publicized in 1843 the pressing need for a library building, the alumni association, formed in the previous decade, was able to raise only $2,000 in three years. Appeals to the Yale alumni on more than one occasion fell short of the mark. Prior to 1852 no Dartmouth alumnus had given or bequeathed the college more than five thousand dollars. Moreover, until 1895 only ten Dartmouth alumni had given the college five thousand dollars or more, and the total contribution

186

of these ten was only $363,367. During the same period seventeen nonalumni friends contributed more than $1,375,000.[1]

Several hortatory statements of educational leaders in the 1870's and 1880's indicated that in their mind the alumni were not doing their part in repaying to alma mater the debt they owed. "No graduate of the college," declared William Graham Sumner, on his way in 1870 to becoming an undergraduate idol at Yale, "has ever paid in full what it cost the college to educate him. A part of the expense was borne by the funds given by former benefactors of the institution. A great many men can never pay the debt. Very few can, in their turn, become munificent benefactors. There is a very large number, however, between these two," he went on, "who can, and would, cheerfully, give according to their ability in order that the college might hold the same relative position to future generations which it held to their own. The sense of gratitude, the sense of responsibility, the enlightened interest in the cause of education, which are felt by these men, constitute a resource which has never yet been tried, but which would yield richly." [2]

President James B. Angell, in his inaugural address at the University of Michigan in 1871, spoke in the same terms of alumni indebtedness, a point the more interesting in view of the obvious fact that he was speaking to those associated with a state-supported institution. Noting the beneficent results of the gifts of graduates of privately supported colleges in the East, Angell went on to say that while Michigan was chiefly dependent on the state for help, she might "reasonably hope that the men she had been sending forth into all honorable callings and professions might testify to their indebtedness to the University by increasing her power and usefulness." After pointing to the need of books, endowed chairs, and a museum, Angell concluded, "Let it not be thought that the aid furnished by the State leaves no room for munificence." [3]

In advocating alumni giving, Andrew D. White, while not neglecting the theme of indebtedness, developed a different point in his rationale. Such giving, he felt, "would attach the alumni to the university as nothing else could, for, by a subtle principle in human nature, men care readily more, as a rule, for those whom they have benefitted than for those from whom they have received benefits, and the alumni will prove no exception to the rule; they will be far more deeply attached to the university when they shall have bestowed something upon her besides criticism." [4]

On occasion alumni themselves admitted to carelessness in the cultivation of feeling for and meaningful interest in their college. It was easy, a Dartmouth man declared at a college dinner in Washington in 1883, to dismiss pleas for more help on the score that large gifts had been made without realizing that in many instances gifts and bequests were paper matters or at least provided no current funds for pressing needs. [5] Another case to the point was the observation of Henry Seidel Canby who, looking back on Yale, his alma mater, felt that alumni giving, particularly for memorial buildings and athletic facilities, had often been related more closely to a nostalgic desire to recapture a bygone "college spirit" than to far-sighted philanthropy for programs that were actually transforming the college they had known into a university with which they found it hard to identify themselves. [6]

The coming together of alumni with alma mater on a basis transcending mere sentiment depended in part on the attitude of the college toward its graduates. Two examples may illustrate different ways in which this rapprochement began to express itself. In the renewal of Dartmouth under President William Jewett Tucker a conscious effort was made to take alumni into confidence as to actualities and needs. [7] The movement for representation of alumni on boards of trustees, cautiously begun at Cornell, was another indication of a growing sensitivity to the need for enlisting more generous and widespread alumni interest and support.

The older New England colleges seemed to fare best in alumni donations. Amherst's benefactors included Dr. William Turner, who gave two hundred thousand dollars during his lifetime and who, with his sister, bequeathed the college a million dollars. [8] Dwight Morrow, with an estate estimated to total twenty million dollars, bequeathed two hundred thousand dollars to Amherst. The college also received the beautiful Long Island estate of Charles E. Merrill of the class of 1908, founder of a famous investment company, as a meeting center for the advanced study of economics with the wise provision that if the trustees deemed it feasible, it might sell the property and use the proceeds for more important needs. Merrill added numerous other gifts and sent his sons to his alma mater. [9] The magnificent Folger Shakespeare Library, the gift of Henry

Clay Folger, '79, handsomely housed near the Library of Congress in Washington, gave the college new prestige among scholars.[10]

Although in the 1890's Dartmouth received the Ralph Butterfield Museum of archaeology and ethnology, the turning point came in 1899 when, unsolicited, Edward Tuck, '62, a wealthy banker long resident in Paris, made the first of his many gifts to Dartmouth: three hundred thousand dollars. This generous donor also gave the Amos Tuck School of Administration and Finance, Tuck Drive, the president's house, valued at one hundred thousand dollars, and more than one million dollars for instruction.[11] Edwin Webster Sanborn enriched the facilities of Dartmouth's library building, given by George F. Baker, who was not a college man, with the Sanborn House for English studies. William N. Cohen, '79, gave an unrestricted gift for endowment of more than a million dollars. All these and other gifts enabled President Tucker and his successors to make Dartmouth into one of the strongest undergraduate colleges.

The nicely spaced gifts of John D. Rockefeller, Jr., Brown '97, contributed directly and indirectly to his alma mater's success in raising the six million dollars it indicated was necessary for housing and development in the late 1940's. In 1955 Rockefeller made an additional gift of four million dollars, of which about a fourth was earmarked for a new psychology building. The gift, he observed, was a testimony to his confidence in the integrity of the university and of its stability, program, and purpose.[12]

Brown and Dartmouth were not the only older eastern institutions to benefit from the loyalty and generosity of well-known alumni. Elihu Root, for example, did a great deal for Hamilton College. In addition to his own gifts of $250,000 and his bequest of two hundred thousand dollars (the largest in his will), he asked Andrew Carnegie to give one hundred thousand dollars which the canny Scot did in recognition of Root's sacrifice for the public as Secretary of War. When Root appealed again six years later, he observed that if Carnegie thought his work for peace as Secretary of State was worth less than his work for war, he was wrong. Carnegie thereupon gave Hamilton two hundred thousand dollars more in honor of Root's later achievements.[13]

In 1946 an anonymous alumnus of Bucknell offered a million dollars for an endowment, conditional on other gifts.[14] Frank Bailey, son of a country doctor and a successful real estate operator in

New York, not only served wisely as treasurer of Union College for forty-eight years, building up the endowment funds from $500,000 in 1901 to seven million dollars in 1949, but himself endowed professorships, provided buildings, and made other contributions totaling more than a million dollars.[15] James B. Colgate and his daughter Evelyn gave the college bearing the family name a half million dollars for a new chemistry building; Colgate's gifts of more than $1,000,000 and his active association with the institution for fifty years directly and indirectly benefited its program.[16]

Haverford and Swarthmore, too, were recipients of welcome and useful benefactions. William Lyle Phillips, Haverford '02, who made his money in law and banking in New York, left the bulk of an estate of two million dollars to educational and charitable institutions, Haverford receiving the major portion as well as rare books of considerable value.[17] Charles Wharton Stork, a Swarthmore alumnus and a poet and dramatist, gave the college $150,000 to be used for the establishment of an art museum. Another welcome gift to Swarthmore was that of Harriet Cox McDowell, who completed just before her seventieth reunion a sequence of gifts endowing a professorship of religion and philosophy.[18]

The financial histories of three colleges west of the Alleghenies may suggest the character of philanthropic aid from alumni. In the early 1920's Antioch was at low ebb with fifty students, an annual budget of less than twenty thousand dollars, and much indebtedness. Old and new friends rallied with gifts that saved the college and pointed it toward new achievements, a remarkable result of a determined administration and the teamwork of faculty, students, alumni, and foundations. President Arthur E. Morgan used the money to promote a cooperative work-study plan and to institute community government by students and faculty which have become Antioch trademarks. The most striking benefaction came from its oldest alumnus, Hugh T. Birch, who had been a student in the days of Horace Mann's presidency on the eve of the Civil War. Birch married into the Marshall Field family and acquired wealth through real estate on the edges of Fort Lauderdale, Florida. His wife and children died before him and, on renewing his interest in Antioch, Birch gave it a thousand-acre wooded tract, Glen Helen, with a $500,000 endowment fund for upkeep. He also bequeathed his alma mater 220 acres of Fort Lauderdale land, which the college developed and sold at a profit of more than two million dollars. Other land behind the intercoastal canal, which the college also acquired from the Birch estate, was likewise developed and sold for a handsome sum, which further augmented the endowment.[19]

Another Ohio college, Oberlin, was fortunate in having Charles Martin Hall as a loyal alumnus of the class of 1885. Working on a chemical problem suggested by Professor F. F. Jewett, Hall discovered, at the age of twenty-two, the only way to produce aluminum commercially. The Mellons and other investors applied the method with such spectacular results that aluminum became widely used. Although Hall had many trials in the venture, he became a rich man. Elected to the Oberlin board of trustees in 1905 and having no family to engage him, he centered his philanthropy on the college. In addition to many gifts while he was living, he bequeathed Oberlin a third of his estate, which by the 1920's approached fifteen million dollars. This was by no means Oberlin's only large gift or bequest, but it helped account for the growing strength of one of the oldest and most celebrated liberal-arts colleges in the Middle West.[20]

In 1939, Centre College of Kentucky, whose football team had attracted national attention, received the largest gift in its history: four hundred thousand dollars from Guy Eastman Wiseman, '85. Wiseman had served on the board of trustees since 1901 and had taken a leading part in the movement to raise a million dollars for his alma mater. The larger part of his bequest supplemented the existing endowment, though a men's dormitory, Wiseman Memorial, was also erected.[21]

As individuals, alumni in the legal profession sometimes interested clients in making bequests to their own colleges when these clients had no academic affiliation of their own. In the 1880's, for example, John Sterling, Yale '64, interested a client, Mrs. Miriam Osborn, in giving to Yale the Osborn Laboratories in honor of her financier husband. Sterling's influence also led Lord Strathcona, an Englishman and one of the owners of the Canadian Pacific Railroad, to bequeath Yale half a million dollars for a chair for the study and investigation of problems relating to transportation.[22]

One of the most unusual cases involved the lawyer who persuaded Mrs. Lucius Nieman, widow of the publisher of the *Mil-*

waukee Journal, to give a million dollars to Harvard "to promote and elevate the standards of journalism in the United States and educate persons deemed especially qualified for journalism." Since Harvard did not want a school of journalism it established fellowships for study in Cambridge to enable outstanding young newspapermen to broaden and deepen their intellectual horizons.[23]

In their own giving as individuals, alumni generally preferred to specify a particular purpose, though now and then gifts were made without strings. President Eliot of Harvard was thus especially grateful to Walter Hastings, whose will provided that, after the cost of buildings in memory of his family had been met, the rest of the $750,000 bequest was to go into an unrestricted Walter Hastings Fund. Several unrestricted gifts from Andrew Paul Keith, '01, helped President Lowell over a number of tight places.[24] By and large, however, such unrestricted giving was long the exception rather than the rule.

Alumni gifts may be considered in terms of the donors' purposes. Buildings were traditionally one of the most favored objects of benefaction. President Eliot early in the twentieth century, in connection with the Robinson gift for a memorial building for instruction in architecture, noted the importance of including provisions for upkeep in gifts for buildings, and such provisions increasingly came to be customary. The campuses of the country were enlarged (and occasionally beautified) by dormitories, libraries, student centers, and gymnasiums provided by individual "old grads."

Of buildings, those intended to promote the well-being and comfort of students, with the presumable benefit of character development, bulked large. Prominent were the dormitories given Yale by Frederick Vanderbilt, '76, with support from Cornelius Vanderbilt II, and the M. Hartley Hall in 1903. Occasionally philanthropy revolutionized student living conditions. Convinced of the need of assembling freshmen in their own dormitories, Harvard's President Lowell succeeded before World War I in attracting gifts that enabled first-year undergraduates to live with some elegance in new dormitories along the Charles River. But this was only the start.

A Yale man, Edward Harkness, who inherited a great fortune in Standard Oil, had independently come to a view about undergraduate living very much like that of President Lowell, but when he made a handsome offer to Yale to supplement the conception the university's officers were unable to decide on how the conditions necessary to an acceptance were to be met. Harkness went impatiently to Lowell, who accepted, allegedly in ten seconds, the offer of $13,000,000 that enabled Harvard to establish a "house" system. Named for Harvard presidents and scholars, the houses were in some ways modeled on the colleges of Cambridge and Oxford. Lowell pointed out that Harkness made the development at Harvard possible not because of a special interest in Harvard but because of his interest in the idea itself and his desire to see other campuses follow this example. Subsequently Harkness renewed his offer to Yale, which this time accepted it and instituted the Yale "colleges," equivalent to the Harvard "houses." [25]

But dormitories were by no means the only examples of alumni gifts for enriching student living. Henry Lee Higginson, patriot, soldier, and civic leader, in 1890 presented Harvard with Soldiers Field, to be a great athletic center on the Charles, and a decade later with the Harvard Union, planned to promote social democracy among undergraduates, a purpose only partly realized.[26] At Columbia, Frances Levien of the class of 1926 contributed a million dollars toward a nine-million-dollar athletic plant.

Scholarships had long been favorite gifts from alumni. This continued to be the case, as an inspection of university and college catalogs indicates. A few examples may suggest the range. James Loeb, Harvard '88, established the Charles Eliot Norton Fellowships in honor of his cherished friend and teacher for work at the American School of Classical Studies in Athens.[27] Fellowships were included in the multipurpose bequest John Sterling left to Yale in 1918, which at more than twenty million dollars was the largest single bequest an American university had received.[28] In 1939 a bequest of Frank Patterson, Yale '96, enabled the university to establish additional scholarships. Princeton, too, received large gifts for helping students through scholarship grants. Charles Custus Harrison, Pennsylvania '63, a trustee and provost, who in tapping Philadelphia's men of wealth for ten million dollars continued the revitalizing program of his predecessor, Provost William Pepper, a leading physician and benefactor of the university. Harrison's gifts included half a million dollars for the George Leib Harrison Foundation, established in memory of his father and devoted largely to scholarships and fellowships.[29] Columbia's scholarship program drew strength from many gifts and bequests, an especially notable one being the six-million-dollar bequest of Henry Krumb, '98. "I would not have been a mining engineer if I had not had a scholarship which paid my tuition fee," Krumb said in speaking of the motivation for his gift.[30] Of special interest was the fund established in 1952 by Evan Edward Worthing, a football star at Texas A. & M. in the early 1900's, to provide tuition, books, and living expenses for deserving students graduating from Negro high schools in Houston.[31]

The contributions of graduates to laboratories for the rapidly growing natural sciences and their application can only be suggested. Their part in the transition from college to university in the older institutions was a major one. During his lifetime, Alexander Agassiz, Harvard '62, contributed $1,500,000, derived from his activities in copper mining, to the Museum of Comparative Zoology his father had founded and to which Harvard men had contributed in its early days. The younger Agassiz also served as director, without pay, during much of his busy life.[32] Desperately in need of a modern physics laboratory, Harvard received $115,000 from Thomas Jefferson Coolidge of the class of 1850, given in memory of his son and opened in 1913. To the Wolcott Gibbs Memorial Laboratory, dedicated to investigation in physical and inorganic chemistry, Dr. Morris Loeb and his brother, James Loeb, made generous gifts. This laboratory, unusual in its equipment for precise research free from dirt and fumes, was finished in 1919 and set a high standard for similar undertakings elsewhere. Albert Fairchild, '88, a mining engineer of Cleveland, gave his magnificent collections of minerals and $75,000 for a mineralogical museum.

At Yale, Henry and Thomas Sloane of the classes of '66 and '68 made possible the Henry Sloane Physical Laboratory and provided in their wills for its improvement. One of Yale's most recent gifts is that of C. Mahlon Kline, '01, a Philadelphia pharmaceutical magnate, whose gift of ten million dollars for the Kline Science Center takes its place as the outstanding benefaction in this field.[33]

Nor was it only in providing laboratories that alumni contributed to scientific research. At Harvard, Robert Treat Paine, in establishing a professorship of practical astronomy, enabled Edward Pickering to revolutionize the photography of stars by using, instead of the conventional telescope and spectroscope, the doublet and objective prism. Responding to President Butler's appeal for funds for developing research at the Columbia School of Mines, William Boyce Thompson, who had studied only one year at this institution, contributed one hundred thousand dollars, the largest alumni gift it had received, from a fortune made in mining.[34] Thomas Davis Jones, Princeton '76, gave half a million dollars for the Henry Burchard Fine Hall of Mathematics and an equal sum for scientific research at his alma mater. Ellis L. Phillips, president of the Long Island Lighting Company, gave Cornell $1,650,000 for an electrical engineering building. Dr. Frank R. Oastler, an outstanding naturalist, left most of a net estate of $1,547,054 to the Yale School of Forestry. The great Eastman gifts to the Massachusetts Institute of Technology attracted donations from alumni who had become prominent in technical fields. Such gifts are only examples of what many other graduates with similar interests did for Union, Lehigh, Rensselaer, and dozens of other institutions.

It was some time after the Johns Hopkins bequest for medical training and research that other philanthropists took comparable steps in this field. Nevertheless the beneficence of the Shattucks to the Harvard Medical School and of Dr. William Pepper to the University of Pennsylvania were straws in the wind. Through his own generous gifts and by persuading other Philadelphians of means to open their purses, Dr. Pepper, a provost of the university, was responsible for the establishment of the Laboratory of Hygiene and the Laboratory of Clinical Medicine. In 1937 Yale received Starling W. Childs's gift of ten million dollars for cancer research and a bequest of three million from Ray Tomkins, a former football star.[35] Other gifts and bequests for medical research, from alumni as well as nongraduates, strengthened programs in all the major medical centers.

Law fared less well than medicine or the rising profession of business.[36] Myron Taylor gave half a million dollars to Cornell, his alma mater, for a new law building.[37] By an unforeseen turn of events, law at Columbia came by a four-hundred-thousand-dollar legacy that William Nelson Cromwell, a graduate of the law school, intended for Russian War Relief, an agency that died before he did. The Cromwell bequest helped Columbia realize an ambitious and promising program for bringing law and the social sciences into more fruitful relationships.[38] Rising professions besides the law received support from alumni. Lucius N. Littauer, Harvard '78, after establishing a professorship of Jewish philosophy, in 1937 contributed two million dollars for a school of public administration.[39] In 1929 James Freeman Curtis, '99, established a chair of regional planning at Harvard in memory of his friend Charles Dyer Norton.[40]

Research in science, at least in the decades after the Civil War, was in the nature of innovation, but it was by no means the only kind of pioneering that alumni gifts made possible. The development of academic work in the history and appreciation of the arts was an example of a break with academic tradition that in time deeply enriched American culture. Yale had acquired the Trumbull collection of paintings long before the Civil War. This precedent, together with Augustus Russell Street's conviction, heightened by residence abroad, that Americans were artistically illiterate, led this well-to-do alumnus to provide just before his death for a museum designed not only to house Yale's paintings and to attract other art objects but also to give instruction in the visual arts. The Yale School of Fine Arts, to the endowment of which Mrs. Street added, was opened in 1866, women being admitted along with men. By a fortunate turn of events, Yale soon after acquired a collection of Italian primitives for which James Jackson Jarves, its collector, had been unable to find a purchaser in Boston, New York, and Philadelphia. Later gifts, including the Griggs and Garvan collections, made Yale an important art center.[41] Harvard alumni enriched the collections of the Fogg Art Museum, and Princeton, thanks to Henry C. Marquand, a wealthy New York banker and patron of the arts, received a professorship in the history of art that his scholarly son Alan held with distinction for almost forty years after his appointment to the chair in 1883.

Music attracted a few patrons. At Harvard, John Knowles Paine, organist, composer, and teacher, received a full professorship in 1875 without the benefit of a special endowment—in fact, over the opposition of Francis Parkman, a member of the Corporation, who regularly proposed abolishing work in music whenever the college was faced by a financial problem. But a few years after his death in 1906 Paine was honored by the gifts of such alumni as the Loebs that made possible the building and equipment of the John Knowles Paine Music Building.[42]

The story of music at Columbia has a special interest. In 1896 New York friends of music, including alumni, endowed with a hundred thousand dollars the Robert Center Chair of Music. Edward Alexander MacDowell, a well-trained musician and gifted composer, accepted the chair, determined to carry out the intention of the endowment "to elevate the standard of musical instruction in the United States, and to afford the most favorable opportunity for acquiring instruction of the highest order." MacDowell organized a first-rate orchestra and male vocal group, probably the first academic chorus to sing serious music. His lectures were learned and inspiring. But his students were too often ill-prepared for what he wanted to give them, and his colleagues were reluctant to accept his dictum that the arts rated the same academic recognition as other subjects. Nor was he able to persuade alumni or friends of the arts in New York to endow a chair of painting and sculpture and thus create a distinguished faculty of fine arts. Discouraged, MacDowell left Columbia in 1904 after an acrimonious exchange in the public print with President Nicholas Murray Butler. But Columbia, belatedly recognizing the force of MacDowell's arguments, proudly established the Edward Alexander MacDowell Professorship.[43] Princeton was fortunate in receiving $750,000 from William S. Conant, an engineer who had helped develop the internal combustion engine, for an endowed professorship of music and for strengthening related fields.[44]

Philanthropy to the humanities found its greatest expression in the continuing aid to libraries. In 1881 the Stephen Whitney Phoenix gift to Columbia's fledgling library opened a new era. Other donations followed, outstanding among them the Avery Architectural Library, the greatest collection of its kind in the world, which Columbia received in 1890 from Samuel P. Avery in memory of his son, a Columbia student and promising architect.

Harvard's libraries were, as Samuel Eliot Morison observed, a mosaic of countless gifts largely from alumni and their families. In 1912 the mother of Harry Elkins Widener, a Harvard graduate in 1907 who had lost his life in the *Titanic* disaster, gave not only his rare collections but the Widener Library building. By the First World War, the Widener ranked as the finest scholarly library connected with an American university.[45] Subsequent gifts to Harvard included those of Alanson B. Houghton and Thomas Lamont for libraries bearing their names.[46] In 1940 Robert Woods Bliss, Harvard '00, donated Dumbarton Oaks, his home in the George-town section of Washington, D.C., housing one of the world's out-standing libraries and collections for the study of Byzantine cul-ture.[47] At the same time the libraries of Yale, Columbia, Princeton, and other institutions were also being enriched, often at the hands of alumni.

The generosity of alumni as individuals to privately supported institutions has been so impressive that the lesser magnitude of gifts from graduates of public universities has been overshadowed. As might be expected from its long history, the University of Michigan ranked high among state institutions as the recipient of alumni gifts. The earliest alumni endowment fund was the gift of Mary Porter, the first woman to attend the university, though she was never formally registered. In 1887 she gave a farm near Chilli-cothe, Ohio, valued at two thousand dollars. One of the great alumni givers to any public institution was William Wilson Cook, Michigan '82 and a graduate two years later of the university's law school. Cook became a leading corporation lawyer in New York and wrote a widely used text, *Cook on Corporations*. A generous giver during his life, Cook, who died in 1931, provided for a su-perb law quadrangle, scholarships, fellowships, and research in law. His total benefactions to his alma mater ran to more than eight million dollars. Another member of Michigan's class of 1882 who remembered his alma mater was William L. Clements. A great collector in the field of American history and its British back-ground, Clements in 1920 presented his collections, together with a handsome library costing more than a million dollars. He also gave more than a million for the Michigan Union.[48]

The University of Virginia, an older institution that influenced Michigan in its inception, received in 1929 an anonymous gift of a trust fund of six million dollars in corporation securities for scholarships and fellowships. The donor was Philip Francis du Pont, a student at the university between 1897 and 1900.[49]

West Virginia University, much less well off than Michigan and Virginia, was indebted to Dr. Israel C. White, a graduate of the class of 1872 and later a member of the faculty. His gift of 1,900 acres of coal land valued at three million dollars stipulated that the income be divided between the university and the City of

Morgantown.[50] Or take Ralph D. Merson, Ohio State, '00, a notable figure in electrical engineering. Merson was the largest contributor to the Development Fund of Ohio State and in addition left it the bulk of a fortune exceeding seven million dollars.[51]

The role of alumni in the development of the University of Wisconsin has special interest. Generally speaking, the university received few important gifts until after World War I. But William F. Vilas, an early graduate whose fortune rested on lumber and the practice of law and who held two cabinet posts under President Grover Cleveland, left an extraordinary bequest to his alma mater. He provided that, after the death of his wife and daughter, the university was to acquire his residuary estate. This was expected to appreciate to several million dollars and was to endow professorships with salaries of ten thousand dollars a year, a figure twice the prevailing level in America's strongest institutions at the time Vilas made his will in 1906. No less unusual and foresighted was the provision that these professors were to devote almost all their time to research. By 1961 enough money had accumulated so that Wisconsin was finally able to establish the first Vilas Professorships.[52]

Another creative philanthropy of great importance was the establishment of the Wisconsin Alumni Research Foundation. This grew out of the decision of Professor Harry Steenbock, an alumnus whose contributions to biochemistry included the discovery of means for creating Vitamin D in foods by irradiation with ultraviolet light, to assign his patent to a trust. Authorized by the regents in 1925, the Wisconsin Alumni Research Foundation's articles of incorporation provided that receipts from patents for research, after expenses, were to be divided between the inventor, who received fifteen percent, and the fund. The foundation, the members of which were all alumni, invested its share of the proceeds with great skill and success. It made annual grants to the university's Research Committee, which in turn gave faculty grants-in-aid for research, awarded research scholarships and fellowships, and supported designated investigations in the natural sciences. The foundation thus pioneered in working out and implementing a constructive formula for the social uses of new knowledge and in so doing contributed markedly to research programs at Wisconsin. The device occasioned favorable comment in educational circles and had some influence on a few other publicly supported institutions.[53] It was also important in view of the refusal of Wisconsin's Progressive-oriented regents to accept a grant from the Rockefeller Foundation for medical research and training on the ground that the state's university should be supported by the people and should avoid the partisanship that acceptance of "tainted money" might involve or imply.[54]

Although well-to-do citizens whose own connections were often with privately supported institutions sometimes gave generously to municipal universities, the alumni themselves were either unable for economic reasons to do much in the way of large individual giving or fell back on the common assumption that these schools, like state universities, were sufficiently supported by public funds. As late as 1956 the largest alumni gift the City College of New York had received was that of David Aronow, '14, totaling two hundred thousand dollars.[55]

Necessary as gifts and bequests from individual alumni and friends were in enabling colleges and universities to meet rising costs, admit more students, expand plant, and improve programs, they left much to be desired from the point of view of any institution. For one thing, most of the individual gifts were for specified purposes rather than for general endowment, so necessary to increase faculty salaries, to take care of contingencies, and to meet needs related to changing situations. There were exceptions, of course, and when a donor gave for endowment or for faculty salaries the receiving institution publicized it with special expressions of gratitude.[56] Yet it is significant that, when in 1954 the Hanover Bank asked leading and representative college presidents the question "What points would you make if you had a chance to speak to a room full of rich men and women?", almost every response emphasized ways to stress the need for unrestricted giving.[57] Another factor in the increasing feeling about the inadequacy of more or less unplanned giving was that no one knew in a given year just what gifts would be made, with the result that it was difficult to plan ahead. Although many educational leaders took genuine pleasure in gifts to other institutions, the fact that many alumni for various reasons gave to colleges and universities other than, or in addition to, their own,[58] suggested the desirability of focusing attention through organized efforts on alumni as well as on the general public.

The precedents provided by mid-nineteenth century efforts to enlist alumni support to save a distressed institution or to meet a special need were not forgotten. Special academic occasions lent themselves to organized alumni giving. Thus Yale undertook to raise $2,000,000 for Woolsey Hall in connection with its bicentennial in 1901. Alumni were prominent on the list of donors.

Another occasion that lent itself to organized giving was the twenty-fifth class reunion. In 1906 President Eliot announced that the class of 1881, in connection with its anniversary, had presented Harvard with a special gift of $113,777, the income to be used for unrestricted purposes.[59] Such anniversary gifts came to be habitual. More and more work, more and more money, went into the preparation of the reunions. The organizing committee for the twenty-fifth reunion of the class of '38 spent two hundred thousand dollars in getting ready for and carrying through the five-day gala festival. But the class in turn contributed $1,025,000, the first class gift to top the million-dollar mark.[60] Other institutions adopted the twenty-fifth anniversary fund to advantage.

Special needs also occasioned efforts at organized alumni giving. In 1906 President Eliot called on Harvard alumni to raise $2,500,000 needed as endowment for faculty salary increases, special professorships, and retirement allowances. Bishop William Lawrence, president of the alumni association, agreed to head a campaign that was carried through with minimum organization and publicity. "It were better," he believed, "not to complete the full amount" than to stoop to "crowding or jamming for subscriptions." Harvard men responded even without pressure; 2,000 gave a total of $2,400,000. This was the first time an institution of higher learning had raised as much as a million dollars at one time.[61] Concurrently, alumni as well as friends of Princeton responded to President Woodrow Wilson's request for six million dollars to inaugurate the preceptorial system and to meet other needs in transforming a college into a university.

But such campaigns did not meet the need for an increase in sources of income on which the college could rely year after year. The organized effort to institutionalize philanthropic support began in 1890 when a few Yale graduates established the Alumni

Fund. In the first solicitation 385 alumni gave a little more than eleven thousand dollars. It took fifteen years for the fund to reach the $104,500 goal it had originally set. By 1910, however, 8,000 Yale men were giving close to half a million dollars yearly for running expenses. Nevertheless twenty-five years went by after Yale's pioneering attempt before similar funds were operating at Brown, Union, Illinois, Cornell, Dartmouth, and Wesleyan. The slowness with which the idea caught on is evident in the fact that only four new alumni funds were begun in the first decade of the twentieth century.[62]

A good deal of stimulus was given to the alumni fund idea by the increasingly effective organization of the alumni themselves. As organization of innumerable self-conscious groups provided a sense of identity in the ever larger and more complex American communities, as the growing number of college graduates included proportionately fewer teachers and preachers and more men in the better-paid professions and in business, and as denominational support for church-related colleges decreased, alumni organizations took on increased importance as philanthropic sources. Gradually alumni came to be more actively interested in their alma mater, thanks in part to efforts of educational leaders, partly to the growing effectiveness of alumni organizations nationally and in cities all over the country, and in some measure to alumni magazines that kept readers abreast of what was happening on the campus. In 1913 the Association of Alumni Secretaries was formed, two years later the Alumni Magazines Association made its appearance, and in 1925 the Association of Alumni Organizations was launched. In 1927 these separate organizations combined to form the American Alumni Council, with 249 participating institutions. A central office gave the council leadership and coherence, and the group rapidly added new members. Annual meetings of alumni secretaries, editors, and other officers discussed common problems such as admission requirements to college, athletic policy, and opening graduates' pockets wider on behalf of alumni funds and special campaigns, which became an important part of fund-raising in the years following World War I.[63]

The first example of mobilizing alumni in a highly organized campaign took place in 1914–15 when the University of Michigan alumni launched a great movement to raise a million dollars for a student union. The alumni organization reached virtually every Michigan graduate in the country with appeals that brought results. Wisconsin followed Michigan's example in raising money for her own student union a decade later. In 1922, to commemorate Minnesota's war dead, a campaign was launched for a stadium. The business community, as well as students, faculty, and alumni, were solicited in a great "drive." No contributing group did better than the alumni's ninety percent redemption of its pledges. The Minnesota stadium campaign adopted the rapidly growing practice of using a professional fund-raising company. The background of this new development was the extraordinary success such companies had in the years before the First World War in the Young Men's and Young Women's Christian Associations' campaigns and in the "drives" for selling Liberty Bonds and raising funds for the Red Cross. From what he had learned in running such campaigns, John Price Jones published monographs and gave speeches publicizing the idea that a new era in fund-raising was at hand.[64]

The fact that Harvard was the first academic institution to make use of the professional fund-raiser was of great importance because of the prestige of America's oldest university. Thomas Lamont, an influential member of the Harvard Corporation, had agreed just before the war to head a campaign for fifteen million dollars for endowment. Because of the war, the campaign was postponed until 1918. Having been closely associated with the work of John Price Jones, also a Harvard man, in the Liberty Loan "drive," Lamont engaged him as director of publicity. An interesting exchange of letters between Jones and Thomas Nelson Perkins, '91, a director of the Harvard Endowment Fund Committee of 1919, reveals the conflict between the older and newer approaches to fund-raising. Jones defined the aims and methods of fund-raising, as he saw them, and urged Perkins, who objected to the use of the war-time term "drive" in connection with the campaign, to take a more liberal and modern view of the matter. "Publicity," Jones argued, "provides a certain amount of mental ammunition that is shot at the mind and the heart by constant repetition; it makes a prospective giver think again and again of the question of giving, and gradually works upon his mind and his heart in such a way that he finally comes across. It is a scientific fact that advertising saves two-thirds of a salesman's time. The same truth applies to publicity in a campaign of this kind." Jones also reported that in the course of his experience he had modified his ideas in regard to the relative importance of publicity and organization. Of the two, he had decided that organization was the more important.[65]

The Harvard Endowment Fund campaign of 1919 made use of both. Leaders from the local Harvard clubs throughout the country attended a short "summer session" at Cambridge and were briefed on the university's needs and on ways of stimulating generous responses among old grads. Jones then "fed the ammunition" he had prepared into the network of organizations. On his part, Perkins seems to have modified some of Jones's own ideas about the kind of publicity to be used. "I am not seeking," Jones wrote in reply to an admonition, "to promote Harvard by means of publicity." The tone of the publicity, he agreed, must be "in keeping with the quality of the article or the idea which you are promoting." For this, the Harvard drive had best arouse "a quiet enthusiasm and firm determination." The campaign, conducted along these lines, was a great success.[66]

When other colleges wanted to follow the Harvard example, John Price Jones incorporated a professional fund-raising organization. Using the methods developed in the Harvard drive, the new corporation managed fund-raising campaigns for Smith and five other women's colleges. The campaigns began with careful planning, including a survey of the needs of the colleges and of the social and economic status of alumnae and other potential donors. It made use of a speakers' bureau, a press bureau, a quota system for the widely scattered local alumnae clubs, facts and figures, and slogans. Special attention was given to the kind of publicity likely to be most effective in view of the traditions of the college and the psychology and values of the alumnae.

When John Price Jones, Incorporated undertook to raise an endowment for The Johns Hopkins University and Hospital, the problems proved to be unique. Five years earlier the university on its own had tried to raise a much-needed five million dollars; it had secured only $150,000 in pledges and less than half of these had been paid. The John Price Jones people found that there was no complete or even accurate list of alumni and no effective alumni organization. Since many who had studied at Hopkins felt a stronger tie to a particular department than any emotional loyalty to the university as a whole, the campaign emphasized a departmental approach to alumni. It also stressed the significance of research that had been done and was under way. The goal of ten million dollars was not reached, but in view of the circumstances raising seven million dollars was a real achievement. And out of the Hopkins campaign came an effective alumni organization with a high potential for future giving.[67]

Between 1918 and 1925 John Price Jones, Incorporated managed fourteen fund-raising campaigns for colleges and universities. At a cost of $1,576,731 (2.34 percent) these raised nearly sixty-eight million dollars for endowments and plant. Between 1919 and 1955 the Corporation raised $237,206,690 for higher education. Some in academic circles saw dangers in turning over fund-raising to professionals—particularly the possibility that educational policy might be overly influenced from the outside. But the professional fund-raiser had come to stay. Other firms quickly took their place in the business. The firm of Pryne and Lee handled Princeton's campaign for fourteen million dollars. It was launched with the announcement that Henry Clay Frick, the steel magnate, had bequeathed Princeton thirty percent of his estate. Far from discouraging gifts, this revelation stimulated them. The Princeton Lectures informed alumni of what was happening on the campus and what was needed. The campaign raised almost ten million dollars in addition to the Frick bequest. Charles Sumner Ward, a veteran fund-raiser for the Y.M.C.A., directed the University of Pittsburgh's campaign for three million dollars. Marts and Lundy took over Mount Holyoke's campaign, which had raised only $900,000 toward a three-million-dollar goal. "We brought it up to $2,600,000 mark in quite a short time by an individual quota on Mount Holyoke alumnae," the partners reported. Lyman Pierce organized a three-million-dollar campaign for Stanford and the American City Bureau raised $417,000 for Columbia College.[68]

In 1923 John Price Jones sent a questionnaire to 150 colleges and universities in an effort to gather information about the whole problem of fund-raising campaigns. Of the 109 institutions that responded, 64 had conducted campaigns since the end of the World War. The amounts sought ranged from small sums to Harvard's fifteen-million-dollar goal. Of the total sought, $113,664,689, more than half was needed for endowment, the rest mainly for buildings. Thirty-six campaigns reached their goal. As the years passed, campaign after campaign was launched. Generally speaking, economic conditions had a good deal to do with their results. The peak was reached in 1929–30, just before the Great Depression, when $93,007,000 were raised.[69]

Cooperation in fund-raising reflected the increasingly professional approach to the problem. Shortly after World War I nine Wisconsin colleges embarked on a federated fund-raising program, the object being five million dollars for endowment capital. A professional, Lyman L. Pierce, directed the drive, which began in September, 1919, with much carefully planned publicity. The plan was to divide the proceeds between the cooperating colleges on a pro rata basis of enrollment. The eight thousand alumni of the colleges were solicited through respective alumni organizations. Though some pledges were not redeemed the experiment was successful. Privately supported colleges in other states, especially in Indiana and Ohio, developed a similar pattern of cooperative fund-soliciting, a practice encouraged by corporations in business and industry.

Another kind of cooperation was that of the seven leading Eastern women's colleges. They were concerned by the fact that in 1932 women's colleges received only two millions out of the almost sixty-one millions given by Americans to education. Plans were made to develop the case for these institutions. Admitting that the serious business depression militated against academic philanthropy, the colleges pointed out in widely circulated brochures that the stringency in the financial resources of the women's colleges antedated that of the world at large; that it was chronic; and that the disparity in the support enjoyed by men's and women's colleges was a commentary on American values. A total endowment of what might be regarded as the seven leading men's colleges in the East was more than eight times as large as that of the seven women's colleges. The women asked for $29,645,000. No drives were contemplated, but the cause of higher educational parity was publicized in the leading newspapers of the country and the specific needs of the women's colleges made concrete.[70]

Like the men's colleges and the coeducational institutions, some women's colleges undertook, with the aid of fund-raisers, "development plans" to which alumnae were urged to give. One such plan involved the removal of the Goucher campus from its overcrowded plant in Baltimore's business district to a spacious, wooded campus in the suburbs. No efforts were spared in presenting Goucher's claims, both to alumnae and to the public. The results were gratifying.[71]

In recent years the use of professional fund-raisers in development plans involving special campaigns has become common practice. When in 1956 "A Program for Harvard College" was announced and a campaign begun for an unprecedented $82,500,000 to implement the program in endowment, plant, and services, professional fund-raising techniques were fully used. These involved Harvard Clubs all over the world, radio and television programs, and pamphlets refuting the legend that Harvard, unlike other universities, was so rich it needed no more money and the objection that the government was assuming the support of higher education. Other pamphlets compared costs and income over a period of years; it was shown that in 1931 42 percent of Harvard's income came from endowment, but in 1956 only 27 percent came from this source. Moreover, publicity identified Harvard's cause with that of higher education in general, the national interest, and world civilization itself. Graduates were informed that they might have a professorship named in their honor for a donation of four hundred thousand dollars or a house dining hall for $275,000 or a house library for one hundred thousand dollars. A young graduate replied that in view of the present condition of his finances he was unable to avail himself of any of the medium-price range bargains but enclosed a check for five dollars with the request that his name be inscribed with chalk on the floor of the south entry of Weld Hall. It was anticipated, however, that alumni would contribute sixty-two million dollars. The actual alumni contribution was $54,779,179, but almost 60 percent of all Harvard graduates gave, and the "Program" exceeded its goal.[72]

A comparable campaign for M.I.T. also succeeded in raising millions. In an age of automation, with the penetration of technology into every phase of life and preparedness for atomic war, research programs in which M.I.T. led took high rank and philanthropy responded proportionately.

Endowment, which provided a dependable annual income, was

the preferred type of support from the point of view of the beneficiary. But endowment growth proved inadequate to the growing
needs of most colleges and universities. For example, by 1957 Vanderbilt's income from endowment met only one-fifth of annual operating expenses, whereas a generation earlier it had provided two-
thirds. The alumni fund offered a means to bolster endowment yield.
More and more institutions turned to their alumni with outstretched
hands. The number of new alumni funds increased in the second
decade of the century by only seven, but the 1920's saw an addition
of thirty-two and the 1930's, when the need was unusually great and
large single contributions were rare, saw a doubling of the number
of funds. In the 1940's another ten were added, in the 1950's, eleven.
Yet according to an Alumni Council survey in 1955, sixty-five years
after the Yale Fund was organized, less than one-third of American
colleges and universities seemed to have made serious efforts to cultivate alumni philanthropy. Moreover, for every dollar contributed
in 1955 to the annual funds, two alumni dollars reportedly reached
institutions through other channels or by direct gifts.[73]

Nevertheless the record of alumni giving through organized
fund-raising was impressive. In 1936, when annual surveys began,
the eighty-six alumni funds known to exist reported $2,815,130 in
annual gifts. By 1951, 526,621 alumni in 252 reporting colleges
and universities contributed $19,217,094 to the funds, of which
$12,212,967 was allocated for current operating expenses and the
remainder for endowment. Yale's graduates led with a contribution
of more than one million dollars, the first time any alumni fund
had reached this mark. Wellesley, Notre Dame, Harvard, Dartmouth, Princeton, Vassar, Stanford, Ohio State, and Chicago followed in that order. Rivalry between classes, especially those cele-
brating their twenty-fifth reunions, and between alumni organizations of different institutions, together with intensified organizing
effort and continuing prosperity among sections of the population
that had attended college, sent the record higher each year.[74] In
1952, for example, the Alumni Fund Survey reported an increase
of two million dollars in contributions over the preceding year.
Yale led in the total amount given, $1,015,418. Dartmouth held
the record in percentage of alumni contributing: 65 percent. The
several percentages shifted in subsequent years. In 1956, for instance, almost 80 percent of Dartmouth's alumni contributed while

Harvard had the largest number of contributors and raised $1,603,127. Yale was not far behind, while the funds of Princeton, Wellesley, Notre Dame, Dartmouth, Vassar, Cornell, and M.I.T. were all well over $500,000. The year 1956 also marked the first time total alumni fund contributions surveyed exceeded one hundred million dollars. For the academic year 1960–61, 1,042 institutions in the survey reported record receipts of $208,898,409.[75]

Organized alumni giving among the publicly supported institutions was not inconsequential. Ohio State enjoyed an especially good record. Its Development Fund Association, established in 1940, reported receiving in its first fifteen years 167,968 gifts totaling more than four million dollars. Each year more than twenty thousand alumni, a larger number than those ordering football tickets in a given season, contributed through three thousand voluntary alumni solicitors in many parts of the country. The money went to scholarships, fellowships, and the construction of the first electron microscope.[76] It is of interest to note that in competing for voluntary gifts state universities encountered contentions on the part of private institutions that misrepresented actualities. Ernest Stewart, executive director of the American Alumni Council, criticized attempts of private universities to create the impression that state institutions were "inefficient" simply by "comparing total budgets per student and ignoring research and other services included in the overall figure." [77] Efforts to link private colleges with the free-enterprise system and with religious values seemed to carry the inference that state-supported institutions savored of socialism and atheism. In point of fact, the line between private and public institutions dimmed as the former accepted more and more subsidies, in one form or another, from government and as the state universities trained a larger and larger number of instructors on private college faculties.

Organized alumni fund-raising under professional auspices did not have the effect of outside interference on academic policy that some had feared. On the contrary, the influence of a single important alumnus on policy seems to have been reduced. Thus when William F. Buckley, Jr., in his widely read book, *God and Man at Yale*, called on alumni to stop giving to the annual fund until the university took action on the socialistic and atheistic teaching he alleged dominated instruction at Yale, the fund that year went over the million mark for the first time. Likewise, when his sister, Mrs. Aloise Buckley Heath, urged her sister alumnae of Smith to exercise discrimination in contributing to the annual fund until certain liberal and radical members of the faculty were dismissed, the alumnae responded with an outpouring of letters and checks— overwhelming evidence of solid support of alma mater.[78]

Alumni funds and special development campaigns did not exhaust the devices for broadening the support of old graduates. Higher education had always, of course, benefited from wills, but only in the 1920's were formal bequest programs organized. In 1924 Cornell began the first such program. A special bequest committee of eight hundred Cornell-trained lawyers, scattered throughout the country and in foreign nations, encouraged alumni and others to include the university in their testaments. The slogan "Where there's a will there's a way" was widely publicized, with the result that in less than a decade at least a million dollars a year was being written into wills for Cornell's benefit. By 1939 six million had already come to the university through this device and several million more had been committed by persons still living.[79] Other institutions adopted the practice. By 1937 at least thirty colleges and universities were operating formal bequest programs. Northwestern's booklet, *The Story of Educational Philanthropy*, stressed the need of bequests for unrestricted funds. Although publicity in the several programs emphasized the need of tact in approaching prospective donors, the consensus seemed to be that men and women did not resent being thus approached. If a Cornell spokesman was optimistic in holding that the university's major financial problems in the decades ahead would be solved largely by gifts through bequests, this method of fund-soliciting nevertheless achieved importance.[80]

In recent years organized alumni giving in one form or another became firmly entrenched. For the period 1954–61 the Council for Financial Aid to Education's biennial surveys of philanthropy to American colleges and universities showed alumni to be a source of support second only to the foundations.[81] In 1962–63 the council collected data from more than a thousand institutions and found alumni philanthropy in the lead among sources of voluntary aid.[82] The unparalleled magnitude of alumni support since World War II was obviously related to the relatively high income of the college and university graduates and to the tax advantages inherent in giving. But it was clear that with the ever-rising costs of higher education and with an expanding undergraduate and graduate population the gifts of individual alumni and the proceeds from campaigns must rise even higher. It was equally clear that privately supported institutions must also depend on other sources. Foundations had been doing a good deal for some time; business corporations had begun to help, especially since the war. Hopefully, in view of the longer and shorter records of these sources, philanthropy might provide part of what higher education had come to cost.

Chapter X

Foundation Millions

At first colleges were bigger than philanthropists. The accumulated strength of numerous small donations founded and nourished the earliest institutions. But in the first half of the nineteenth century men of means sometimes found it in their power to make single contributions that often proved the salvation of small and struggling colleges. The palmy days following the Civil War provided the setting for the accumulation of great fortunes that built new universities. A few financial giants, however, could not stop even here. In philanthropy, as in business, there seemed to be no limit to what man could accomplish. The thoughts of some donors turned to the entire system of American higher education, and their gifts went not to strengthen a single college or university but to reform and innovate in the larger sphere.

A new philanthropic agency was needed to deal with vast resources. When John D. Rockefeller was providing endowment for Vassar and Brown, or even when he helped build the University of Chicago, it was feasible for him to give directly to the institution. But by the twentieth century Rockefeller's fortune, along with that of several other Americans, had grown too large for the earlier forms of giving. So much money carried with it grave responsibilities when applied to philanthropy. It also subjected the donor to difficult decisions, endless detail, and unceasing requests for aid. Clearly, philanthropy of this scale could no longer be a matter of conversation and letter-writing. The situation demanded full-time experts in the field of giving, and the entrepreneurs who possessed the fortunes had reason to know the importance of specialists.

Foundations were the institutional response to the requirements of large-scale philanthropy. They took the form of independent organizations specializing in the efficient allocation of another person's money for philanthropic purposes. Their high degree of independence from the original donor was usually guaranteed in the deed of gift or charter and constituted the major distinction between them and "foundations" established by business corporations.[1] This same autonomous nature enabled the foundations to operate boldly and often creatively at the cutting edge of advance in a chosen field. The scope of the foundations, in some instances, was international, and their objective no less than the solution of great problems affecting all mankind. Higher education had crucial importance to the new giants of philanthropy in their broadly conceived plans for progress as well as in its own right.

Foundation philanthropy in the twentieth century differed in several respects from previous patterns of giving to higher education in the United States. For one thing, it did not seek to establish new institutions, but concentrated instead on strengthening the older ones. Influencing foundation thinking on this matter was the vast number of colleges, many of inferior grade, bequeathed to modern times by the college boom years. For entrepreneurs used to destroying weaker competitors, a solution to the problem was readily apparent: the weaker colleges had to be eliminated and the survivors made to emerge as institutions of the highest quality. Certainly further proliferation was unnecessary. Moreover, the foundations believed that since their immense financial resources gave them the power to effect changes in existing colleges, it was unnecessary to found a new institution in order to give substance to an idea.

The second point of difference was in the mechanism of giving. The decision to give and the conditions attached to a donation were transferred from the philanthropist to the "philanthropoid," an individual who made a career of giving the money of others. He commonly served the foundations as a collector of information, an evaluator of applications for aid, and a dispenser of advice, encouragement, and criticism. The man who made the money withdrew from active participation in the process of giving, content to let those with greater skill in the art dispense his surplus wealth. One philanthropist who created a number of giant foundations stated that "money is a feeble offering without the study behind it which will make its expenditure effective." [2] Since he himself was not prepared to engage in the research necessary for constructive philanthropy, John D. Rockefeller selected experts to do it in his place. "I have not had the hardihood," he confessed, "even to suggest how people, so much more experienced and wise in those things than I, should work out the details even of those plans with which I have had the honor to be associated." [3] Such ideas marked a new era in American philanthropy with far-reaching implications for educational institutions.

The third departure from much of the previous giving to colleges and universities was the clear, if sometimes only implied, philanthropic philosophy on which the foundations operated. They determined for the most part not to give merely to sustain and perpetuate the status quo in higher education. Neither would they support palliative measures. Instead, foundation officers asserted over and over again that gifts would be directed to reforms and experiments which institutions on their own were too poor or too conservative to adopt. In time this conception came to be spoken of as making foundation assets the "venture capital" of education. The doctrine had enthusiastic defenders who regarded it as the key to progress and determined critics who felt it slighted the colleges' more urgent needs. Added to the controversy was the question of what the foundations' role should be in shaping higher education. Many wondered to what extent it was proper for foundations to influence, even to coerce, the recipients of their grants. On this point foundation officials were themselves uncertain. They wished to respect the autonomy of the colleges, and yet they were committed to a policy of promoting specific innovations and reforms. Also lacking was a clear conception of goals for higher education. For instance, was precedence to be given to research and publication by faculty members, or should their traditional teaching role be emphasized?

A large number of the more than five thousand foundations that exist in the United States today profess a major interest in higher education.[4] Many of these are small and limit their activities to the awarding of an occasional scholarship to a student or professor. Some have the resources to provide telling aid to an entire discipline at a college or university. Only a few foundations are equipped with the cash assets and the staff to undertake projects concerned with higher education as a whole. Among these the names of Rockefeller, Carnegie, and Ford are preeminent. Not only have the foundations bearing these names set suggestive patterns for others, but the grants of the big three together compromise the greater part of all foundation giving to education. On their record, both in its best and worst aspects, the impact of foundations on higher education has in large part depended.

In 1865 John D. Rockefeller's gifts topped a thousand dollars for the first time. They exceeded a hundred thousand dollars in 1884 and passed the million-dollar mark four years later.[5] Even so, the oil magnate's philanthropy was not keeping pace with his gigantic income. On March 1, 1902, as a possible solution to the problem of excess wealth, Rockefeller gave a million dollars to launch the General Education Board. Its object was "to promote education in the United States of America without distinction of sex, race, or creed," and its immediate field of interest was the South.[6] In its size and initial purpose it resembled the funds that George Peabody and John F. Slater created following the Civil War.[7] But Rockefeller had far more ambitious plans for his foundation. "If a combination to do business is effective in saving waste and in getting better results," he wrote in his memoirs, "why is not combination far more important in philanthropic work?"[8] The General Education Board was designed to bring order and efficiency to Rockefeller's philanthropy, which had proved too vast for his own office and the American Baptist Education Society to handle. Another motive for establishing the foundation, to which Rockefeller gave high priority, was a desire to show socialists that capitalism was capable of promoting the greatest "general good."[9]

Robert C. Ogden, an executive in the Wanamaker chain of department stores, initiated the series of events that culminated in the formation of the General Education Board. Ogden organized annual conferences at which the problem of improving education in the South was discussed and solutions proposed. John D. Rockefeller, Jr., was a member of the party of Northern businessmen that in 1901 attended the conference held at Winston-Salem, North Carolina. He came from the conference deeply moved by the plight of the Southerner, both white and colored, and determined to talk with his father about extending the Rockefeller philanthropies in that direction. Frederick T. Gates, the Baptist minister who had advised the senior Rockefeller in his support of the University of Chicago,[10] was also consulted. A board of trustees including Ogden, Gates, Daniel Coit Gilman, Jabez L. M. Curry, and Walter Hines Page organized to receive the first donation. Wallace Buttrick was named executive secretary. Early work centered in the South and was confined to secondary education, farm demonstrations, and primary schools in rural districts.[11] Then on June 30, 1905, the board received a letter from Gates, written on behalf of Rockefeller, bearing notice of a gift of ten million dollars "to promote a comprehensive system of higher education in the United States."[12] This donation and the $118,000,000 Rockefeller allocated to the board in the next sixteen years gave it the means to exert a considerable influence on American colleges and universities.

The General Education Board was determined to use the great resources at its disposal in a creative fashion. As a preliminary it conducted an intensive survey of the facilities for higher education in the United States. The results confirmed what many had suspected: the nation had an overabundance of colleges, most of which lacked the income and equipment to perform their task even passably well. It appeared, for instance, that "the State of Ohio, with a total population of 4,767,121, contains over 40 so-called colleges and universities, almost twice as many as the entire German Empire with a population of 64,903,423." What was lacking was a "general design" for higher education, national in scope, that would order the chaos.[13] The board wanted to help remedy this defect but was torn between two ideals. On the one hand, the trustees declared it their policy "to put no pressure, direct or indirect, upon any college or university with a view to influencing its course of action. . . ." Instead, institutions would be left to "work out their own salvation." Yet the board knew "that they are most likely to do this effectually if they are comfortable financially."[14] And with their millions, the trustees had within their power the ability to confer such comfort and even to determine whether an institution would continue to exist. Coercion may not have been overt, but in making grants the board naturally selected those institutions whose policies and program they approved. As a result these practices became unofficial standards for many other colleges. The desire to shape higher education inevitably worked against the determination to refrain from pressuring individual colleges.

In attempting to decide which colleges they would support and which, in Gates's words, "must perish and ought to do so," [15] the board relied on the principle of optimum location. Among other things this meant a college's possession of a loyal constituency willing to support it with gifts and bequests. Institutions situated in populous and wealthy areas seemed to the board to be assured of adequate enrollments and sufficient patronage to merit survival. Colleges on the fringes of such areas and those that overlapped the hinterland of more successful institutions had poorer chances. An elaborate series of maps was prepared to illustrate what the board termed these "laws of college growth." [16]

With a philanthropic philosophy in hand, the General Education Board began its appropriations, and by 1925 they totaled approximately sixty million dollars almost entirely in the form of gifts to endowment. Harvard, Amherst, Wellesley, and similar colleges were certain inclusions in the grants. The criterion for other institutions came to be the vague notion of their "promise." [17] This was demonstrated, in part, by their ability to raise on their own sums equal to or greater than the board's grant. Unquestionably this matching-gift policy stimulated philanthropy outside the foundation. Colleges could raise funds with the argument that the contribution of one dollar really amounted to two in the treasury. It was a source of pride to the board that the 103 colleges to which $10,582,592 had been given as of June 30, 1914, raised matching sums of almost forty million dollars.[18] The Rockefeller trustees looked coldly on colleges that begged for a gift on the grounds that they would be obliged to close without it. It seemed to Wallace Buttrick that an institution in such straits did not deserve support. As a result of this point of view the General Education Board confined its gifts to major colleges and universities to the extent that by 1920 twenty institutions had received about 75 percent of all foundation philanthropy.[19]

By 1926 the board had concluded its major program in support of college endowments. The report of that year pointed out that the reason for turning elsewhere was not because the problem had ceased but because the public had been fully awakened to the need to carry on alone. In addition the amounts needed for adequate endowments had become so large that the board could no longer make telling gifts in that area.[20] There were other aspects of higher education, however, that foundation philanthropy could help reform and, indeed, already had.

One of the great shortcomings of American higher education at the turn of the century was the deplorable condition of medical schools. Abraham Flexner's famous report of 1910 described the problem in vivid terms. In fact, Flexner recommended that all but 31 of the existing 155 medical schools be abolished.[21] The members of the General Education Board were intensely interested in these statistics. Rockefeller had already shown his interest in medicine when in 1901 he established the Rockefeller Institute for Medical Research in New York City. Now Flexner's findings suggested that the teaching of medicine also needed a philanthropic assist. A comprehensive plan emerged from conferences of Flexner and Gates. The most promising medical school in the country, that at The Johns Hopkins University, would be built into a first-rate institution to serve as a model and stimulus. In 1913 Hopkins's Dr. William H. Welch, the leading figure in American medicine, received one and a half million dollars from the board. The gift's terms required that it be used to pay the medical staff a full academic salary and thus eliminate the need for them to maintain an outside private practice. So insistent were Gates and Flexner that the policy of "full-time," as it was called, was medical education's panacea that the board obliged the institutions it benefited to sign detailed contracts specifying that the policy would be adopted. Such attempts at coercion brought immediate opposition from eminent educators, including Charles W. Eliot, Harvard's former president and an adviser of the board, and in time dogmatic insistence on "full-time" was relaxed.[22]

Between 1919 and 1921 John D. Rockefeller gave the General Education Board forty-five million dollars more earmarked for medical education. Occasionally assistance also came from the vast resources of The Rockefeller Foundation, the major concern of which at this time was public health on an international scale. The money went to promote excellence in medical education at various centers over the country. Besides the gift to Hopkins, millions were given to Yale, Washington University in St. Louis, the University of Chicago, and Vanderbilt. The board felt that these and a score of other institutions it assisted would oblige the remainder of the nation's medical schools to either raise their standards or close. Always anxious to generate local support for the projects they aided, the trustees were gratified to see individuals such as George Eastman in Rochester,[23] Julius Rosenwald in Chicago, and Stephen V. Harkness in New York supplement their gifts. In 1929, when the board closed out its giving to medical education, its members could take satisfaction from the accomplishment seventy-eight million dollars had obtained. Its gifts had primed the philanthropic pump, from which roughly one hundred million dollars had come for medical education. In less than two decades after Flexner's scathing report, America's medical schools had been reduced in number and so improved as to place them among the world's finest.[24] Here, surely, was a convincing illustration of Abraham Flexner's maxim that, to be effective, foundations "must 'bunch their hits,' not scatter their fire like buckshot." [25]

Like Rockefeller, Andrew Carnegie entered the twentieth century with the problem of surplus wealth. In the Scot's case, however, the pressure to give and give creatively was more acute because he himself had previously outlined a philanthropic philosophy that made such donations imperative. In 1889 Carnegie published two articles that generated widespread excitement because they confronted directly the questions raised by that relatively new phenomenon, the American millionaire. In his first essay Carnegie maintained that it was the duty of the rich man to consider his fortune as a trust held in the name of the less fortunate. This obliged him to give during his own lifetime everything not needed by his own family. Moreover, the philanthropy had to be constructive, and it should promote self-help. Carnegie concluded his article with a ringing peroration: "The man who dies thus rich dies disgraced." [26]

In Carnegie's estimation, higher education was a proper field for philanthropy. He singled out Leland Stanford, Peter Cooper, Johns Hopkins, and Ezra Cornell as men of wealth who admirably fulfilled the duties of stewardship.[27] Carnegie himself had certainly not been niggardly in his giving, and numerous colleges were among the recipients, but his philanthropy lacked the planned direction he regarded as essential for it to be most beneficial.

In 1904 Carnegie received a proposal from President Henry S. Pritchett of the Massachusetts Institute of Technology that appealed to his philanthropic tastes. Pritchett proposed that the steel magnate provide retirement pensions for the M.I.T. faculty. Carnegie had long recognized that this was a worthy cause. In 1890, as a newly appointed trustee of Cornell University, he had been astonished to discover that the professors were paid less than many of his clerks.[28] But why stop at M.I.T., Carnegie wondered, and he asked Pritchett to look into the possibility of a nationwide system of pensions. The resulting report indicated that the faculty in ninety-two colleges and universities could be provided for with the income from a gift of ten million dollars. In April, 1903, Carnegie donated that amount in United States Steel Corporation bonds and selected twenty-five leaders in higher education to serve as trustees. Pritchett resigned from M.I.T. to become president of the Carnegie Foundation for the Advancement of Teaching.[29]

On taking control of the foundation, Henry S. Pritchett saw at once that it was within his power to do far more than merely provide an income for retired professors. The colleges were eager to be included in Carnegie's pension system. Why not, reasoned Pritchett, use the privilege of membership as a reward for those institutions that conformed to certain standards? One of the most glaring defects of American higher education at the turn of the century was the lack of a consistent policy on the requirements for admission to college. This meant that any institution could purport to dispense higher education even if its students were inadequately prepared for college work. The Carnegie Foundation determined to remedy this situation with the provision that if its professors were to receive pensions a college must confine its admissions only to those students with four complete years of secondary education. So that this requirement would not be misunderstood, the foundation sponsored a conference in 1908 that devised the "Carnegie unit" as a measurement device. Fifteen units of work were demanded of those desiring to matriculate at a bona fide college or university, or at least one associated with the pension system.[30]

The Carnegie Foundation also demanded that those colleges it benefited with pensions have at least six full professors (after 1921 eight were required), which usually meant that number of departments. In addition, member institutions had to meet the requirement of an endowment of two hundred thousand dollars (five hundred thousand after 1921) and had to be free from debt. The foundation believed that the weakest links in American higher education were the denominational colleges, whose sectarianism prevented adequate growth and support from a diverse public. In an effort to eliminate church control of colleges the foundation had been chartered with the stipulation that no pensions would be given to the faculties of institutions under sectarian control.

This policy was in marked contrast to that of the General Education Board, which welcomed denominational assistance in raising standards, but in other respects the two foundations pursued similar ends. Both selected colleges to support that appeared on the basis of location and record to have the greatest potential for growth. In each case the number was about a hundred. And both Pritchett and Buttrick were aware that they could frequently influence institutions, even without giving them benefits directly, by the lure of philanthropy and the example of others.[31]

There was no lack of criticism leveled at the General Education Board and the Carnegie Foundation in their bold attempts to reshape the system of American higher education. From the South came screams of protest against the work of the board. One was an invective by a Methodist clergyman with the subtitle: *A vast scheme for capturing and controlling the colleges and universities of the country.*[32] The Carnegie pensions were challenged from the professor's viewpoint as sops given in the place of salary increases, and a few resented the lack of faculty control of the operation.[33] Most teachers, however, were grateful for the increased security Carnegie's philanthropy made possible. The state universities resented their omission from the foundation's pension plan and protested so vigorously that Carnegie himself, in one of his rare violations of his trustees' autonomy, countered Pritchett's policy and in 1908 gave five million dollars more to provide for faculty in state institutions.[34] Even the highly successful medical program came in for criticism. A Harvard scholar, who was generally favorable to the work foundations were doing, felt compelled to record his foreboding that "the guidance of medical education is to a considerable extent passing out of the hands of the universities" and into those of a "superacademic general staff." [35] In answer to such critics, however, was the successful resistance of many medical schools to the board's attempts to press the "full-time" arrangement on them.

From all quarters came charges that the foundations were attempting to "standardize" higher education. In many cases the critics represented colleges that did not meet the standards, and could be answered with Carnegie's concept of the law of competition which, he explained in 1889, "may be sometimes hard for the individual, [but] . . . is best for the race because it insures the survival of the fittest in every department." [36] But occasionally Pritchett's grandiose plans and dictatorial tactics obscured his recognition of the virtues of smaller colleges. [37] And in 1916 Pritchett published a report that admitted the inadequacies of using free pensions to construct a system of higher education composed of a few favored institutions. [38] Two years later the entire pension program of the Carnegie Foundation, which had committed itself beyond its resources, was reorganized around the Teachers Insurance and Annuity Association. The major innovations of the new pension program were the dropping of the college standards necessary for participation and the provision that a professor contribute 5 percent of his salary toward retirement benefits.

In the interwar period, foundation philanthropy to higher education continued to be dominated by the creations of John D. Rockefeller and Andrew Carnegie. Also continuing was the policy of selecting the strongest and most promising centers of learning as recipients. Between 1923 and 1929, for example, of the $103,000,000 that the five largest foundations gave to private institutions, $88,-500,000, or about 86 percent, went to only thirty-six colleges and universities. [39] Out of a total of more than a thousand institutions in the United States, this was indeed concentrated giving. In the following six-year period fifteen institutions received about three-quarters of foundation allotments, and in 1940 Ernest V. Hollis could state that twenty schools received 73.2 percent of foundation benefactions, 425 divided the remainder, and some eight hundred colleges got nothing. [40] The General Education Board, it should be said, made some attempt to diversify the allocation of a fifty million dollar gift it received from Rockefeller in 1919 for improving academic salaries. A total of 173 colleges received aid, but the criteria for selection were stiff. Moreover, the money was given only on the condition that the recipient institution raise from outside sources at least double and in some cases four times as much as the board gave.[41] Clearly the board did not take many risks in its philanthropy; there was no sustenance for moribund colleges.

Rockefeller's fifty million dollars for salaries was one of the last donations that went to bolster endowment in the name of broad, strengthening purposes. Increasingly after 1920 the foundations focused their giving on specific projects. Conscious of their self-appointed role to provide "venture capital" for the colleges, the foundations sought to support innovations on many campuses. Almost all of the projects tended to direct higher education away from its traditional teaching function and to give emphasis to scholarly investigation and publication.

One of the leaders in pioneering and experimenting was the Carnegie Corporation of New York. A foundation despite its name, this organization had been created in 1911 on the strength of a twenty-five million dollar gift from Andrew Carnegie "to promote the advancement and diffusion of knowledge and understanding."[42] In 1912 further Carnegie gifts of one hundred million dollars swelled its resources. Actually, until Frederick Paul Keppel was elected president of the corporation in 1922, it was little more than a device for Carnegie to gain assistance in his personal giving to libraries, churches, and other philanthropic enterprises. But with the far-sighted Keppel at the head of the foundation, and with Carnegie dead, the corporation looked to other fields.[43] In so doing it was encouraged by a statement in Carnegie's original letter of gift: "Conditions upon the erth [sic] inevitably change; hence no wise man will bind Trustees forever to certain paths, causes or instructions." As a consequence of this belief, Carnegie gave complete freedom to the men responsible for allocating his wealth and added that "they shall best conform to my wishes by using their own judgment."[44]

The Carnegie Corporation plunged vigorously into new enterprises. Typical of them was the Food Research Institute at Stanford University, which the corporation began aiding in 1922 and ultimately supplied with more than one and a half million dollars. No teaching was carried on at the institute, but rather intensive scientific study of the production, distribution, and consumption of food.[45] Smaller grants in the field of science were made to men whose work seemed to hold promise of important breakthroughs, such as R. A. Millikan, who in the 1920's was performing research in atomic structure and cosmic rays at the California Institute of Technology.[46] In 1926 the corporation expressed satisfaction that its grants had opened new lines of inquiry in engineering education, and it continued to aid in the development of such fields as aerodynamics, notably at the Massachusetts Institute of Technology.[47] Grants of this sort were made through, rather than to, the college or university that furnished the equipment and personnel for advanced research.

The fine arts were another new field into which the Carnegie Corporation poured money and encouragement. Specifically, attempts were made to interest colleges in cultivating an appreciation of the arts in their students. Grants went to help organize art departments and to provide sets of slides and books on the subject. President Keppel, who was personally interested in the arts, strongly supported this phase of the program, although even he had moments of doubt as to whether the program was "a passing fad" or "a permanent cultural advance." [48] Extensive aid from the corporation also went to college libraries and a novelty, graduate schools of librarianship such as the one at the University of California, which received a million-dollar endowment in 1926.[49] Another novel undertaking was the Employment Stabilization Research Institute at the University of Minnesota, which received support at the height of the Depression.[50]

In promoting innovation in the process of education the Carnegie Corporation frequently joined forces with other foundations. The object of the benefactions was the new "experimental" colleges and programs of reform in the older establishments. At Swarthmore a program was initiated to give first-rate students almost complete freedom for independent study under faculty guidance. The corporation supported it with $275,000, the Rosenwald Fund with $364,000, and the General Education Board with $675,000.[51] Similarly, the University of Minnesota's General College, for students not inclined to or suited for regular college work, received aid from a number of foundations. The Carnegie Corporation by 1938 had appropriated more than five million for progressive institutions such as Bennington, Antioch, Bard, Stephens, Southwestern, and Teachers College at Columbia University.[52]

In the period between the wars the other foundations also tested the limits of their effectiveness. The General Education Board, whose donations were by far the largest, pursued the same policy as the Carnegie Corporation in focusing its giving on a few chosen institutions for specific programs. The sciences in particular received emphasis. Between 1925 and 1932, for example, the California Institute of Technology received $3,300,000 for the expansion of its offerings in physics, chemistry, mathematics, and biology. Large sums for the advancement of science also went to Harvard, Stanford, and Princeton. At Yale, Arnold Gesell received board money to further his studies in child growth and development.[53]

One notable exception to the General Education Board's emphasis of the natural sciences was the support given the Oriental Institute at the University of Chicago. James Breasted was the leading figure in this archaeological center, and he commanded so much respect that eleven million dollars came to the institute from the various Rockefeller philanthropies, including $3,500,000 from the board. So much money enabled Breasted to raise the institute into world prominence, with expeditions constantly in the field in such areas as the Near East, Egypt, or along the African coast. At one point the institute had an annual budget of seven hundred thousand dollars, and criticism was rife that this "bizarre undertaking" destroyed the proper balance between departments of a university.[54] After Breasted's death in 1935 the Oriental Institute receded to a more modest place at Chicago, but its success in finding funds indicated the stress that foundations placed on academic showcases where leading scholars could pursue their specialties.

The giant Rockefeller Foundation, chartered in 1913 "to promote the well-being of mankind throughout the world," concentrated its activities in the field of public health, frequently in foreign lands.[55] Yet its vast resources permitted it to help shape higher education at home. Again the sciences received primary attention, and again it was prominent men such as Thomas Hunt Morgan and Linus Pauling at the California Institute of Technology who received the grants. The field of enzymology alone drew $1,600,000 from the foundation, spread among thirty-five institutions. West Coast centers had particular luck with the Rockefeller Foundation. The University of California got $1,000,000 for a cyclotron, but Cal Tech landed the real prize—the Mount Wilson Observatory, erected at a cost of six million, which when completed was the finest astronomical facility in the nation. After 1929, when the foundation absorbed the Laura Spellman Rockefeller Memorial, the social sciences and humanities received increased emphasis. Grants were especially easy to obtain for studies of other countries, such as those conducted at Yale's Institute of International Studies, established in 1935. Aid also went to Columbia's Russian Institute a decade later. In all its grants, totaling many millions, the Rockefeller Foundation stressed research and discovery—the giant newcomer on the American college scene.[56]

Foundations with smaller resources had to be content with preparing reports on particular problems in the field of higher education or with aiding a few limited projects. In 1929 the Carnegie Foundation for the Advancement of Teaching sought to duplicate the success of its 1910 exposure of medical education with a report, which cost $110,000 to make, on the dangers of commercialism in intercollegiate athletics. In this case, however, philanthropy did not hasten to reform the situation.[57] Other projects examined the problem of "quality" in American education, investigated the efficiency of the process of transition between secondary schools and colleges, and conducted studies on educational testing that led to the development of the Graduate Record Examination.[58] The Lilly Endowment, established in 1937, interested itself especially in the private, church-related colleges of Indiana, an interest which took the form of several million dollars in grants for salary increases.[59] Mrs. Stephen V. Harkness's Commonwealth Fund, established in 1918 "to do something for the welfare of mankind," was primarily interested in health and medical research, and its support of numerous colleges and universities went to further these fields.[60] And the chain store magnate, Sebastian Kresge, created a foundation that aided the training in medicine and business of a number of prominent institutions.[61]

On summing up the impact of philanthropic foundations on higher education on the eve of World War II, Ernest V. Hollis termed them "the most influential of the external agencies that have modified higher education as a process or institution." He went on to praise their creativity, saying that "the trend of foundation influence in higher education has increasingly been toward supporting ideas and institutions that are usually considered close to the growing edge of culture." [62] And he cited examples such as their pioneering work with fine arts, librarianship, medicine, engineering, adult education, the art of teaching, and the formulation of standards for colleges. Certainly the expenditure of some $220,-000,000 by all the foundations in the field of higher education up to 1938 had achieved important results. And the foundations felt they had done justice to novelty. Speaking in 1937 of the opportunities of obtaining grants for new research and demonstrations, President Keppel of the Carnegie Corporation declared that "if the really exceptional enterprise or the exceptional individual is overlooked today, it is not because the necessary funds are not somewhere available." But some educators, such as those pioneering new methods at Bard College, had grounds for disagreeing with Keppel.

Along with the knowledge of their power to innovate, the foundations gained a maturity from several decades of making grants. In his final report, Keppel remarked on the confidence of the typical foundation in the early 1920's. "It still has confidence today," he continued, "but of a different kind. It has less trust in what money can do, far less certainty of its own wisdom, but it knows from experience that, while many of its most cherished plans may go astray, others will prove useful to humanity to a degree far beyond original hopes." [64]

One of the facts that foundations had to face as they moved into the period following World War II was that the rising costs of higher education were reducing the extent of what they could accomplish with their grants. In the early days of its work the Carnegie Corporation's annual appropriations were a 15th of the yearly income of higher educational institutions. By 1940 the fraction had decreased to a 140th.[65] Consequently the foundations would have to take special pains to place their gifts where they would "count" the most as venture capital.

In dispensing their bounty after the war, the foundations also had the worry of answering a host of critics. Some deprecated the entire concept of a philanthropic trust as tax evasion and bribes for public esteem on the part of those who scarcely deserved it.[66] Others endeavored to link large-scale philanthropy with socialism.[67] Especially painful was criticism from within the foundation family. Abraham Flexner took the foundations to task for neglecting the humanities in favor of the natural and social sciences. It was a waste of money, he declared, to place a few thousand dollars in various universities in support of literature, philosophy, or music. Flexner called for a program of giving to the humanities on the scale of the earlier assistance to medical education, and although he was too old to blaze the way with another critical report, the foundations listened intently to his advice.[68] Another foundation officer, Edwin R. Embree, who had served both the Rockefeller Foundation and the Rosenwald Fund, made provoking charges in the March, 1949 issue of *Harper's*. Embree believed that foundations should pioneer in the support of innovations, and he charged that they had abdicated their risk-taking role. Instead, he said, under the guidance of conservative trustees they were primarily concerned with self-preservation and were infected by "traditionalism." Grants went to causes that were once ventures but no longer needed foundation stimulation, such as medicine, research in the physical sciences, and general endowment for colleges. Any grants that might be made to new ideas were weakened by the foundation practice of "scatteration," or sprinkling small allotments over a number of institutions. Embree advocated large-scale giving to carefully chosen innovations with the hope of making a significant contribution.[69] Still there were practical difficulties to being bold that frequently made the middle of the road seem a far more desirable position to foundation administrators.[70]

The 1950's marked the beginning of giving from several foundations to higher education on a colossal scale. The most important by far, since it was the largest philanthropic enterprise in world history and came to stand in the popular mind for American philanthropy as a whole, was the Ford Foundation. Disinterested benevolence did not figure as a primary motive when Henry Ford and his son Edsel established their philanthropic agency on January 15, 1936. Far more pressing than the desire to do good were the new laws the Roosevelt administration had devised in an effort to trim the surplus wealth from America's richest families. One of the new taxes fell on estates. The Fords, who had traditionally refused to extend ownership in their company beyond the immediate family, perceived in the inheritance tax an end to family control since to pay it would necessitate selling a large portion of the Ford stock to outsiders.[71]

Hurried consultation with company lawyers in 1935 produced an ingenious solution to the Fords' problem. A philanthropic foundation would be established to which both Henry and his son, Edsel, could bequeath their common-stock holdings and thereby avoid payment of estate taxes. While the Fords lived the foundation was relatively small and active only in the Detroit area. But with the death of Edsel in 1943 and his father four years later, the Ford Foundation acquired about 90 percent of the Ford Motor Company stock with an estimated value of more than two billion dollars. The problem of the Fords was solved, but that of their foundation's trustees was only beginning. Primary among their concerns was the necessity of dispensing the income from the Ford stock before it ballooned to a point where it would arouse the concern of federal tax agencies. Added to the administrators' dilemma was the fact that any gifts they made would from their size alone be eminently newsworthy and subject to wide and critical discussion.

As a partial answer to their predicament, the Ford Foundation officers issued a public report on the results of their study of the fields open to large-scale philanthropy.[72] This document and the ideas of Paul Hoffman, president of the foundation, and Robert M. Hutchins, associate director, made two points clear: higher education would be supported as a basic tool in the solution of mankind's problems, and novel, experimental programs would be favored in making grants to colleges and universities.

In order to handle appropriations for education, the Ford Foundation in 1951 created the Fund for the Advancement of Education. Its first president, Clarence H. Faust, gave full support to the principle of venture capital. To his way of thinking, foundation philanthropy should go to carefully selected innovations in education and in amounts sufficient to give them a thorough trial. Faust advocated giving according to the "principle of ferment," by which foundation support called attention to a problem and set other agencies to action. Money would not go, he declared, to developments in education for which tax funds and the resources of private institutions were available.[73]

The record of the Fund for the Advancement of Education in the

1950's was consistent with its philanthropic philosophy. Among the departures it aided was a "fifth-year" teacher-training program in which liberal-arts graduates of colleges in a region might attend a central graduate school of education for a year of intensive training before taking positions in secondary schools. Starting with a number of colleges in Arkansas, the program gained great momentum when Harvard's Graduate School of Education agreed to act as training center for graduates of twenty-eight private Eastern colleges. In 1959 the fund spent more than fourteen million dollars on the fifth-year program and termed the results a "breakthrough" in teacher training. Opposition to the program developed in non-participating graduate schools of education, who regarded the fund as an interloper in their domain, but fund officers expected innovation to engender criticism and had the satisfaction of seeing what once was novel become widely accepted as a means of meeting serious teacher shortages.[74]

In the early 1950's, as the Fund for the Advancement of Education began its allocations, President Faust laid down a guiding principle: "If to avoid the risk of criticism or error, a foundation supports only programs or projects that are already widely approved and generally accepted, it does not fulfil the mission which its unique position both enables and requires it to perform."[75] In its decade of experimenting the fund encountered both attack and failure. The series of grants made from 1952 to 1954 to enable selected institutions of higher learning to undertake studies of their own effectiveness did not produce the results that had been expected and was dropped.[76] Heated controversy arose over fund-sponsored attempts to determine the effects of admitting exceptional students to colleges and graduate schools before they had attained the traditional age.[77] But the greatest uproar developed over the fund's activities in promoting experimentation with new teaching methods, such as educational television and teaching machines. Critics charged the Ford Foundation and the fund with using its great resources as a means of "pushing" the new techniques on institutions that were not convinced of their value.[78] The literature issued by the foundation, however, indicated that its approach to the new methods was one of objective experimentation rather than all-out advocacy. The first attempts to use television at the college level, said a fund report, "were designed to determine . . . whether or not television could be used effectively . . . and the effects of its use on instructors, students, and on the institutions themselves." [79] Of course the only way to find the answers was to try the method, and the fund undertook projects such as the Midwest Program on Airborne Television Instruction with a vigor that misled its critics into thinking philanthropy was insidiously attempting to put something over on higher education.

While the Fund for the Advancement of Education was supporting innovations, the Ford Foundation made important grants to education on its own. Some were of the venture variety, such as the three and a half million that went to the Center for Advanced Study in the Behavioral Sciences associated with Stanford University.[80] But many grants were of a conservative nature scarcely in keeping with the foundation's avowed policies but possibly a reaction to the embarrassing Congressional investigations conducted at the time. In this category was the gigantic $210,000,000 gift to 630 private liberal-arts institutions that the foundation announced late in 1955 as part of a five hundred million dollar benefaction of American hospitals, colleges, and medical schools. This philanthropic act was of unprecedented size in world history, but it carefully avoided any attempt to make a basic change or introduce an innovation in the recipient institutions. The only conditions under which the colleges received the money were that it should be invested and the income used to raise faculty salaries. The $210,-000,000 was distributed on a mathematical basis (an amount equal to the 1954–55 faculty payroll of each institution). There was no attempt to direct the benefactions so as to encourage colleges which met certain standards—the usual procedure of foundations in the past. Another Ford grant, of fifty million did go to a select group of 126 institutions that had taken steps on their own initiative to increase salaries since World War II. This money, however, was given for general use and practically without condition.[81]

By its very size a $260,000,000 gift would have some effect, but critics were quick to point out that the Ford Foundation's giving was subject to the same charges of "scatteration" that Edwin Embree had leveled at foundations in 1949, and which the Ford Foundation report of the same year had promised to avoid. Even recipients of the money were grieved that it had gone to such a safe, noncontroversial cause as faculty salaries. One professor with a talent for long division figured that the $260,000,000 spread out over 630 institutions would mean an increase in the pay of an individual faculty member of only four dollars a week. Such a pittance, he continued, was unlikely to do much good, whereas if the money had been concentrated the total accomplishment could have been much greater.[82] In reply to these charges, some pointed out that the Ford grant had dramatized the problem of faculty pay and had, through its wide dispersal, minimized elitism and kept alive plurality in the American system of higher learning.[83] Such arguments were unconvincing, however, especially in the light of the reforms and changes the Carnegie and Rockefeller philanthropies had been able to accomplish through clear statement of aims and judicious placement of funds. Yet in fairness to the Ford Foundation and President H. Rowan Gaither, there was some discrimination in making the $260,000,000 appropriation. Hundreds of small, frequently church-related colleges received nothing and faced bleak futures if not termination.[84]

Subsequently the foundation took a few steps toward concentrating its benefactions under its Special Program in Education through which a few dozen selected colleges and universities were given a minimum of one and a half million dollars each to advance their development as "regional and national centers of excellence." [85] In every case the grant was conditional on its being matched by money the recipient institution raised on its own from alumni and friends. Rather than dictate how its money was to be used, the foundation permitted each college to undertake what seemed best calculated to improve its service.[86] It was just such forbearance that earlier critics of the foundations had found wanting.

As it faced the 1960's the Ford Foundation emphasized that it would "resist pressures and temptations to support only conventional activities, however worthwhile" and would "take risks in ventures that it hopes may yield substantial advances for human welfare." [87] But the disposition of the $744,000,000 the foundation gave to education at all levels during the 1950's left some doubt as to its determination to live up to its stated aims. There was no doubt, however, that the $2,600,000,000 remaining in the foundation treasury gave it immense power and commensurate responsibility in the field of higher education in the years ahead.

Although dwarfed by the mammoth Ford Foundation, other philanthropic organizations made contributions to higher education
after World War II. The General Education Board began the process of closing out its philanthropic activity, which since 1902 had
brought more than two hundred million dollars to American colleges
and universities. As a final undertaking the board attempted to make
Emory University in Atlanta, Georgia, into a center of research and
graduate training serving the Deep South. Emory was promised
seven million dollars but found itself unable to raise the twenty-six-
million-dollar matching amount necessary to qualify for the full
grant. In the end the board obtained much less than it had hoped in
the way of building a great center of higher learning in Atlanta.[88] The
other Rockefeller philanthropy, the foundation, concentrated on
its aid to higher education in the field of international studies.
Grants took the form of fellowships to individuals and support of
centers for advanced work in international affairs at Columbia, Harvard, and Princeton.[89] In 1952 both Rockefeller organizations
recognized the importance of college and university autonomy by
providing that after five years the recipient institution could begin spending the principal of a Rockefeller gift for whatever purpose
it desired regardless of the original conditions.[90]

The Carnegie Corporation maintained a program of vigorous philanthropy in the postwar years. In 1945 President Devereux C.
Josephs declared that the corporation would continue pioneering in
new educational fields by searching out for support the man or
institution with inspired and vital ideas.[91] "There is small probabil-
ity," he added two years later, "that grants will be made for endowments, for buildings, for equipment, or for the current support
of established enterprises."[92] The social sciences benefited from
this policy. Harvard's new department of social relations received
support, as did its Russian Research Center. Efforts in establishing
"general education" programs, as compromises between the liberal
arts and the specialized sciences, and in building offerings in inter-
disciplinary "American studies" were encouraged on a number of
campuses. Although the Carnegie Corporation's reports stressed the
importance of the teaching of undergraduates, most of its grants to
higher education, which totaled more than nine million dollars in
1962, went to various centers for advanced study in which faculty
members performed as research specialists and writers. In addi-

tion, the corporation continued its support of the Teachers Insurance Annuity Association with annual grants in the millions.

While the Rockefeller, Carnegie, and Ford enterprises dominated the field, other foundations, small only in comparison, made important contributions. Even more than the big three, they realized by the 1950's that reform or direction of the entire system of American higher education was beyond their capabilities. Consequently, their philanthropy was concentrated on specific fields or institutions. Alfred P. Sloan, Jr., chairman of the board of the General Motors Corporation, focused the grants of the Sloan Foundation on the problems peculiar to conducting a giant industrial complex. The Massachusetts Institute of Technology, his alma mater, in 1950 received $5,250,000 to establish a school of industrial management and later an additional one million dollars for operating funds. The Sloan Foundation also gave M.I.T. $1,000,000 for a metals laboratory. Recently its attention has shifted to the West Coast, where Stanford was enabled to undertake a program in executive training for industry and the California Institute of Technology received a new mathematics and physics laboratory.[93] In making its grants the Sloan Foundation declared that it was guided by the belief that its resources should be "social venture capital."[94] Like most foundations active in higher education, it justified its grants with the argument that they went to support departures in subject matter or method.

The A. W. Mellon Educational and Charitable Trust, established in 1930, decided in 1946 to expend its assets for the benefit of the Pittsburgh region. In 1949 a $13,600,000 gift went to the University of Pittsburgh's Graduate School of Public Health. Five years later Pitt received fifteen million dollars as an endowment fund from which to pay the salaries of full-time teachers in its medical school.[95] At about the same time the university received another indication of the advantage of being located in a community of wealthy industrialists when the Buhl Foundation granted it one million dollars for a building program in engineering and the health sciences.[96] The Commonwealth Fund continued its support of medical education with the added resources that accrued to it in 1950 from the estate of Edward S. Harkness. At Western Reserve University a grant of $1,600,000 financed an attempt to teach medicine as a coherent whole rather than in parts. In 1955 and 1956 gifts of $12,600,-

ooo were made to a number of private medical schools to be applied to salaries, expansion, and pilot experiments in medical education.[97]

Over the past decade foundation grants have proven to be the most lucrative source of voluntary aid to higher education.[98] And since foundations generally place conditions on their grants in order to promote specific ends that frequently depart from traditional practice, they have received more critical examination than other sources of philanthropic support. Few, except those who received no money, have objected to the role of foundations in raising standards of American colleges and universities. Rather, it is the relationship between the foundation and the professor or institutional administrator that has been subjected to scrutiny. On the one side are the foundation millions; on the other are the college people who know first-hand the financial burdens of modern scholarship and the desirability of securing a grant. Add to this the fact that foundations cannot possibly support all the projects that come to their attention and the result is a situation in which the temptation to tailor a proposal to foundation tastes is very great. Conversely, the situation gives the foundation official a lever to move the academic community that is no less real because of its subtlety.

Harold J. Laski was one of the first to suggest that the existence of foundations tended to produce what he called the " 'executive' type of professor" rather than the true scholar. Skill, Laski warned, would become a function of getting grants rather than command over an academic discipline.[99] Twenty-five years later, when William H. Whyte, Jr. wrote *The Organization Man,* the effect of foundation philanthropy was much clearer. Whyte charged the foundations with intensifying the bureaucratization of research in centers of higher education at the expense of the individual scholar. Putting his finger on something that had been apparent since the advent of large foundations, Whyte observed that it was easier to get a half million than five thousand dollars from a foundation. Large-scale philanthropy seemed to prefer thinking in terms of large-scale scholarship such as that carried on at "centers" by "teams" of researchers and elaborate staffs. What Whyte termed "projectism" was making a strong bid to become dominant in the humanities and social sciences as well as the natural sciences.[100]

Jacques Barzun echoed these complaints at collectivized scholarship. The attitude of too many professors, he observed, was: "Oh, to be the director of a project and lead an airport existence!" "To stay on the spot and teach or meditate is the sign of the unenterprising if not the mediocre," Barzun ruefully concluded.[101] And Arthur Schlesinger, Jr., declared after surveying the opinions of his fellow historians on foundation philanthropy that most scholars felt the useful, practical, problem-solving aspects of scholarship had received an unfortunate emphasis. Yet these same historians admitted that on occasion they themselves "dressed up" proposals and invented gimmicks suitable to foundation tastes in order to secure financial aid.[102]

Here, clearly, was a tragic dilemma for the serious scholar. While he might appreciate the necessity of complete freedom to pursue the subject of *his* choice, he nonetheless realized that without money to provide that most essential element in scholarship—free time—his chances of making a contribution to knowledge were slim indeed. Foundation "control" over research was a subject of much concern to academicians who discussed it in strident or hushed voices, depending on the setting. It was an unpalatable situation. Philanthropy, which had done so much for higher education, could well become its worst enemy, compromising the freedom of investigation that was its strength.

Some institutions of higher learning attempted to avoid the drawbacks to foundation philanthropy by establishing certain rules under which they would accept assistance. In many cases these required an institution to accept grants on a "no strings" basis and dispense them to its faculty itself. Sometimes this was accomplished by means of establishing a fund-receiving trusteeship affiliated with the college. It was hoped that this would eliminate any division of faculty loyalty between the college and an outside philanthropic body.[103]

From the standpoint of the shaping of American higher education, foundation philanthropy's principal importance has been helping to make the college or university a center for research and advanced study. In the old-time college the professor was primarily a teacher of young men entrusted with the task of sharpening their mental faculties and imparting to them a portion of what man knew. The impact of German ideas about scholarship and the rise of the university on American soil shifted emphasis to the research function of faculty members. The foundations, which declared new ventures to be their special concern, were especially eager to support the professor as researcher. Translated into grant-making policy, this meant giving to projects that promised to add to knowledge rather than merely transmit it.

It is true that foundations, notably Carnegie's, on occasion have given to improve undergraduate instruction in such fields as the fine arts and American studies. And the Ford Foundation has poured a large portion of its resources into experimental teaching techniques as well as into direct salary increases. But the great majority of foundation grants go to the man or group of men with an idea. Handsome new facilities, "centers" as they are generally called, have been built on many campuses. The foundations and the learned societies they in large part support have also provided research funds and leaves of absence from teaching duties. Colleges and especially universities have tended to become places where talented scholars hang their hats while pursuing the answers to problems of advanced research rather than institutions primarily concerned with instruction.

Deemphasis of the professor's teaching function is the price that must be paid if philanthropy is to concentrate on advancing knowledge through the medium of higher education. Of course, advanced investigation does not necessarily detract from teaching effectiveness. The opposite is often the result. But frequently the star researcher has found himself, willingly or not, completely relieved of teaching responsibility at least as it concerned undergraduates. For better and for worse, the millions of dollars of foundation philanthropy have encouraged a gradual redefinition of the role of the professor within the framework of American higher education.

Chapter XI

Corporations and Higher Learning*

Since the Civil War most of the money that came to the colleges
and universities in the form of philanthropy, whether from friends,
alumni, foundations, or corporations, was made in the world of
commerce, finance, and industry. In the case of the foundations,
independence from the source of wealth was obtained through the
creation of autonomous agencies to dispense the philanthropy.
Some philanthropists such as Rockefeller and Henry and Edsel Ford
severed personal and company connections in establishing their
foundations. But many companies were unwilling to dissociate
themselves from their philanthropy so completely. Instead they
turned either to direct giving or to company "foundations," organizations directed by officers of the parent corporations as part of
their executive duties. In some cases the corporation and its foundation might be legally separate, but the same men sat on the
respective boards of trustees.[1] The combined efforts of corporations
and their philanthropic agencies grew phenomenally during and
after World War II, quickly becoming a major source of revenue
for American colleges and universities.

The increasing importance of corporation support of higher education in the 1940's and especially in the 1950's can be understood
only in the context of the place of American business in the national

* We are especially indebted in this chapter to an unpublished paper by
David Allmendinger, research assistant in the University of Wisconsin History
of Philanthropy Project.

culture in these decades and of an emerging image of the business corporation projected by a small but important segment of corporation leadership. This image, picturing the corporation as a quasi-public institution with large responsibilities for the general welfare, was not without a history. But the traditional and still predominant view of businessmen, including most corporation leaders, regarded the powers exercised in the name of a corporation as powers held in trust for the shareholders. The purpose of business large and small, according to this view, was to make profits and produce needed or desired goods and services for the ultimate consumer.

Within this limited frame a few corporations, largely in an ad hoc way, supported local charities when these seemed to bear directly on the welfare of employees. Thus in the later decades of the nineteenth century railroads contributed to Young Men's Christian Associations, since these provided needed facilities for a mobile personnel.[2] In the towns of the Mesabi iron range in Minnesota, to cite another example, the Oliver Iron Mining Company, a subsidiary of the United States Steel Corporation, cooperated with the public schools in developing programs designed to improve the health and recreational facilities of the community and to encourage foreign-born employees to take advantage of evening classes in both language training and vocational subjects.[3] Many corporations during the World War I crusade for "Americanization" supported language instruction and citizenship training in the public schools or, when such facilities were inadequate, undertook similar programs at the plant or in nearby social clubs.[4] But the conception of responsibility to the community remained limited.

In an effort to overcome public suspicion of and hostility toward great corporations, which reached high tide during the Progressive era, and to develop an image of the corporation as beneficial to the whole population, the practice of employing public relations experts became increasingly common in the 1920's. These people publicized the programs of welfare capitalism that were making headway in many corporations. At the same time there was a good deal of reliance on the efficacy of slogans, advertisements, and stories designed to convey the impression of an open ladder for talent within the corporation and of the public-mindedness of big business. Few, however, went beyond the commonly held view that corporations' responsibility for the general welfare ended with programs in the workers' interests in the plant, the school, the home, the club, and in contributions to local charities, including the Red Cross, the Y.M. or Y.W.C.A. and, increasingly, the Community Chest.

The optimistic belief that big business had won an enduringly favorable place in the American mind was rudely shaken during the Great Depression. Public-relations experts increasingly warned corporation executives that words were not enough to restore confidence in the image that had been shaped in the golden 1920's, that much more must be done than contribute to the local charities and to welfare programs for employees if good public relations were to be recaptured and if a buffer was to be set up against the ever-expanding territory of the welfare state. The characteristic American response to social crisis was to emphasize the fuller role that education might play; hence aid to education was almost bound to suggest itself as a means of rehabilitating the reputation of big business and of creating a more effective alliance with intellectuals and especially with academic leadership. The fear on the part of business leaders that these groups were becoming alienated from capitalism, heightened by the ideological disputes of the Cold War and McCarthyism, figured heavily in the great spurt of corporation giving to higher education after World War II.[5]

A few precedents existed for what was to become an increasingly important idea. Several programs in aid to education, all pragmatic in character, were already under way. Du Pont began its interest in 1918; General Electric entered the scene the next year; in 1930 General Motors made a start. These beginnings were confined to supporting technical training or subsidizing ad hoc research projects clearly related to the limited conception of improving production and distribution of the product. In 1930 Sears, Roebuck took an important step in adopting a broader plan for aiding education on the higher levels,[6] and four years later Allied Chemicals set up its fellowship program.[7] Data provided by the United States Treasury revealed that in 1936, corporation giving for all purposes totaled thirty million dollars; by 1945 it had reached the $266,000,000 mark.[8]

During World War II, spokesmen for colleges and universities, in planning for anticipated problems once the fighting stopped, gave much thought to how higher education was to be financed under the pressure of rising costs and expanding enrollments. Even though the federal government's program of helping veterans attend college promised temporary help, it seemed clear that the traditional sources of private support were bound to be inadequate for the expansion of plant and services in a period of certain inflation. Administrators of private institutions feared that further increases in tuition and fees would hamper them in the competition for able students. They also feared that existing sources of income would be inadequate to enable private institutions to compete for outstanding faculty. As changes in the corporate structure of the economy and heavy personal income taxes indicated that great individual fortunes comparable to those of Rockefeller, Carnegie, and Ford were, save perhaps in Texas, likely to be a thing of the past, it was natural to turn to corporations. But it was no less clear that the restricted grants a few great firms had been giving to higher education would not be of much help even if greatly increased. The need for unrestricted grants was imperative.

Whether or not corporations would respond at all adequately depended on a number of factors. Certainly the support of leading corporation executives was indispensable; and, in the American way of doing things, some sort of organization for soliciting corporate gifts was also necessary. No less important was the development of a rationale extending the concept of welfare capitalism from the immediate to the larger community—ultimately the entire nation—together with expansion of the concept of wide public responsibility of the corporation as a quasi-public institution of overweening power and influence. The legal clarification of the right of corporations to give unrestricted funds to higher education, in place of the limited *quid pro quo* grants for research and specialized training in the company's field of interest, was equally necessary.

Before 1936, corporations could not deduct charitable contributions from taxable income. In the Revenue Code of 1935, Congress inserted a provision that permitted corporations to deduct up to five percent of their net taxable income for contributions to charitable institutions and causes. There was little or no discussion of corporation contributions to higher education. Consequently the legal grounds for making contributions to higher education were not firm as late as the early 1950's.[9]

The way in which such clarification was sought and obtained is an interesting story. Frank Abrams of the Standard Oil Company of New Jersey, who was to play a leading role among corporation executives in urging contributions to higher education, had made an address boldly favoring corporate aid to higher education without consulting his legal counsel. The head of Jersey Standard's legal staff then pointed out that the company's operating charter would not permit such gifts without the approval of every stockholder. In 1950, some time after Abrams's interest in corporate giving to colleges and universities had become well known, New Jersey amended its corporation law to empower corporations chartered in the state to contribute, as public policy, to educational institutions. On July 24, 1951, the board of directors of the A. P. Smith Company, a New Jersey manufacturer of valves, fire hydrants, and equipment for water and gas industries, voted to give a token amount—$1,500—to Princeton University. A group of Smith stockholders challenged the gift in what may have been a maneuver planned by the New Jersey corporations themselves to provoke a test case. The stockholders asserted that the 1950 amendment was unconstitutional if applied to the Smith Company, which had been chartered long before. The company then sought a declaratory judgment in the Superior Court of New Jersey, Chancery Division. An array of distinguished and costly legal talent represented both parties in the litigation, which obviously was of great interest to all corporation executives. Both the Superior Court and the Supreme Court of the state upheld the company's right to contribute in language that might well have encouraged corporations' contributions all over the country.[10]

In his opinion in the Superior Court, Judge Alfred P. Stein declared such contributions necessary to assure a "friendly reservoir" of trained men and women from which industry might draw. Stein's words were well considered:

I am strongly persuaded by the evidence that the only hope for the survival of the privately supported American college and university lies in the willingness of corporate wealth to furnish in moderation some support to institutions which are so essential to public welfare and therefore, of necessity, to corporate welfare. . . . I cannot conceive of any greater benefit to corporations in this country than to build and continue to build, respect for and adherence to a system of free enterprise and democratic government, the serious impairment of either of which may well spell the destruction of all corporate enterprise.[11]

Reactions to the decision were significant. The *New York Times* editorially commended Judge Stein for making "the right decision." It is to be hoped, the editorial went on, that "corporation executives generally will appreciate the wisdom of the position he has stated and help enlarge the role corporations now play in financing the hard-pressed private institutions of this nation." [12] In writing to Arthur W. Page, a key public-relations figure in corporate philanthropy, Douglas Williams, vice-president of the Southwestern Bell Telephone Company in St. Louis, noted that he had read Judge Stein's opinion and felt that a strong case had been made for corporate support of education. He further declared that greater expression ought "to be given to this train of thought" and proposed that articles in *Harper's Magazine* and the *Atlantic* might "give some impetus to the idea generally." [13]

With the Smith decision and the passage of legislation similar to New Jersey's by a majority of the states, the legal barriers to corporate giving to higher education were removed. Nevertheless, not all corporations were ready to give. Arthur W. Page, who was a trustee of the Carnegie Corporation and a veteran fund-raiser in addition to his duties as a vice-president of the American Telephone and Telegraph Company, said he had found that directors were reluctant to give to colleges "unless the corporation will get a direct and tangible benefit therefrom." [14] Many corporation directors insisted that their aid must contribute directly to the expansion of their production or profits. A 1951 study by the Standard Oil Company of California showed that the general attitude of responding companies was not to support colleges except on a *quid pro quo* basis, and a 1953 survey showed similar feelings.[15] A Westinghouse executive declared that his corporation did not grant funds for current expenses of educational institutions, nor would it do so in the future. Furthermore, Westinghouse would make grants only to the schools most helpful to its special interests.[16]

In 1953 the Opinion Research Corporation published a confidential study of stockholder attitudes toward giving to higher education. It found that few executives felt a moral obligation to support higher education, and that while stockholders did not oppose gifts to colleges, only 31 percent endorsed giving for unrestricted purposes. Their enthusiasm declined when direct benefits were not clear. According to the survey, 91% approved providing scholarships for company employees, 89% scholarships for students in the company's field, 88% financing college research to improve products, and 81% giving to colleges furnishing the company with technical and professional personnel. Fifty-three percent approved grants-in-aid to defray expenses of scholarships, 54% contributions to college building campaigns, 43% contributions to colleges outside the company's field, 42% of a steel company's giving to small liberal-arts colleges, and 31% approved gifts to colleges to use as they saw fit.[17]

Another 1954 survey reported that companies in two broad fields, each subject to government regulation, did not feel free to give despite the decision in the Smith case. They were corporations involved in transportation, communications, and public utilities and those concerned with finance, insurance, and real estate. Their reluctance was based on public rate-regulation and banking laws.[18]

In view of such sentiment, aggressive initiative and vigorous leadership by the segment of the corporate world that was committed to the broad view of public responsibility in general and aid to higher education in particular was indispensable. Most of those taking roles of leadership in inspiring the drive for corporation aid to higher education had close connections with both prospective donor and recipient institutions. In the vanguard were Frank Sparks, Wilson Compton, Frank Abrams, Alfred P. Sloan, Jr., Irving S. Olds, Henning W. Prentis, Jr., and Walter Paepcke. In the years after World War II, these men organized meetings, gave speeches, and founded organizations to help the mounting campaign for corporation funds.

In 1948 Frank Sparks founded the Associated Colleges of Indiana, the first of the regional college fund-raising cooperatives. Sparks had connections both in business and in higher education. He was co-founder and treasurer of the Indianapolis Pump and Tube Company, later Noblitt-Sparks, Inc., and was a member of the board of Arvin Industries, Inc. Despite his business success, Sparks had a curious yearning to be president of a college. In 1941 he received a Ph.D. at the University of Southern California and became president of Wabash College in Crawfordsville, Indiana, a well-known and long-established college with about five hundred students. Until 1948 Sparks relied on traditional sources of revenue for Wabash, but like many college presidents he was caught in the postwar price squeeze, which sent him in search of new sources of money. Federal support was out. Sparks was one of many who argued that government aid would bring unwanted government control. *"Federal aid to education will mean a basic change in the principle that has produced in America the most complete and the highest quality school system attained anywhere at any time,"* he warned in 1947. *"Federal aid to education almost certainly will mean the disappearance from our educational system of the independent, privately financed, liberal arts college."* [19] Perhaps beneath this attitude lay a fear on the part of private enterprise that if the government gained control of higher education its appetite might enlarge to the point of relishing business and industry also. Preserving higher education as a nongovernmental area seemed a worthwhile precaution as well as a step toward improving the climate for private enterprise.

Sparks found an ally in President Thomas Elisa Jones of Earlham College. Together they toured Indiana, soliciting aid from corporations and building membership in the Associated Colleges of Indiana. They stressed appeals that were to become commonplace in soliciting American business: liberal-arts colleges preserve freedom; they produce many essential scientists and business executives; tax laws make it inexpensive to give, since corporations could deduct up to five percent of their net income for contributions to charitable institutions and causes.[20]

By 1957 the Indiana Association had collected $3,724,529 in 1,770 gifts. Soon the joint fund idea spread to other states. In Michigan, Simon D. Den Uyl, president of the Bohn Aluminum and Brass Corporation and another outspoken foe of federal aid, urged several college presidents in the state to join the Detroit Board of Commerce in a joint campaign for funds. But it was businessmen who actually took the lead in 1950 in organizing the Michigan Colleges Foundation, Inc. Its members had by 1957 raised a total of $1,456,190 in 1,665 gifts. Sixty percent of it was distributed in equal parts among the colleges, forty percent on a basis of enrollment. The Ohio Foundation of Independent Colleges, Inc., founded in 1951, amassed by 1957 $3,375,552 from 3,324 gifts. Its leadership, too, was a mixture of business and college men.[21]

Frank Sparks also headed the Commission on College and Industry of the Association of American Universities from 1953 to 1958. The commission was created in 1949 when trustees at the Rockefeller Foundation voted four hundred thousand dollars to the association; the Carnegie Corporation added fifty thousand dollars. These grants enabled the commission to sponsor nine studies of the financial problems facing American education.[22] The commission was composed of several lawyers, industrialists, and presidents of universities, mostly private.[23] In 1951 it sponsored a dinner meeting in New York for industrialists and business executives, who discussed ways to encourage larger corporation support for the current operations of colleges and the kind of machinery desirable for channeling that support into the colleges.[24]

Perhaps the most influential fund-raising organization to come into being after World War II was the Council for Financial Aid to Education, incorporated as a nonprofit organization in 1952 with funds supplied by the General Education Board, the Alfred P. Sloan Foundation, the Carnegie Corporation, and the Ford Foundation's Fund for Advancement of Education.[25] A board of directors composed of sixteen business leaders and twelve college or university presidents directed the C.F.A.E. Wilson Compton, former president of the State College of Washington (now Washington State University), became its first president. Compton also had ties with the business world; he was secretary and general manager of the National Lumber Manufacturers Association from 1918 to 1944 and was vice-president and manager of the American Forest Products Industry from 1932 to 1944. During the New Deal he helped draft the National Recovery Administration's lumber code. When he became C.F.A.E. president he was chairman of the board of Cameron Machine Company, Dover, New Jersey. He was a graduate of Wooster College and held a Ph.D. in economics from Princeton.

The council became a clearinghouse of information and research on all aid to higher education, but especially for corporation philanthropy. It advised prospective contributors on adopting programs of financial support for colleges and universities, but did not solicit funds for individual institutions.[26] While representing all institutions, its major interest seemed to lie in shoring up private higher education, especially in its early years.[27] Starting with the academic year 1954–55 the C.F.A.E. published biennial surveys of corporate and other giving to higher education, as well as a series of pamphlets dealing with the financial problems of colleges and universities. In 1956 it also conducted a two-million-dollar advertising campaign dramatizing the financial plight of higher education.[28]

The impetus behind the council came from corporation executives who also had close connections with colleges and universities: Frank Abrams, Alfred P. Sloan, and Irving Olds were especially influential in founding the C.F.A.E.; Walter Paepcke and Henning W. Prentis, Jr. also took important parts. These five helped organize the council in 1952 and developed a rationale for giving to higher education in a series of articles and speeches at commencements and business meetings.[29] Other men probably stood backstage and directed these activities; the speeches may have been written by public relations men and university administrators may have persuaded the executives to join the cause. Abrams once suggested this when he said:

I know I can't take any credit for this. I'm just an ordinary business guy that got shoved into something. It's like being thrown into a Billy Sunday meeting, I suppose, and getting converted. You didn't want to go in, but somebody pushed you—they thought you needed it. And it has been rather overwhelming and highly satisfying.[30]

Yet the minutes of the early meetings of what became the C.F.A.E. indicate that corporation executives were actively and sincerely interested in higher education.

Frank Abrams became the chairman of the executive committee of the Council for Financial Aid to Education. He was chairman of the board of the Standard Oil Company of New Jersey from 1946 to 1953 and a trustee of Syracuse University, where he had taken a civil-engineering degree in 1912. He was also a trustee of the Ford and Sloan Foundations and among the first to begin the campaign to win corporate aid for the colleges. As early as September, 1947, he gave an offhand luncheon speech about the needs of higher education, developing the idea that "business was a kind of absentee stockholder in education and ought to pay some attention to its investment."[31]

Another of the C.F.A.E. founders, Alfred P. Sloan, a former chairman of the board of General Motors, became a director of the council. Sloan had long been interested in the problems of higher education. He was a member of the board of Massachusetts Institute of Technology, from which in 1895 he took a bachelor of science degree. In 1934 he established the Sloan Foundation, whose primary interest was American economic education and research. Later the foundation made grants for cancer research and for studies in the physical sciences and ophthalmology and developed an undergraduate scholarship program.[32]

To a man, leaders of the Council for Financial Aid to Education shared an interest and had considerable importance in both business and education. Irving S. Olds, Yale '07, became chairman of the council's board of directors. A lawyer in the New York firm of White and Case, Olds had served as chairman of the board of United States Steel Corporation. At the same time he was a fellow of the Yale Corporation. Olds became a member at large of the Yale Alumni Board in 1940 and was chairman of the Yale Alumni Placement Service from 1944 to 1947. He was an original incorporator of the College Retirement Equity Fund, and in the late 1950's became a member of an informal committee to aid higher education composed of corporation trustees. Walter Paepcke was chairman of the board of the Container Corporation of America and a trustee of the University of Chicago when he became a director of the council in 1953. He graduated from Yale in 1917, Phi Beta Kappa. Henning W. Prentis, Jr. was chairman of the board of the Armstrong Cork Company and a former president of the National Association of Manufacturers. His interest in higher education was evident from his long service as a trustee of Franklin and Marshall College. Prentis, too, became a director of the council, at the same time serving as president of the board of trustees at Wilson College, Chambersburg, Pennsylvania.

In 1957 another organization was formed, calling itself the Informal Committee for Corporate Aid to American Universities. It was composed of other men with connections in both business and education. The committee actually had its origins in Harvard's $82,500,-000 campaign of 1957–60, when Harvard fund-raisers discovered agents from other universities knocking on the same corporation doors. Alexander White, an investment banker, was leading the Harvard drive at the time. After the 1956 Harvard-Yale football game, White met with Yale's Juan Trippe, president of Pan American Airways, and together they produced the idea of a cooperative campaign to stimulate corporation philanthropy. "Later we invited others who were all very active in their respective universities whose names and voices we felt would be listened to by industry," Trippe said.[33] Eventually, about twenty businessmen comprised the committee and met for dinner at the Links Club in New York about four times a year. Among them were Devereux C. Josephs, a Harvard graduate, chairman of the board of the New York Life Insurance Company, president of the Carnegie Corporation (1945–1948), and trustee of the Johns Hopkins University; Clarence B. Randall, president of Inland Steel and author of several books and articles dealing with higher education; Thomas S. Lamont, Harvard, banker; Arthur W. Page, Harvard, vice-president, American Telephone and Telegraph; Neil McElroy, president, Procter and Gamble; and Irving S. Olds.[34]

The Informal Committee kept no minutes, adopted no official name, and had no offices, budget, or letterhead. Richard Chapin of the Harvard Business School acted as part-time executive assistant, and drew up a list of 500 corporations for members to approach; they agreed to see 190. Members made their own contacts and wrote their own letters. They concentrated on obtaining aid for the major universities that maintained graduate schools and conducted research. Josephs and Olds composed a list of twenty-three privately supported and fifteen publicly supported members of the Association of American Universities as worthy of corporation support. Josephs explained this policy:

The informal committee . . . believes that the great universities, scientific institutions, and leading colleges that have graduate departments differ in an important way from the schools that are concerned mostly with young people in search of a bachelor's degree. These latter schools indeed underwrite the diffusion of knowledge, but the universities and scientific institutes go much further: collectively they underwrite the advancement of basic knowledge that enriches, recreates, and expands U.S. life.[35]

As of April, 1959, the Informal Committee for Corporate Aid to American Universities had secured contributions for the California

Institute of Technology, Chicago, Colby, Columbia, Cornell, Dartmouth, Duke, Harvard, Johns Hopkins, Kenyon, M.I.T., New York University, Northwestern, Pennsylvania, Princeton, Stanford, and Yale. Total grants came to about $1,140,000 a year. The committee's first success came when Procter and Gamble, under Neil McElroy, gave twenty thousand dollars in unrestricted funds to each of ten universities—Harvard, Chicago, Columbia, Stanford, Princeton, Cornell, Yale, M.I.T., Northwestern, and Pennsylvania. The second grant came from U.S. Steel, for student aid, operating funds for state and regional college associations, and project aid. In addition, the company gave $100,000 each to M.I.T., Cal Tech, Cornell, Johns Hopkins, and Harvard. General Foods provided the third grant, a program of matching contributions by employees, a scholarship and fellowship program, and gifts to state and regional college associations. It also gave $25,000 each to Harvard, N.Y.U., Princeton, and Yale. Other philanthropy followed from the Columbia Broadcasting System, Time, Inc., J. Walter Thompson, the Chase Manhattan Bank, Hewlett-Packard, National Dairy Products, B. F. Goodrich, Pan American Airways, Champion Paper and Fiber, and the Chemical Corn Exchange Bank.[36]

Encouraging though these responses were, most corporate executives still believed that giving to education should rest on a *quid pro quo* base. In their effort to break down this conviction, executives in the vanguard developed a more comprehensive rationale for giving to higher education. No one suggested that corporations should underwrite social experimentation; the aims were remedial and palliative. Some executives stressed the cheap cost of such gifts, which were, of course, deductible from taxes. Actually, as one writer pointed out, Uncle Sam was a kind of silent partner for, under existing regulations, fifty-two cents of every dollar a company gave would otherwise go to the government; only forty-eight cents would actually stay with the company for reinvestment.[37]

Although several corporate leaders contributed to the positive rationale for unrestricted giving,[38] the most important ideologue of the corporations was Richard Eells, a consultant on public policy for General Electric. Eells stressed the need of corporations to create a favorable social environment in the interest of survival and prosperity, not to speak of private enterprise. The major aim of corporate aid should be to strengthen nongovernmental areas of society—the family, local community, private schools, and colleges and universities—"the whole spectrum of voluntary associations." Under such conditions corporate aid could not be considered charity or philanthropy, Eells contended, but rather prudent investment.[39]

In due course countless executives and fund-raisers made similar appeals, connecting the survival of private enterprise with the survival of higher education. "It is my contention that financial support of higher education by corporations, if reasonable in amount and properly administered, is not engaging in pure philanthropy," declared Olds. It was, in short, a business matter.[40] "Capitalism and free enterprise owe their survival in no small degree to the existence of our private, independent universities," Olds argued elsewhere. "If the day ever comes when our tax-supported competitors can offer the youth of America a better education than we can —and at a lower price—we are through. . . ." At the same time, he warned, it was in the interest of the universities "to preserve those fundamental principles of freedom upon which Academic Freedom itself depends. . . ." And he would not have the corporation withdraw aid if universities criticized capitalism.[41] Many others joined in developing these points.[42]

Also stimulating corporations' interest in aiding higher education was a fear held by business executives of academicians opposing capitalism. Frank Abrams revealed a concern over the alienation of some intellectuals from the corporate society. "Our teachers," he said, "must be strengthened in their belief in the American system of democratic capitalism by a more equitable participation in the rewards of that system." [43] Clarence B. Randall, Courtney C. Brown, and Leston B. Faneuf expressed similar concerns.[44] Abrams, like nearly all the executives, explicitly denied any desire to control the universities, to make them teach a certain dogma. Yet there are also statements in his writings—and others'—that clearly show that he expected corporations' aid to pay dividends, if only by preserving a climate favorable to corporate enterprise. The financial support was to be accompanied by only an indirect and sophisticated influence. "We simply have to face the fact that if we expect our teachers to believe in the superior values of a society based on individual responsibility and the voluntary cooperation of free men society must act in ways to justify the belief," Abrams contended.[45] Some-

times corporation executives and fund-raisers accompanied their support with not-so-subtle indications of their expectations. A. Crawford Greene wrote: "Our institutions can expect support from a free
people only if they themselves are vigilant guardians of freedom.
Their faculties are not entitled to invoke the protection of academic
freedom if they are not teaching freedom and ever on the alert to
protect it." [46] More pointedly, Arthur Page confided to Greene that
"as a corporate director I would find it hard to vote to give money to
a college where they taught that the company should be taken over
by the government." [47] In 1950, the Committee to Visit the Department of Economics at Harvard criticized the department's balance
"with respect to the viewpoint of its members." Randall chaired this
committee which asserted that there were "one or more socialists" in
the department, and that other viewpoints were under-represented. Harvard's President Conant disagreed and said he would
refuse to hire faculty members on the basis of their position in
political or social spectrums.[48] As a rule, however, corporation
executives denied any desire to control curriculum or faculty composition in any overt way. But cases were not unknown in which
the officers of a company used the power of their financial support
of a small college to force the dismissal of a faculty member whose
opinion they opposed.[49] Yet for the most part corporations achieved
their most telling effect in shaping higher education through grants
to specific research programs.[50]

Many college and university administrators and fund-raisers
were only too happy to use the appeal of private education as a
bulwark of private enterprise in seeking corporation philanthropy.
President Harold W. Dodds of Princeton declared at the time the
A. P. Smith decision was announced in 1953: "[D]emocratic society will not long endure if it does not nourish within itself strong
centers of non-governmental fountains of knowledge, opinions of
all sorts not governmentally or politically originated. If the time
comes when all these centers are absorbed into government, then
freedom as we know it, I submit, is at an end." [51] The regional and
state associations of colleges used the appeal constantly.[52] Among
the most flagrant exploiters of the theme was Harding College in
Searcy, Arkansas, which geared all its appeals for funds to the war
against communism.[53] Harvard used more restraint in not insisting
that government aid meant government control. The Harvard

Alumni Bulletin said simply: "An alternative to government support would appear to be desirable. That governments support private education in certain other countries, sometimes in perfect amity and with impeccable aloofness, is not the whole point. Washington has enough to do today. It should not be saddled with the task of raising tax money for the benefit of the privately-supported colleges and universities which historically have proved such important counterpoises to our public institutions of learning." [54]

At least one public institution, the University of Vermont, protested against the appeals made by private institutions for corporate funds. "Some of them have been carried away by their zeal to the extent that they have invoked the blessings of God, Country, and Private Enterprise," a Vermont brochure charged. It implied that the connection between private colleges and private enterprise might not be as close as some were maintaining. "The facts are," it said, "that private education has accepted help from the government and is seeking additional help." The brochure asserted that all education must be kept free, and that the distinction between public and private was not important. It denied that public education had sufficient support, or that it was inferior to private education. "Are we, in these attitudes," it asked, "perhaps creating an 'Ivy Curtain' when we need so badly to work together toward our common dilemma?" [55]

Before 1952, most corporations contributed to education by means of scholarships, often for employees of their children, and especially for education or training in the natural sciences. Du Pont included a section on aid to education in its 1948 report, declaring the purpose of its program to be the promotion of "the effectiveness of both education and fundamental research in the fields of science and engineering." In 1952 Union Carbide opened its scholarships to everyone, and began to contribute grants-in-aid to general funds of the colleges. By 1953 many were channeling their funds into state and regional fund-raising associations. Standard Oil of New Jersey removed all strings from its $450,000 allocation among 138 private colleges in 1954, and a year later General Motors gave two million dollars for unrestricted scholarships. General Motors also began the practice of matching all alumni gifts, which had the advantage of avoiding the necessity of choosing particular colleges for support and consequently arousing the wrath of the neglected. [56]

In all the early exhortations by the vanguard of college fund-raisers, corporations were urged to give more and to make their grants unrestricted. Executives were advised to broaden their programs from the narrow *quid pro quo* basis. According to a C.F.A.E. survey in 1954, colleges most wanted unrestricted grants so they could carry on their own programs, using funds as they saw fit without influence from the corporations. In descending order, colleges and universities wanted capital funds for buildings, endowment, salary increases, scholarships, and new equipment.[57]

How successful corporation leaders were in initiating trends toward these goals is shown in a C.F.A.E. report published in January, 1962. A core group of 207 companies participated in C.F.A.E. surveys for 1956, 1958 and 1960. They contributed to education the following amounts: 1956, $33,973,100; 1958, $42,437,114; 1960, $50,-336,080.[58] Their average contributions to education increased from $164,121 in 1956 to $205,010 in 1958 and to $234,169 in 1960. From another standpoint, the C.F.A.E. biennial surveys reveal that in 1954–55, 728 American colleges and universities received $39,432,625 from business corporations. In 1962–63 the figures jumped to $146,-687,587 for 1,036 institutions.[59] Not only did the share of higher education increase in the overall pattern of corporation giving, but the gifts tended more and more to be unrestricted—whereas in 1956 unconditional gifts amounted to 35.7 percent of corporation philanthropy, four years later the figure was about fifty-two percent. The remainder went in decreasing order to student aid, buildings and equipment, research, faculty salaries, departmental grants, and endowment.[60]

The council's 1960 report on 670 companies indicated, however, that the corporate movement to aid higher education was still a movement among only a small proportion of the million American business operations. In 1960 the leading givers, by kind of business, were: [61]

Transportation equipment (36 firms)	$11,470,351
Chemicals (57 firms)	10,191,234
Petroleum (37 firms)	8,664,248
Electrical machinery (26 firms)	6,310,688
Primary metal (46 firms)	6,236,633

In spite of this showing, C.F.A.E. constantly sought to involve more companies and increase the total gifts. One of the council's arguments was simply that the American business corporation was a major beneficiary of the nation's system of higher education in that they employed the services of about forty percent of its working graduates.[62] Alfred P. Sloan, Jr. suggested another effective line of approach to corporation generosity with his observation that "we must remember that to a major extent our institutions of higher learning provide the basic knowledge which productive enterprise applies to its material advantage. . . . It seems to me that in its own interest, corporate enterprise should support the sources from which fundamental knowledge flows." [63]

The chief purpose of corporate aid remained the support of the existing system of higher education, especially the private sector, through gifts college and university officials could use as capital and for current expenses. The rise in unrestricted grants meant that institutions were freed to carry out their own programs, generated by the ideas of their faculties and staffs. In the case of restricted grants by corporations, the funds were expended for traditional sustaining purposes—student support, new buildings, or salaries. Research grants were usually made for projects closely related to corporate interests, and most often in fields of applied science.

The 1960 C.F.A.E. survey reported that most companies were motivated in giving to higher education by a desire to meet community responsibilities. Perhaps this indicated that the older preoccupation with the survival of the free-enterprise system was broadening into a concern for the general welfare of the nation. C.F.A.E. found the following rank and motivations: [64]

No. Firms	Objectives
196	Meeting community responsibilities
147	Creation of educated manpower
99	Insuring free enterprise system
92	Public relations
59	Aiding higher education
57	Fostering new knowledge
14	Research
6	Tax savings

The desire to create a favorable "image" before the public probably resulted in a deemphasis of the tax advantages and the benefits from research conducted in colleges and universities. Moreover, the table of declared motivations revealed that plain support of higher education, which had long taken top priority with philanthropists including foundations, ranked far behind concerns of more direct interest to corporations.

In 1960 the corporations did not seem to fear federal aid to higher education as much as they once did. The C.F.A.E. asked companies what effect an expanded federal program of aid to education would have on their philanthropy to higher learning. Most replied "none" or "unknown." [65] At the same time, colleges and universities seemed ready to go beyond their earlier campaign for corporate philanthropy and seek for increased federal funds. In a study released July 6, 1963, twenty-six major universities and colleges concluded that federal aid had been "highly beneficial" to them. The *New York Times* quoted the study on an interesting point: "Basically, what is needed, many of them pointed out, is a different raison d'être from that on which most Federal support of higher education is now based." [66] The institutions felt that the wartime partnership with the federal government, based upon a *quid pro quo* relationship in which the universities conducted scientific research for the government, was no longer adequate. In their view the government should recognize higher education as worthy of support in itself. The study urged a broader, more general aid program beyond such fields of immediate national interest as health, basic science, and defense.

If by the end of 1963 the federal government seemed loath to broaden its support to privately endowed colleges and universities except for plant and for such specialized training as medicine, corporations were giving evidence of enlarging their share of the total gifts to education and of imposing fewer restrictions on them. In 1962, according to a survey of the National Industrial Conference Board, corporate contributions to education for the first time since 1945–46, when the surveys were initiated, exceeded gifts to health and welfare. In 1962, 420 corporations, whose contributions totaled $154,000,000, allocated $64,531,000, or 42 percent of the total, to education. The survey also revealed that privately owned companies gave more than publicly owned concerns, that manufacturing enterprises allocated the bulk of their gifts to education while nonmanufacturing corporations favored health and welfare, and that the highest rate of giving was by the smaller companies: 1.1 percent of their pre-tax incomes as against the average rate for all reporting corporations of seventy-six hundredths of a percent.[67]

Regardless of the philanthropic philosophy of American corporations and in spite of the increases registered in their giving, the potentiality of corporations for shaping American higher education was severely limited by the increasing expenses of America's colleges and universities. Indeed, as a force for innovation in higher education, every source of philanthropy felt the loss of power that came with providing an ever smaller percentage of its financial needs. While there was a time when philanthropy carried the major burden of the expense of higher learning and when a few wealthy men could revolutionize the field, the twentieth century found even the giant foundations unable to do much more than make pilot and experimental studies. The Council for Financial Aid to Education predicted in 1963 that by the end of the decade, private gifts and grants would constitute only about a fifth of the estimated nine billion dollars higher education would consume. Even tuition and fees were expected to be greater than the proceeds from philanthropy, while the government's burden would be almost twice as great.[68] Thus while the percentage of the total giving furnished by corporations was expected to continue its upward trend, the shaping role of the corporations on higher learning, along with other philanthropy, was certain to be less than in the past. This knowledge itself might have the effect of diminishing the flow of philanthropy.

In contrast to foundations interested in the field of higher education, corporations with similar interests have concerned themselves with conventional and traditional programs. While the foundations generally refused to support what was not a new course or "venture" in education, company giving was predominantly unrestricted or was earmarked for broad categories, such as capital funds or general building programs. Only in selecting research programs to aid with equipment and fellowships did the corporations exercise specific power as philanthropists. And even here the fields aided were usually well established at the particular college or university at the time of the gift. Conservatism apparently dominated the philanthropy of American businessmen as it did their politics. Like most of those who supported the colonial colleges, corporations in the twentieth century seemed to regard *having* a system of diversified higher education as more important than the shape it assumed.

Chapter XII

Balance Sheet

The role of the individual in his essentially private capacity has helped to shape American civilization through the influence of his brawn, his pen, his sword, his laboratory, and his power to make decisions in the countinghouse and executive suite. Through voluntary giving the individual has also affected the general welfare. Philanthropy, especially the large-scale variety, has enabled the donor to play a special role in transforming his ideas into social institutions. What he does may be praised or deprecated, but it cannot be ignored. The consequences of his action, as they stimulate others, may ripple outward in everwidening circles far beyond his single creative or influential act. By definition philanthropy touches the lives of others and in this quasi-public aspect demands responsibility. Giving money wisely, as so many who tried it have observed, is usually far more difficult than making it.

Few institutions in the United States bear the marks of private, voluntary giving as noticeably as higher education. In creating and in providing means for its growth and diversification, philanthropy has exerted a powerful shaping influence. There have been others, of course, but time and again philanthropy has provided the telling force behind the ideas that characterize American higher education today.

Over the decades, colleges and universities have found their relationship with private wealth to have had both inestimable advantages and definite liabilities. Colonial educators quickly learned that philanthropy was indispensable in their efforts to transplant higher education to the New World. For the most part, gifts and bequests were the bread and butter of the colonial colleges and remained the mainstay of institutions of higher learning as they multiplied in the growing nation after Independence. In permitting the creation of new colleges and the growth and improvement of those already established, philanthropy overshadowed the feeble record of public support, which remained a minor matter until the later decades of the nineteenth century. But a good thing could be carried too far. Even when American life centered in the immediate locality and when the multiplication of colleges was necessary to implement the ideal of equality of educational opportunity, the burden of supporting a great number of institutions militated against the achievement of high qualitative standards in any. The competing philanthropy that marked the educational efforts of various religious groups also worked against the development of first-rate institutions. Instead, the nation, and notably the Middle West, became burdened with small, inferior colleges whose chances for growth and improvement were slight. Yet many who gave seemed determined to start new institutions rather than to support those that had already gained a foothold.

Colleges and universities have always coveted the unrestricted donation, since it permitted them to use the money as their own experience and need directed. Given the assumption that an educational institution, rather than someone from the outside, was best fitted to guide its own development, such unconditional philanthropy was ideal. Certainly it was the easiest way to give. But many donors to higher education were not content to let the recipient decide on the use of their benefactions. Instead they sought to reform or to innovate.

Again and again in the history of American higher education, philanthropy has given force to the cutting edge of new ideas. Fields of study were added to the curriculum through the generosity of men and women with an interest in a particular discipline. Buildings and equipment have expanded the physical plant of numerous campuses and have permitted researchers to probe to greater depths in fields as diverse as physics and archaeology. Philanthropy occasionally added an entire new college to a university community. And the living conditions of undergraduates have been altered with substantial effects on the college atmosphere. In some cases entire campuses have been relocated.

Even more significant than these innovations have been the changes philanthropy has promoted in the whole system of higher education. In 1824 Stephen Van Rensselaer's support of an institution for training in practical and applied knowledge with emphasis on the sciences started a movement that before the end of the century drastically altered the old classical curriculum. The names and gifts of Abbott Lawrence, Joseph Sheffield, Peter Cooper, Joseph Wharton, and Philip D. Armour figured prominently in this transformation, which, to be sure, the utilitarian-minded land-grant colleges also accelerated. In developing a practical higher education, philanthropy sometimes responded to the requests of progressive college or university officers. But there were also instances in which money overcame the resistance of educators committed to the classical studies. The result was a reorientation of the nature and purpose of higher education. Whatever its limitations, this reorientation was advantageous to the nation as it entered an era in which applied science and technology played so large a part.

The stimulus given to utilitarian values and skills in higher education was not the only example of the role of philanthropy in promoting significant innovations. In the middle decades of the nineteenth century almost every college and university threw up a solid barrier of opposition to the admission of women. But wealthy individuals who believed that women should be entitled to the same training as men used philanthropy to circumvent established interests and tradition. Vassar, Smith, Wellesley, and Bryn Mawr, to name only the most prominent institutions, owed their existence to philanthropy. Women's access to higher learning would certainly have come about if left to existing colleges and to the legislative agencies supporting state institutions, but philanthropy greatly speeded the development. It was far easier to find one man who accepted the new idea than to win over a majority of a board of directors or a legislature.

Philanthropy also financed the extension of higher education to the Negro. But here the idealism of philanthropists at first outstripped the preparation of the recipients, and the resulting confusion was in some ways a liability that the slower pace of government-financed support might have avoided. To its credit, however, philanthropy did not abandon the Negro after the misguided beginnings. Instead it poured millions into Negro colleges, which in time developed a strength and reputation considerably greater than the segregated institutions that the states supported. The criticism that philanthropy was designed to promote white supremacy, or at least had that effect, overlooked the dominant motive of those who gave to Negro colleges—helping colored Americans realize their potentialities as citizens and human beings.

If philanthropy in multiplying the number of colleges sometimes tended to keep academic quality low by spreading resources too thinly, it occasionally aided in the raising of standards. Existing colleges seldom had the financial resources to meet demands for a true university. But post-Civil War millionaires such as Johns Hopkins, Ezra Cornell, John D. Rockefeller, and the Leland Stanfords had the means to translate the ideal of a university into going institutions. With characteristic American exuberance, not just one but a dozen universities took their places as first-rate centers of learning ranking with the older European institutions. Public funds, of course, built many great state institutions, but private giving had helped to dramatize the need for true universities and had erected models which greatly influenced the state.

Part of the problem of standards was the need to limit the number of American colleges, which by the twentieth century was far out of proportion to the size of the country. In large measure the scattering of small, inferior institutions across the continent had been the result of overzealous and overindependent philanthropy. Yet it was also philanthropy, on the unprecedented scale of which the educational foundations were capable, that remedied the situation. The General Education Board, the Carnegie Corporation, and later the Ford Foundation carefully distributed their bounty only to those institutions that deserved, in their opinion, to remain alive. By concentrating on a select number of colleges and universities, philanthropy helped raise their quality. The outsiders complained bitterly, but in many instances were obliged to improve or die. The result was a survival of the fittest in higher education thoroughly compatible with the social ideas of the industrialists-philanthropists responsible for the foundations. While the trimming process did not so reduce the number of institutions as to limit diversity, it did perform a needed function in tightening the system of American higher education.

The association of a philanthropist with a college or university proved to be both a great asset and a serious liability, depending in large part on his attitude as a donor and on his ability to work with educational leaders and experts. The optimum relationship seems over the years to have been one in which the donor gave little but his money. Especially fruitful were collaborations in which a man of wealth and a man with ideas and administrative ability worked together in an atmosphere of mutual respect. In this way Amos Eaton cooperated with Stephen Van Rensselaer, Andrew D. White with Ezra Cornell, and William Rainey Harper with John D. Rockefeller. When a philanthropist sought to intervene personally with the object of his benefactions, as was the case with Jonas Clark, the Leland Stanfords, and Henry Durant, the freedom that higher education demands for greatness was seriously compromised. Even after death the stipulations of a philanthropist could be a liability, as The Johns Hopkins University, Bryn Mawr College, and Duke University learned. Occasionally a philanthropist such as Joseph Wharton requested that particular views, in his case the protective-tariff dogma, be taught in the classes of the institution he created. Such a request ignored the fact that an institution of higher education was not the personal possession of the man who financed it. But the quasi-public nature of a college or university usually limited the degree to which a philanthropist personally directed its conduct.

The line between creative giving and coercion is thin. As philanthropic foundations in the twentieth century have learned, the promotion of a new idea or experiment in higher education invariably encountered old-guard opposition that phrased its protest as a defense against an encroachment on academic freedom. Such a response only confused the issue, since any reform or innovation had to be "pushed" if it was to overcome the inertia of tradition. The programs that foundations, or individual philanthropists, promoted must be judged on the basis of their contribution to the ends of higher education. Not to do so is to lose sight of the importance philanthropy has had in winning acceptance for novelty.

The American experience demonstrates that private gifts and bequests have been vital in the continual reshaping that has marked the development of colleges and universities. Too often ideas alone are given credit as the moving force in history without recognition of the crucial role of material resources in transforming abstractions into realities. Of course ideas are indispensable, and so is leadership, but without money the necessary impetus for innovation is often lacking. The history of American higher education provides many instances of the interaction of these three factors. Sometimes the philanthropist himself had the idea and the administrative ability, but often his benefactions went to aid the educator with a theory or a dream. Together, the idea, the leader, and the dollar brought about change in response to changing conditions.

NOTES FOR CHAPTER I

[1] Wilbur K. Jordan, *Philanthropy in England, 1480–1660: A Study of the Changing Pattern of English Social Aspirations* (London, 1959), pp. 56 ff., 253 ff., 282, 368–69.

[2] For general discussions see Frederick Rudolph, *The American College and University: A History* (New York, 1962), pp. 3–22, and Richard Hofstadter and Walter P. Metzger, *The Development of Academic Freedom in the United States* (New York, 1955), pp. 148–51.

[3] Leonard Labaree, *Conservatism in Early American History* (New York, 1948), p. 101, has made this criticism.

[4] Beverly McAnear, "The Raising of Funds by the Colonial Colleges," *Mississippi Valley Historical Review*, XXXVIII (1952), 591–612.

[5] Franklin M. Wright, "A College First Proposed, 1633: Unpublished Letters of Apostle Eliot and William Hammond to Sir Simonds D'Ewes," *Harvard Library Bulletin*, VIII (1954), 274.

[6] Jordan, pp. 152–54.

[7] Wright, p. 277.

[8] The most detailed investigation of Harvard's life in the colonies is Andrew F. Davis, "John Harvard's Life in America; or Social and Political Life in New England in 1637–1638," *Colonial Society of Massachusetts Transactions*, XII (1908), pp. 4–45. Two partly imaginative recreations of his life and times are Henry C. Shelly, *John Harvard and His Times* (Boston, 1907) and George Hodges, "The Education of John Harvard," *The Apprenticeship of Washington and Other Sketches of Significant Colonial Personages* (New York, 1909), pp. 149 ff.

[9] Evelyn S. Shuckburgh, *Emmanuel College*, University of Cambridge: College Histories (London, 1904), pp. 17 ff.

[10] Samuel Eliot Morison, *The Founding of Harvard College* (Cambridge, Mass., 1955), p. 219.

[11] A full discussion of the Harvard bequest is contained in Josiah Quincy, *The History of Harvard University* (Boston, 1860), I, 459–62.

[12] George G. Bush, *History of Higher Education in Massachusetts*, U.S. Bureau of Education Circular of Information, No. 6, 1891, Contributions to American Educational History, ed. Herbert B. Adams, No. 13 (Washington), p. 49.

[13] Louis Shores, *Origins of the American College Library, 1638–1800*, George Peabody College for Teachers Contributions to Education, No. 134 (Nashville, 1934), pp. 11 ff., 121 ff., 228–44, discusses Harvard's gift and lists those titles known to have been included.

¹⁴ Cotton Mather, *Magnalia Christi Americana* (Hartford, 1820), II, 7.

¹⁵ Jordan, pp. 295–96.

¹⁶ Worthington C. Ford in "The Authorship of *New England's First Fruits,*" *Massachusetts Historical Society Proceedings,* XLII (1909), 259–66, suggests these men as probable authors. The fullest account of the fund-raising campaign is Raymond P. Stearns, "The Weld-Peter Mission to England," *Colonial Society of Massachusetts Transactions,* XXXII (1934), 188–246.

¹⁷ *New England's First Fruits* appears in Joseph Sabin, *Sabin's Reprints,* quarto series, VII (New York, 1865). The section concerning the college alone is in *Massachusetts Historical Society Collections,* I (1792), 242–50.

¹⁸ The complete text of the bond is printed in Morison, *op. cit.,* pp. 309–10. See also Andrew M. Davis, "The First Scholarship at Harvard College," *Proceedings of the American Antiquarian Society,* V N.S. (1887), 129–39.

¹⁹ Jordan, p. 294.

²⁰ Samuel Eliot Morison, "American Colonial Colleges," *Rice Institute Pamphlet,* XXIII (1936), 273.

²¹ Quincy, I, 465.

²² Morison, *Founding of Harvard College,* p. 311. Lady Mowlson's maiden name was conferred on Harvard's Annex when it became Radcliffe College in 1893.

²³ [Jonathan Mitchell] "A Modell for the Maintaining of Students and Fellows of Choise Abilities at the Colledge in Cambridge," *Colonial Society of Massachusetts Collections,* XXI (1935), 311, 320, 322.

²⁴ Samuel A. Eliot, *A Sketch of the History of Harvard College* (Boston, 1848), p. 159. The extant "College Books" that have been printed and indexed in the *Colonial Society of Massachusetts Collections,* XV, XVI (1925) are the best source information about benefactions to Harvard to 1750. The lists of donations in Quincy, I, 449 ff., 506 ff.; II, 525 ff.; in Eliot, p. 158 ff.; and in *American Journal of Education,* IX (1860), 139–60, all derive from the "College Books."

²⁵ See Benjamin Peirce, *History of Harvard University* (Cambridge, Mass., 1833), p. 17.

²⁶ Quincy, I, 506.

²⁷ The original requisition appears in *Records of the Governor and Company of the Massachusetts Bay,* ed. Nathaniel B. Shurtleff (Boston, 1853–54), II, 86.

²⁸ Original records of the receipts are in *Colonial Society of Massachusetts Collections,* XV (1925), 179–80.

²⁹ Samuel Eliot Morison, *Harvard College in the Seventeenth Century* (Cambridge, Mass., 1936), II, 374.

³⁰ Morison, "American Colonial Colleges," pp. 273–74.

³¹ Quincy, I, 508–9. Harvard encountered considerable difficulty in collecting the promised subscriptions, and as a result the building was not completed until 1682.

³² The bequest of £1,000 was from an English merchant, Matthew Holworthy: *Colonial Society of Massachusetts Collection,* XV (1925), 39; Albert Matthews, "Sir Matthew and Lady Holworthy," *Colonial Society of Massachusetts Transactions,* XIII (1910), 153–80.

³³ *Colonial Society of Massachusetts Collections,* XVI (1925), 837.

³⁴ *Ibid.,* p. 834.

³⁵ *Ibid.,* pp. 847, 851.

[36] *Ibid.*, pp. 836–37.

[37] William L. Sachse, *The Colonial American in Britain* (Madison, Wis., 1956), p. 107.

[38] "Edward Hopkins, and the Hopkins Bequests," *American Journal of Education*, XXVIII (1878), 177–83; Anne S. Pratt, "The Books Sent from England by Jeremiah Dummer to Yale College," *Papers in Honor of Andrew Keogh* (New Haven, 1938), pp. 7–44.

[39] Peirce, p. 47; Morison, *Harvard College in the Seventeenth Century*, I, 290–91; Quincy, I, 184–85.

[40] *Colonial Society of Massachusetts Collections*, XVI (1925), 838–39.

[41] This account comes from a contemporary, John Winthrop, who entered it in his journal under the date of November 9, 1639. *Winthrop's Journal "History of New England," 1630–1649*, ed. James K. Hosmer (New York, 1908), I, 317.

[42] "The Last Will and Testament of Me, Robert Keayne," *Report of the Record Commissioners of the City of Boston*, X (1886), 2. Such contradictions were frequently the result of the operation of the Puritan mind, which somewhat awkwardly attempted to make a place in its theology for both God's omnipotence and the effectiveness of man's action.

[43] *Ibid.*, pp. 13–14.

[44] *Sketch of Harvard College*, p. 163. On Keayne and his troubles see Bernard Bailyn, "The Apologia of Robert Keayne," *William and Mary Quarterly*, VIII (3d series [1950]), 568–87, and Bailyn's *The New England Merchants in the Seventeenth Century* (Cambridge, Mass., 1955), p. 35 ff.

[45] The predominance of benefactors with mercantile interests has been demonstrated in the most recent study of the economics of colonial Harvard: Margery Somers Foster, *"Out of Small Beginnings . . .": An Economic History of Harvard College in the Puritan Period, 1636–1712* (Cambridge, Mass., 1962), p. 106–28. Morison has attributed it in part to the political controversies of 17th-century Massachusetts Bay: *Harvard College in the Seventeenth Century*, I, 38, II, 389.

[46] Quincy, I, 181, 417–19.

[47] Morison, *Harvard College in the Seventeenth Century*, I, 38, fn. 1.

[48] Jordan, 353, fn. 1.

[49] Perry Miller, *Errand Into the Wilderness* (Cambridge, Mass., 1958), p. 143.

[50] Bailyn, *New England Merchants, passim.*

[51] Foster, p. 122.

[52] The broad outline of the following discussion rests on the careful reconstruction of the Hollis controversy from the Harvard Archives in Quincy, I, 230–64. Several accounts of Hollis's life and character made at the time of his death were later reprinted in *Christian Examiner*, VII (Sept., 1892), 84–104. The authors are indebted to Mark Haller's unpublished paper on the subject.

[53] Ebenezer Turell, *The Life and Character of the Reverend Benjamin Colman* (Boston, 1749), pp. 115–16; Perry Miller, *Jonathan Edwards* (New York, 1959), pp. 8 ff.

[54] An attempt to calculate the exact amounts of the Hollis donations to Harvard, approximately £5,000, has been made in Eliot, pp. 168 ff. See also [Francis Blackburne] *Memoirs of Thomas Hollis* (London, 1780), which deals with a grand nephew of Hollis with the same name, and Quincy, II, 525–26.

[55] Alfred C. Potter, "The Harvard College Library, 1723–35," *Colonial Society of Massachusetts Publications*, XXV (1922), 11–12.

[56] Quincy, I, 232.

[57] *Ibid.*, p. 234.

[58] The full text of Hollis's "Orders" of Feb. 14, 1721 appears in Quincy, I, 530–31. The italics are Hollis's.

[59] The liberal-orthodox controversy and its bearing on Harvard is well covered in Hofstadter and Metzger, *op. cit.* (above, fn. 2), pp. 98 ff., and in Morison, *op cit.*, II, *passim*.

[60] *Colonial Society of Massachusetts Collections*, XVI, 460. These proceedings of the Corporation bear the date June 21, 1721.

[61] Quincy, I, 537.

[62] Quincy felt that the wording "sound and orthodox principles" came from the Overseers in their draft with the express intent of providing a loophole with which to twist the donor's purposes. It is the authors' opinion that the wording was Hollis's with liberal intentions and that the Overseers subsequently seized on the phrase as a means to achieve their ends. In either case, Hollis must have attached a liberal meaning to it.

[63] The "Plan or Form for the Professor of Divinity to Agree to at his Inauguration" may be found in Quincy, I, 337–38.

[64] "Diary of Samuel Sewall," *Collections of the Massachusetts Historical Society*, VI (5th series [1882]), 298–99. It is only necessary to recall the furor in New England over the question of infant baptism aroused in connection with the Half-Way Covenant of 1662, and to remember that Harvard's President Henry Dunster narrowly escaped dismissal because he questioned the Scriptural validity of infant baptism, to appreciate the seriousness of this matter at the time.

[65] Quincy, I, 538–39.

[66] As quoted in Peirce, p. 157. After Wigglesworth had been installed as professor of divinity, Hollis made an attempt to secure from the college a formal promise to respect the terms of his benefaction. He succeeded only after threatening to alter his will in which Harvard was a beneficiary: Quincy, I, 261–62; *Colonial Society of Massachusetts Collections*, XVI (1925), 526–28.

[67] As quoted in Quincy, I, 399.

[68] Peirce, pp. 97–100, provides the complete document.

[69] *Ibid.*, p. 99.

[70] Quincy, II, 21.

[71] Quincy, II, 26–27; Peirce, p. 190.

[72] Theodore Hornberger, *Scientific Thought in the American Colleges, 1638–1800* (Austin, Texas, 1945), pp. 44 ff., 49 ff., discusses the contributions of Greenwood and Winthrop.

[73] A quantitative treatment of the sources of Harvard's income to 1712 may be found in Foster.

[74] Eliot, pp. 153 ff. and 158 ff. These figures do not contain money collected in subscriptions from communities as a whole and should be compared to the compilations in Quincy, I, 506 ff., 462 ff., II, 525 ff. Also pertinent is Elsie W. Clews, *Educational Legislation and Administration of the Colonial Governments*, Columbia University Contributions to Philosophy, Psychology and Education, Vol. VI, Nos. 1–4 (New York, 1899), pp. 7–72, 501.

[75] Frank F. Blackmar, *The History of Federal and State Aid to Higher*

Education, Bureau of Education Circular of Information, No. 1, 1890 (Washington), p. 92. The statistics in Jesse B. Sears, *Philanthropy in the History of American Higher Education*, Bureau of Education Bulletin, No. 26 (Washington, 1922), p. 23, also show a ratio of private to state support of more than 2 to 1.

[76] Foster, *op. cit.* (above, fn. 45), pp. 125–27, 148.

NOTES FOR CHAPTER II

[1] Wilbur K. Jordan, *The Charities of London, 1480–1660: The Aspirations and Achievements of the Urban Society* (London, 1960), pp. 255 ff., and Jordan, *Philanthropy in England, 1480–1660: A Study of the Changing Patterns of English Social Aspirations* (London, 1959), pp. 294 ff.

[2] *Samuel Johnson, President of King's College: His Career and Writings*, ed. Herbert and Carol Schneider (New York, 1929), I, 135.

[3] The subject of state aid to higher education in the colonies is fully treated in William Wallace Smith, "The Relations of College and State in Colonial America" (unpubl. diss., Columbia, 1949). Also useful are Beverly McAnear, "College Founding in the American Colonies, 1745–75," *Mississippi Valley Historical Review*, XLII (1955), 24–44; Jesse B. Sears, *Philanthropy in the History of American Higher Education*, U.S. Bureau of Education Bulletin, No. 26 (Washington, 1922), pp. 10–32; and Elsie W. Clews, *Educational Legislation and Administration of the Colonial Governments*, Columbia University Contributions to Philosophy, Psychology and Education, Vol. VI, Nos. 1–4 (New York, 1899).

[4] The best accounts of Dummer's life are in Anne S. Pratt, "The Books Sent from England by Jeremiah Dummer to Yale College," *Papers in Honor of Andrew Keogh* (New Haven, 1938), p. 8, and the *Dictionary of American Biography*, V. See also William L. Sachse, *The Colonial American in Britain* (Madison, Wis., 1956), pp. 107–8.

[5] Edwin Oviatt, *The Beginnings of Yale, 1701–26* (New Haven, 1916), p. 294; Franklin B. Dexter, *Documentary History of Yale University under the Original Charter of the Collegiate School of Connecticut, 1701–45* (New Haven, 1916), p. 58.

[6] Pratt, pp. 7–44, discusses the contribution in full, and Louise May Bryant and Mary Patterson, "The List of Books Sent by Jeremiah Dummer," *Papers in Honor of Andrew Keogh*, pp. 423–92, lists the books individually. Additional information may be found in Louis Shores, *Origins of the American College Library, 1638–1800*, George Peabody College for Teachers Contributions to Education, No. 134 (Nashville, 1934), pp. 20 ff., 127 ff. Shores has compiled a list of benefactions to all colonial college libraries: pp. 233–36.

[7] Hiram Bingham, "Elihu Yale: Governor, Collector and Benefactor," *American Antiquarian Society Proceedings*, XLVII N.S. (April, 1937), 128; Addison Van Name, "The Library," *Yale College: A Sketch of Its History*, ed. William L. Kinsley (New York, 1879), I, 1844 ff.

[8] Dexter, *op. cit.* (above, fn. 5), p. 56, prints the letter from Dummer to Pierpont of May 22, 1711.

[9] For Yale's life see Hiram Bingham, *Elihu Yale: The American Nabob of*

Queen Square (New York, 1939); Dexter, "Governor Elihu Yale," *New Haven Colony Historical Society Papers,* III (1882), 227–48; and Bingham, "Elihu Yale: Governor," pp. 93–114.

[10] Bingham, "Elihu Yale: Governor," p. 123; Bingham, "Elihu Yale," *American Journal of Education,* V (1858), 716.

[11] A letter from Mather to Connecticut's Governor Gordon Saltonstall of June 25, 1718 expressed his displeasure with the "senseless, useless, noisy impertinency" in Cambridge and the expectation that Yale would be more "serious and mature" in its service of education and religion: Josiah Quincy, *The History of Harvard University* (Boston, 1860), II, 526–27.

[12] Quincy, I, 524–26.

[13] Dexter, *Documentary History of Yale,* p. 193.

[14] *Ibid.,* pp. 157–59.

[15] Quincy, I, 526–27.

[16] Bingham, "Elihu Yale: Governor," pp. 138–39, puts the total contribution of Elihu Yale at £1,162, or about $28,000 in modern currency.

[17] Bingham, *Elihu Yale,* p. 335.

[18] Dexter, "Governor Elihu Yale," p. 241.

[19] Although Johnson had been dismissed from Yale for his part in the defection of Congregationalists at Yale to the Church of England in 1722, known as the "Great Apostasy," he remained sympathetic toward the college and was treated respectfully in New Haven: *Samuel Johnson,* I, 26.

[20] A. A. Luce, *The Life of George Berkeley, Bishop of Cloyne* (London, 1949), pp. 94 ff., 136 ff.; Benjamin Rand, *Berkeley's American Sojourn* (Cambridge, Mass., 1932).

[21] Dexter, *Documentary History of Yale,* pp. 284–85.

[22] Henry M. Fuller, "Bishop Berkeley as a Benefactor of Yale," *Yale University Library Gazette,* XXVIII (July, 1953), 8.

[23] Dexter, *op. cit.,* p. 289.

[24] The deed is quoted in full in Daniel C. Gilman, "Bishop Berkeley's Gifts to Yale College," *New Haven Colony Historical Society Papers,* I (1865), 153–56.

[25] Ebenezer Turell, *The Life and Character of the Reverend Benjamin Colman, D.D.* (Boston, 1749), p. 60.

[26] *Samuel Johnson,* I, 27.

[27] Notable recipients in the field of American higher education were Eleazar Wheelock, Aaron Burr, William Samuel Johnson, Napthali Daggett and Timothy Dwight: Gilman, pp. 157 ff.

[28] Luce, "Berkeley's Bermuda Project and his Benefactions to American Universities," *Royal Irish Academy Proceedings,* XLII (1934–35), 109. Gilman, pp. 162–65, lists the books individually. Berkeley also sent a smaller gift of books to Harvard, whose library he thought was less in need than Yale's: Harold J. Cadbury, "Bishop Berkeley's Gifts to the Harvard Library," *Harvard Library Bulletin,* VII (1953), 73–87.

[29] *The Literary Diary of Ezra Stiles,* ed. Franklin B. Dexter (New York, 1901), I, 205–6. Stiles received this information from Jared Eliot, who undeservedly took the credit due Johnson for securing Berkeley's gifts for Yale. For a modern acceptance of this version see Roland H. Bainton, *Yale and the Ministry* (New York, 1957), p. 12.

[30] Gilman, p. 166.

[31] *Samuel Johnson*, I, 177.

[32] Varnum Lansing Collins, *Princeton* (New York, 1914), pp. 35–37; Thomas Jefferson Wertenbaker, *Princeton, 1746–1896* (Princeton, N.J., 1946), p. 36.

[33] William H. S. Demarest, *A History of Rutgers College, 1766–1924* (New Brunswick, N.J., 1924), pp. 79–80.

[34] Walter C. Bronson, *The History of Brown University, 1764–1914* (Providence, R.I., 1914), p. 49; Reuben A. Guild, *Early History of Brown University including the Life, Times and Correspondence of President Manning, 1756–1791*, 2d rev. ed. (Providence, R.I., 1897), pp. 108 ff.; Stiles, I, 31.

[35] James B. Hedges, *The Browns of Providence Plantations: Colonial Years* (Cambridge, Mass., 1952), p. 197; Augustine Jones, *Moses Brown: His Life and Services: A Sketch Read Before the Rhode Island Historical Society, October 18, 1892* (Providence, R.I., 1892), pp. 22–23.

[36] Guild, p. 160.

[37] Bernard C. Steiner, *The History of Education in Connecticut*, U.S. Bureau of Education Circular of Information, No. 2, 1893, Contributions to American Educational History, ed. Herbert B. Adams, No. 14 (Washington), p. 92.

[38] Guild, p. 174.

[39] Guild, p. 23.

[40] Guild, pp. 172–74. Manning even provided a form for bequests to the Baptist minister of London to simplify the process of making a contribution.

[41] The Charter of 1764 is printed in full in Bronson, p. 502.

[42] Guild, pp. 368–70.

[43] A complete account of this venture is Robert H. Land, "Henrico and Its College," *William and Mary Quarterly*, XVIII (1938), 453–98.

[44] As quoted in Herbert B. Adams, *The College of William and Mary: A Contribution to the History of Higher Education with Suggestions for its National Promotion*, U.S. Bureau of Education Circular of Information, No. 1, 1887, Cont. Am. Ed. Hist., No. 1 (Washington), p. 15.

[45] *Ibid.;* Smith, "Relations of College and State," pp. 77 ff.; Frank W. Blackmar, *The History of Federal and State Aid to Higher Education*, U.S. Bureau of Education Circular of Information, No. 1, 1890, Cont. Am. Ed. Hist., No. 9 (Washington), pp. 167–70; Arnaud C. Marts, *Philanthropy's Role in Civilization* (New York, 1953), pp. 31–32; Albea Godbold, *The Church College of the Old South* (Durham, N.C., 1954), p. 4.

[46] *A Documentary History of Education in the South before 1860*, ed. Edgar W. Knight (Chapel Hill, N.C., 1949), I, 440–41; Adams, *College of William and Mary*, pp. 15–16.

[47] Stiles, II, 445; Adams, *College of William and Mary*, p. 16; "William and Mary College," *Scribner's Monthly*, XI (1875), 9.

[48] Beverly McAnear, "The Raising of Funds by the Colonial Colleges," *Mississippi Valley Historical Review*, XXXVIII (1952), 604 ff., has examined the English fund-raising missions, but his statements of amounts collected are frequently inaccurate, ambiguous and, at times, contradictory. See too Sachse, *op. cit.* (above, fn. 4), pp. 108–15, and Michael Kraus, *The Atlantic Civilization: Eighteenth Century Origins* (Ithaca, N.Y., 1949), pp. 72 ff.

[49] *American Higher Education: A Documentary History*, ed. Richard Hofstadter and Wilson Smith (Chicago, 1961), I, 94.

[50] Collins, *op. cit.* (above, fn. 32), p. 72; Wertenbaker, pp. 32–35; John

Maclean, *History of the College of New Jersey from its Origin in 1754 to the Commencement of 1854* (Philadelphia, 1877), I, 148.

[51] Shores, *op. cit.* (above, fn. 6), pp. 138–40, 234.

[52] Quoted in Horace W. Smith, *Life and Correspondence of the Rev. William Smith, D.D.* (Philadelphia, 1880), 300–1.

[53] *Benjamin Franklin and the University of Pennsylvania*, ed. Francis N. Thorpe, U.S. Bureau of Education Circular of Information, No. 2, 1892 (Washington), pp. 77–79.

[54] Edward Potts Cheyney, *History of the University of Pennsylvania, 1740–1940* (Philadelphia, 1940), p. 66. Albert Frank Gegenheimer, *William Smith: Education and Churchman, 1727–1803* (Philadelphia, 1953), p. 73, contends the amount was £4,800.

[55] Cheyney, p. 65.

[56] Sachse, pp. 109–12; McAnear, "The Raising of Funds," pp. 605–8; Cheyney, p. 66; *Benjamin Franklin and the University of Pennsylvania*, p. 237, and Gegenheimer, p. 73, all present slightly different figures for the final returns.

[57] Harold W. Blodgett, *Samson Occom* (Hanover, N.H., 1935), p. 84.

[58] Roy Harvey Pearce, *The Savages of America: A Study of the Indian and the Idea of Civilization* (Baltimore, 1953), pp. 3–49.

[59] Samuel Eliot Morison, *Builders of the Bay Colony* (Boston, 1930), pp. 287–319, and *The Founding of Harvard College* (Cambridge, Mass., 1935), p. 313.

[60] Blodgett is an adequate biography. Leon D. Richardson, *An Indian Preacher in England* (Hanover, N.H., 1932), presents selections from Occom's letters and diaries.

[61] For accounts of the Occom-Whitaker mission see James D. McCallum, *Eleazar Wheelock: Founder of Dartmouth College* (Hanover, N.H., 1939), pp. 147–66; Leon B. Richardson, *History of Dartmouth College* (Hanover, N.H., 1932), pp. 33–67; David McClure and Elijah Parish, *Memoirs of Rev. Eleazar Wheelock, D.D., Founder and President of Dartmouth College and Moor's Charity School with a Summary History* . . . (Newburyport, R.I., 1811), pp. 46 ff.; Blodgett, pp. 84 ff.; Sachse, pp. 112–14.

[62] George G. Bush, *History of Education in New Hampshire*, U.S. Bureau of Education Circular of Information, No. 3, 1898, Cont. Am. Ed. Hist., No. 22 (Washington), p. 143.

[63] Wheelock probably selected the name in the hopes that the influential Earl of Dartmouth would extend his interest in and benefactions toward the college. But, as in the case of Elihu Yale, little more was forthcoming.

[64] Samuel Eliot Morison, *American Colonial Colleges*, Rice Institute Pamphlet, No. 23 (Houston, 1936), pp. 280–82.

[65] Richardson, *An Indian Preacher in England*, p. 9.

[66] McCallum, pp. 175, 193; Wilder D. Quint, *The Story of Dartmouth* (Boston, 1914), pp. 28–29.

[67] McCallum, pp. 194, 196.

[68] Varnum Lansing Collins, *President Witherspoon: A Biography* (Princeton, 1925), II, 85 ff.; Wertenbaker, *op. cit.* (fn. 32), pp. 25 ff.

[69] *American Higher Education*, p. 146.

[70] Wertenbaker, pp. 54–55. Other colleges harvested what Witherspoon had sown. In 1773 an agent of the College of Philadelphia returned from the

West Indies with almost £1,000. He might have collected much more had not a hurricane devastated the islands and made fund-raising for colleges an impropriety: Cheyney, *op. cit.* (above, fn. 54), p. 69.

[71] Guild, *op. cit.* (above, fn. 34), p. 149.

[72] Cheyney, pp. 67–68; J. H. Easterby, *A History of the College of Charleston* (Charleston, S.C., 1935), 12–13, 23.

[73] Wertenbaker, p. 53.

[74] McAnear, "The Raising of Funds," p. 595. The numerous lotteries colonial colleges staged were also a form of local support but not a true philanthropy, in that the purchaser of a lottery ticket hoped for a monetary return. It was probably true, however, that in colonial times as today people purchased lottery tickets as a means of patronizing a cause with no thought of a pay-off. The authority on lotteries for colonial colleges is Philip G. Nordell, whose "Lotteries in Princeton's History," *Princeton University Library Chronicle*, XV (1953), 16–37, is an example of the work he has done on several institutions.

[75] John Howard Van Amringe, "King's College and Columbia College," *A History of Columbia University, 1754–1904* (New York, 1904), p. 11.

[76] Horace Coon, *Columbia: Colossus on the Hudson* (New York, 1947), pp. 38–40. The most detailed account of the controversy over the founding of King's is in *Samuel Johnson* (above, fn. 2), IV, 119 ff.

[77] For Murray's will see "Abstracts of Wills on File in the Surrogate's Office, City of New York," *New York Historical Society Collection*, XXIX (1896), 166–67. The estimates of historians put the value as high as £9,000: Van Amringe, p. 34, or £10,000: *American Journal of Education*, VII (1859), 461–70. McAnear, "The Raising of Funds," p. 598, contends that the bequest was £5,555 sterling.

[78] *Colonial Society of Massachusetts Collections*, XVI (1925), 853–54.

[79] Quincy, *op. cit.* (above, fn. 11), I, 214 ff., II, 138–40; Samuel Eliot Morison, *Three Centuries of Harvard* (Cambridge, Mass., 1936), pp. 64–66.

[80] *Colonial Society of Massachusetts Collections*, XVI (1925), 856.

[81] *Ibid.*, pp. 855–56.

[82] Benjamin Peirce, *History of Harvard University* (Cambridge, Mass., 1833), pp. 100–1.

[83] *Colonial Society of Massachusetts Collections*, XVI (1925), 859.

[84] Quincy, II, 212, 267.

[85] *Ibid.*, pp. 214, 290–91.

[86] *Ibid.*, pp. 216–17.

[87] Guild, *op. cit.* (above, fn. 34), p. 150.

[88] See Caroline Robbins, "Library of Liberty—Assembled for Harvard College by Thomas Hollis of Lincoln's Inn," *Harvard Library Bulletin*, V (1951), 5–23, 181–96, and her "The Strenuous Whig, Thomas Hollis of Lincoln's Inn," *William and Mary Quarterly*, VII (3d series [1950]), 406–53. Francis Blackburne, *Memoirs of Thomas Hollis* (London, 1780), is a biographical account with letters.

[89] Thomas H. Montgomery, *A History of the University of Pennsylvania from Its Foundations to A.D. 1770* (Philadelphia, 1900), pp. 495–500.

[90] *Ibid.*

[91] *The Works of Benjamin Franklin*, ed. John Bigelow (New York, 1904), I, 238–39.

[92] William Smith, *Account of the College, Academy and Charitable School*

of Philadelphia in Pennsylvania, ed. Thomas R. Adams (Philadelphia, 1951, orig. publ. 1756); *Benjamin Franklin and the University of Pennsylvania* (above, fn. 53), p. 235, and Francis H. Thorpe, "William Smith, D.D. and Collegiate Education," *American Journal of Education*, XXVII (1877), 473. Cheyney, *op. cit.* (above, fn. 54), p. 36, puts the figure somewhat lower. Franklin remembered it as "no less—than five thousand pounds": *Works*, I, 239.

⁹³ Montgomery, p. 503.

⁹⁴ The constitution is printed in Montgomery, pp. 46–51. See also Cheyney, pp. 29–31.

⁹⁵ See Morison, *American Colonial Colleges*, pp. 265–68, and Montgomery, pp. 244 ff.

⁹⁶ In 1789 Franklin wrote "Observations Relative to the Intentions of the Original Founders of the Academy in Philadelphia," reviewing and criticizing the lapse from his first plans: *The Works of Benjamin Franklin*, ed. Jared Sparks (Chicago, 1882), II, 133–59.

NOTES FOR CHAPTER III

¹ Varnum Lansing Collins, *President Witherspoon: A Biography* (Princeton, N.J., 1925), II, 142.

² Donald G. Tewksbury, *The Founding of American Colleges and Universities Before the Civil War*, Columbia University Teachers College Contributions to Education, No. 543 (New York, 1932), pp. 34–54. Tewksbury has compiled a list of 516 foundings for only 16 states and calculated a "mortality rate" of 81%. In other words, four out of every five colleges founded before the Civil War closed before 1928, the concluding date of Tewksbury's study. C. Harve Geiger, *The Program of Higher Education of the Presbyterian Church in the United States of America* (Cedar Rapids, Iowa, 1940), pp. 80–81, calculates the mortality rate of colleges related to the Presbyterian Church at 62%.

³ Absalom Peters, *Colleges Religious Institutions: A Discourse Delivered in the Park Presbyterian Church, Newark, N.J., October 29, 1851 before the Society for the Promotion of Collegiate and Theological Education at the West* (New York, 1851), p. 13.

⁴ *The Colleges and the Public, 1787–1862*, ed. Theodore Rawson Crane, Classics in Education, No. 15 (New York, 1963), p. 74.

⁵ Albert Frank Gegenheimer, *William Smith: Educator and Churchman, 1727–1803* (Philadelphia, 1943), pp. 82–87; Bernard C. Steiner, *History of Education in Maryland*, U.S. Bureau of Education Circular of Information, No. 2, 1894, Contributions to American Educational History, ed. Herbert B. Adams, No. 19 (Washington), pp. 75–95; Horace W. Smith, *Life and Correspondence of the Rev. William Smith* (Philadelphia, 1880), II, 64 ff.

⁶ W. Storrs Lee, *Father Went to College: The Story of Middlebury* (New York, 1936), pp. 17, 65–69, 114–15.

⁷ Louis C. Hatch, *The History of Bowdoin College* (Portland, Me., 1927), pp. 4–8, 40, 425.

⁸ Leverett Wilson Spring, *A History of Williams College* (Boston, 1917), pp. 16, 34.

[9] William S. Tyler, *History of Amherst College during its First Half Century, 1821–1871* (Springfield, Mass., 1873), pp. 649–54, prints a list of the subscribers and their donations to the "Charity Fund."

[10] Claude Moore Fuess, *Amherst: The Story of a New England College* (Boston, 1935), pp. 36–37; Stanley King, *A History of the Endowment of Amherst College* (Amherst, Mass., 1950), p. 11.

[11] Spring, pp. 95, 109, 113.

[12] Fuess, pp. 38–39, 78, 93–94, 96.

[13] Tyler, p. 569. For Williston see Sarah Bolton, *Famous Givers and Their Gifts* (New York, 1896), pp. 332 ff., and *Dictionary of American Biography,* XIX.

[14] King, pp. 40–48. Hitchcock's interest in Amherst was aroused through the good offices of Amos Lawrence, himself a wealthy industrialist and educational philanthropist. Although confining his own giving to Williams and Bowdoin, Lawrence persuaded Hitchcock to give Amherst $20,000 for a new professorship with the argument that the donor's soul would benefit from the philanthropy: Edward Hitchcock to Amos Lawrence, August 30, 1847, Lawrence Family Manuscripts, Massachusetts Historical Society, Boston.

[15] King, pp. 61–62; *Boston Transcript,* April 7, 1865; *Dictionary of American Biography,* XIX.

[16] Amos Lawrence's Book No. 17, Lawrence Family Manuscripts. The emphasis is Lawrence's. He repeated the same idea frequently in letters, journals, and his will.

[17] Mark Hopkins, *A Discourse Commemorative of Amos Lawrence Delivered by Request of the Students in the Chapel of Williams College, February 21, 1853* (Boston, 1853), pp. 15–23; Frederick Rudolph, *Mark Hopkins and the Log: Williams College, 1836–1872* (New Haven, Conn., 1956), pp. 175–80; J. H. Denison, *Mark Hopkins: A Biography* (New York, 1935), pp. 295 ff.

The importance of state aid to Williams should not be slighted, as Frederick Rudolph has shown, since it approximately equaled the receipts from philanthropy until it ceased in the 1870's.

[18] Mark Hopkins–Amos Lawrence Letterbook, XXI, Massachusetts Historical Society, Boston.

[19] Rudolph, pp. 179, 182.

[20] Amos Lawrence to Amos Adams Lawrence, June 26, 1846, Amos Adams Lawrence Letterbook No. 6, Massachusetts Historical Society, Boston.

[21] William H. S. Demarest, *A History of Rutgers College, 1766–1924* (New Brunswick, N.J., 1924), pp. 275–76.

[22] Reuben A. Guild, *Life, Times, and Correspondence of James Manning* (Boston, 1864), pp. 394–95; Walter C. Bronson, *The History of Brown University, 1764–1914* (Providence, R.I., 1914), pp. 155 ff.

[23] *The Writings of Benjamin Franklin,* ed. Albert Henry Smyth (New York, 1905), I, 210.

[24] Henry F. Colby, "Sketch of the Life and Character," *A Tribute to the Memory of Gardner Colby* (Boston, 1879), pp. 39 ff.; Edward W. Hall, "Colby College," *The Centennial History of Waterville, Kennebec County, Maine* (Waterville, Me., 1902), pp. 296–305.

[25] Edward W. Hall, *History of Higher Education in Maine,* U.S. Bureau of Education Circular of Information, No. 3, 1903, Cont. Am. Ed. Hist., No. 36 (Washington), pp. 136–46.

[26] *History of Tufts College,* ed. Alaric Bertrand Start (Medford, Mass., 1896), pp. 18–22.

[27] Howard D. Williams, "The Origins of Colgate University," *New York History,* XIX (1938), 239–54; *The First Half Century of Madison University, 1819–1869* (New York, 1872), pp. 25 ff.; Jesse Leonard Rosenberger, *Rochester and Colgate: Historical Backgrounds of Two Universities* (Chicago, 1925), pp. 33 ff.

[28] Bolton, *op. cit.* (above, fn. 13), pp. 315 ff.; *Dictionary of American Biography,* XV.

[29] C. Van Santvoord, *Memoirs of Eliphalet Nott* (New York, 1876), p. 390; George P. Schmidt, *The Liberal Arts College: A Chapter in American Cultural History* (New Brunswick, N.J., 1957), p. 114.

[30] Robert Davidson, *A Vindication of Colleges and College Endowments* (Lexington, Ky., 1841), pp. 20–22.

[31] Robert Peter and Johanna Peter, *Transylvania University: Its Origin, Rise, Decline, and Fall* (Louisville, 1896), pp. 134 ff.; Walter Wilson Jennings, *Transylvania: Pioneer University of the West* (New York, 1953), pp. 129 ff.; Tom K. Barton, "Politics and Higher Education in Kentucky, 1817–1822" (unpubl. master's essay, University of Wisconsin, 1961).

[32] Alvin Fayette Lewis, *History of Higher Education in Kentucky,* U.S. Bureau of Education Circular of Information, No. 3, 1899, Cont. Am. Ed. Hist., No. 25 (Washington), pp. 35–51.

[33] *Bishop Chase's Reminiscences: An Autobiography,* 2d ed. (Boston, 1848), I, 472–73.

[34] G. Wallace Chessman, *Denison: The Story of an Ohio College* (Granville, Ohio, 1957), pp. 10–57.

[35] George W. Paschal, *History of Wake Forest College* (Wake Forest, N.C., 1935), I, 275.

[36] Samuel Eliot Morison, *American Colonial Colleges,* Rice Institute Pamphlet, No. 23 (1936), pp. 273–74. Numerous similar examples for other colleges could be cited, for example Josiah Bushnell Grinnell, *Men and Events of Forty Years: Autobiographical Reminiscences* (Boston, 1891), pp. 327 ff. on the early years of Grinnell College, Iowa.

[37] Estelle Frances Ward, *The Story of Northwestern University* (New York, 1924), pp. 11–21.

[38] James Albert Woodson, *Higher Education in Indiana,* U.S. Bureau of Education Circular of Information, No. 1, 1891, Cont. Am. Ed. Hist., No. 10 (Washington), pp. 158–61.

[39] William Warren Sweet, *Indiana Asbury–DePauw University, 1837–1937* (New York, 1937), *passim;* George R. Crooks, *The Life of Bishop Matthew Simpson* (New York, 1890), pp. 157, 254; John Clark Ridpath, "Washington Charles DePauw: Founder of DePauw University," *Methodist Review,* LXXII (1890), 383–98.

[40] See as examples Edward N. Kirk, *The Church and the College: A Discourse Delivered at the Thirteenth Anniversary of the Society for the Promotion of Collegiate and Theological Education at the West in the First Congregational Church, Bridgeport, Conn., November 11, 1856* (New York, 1856), and John Todd, *Colleges Essential to the Church of God: Plain Letters Addressed to a Parishioner in Behalf of the Society for the Promotion of Collegiate and Theological Education at the West* (New York, 1847).

[41] Professor Post, "A Plea for the Colleges," *First Report of the Society for the Promotion of Collegiate and Theological Education at the West* (New York, 1844), pp. 22, 25 ff.

[42] Edward N. Kirk, *The Church and the College: An Address before the Society for the Promotion of Collegiate and Theological Education at the West delivered in Park Street Church in Newark, N.J., October 30, 1851* (Boston, 1851), p. 22.

[43] Kirk, *The Church and the College . . . 1856*, p. 29.

[44] Chase, I, 510–12.

[45] Charles Henry Rammelkamp, *Illinois College: A Centennial History, 1829–1929* (New Haven, Conn., 1928), pp. 84–86; *Julian M. Sturtevant: An Autobiography*, ed. Julian M. Sturtevant, Jr. (New York, 1896), pp. 177–78, 209, 234, 238.

[46] James Insley Osborne and Theodore Gregory Gronert, *Wabash College: The First Hundred Years, 1832–1932* (Crawfordsville, Ind., 1932), pp. 39 ff.

[47] Allen E. Ragan, *A History of Tusculum College, 1794–1944* (Bristol, Tenn., 1945), p. 15.

[48] Frederick Clayton Waite, *Western Reserve University: The Hudson Era, 1826–1882* (Cleveland, 1943), pp. 88, 117–21.

[49] Stephen Olin, *The Life and Letters of Stephen Olin . . . Late President of the Wesleyan University* (New York, 1854), II, 343.

[50] Peters, *op. cit.* (above, fn. 3), p. 22.

[51] A historical sketch of the Society appeared in *Proceedings at the Quarter-Century Anniversary of the Society for the Promotion of Collegiate and Theological Education at the West held at Marietta, Ohio, November 7–16, 1868* (New York, 1868), pp. 38–57. Western Reserve College joined the group shortly after its formation.

[52] *First Report of the Society for the Promotion of Collegiate and Theological Education at the West* (New York, 1844), pp. 7 ff.

[53] *Thirty-First Annual Report of the Society for the Promotion of Collegiate and Theological Education* (New York, 1874), p. 40. In 1874 the society joined with the American Education Society, which since 1815 had provided scholarships to ministerial candidates, to form the American College and Education Society.

[54] *Fourteenth Annual Report of the Society for the Promotion of Collegiate and Theological Education at the West* (New York, 1857), p. 18.

[55] *Seventh Annual Report of the Society for the Promotion of Collegiate and Theological Education at the West* (New York, 1850), pp. 38–39; *Eighteenth Annual Report of the Society for the Promotion of Collegiate and Theological Education at the West* (New York, 1862), pp. 21–23.

[56] A case in point was Knox College, which was finally accepted in 1846 after an investigation eased qualms about its antislavery views and its proximity to Illinois College: Hermann R. Muelder, *Fighters for Freedom: The History of Anti-Slavery Activities of Men and Women Associated with Knox College* (New York, 1959), pp. 248–56. Oberlin's application for aid was denied until 1862 because the society's Eastern directors considered its favorable stand in regard to abolitionism and coeducation "dangerous": Robert Samuel Fletcher, *A History of Oberlin College from Its Foundation Through the Civil War* (Oberlin, Ohio, 1943), I, 436, II, 896.

[57] William Lawrence, *Life of Amos A. Lawrence* (Boston, 1889), p. 70. The words are Amos A. Lawrence's.

[58] *Ibid.*, pp. 70–71; Marguerite Ellen Schumann, *Creation of a Campus* (Appleton, Wis., 1957), p. 14. Lawrence did request that instruction be non-sectarian and that a large minority of the trustees be of other denominations than Methodist.

[59] Lawrence, p. 72. In addition to his donation of $20,000 to the Wisconsin founding, Amos A. Lawrence established a college at Lawrence, Kansas that later became the nucleus of the state university.

[60] Delavan L. Leonard, *The History of Carleton College* (Chicago, 1904), pp. 177–89.

[61] Arthur G. Beach, *A Pioneer College: The Story of Marietta* (Chicago, 1935), p. 46; Grinnell, p. 336.

[62] Fletcher, *op. cit.* (above, fn. 56), I, 168 ff.; Gilbert Hobbs Barnes, *The Antislavery Impulse, 1830–1844* (New York, 1933), pp. 75–76.

[63] *Memoirs of Rev. Charles G. Finney* (New York, 1876), p. 334.

[64] Fletcher, I, 179–80.

[65] *Ibid.*, pp. 456 ff. Even after its English campaign Oberlin fell into serious financial difficulty. Not until 1860, after repeated strenuous drives among abolitionists, was an endowment obtained and the budget balanced.

[66] Francis Patrick Cassidy, *Catholic College Foundations and Development in the United States* (Washington, 1924), p. 16.

[67] Chase, I, 355.

[68] George Franklin Smyth, *Kenyon College: Its First Century* (New Haven, 1924); Laura Chase Smith, *The Life of Philander Chase, First Bishop of Ohio and Illinois, Founder of Kenyon and Jubilee Colleges* (New York, 1903), pp. 163 ff. Chase made a second trip to England in 1835 on behalf of Jubilee College in Illinois but had little success, and the college died.

[69] James Bryce, *The American Commonwealth* (London, 1889), II, 566.

[70] Martin Brewer Anderson, *Voluntaryism in Higher Education: A Paper read before the New York Convocation of Teachers in Albany, July 14, 1876* (New York, 1877).

NOTES FOR CHAPTER IV

[1] Merle Curti, "America at the World Fairs, 1851–1893," *American Historical Review*, LV (1950), 833–56.

[2] Richard H. Shryock has applied a similar concept of social transformation to explain the concern in nineteenth-century America with applied science at the expense of pure scientific research: "American Indifference to Basic Science During the Nineteenth Century," *Archives Internationales d'Histoire des Sciences*, II (Oct., 1948), 50–65.

[3] Irvin G. Wyllie, *The Self-Made Man in America: The Myth of Rags to Riches* (New Brunswick, N.J., 1954), pp. 95–112, notes this fact as well as the self-made businessmen's dislike of the classical colleges.

[4] Charles A. Bennett, *History of Manual and Industrial Education up to 1870* (Peoria, Ill., 1926); William P. Sears, *The Roots of Vocational Education* (New York, 1931); Lewis F. Anderson, *History of Manual and Industrial School Education* (New York, 1926).

[5] Theodore Hornberger, *Scientific Thought in the American Colleges, 1638–1800* (Austin, 1945); Brooke Hindle, *The Pursuit of Science in Revolutionary America, 1735–1789* (Chapel Hill, N.C., 1956); Louis F. Snow, *The College Curriculum in the United States* (New York, 1907), pp. 38–55.

[6] Josiah Quincy, *The History of Harvard University* (Boston, 1860), II, 292.

[7] James A. Thompson, *Count Rumford of Massachusetts* (New York, 1935), p. 24.

[8] "Will of Benjamin Bussey of Roxbury made on July 30, 1835" in the Harvard University Archives, Cambridge, Massachusetts. Although the will was probated in 1842, it was not until the 1870's that Harvard established the Bussey Institution of Practical Agriculture and appointed professors of horticulture, agricultural chemistry, and applied zoology: Alfred C. True, *A History of Agriculture Education in the United States*, U.S. Dept. of Agriculture Misc. Publication, No. 36 (Washington, 1929), p. 43; *The Harvard Book: A Series of Historical, Biographical and Descriptive Sketches by Various Authors*, comp. F. O. Vaille and H. A. Clark (Cambridge, Mass., 1875), II, 321–23.

[9] Bennett, p. 349.

[10] Bennett, pp. 349–64; William Willis, "Inaugural Address," *Collections of the Maine Historical Society*, V (1857), xvii–lxvii; "Gardiner Lyceum, Gardiner, Maine," *American Journal of Education*, II (1857), 216–19; True, pp. 35–36.

[11] Isaac E. Clarke, *Art and Industry: Education in the Industrial and Fine Arts in the United States* (Washington, 1895–98), III, 103 ff.; John E. Semmes, *John H. B. Latrobe and his Times, 1803–1891* (Baltimore, 1917), pp. 412–15.

[12] Ellwood Hendrick, *Modern Views of Physical Science: Being a Record of the Proceedings of the Centenary Meeting of the Franklin Institute at Philadelphia, September 17, 18 and 19, 1924* (Philadelphia, 1925), pp. 6 ff.; "Observations on the Rise and Progress of the Franklin Institute," *Franklin Journal*, I (1826), 66–71, 129–34; Franklin Institute, *1923 Year Book* (Philadelphia, 1923), pp. 18 ff.; *Dictionary of American Biography*, X, XII; *Public Ledger* (Philadelphia), Aug. 19, 1870; Clarke, III, 9 ff.

[13] Engineering instruction in this country began in 1817 at the United States Military Academy, West Point, N.Y., with the support of federal appropriations.

[14] Daniel D. Barnard, *A Discourse on the Life, Services and Character of Stephen Van Rensselaer* (Albany, N.Y., 1839); Palmer C. Ricketts, *History of the Rensselaer Polytechnic Institute, 1824–1894* (New York, 1895), pp. 12–17; Dixon Ryan Fox, *The Decline of Aristocracy in the Politics of New York*, Columbia University Studies in History, Economics and Public Law, No. 86 (New York, 1919), pp. 32–33.

[15] Ricketts, pp. 6–7. Ethel M. McAllister, *Amos Eaton: Scientist and Educator* (Philadelphia, 1941), pp. 317–68, presents convincing evidence that Eaton drafted the letter for Van Rensselaer.

[16] Ray Palmer Baker, *A Chapter in American Education: Rensselaer Polytechnic Institute, 1824–1924* (New York, 1924), p. 26.

[17] True, pp. 39–43.

[18] Ricketts, pp. 17, 67, 129.

[19] Hamilton A. Hill, *Memoir of Abbott Lawrence*, 2d ed. (Boston, 1884), p. 116.

20 Edward Lurie, *Louis Agassiz: A Life in Science* (Chicago, 1960), pp. 136–37; Richard J. Storr, *The Beginnings of Graduate Education in America* (Chicago, 1953), pp. 49–53.

21 Hill, pp. 1–26; "Abbott Lawrence," *American Journal of Education,* I (1856), 205–15; *Boston Daily Advertiser,* Aug. 30, 1855.

22 Abbott Lawrence to Samuel A. Eliot, June 7, 1847, Records of the Corporation and Fellows of Harvard College, VIII, 360–63, in the Harvard University Archives, Cambridge, Mass.

23 *Ibid.* A revealing sidelight to Abbott Lawrence's donation was the note of congratulation his brother, Amos, sent on June 9, 1847: "[T]his last best work ever done by one of our name . . . will prove a better title to true nobility than any from the potentates of the world. . . . It is to impress upon unborn millions the great truth that our talents are trusts committed to us for use, and to be accounted for when the Master calls." *Extracts from the Diary and Correspondence of the Late Amos Lawrence,* ed. William R. Lawrence (Boston, 1855), pp. 244–45.

Writing to a friend about his brother's gift, Amos Lawrence declared: "Instead of our sons going to France and other foreign lands for instruction, [the Lawrence Scientific School] will be a place, second to no other on earth, for such teaching as our country stands now in absolute need of." The importance of this establishment Lawrence made clear in his next sentence: "Here, at this moment, it is not in the power of the great railroad companies to secure a competent engineer to carry forward their work, so much are the services of such men in demand": Amos Lawrence to Mark Hopkins, June 9, 1849, Lawrence–Hopkins Letterbook 21, Massachusetts Historical Society, Boston.

24 Lurie, pp. 138–41.

25 Elizabeth Cary Agassiz, *Louis Agassiz: His Life and Correspondence* (London, 1885), II, 457; Lurie, pp. 164, 172, 190.

26 "Lawrence Scientific School," *American Journal of Education,* I (1856), 217–24; *The Harvard Book,* II, 280 ff.

27 Samuel C. Prescott, *When M.I.T. was "Boston Tech." 1861–1916* (Cambridge, Mass., 1954), pp. 69–87; Henry James, *Charles W. Eliot, President of Harvard University, 1869–1909* (Boston, 1930), I, 294.

28 Leon B. Richardson, *History of Dartmouth College* (Hanover, N.H., 1932), I, 422.

29 John King Lord, *A History of Dartmouth College, 1815–1909* (Concord, N.H., 1913), pp. 293–95; Oliver P. Hubbard, "The Chandler Scientific Department of Dartmouth College," *Granite Monthly,* III (1880), 252–62.

30 Thomas C. Mendenhall, *Scientific, Technical and Engineering Education,* Monographs in Education in the United States, ed. Nicholas Murray Butler, Vol. II, No. 11 (Albany, N.Y., 1904), pp. 27–28; Richardson, II, 520, 541–42.

31 Richardson, I, 389.

32 Hubbard, p. 259.

33 Russell H. Chittenden, *History of the Sheffield Scientific School, 1846–1922* (New Haven, Conn., 1928), I, 37–38.

34 *Yale College: A Sketch of Its History,* ed. William L. Kinsley (New York, 1879), II, 164–66; Chittenden, I, 37–65; Storr, *op. cit.* (above, fn. 20), pp. 54–58.

35 Chittenden, I, 65–66.

[36] "Department of Philosophy and the Arts in Yale College," *American Journal of Education*, I (1856), 363.

[37] "Scientific Schools in Europe," *American Journal of Education*, I (1856), 327. Curti, *op. cit.* (above, fn. 1), presents further evidence of American uneasiness in the face of European industrial superiority.

[38] Chittenden, I, 51.

[39] *Dictionary of American Biography*, XVII; *Christian Union*, XXV (Feb. 23, 1882), 175.

[40] Chittenden, I, 213.

[41] *Ibid.*, p. 168.

[42] *Ibid.*, p. 211.

[43] David B. Skillman, *The Biography of a College: Being the History of the First Century of the Life of Lafayette College* (Easton, Pa., 1932), I, 269–70.

[44] Emory R. Johnson, *The Wharton School: Its First Fifty Years, 1881–1931* (Philadelphia, 1931), pp. 7–8.

[45] Emory R. Johnson, *Life of a University Professor: An Autobiography* (Philadelphia, 1943), pp. 23–24.

[46] *Speeches and Poems by Joseph Wharton*, ed. Joanna Wharton Lippincott (Philadelphia, 1926), p. 241.

[47] Joanna Wharton Lippincott, *Biographical Memoranda Concerning Joseph Wharton, 1826–1909* (Philadelphia, 1909); *Dictionary of American Biography*, XX.

[48] *Speeches and Poems by Joseph Wharton*, pp. 258–59.

[49] *Ibid.*, p. 471.

[50] *Ibid.*, pp. 262–63.

[51] Thomas W. Goodspeed, *A History of the University of Chicago Founded by John D. Rockefeller: The First Quarter Century* (Chicago, 1916), pp. 323–24; Theodore F. Jones, *New York University, 1832–1932* (New York, 1933), pp. 356–78.

[52] William Jewett Tucker, *My Generation: An Autobiographical Interpretation* (Boston, 1919), p. 356. See also Horatio S. Krans, "Edward Tuck: A Biographical Sketch," *Dartmouth Alumni Magazine*, XXIV (1932), pp. 603–20; Richardson, II, 734 ff.

[53] Melvin T. Copeland, *And Mark an Era: The Story of the Harvard Business School* (Boston, 1958); William Lawrence, "Memorandum about the gift of Mr. George F. Baker of $5,000,000 for the foundation of the Harvard Business School," Oct. 1924, Baker Library Archives, Harvard Business School, Boston.

[54] Edward C. Mack, *Peter Cooper: Citizen of New York* (New York, 1949) is the authoritative biography. Less useful are Rossiter W. Raymond, *Peter Cooper* (New York, 1901) and John C. Zachos, *A Sketch of the Life and Opinions of Mr. Peter Cooper* (New York, 1876). Of more personal nature is Cooper's *A Sketch of the Early Days and Business Life of Peter Cooper: An Autobiography* (New York, 1877). The authors thank C. Merrill Hough and John Hirsch for the use of unpublished papers on Cooper and his Union.

[55] Clarke, *op. cit.* (above, fn. 11), III, 57.

[56] *Fifteenth Annual Report of the Trustees of the Cooper Union for the Advancement of Science and Art* (New York, 1874), pp. 18–19. A slightly different quotation of Cooper's statement is made in Zachos, pp. 40–41.

[57] *Charter, Trust Deed, and By-Laws of the Cooper Union for the Ad-*

vancement of Science and Art, with the Letter of Peter Cooper, accompanying the Trust Deed (New York, 1859), p. 26. Cooper had no desire for the union to be named after himself and, in fact, expressly requested the New York legislature, which granted the charter, not to do so: Clarke, III, 375; Allan Nevins, *Abram S. Hewitt, With Some Account of Peter Cooper* (New York, 1935), p. 375. Hewitt was Cooper's son-in-law and executive secretary of the Cooper Union from its opening until his death in 1903.

[58] George T. Strong, *Diary*, ed. Allan Nevins and Milton Halsey Thomas (New York, 1952), II, 259.

[59] Nevins, *Hewitt*, p. 446.

[60] Prescott, *op. cit.* (above, fn. 27), pp. 34 ff.; James Phinney Munroe, *A Life of Francis Amasa Walker* (New York, 1923), pp. 211–18.

[61] Richard Maclaurin to George Eastman, Feb. 29, 1912, George Eastman Papers, Eastman Kodak Co., Rochester, N.Y. The complete correspondence documenting Eastman's relation with M.I.T. has been preserved in this collection.

[62] Carl W. Ackerman, *George Eastman* (London, 1930), pp. 324 ff.

[63] "Seventy-Five Years of Lehigh University," comp. William A. Cornelius, *Lehigh University Publications*, XVI (Jan., 1942), 6 ff.; Catherine Drinker Bowen, *A History of Lehigh University* (Bethlehem, Pa., 1924); Sarah K. Bolton, *Famous Givers and Their Gifts* (New York, 1896), pp. 301 ff.; *Dictionary of American Biography*, XIV.

In marked contrast to Asa Packer, John Purdue was a philanthropist whose $150,000 donation of 1869 to Indiana's incipient land-grant college, which emphasized engineering, was made conditional on its adopting his name: William Murray Hepburn and Louis Martin Sears, *Purdue University: Fifty Years of Progress* (Indianapolis, 1925), pp. 31–33.

[64] *Morton Memorial: A History of the Stevens Institute of Technology*, ed. Franklin D. Furman (Hoboken, N.J., 1905), *passim; New York Times*, Aug. 11, 1868; *New York Tribune*, Aug. 10, 1868; Mendenhall, *op. cit.* (above, fn. 30), pp. 16–18; *Dictionary of American Biography*, XVII.

[65] James D. Cleveland, "Case School of Applied Science," *Western Reserve Historical Society Tracts*, III (1891), 219–54; Mendenhall, pp. 18–20; George V. Thompson, "Science School: The Founding and Early Years of Case Institute" (unpubl. master's essay, Oberlin College, 1951).

[66] James Insley Osborne and Theodore Gregory Gronert, *Wabash College: The First Hundred Years, 1832–1932* (Crawfordsville, Ind., 1932), pp. 68, 141.

[67] Clarke, IV, 184 ff., 714 ff.; *Indianapolis Sentinel*, Aug. 16, 1887; *Dictionary of American Biography*, XVI.

[68] Clarke, III, 450. See Walter S. Perry, *Pratt Institute: Its Beginnings and Development* (Brooklyn, N.Y., 1926), pp. 4–5, for similar testimony of Pratt's motives from the director of the institute's School of Fine and Applied Arts. For Pratt's life see R. L. Duffus, *The American Renaissance* (New York, 1928), pp. 99–103; *Dictionary of American Biography*, XV; Bolton, *Famous Givers*, pp. 108 ff.; and Frederick B. Pratt *et al., Charles Pratt: An Interpretation* (Brooklyn, N.Y., 1930).

[69] Bolton, p. 108.

[70] Clarke, III, 451.

[71] Clarke, III, 493.

[72] Arthur W. Tarbell, *The Story of Carnegie Tech, 1900–1935* (Pittsburgh, 1937); Robert M. Lester, *Forty Years of Carnegie Giving* (New York, 1941),

pp. 8–18; Carnegie Corporation of New York, *Report of the Acting President for the Year Ended September 30, 1922* (New York), pp. 71–72.

[73] Edward M. McDonald and Edward M. Hinton, *Drexel Institute of Technology, 1891–1941* (Philadelphia, 1942), pp. 13–30; James Creese, *A. J. Drexel, 1826–1893, and his "Industrial University"* (New York, 1949).

[74] Clarke, III, 566–67.

[75] John S. Hittell, *A History of the City of San Francisco* (San Francisco, 1878), pp. 416 ff.; "The Life of James Lick," *Quarterly of the Society of California Pioneers,* I (1924), 14–68; Charles A. Bennett, *History of Manual and Industrial Education, 1870 to 1917* (Peoria, 1937), p. 510.

[76] Clarke, III, 969–87; *New York Herald Tribune,* Aug. 12, 1940.

[77] This version of the conversation is given in Harper Leech and John Charles Carroll, *Armour and His Times* (New York, 1938), p. 212. Gunsaulus fails to mention this incident in his "Philip D. Armour: A Character Sketch," *Review of Reviews,* XXIII (1900), 167–76. The precise date of the sermon is uncertain: James C. Peebles, "Armour Institute of Technology, 1892–1940," MS in Illinois Institute of Technology Archives, Chicago, p. 5.

The authors are indebted to C. Merrill Hough for an unpublished paper on Armour and the Institute.

[78] Charles J. Bushnell, *The Social Problem at the Chicago Stockyards* (Chicago, 1902); John R. Commons, "Labor Conditions in Meat Packing and the Recent Strike," *Quarterly Journal of Economics,* XIX (1904), 1–32; and Louis Unfer, "Gustavus A. Swift and the Development of the Packing Industry, 1875–1912" (unpubl. diss., University of Illinois, 1951), contain details of the Chicago situation.

[79] Courtney R. Hall, *History of American Industrial Science* (New York, 1954), pp. 318–20. Meat packing, however, was not included in the Institute's curriculum.

[80] Leech and Carroll, pp. 207–16; Peebles, *passim;* George F. Redmond, *Financial Giants of America* (Boston, 1922), II, 209 ff.; "American Millionaires and Their Public Gifts," *Review of Reviews,* VII (1893), 52–53; Clarke, III, 907 ff.

[81] For the history of federal aid to practical higher education see True, *op. cit.* (above, fn. 8), pp. 95–191 and Clarke, IV, 227–706. A. Hunter Dupree, *Science in the Federal Government: A History of Policies and Activities to 1940* (Cambridge, Mass., 1957), is an excellent discussion of this topic and includes state patronage of educational institutions.

[82] Roy J. Honeywell, *The Educational Work of Thomas Jefferson,* Harvard Studies in Education, No. 16 (Cambridge, Mass., 1931), pp. 107 ff., discusses the ideas of Jefferson; Philip A. Bruce, *History of the University of Virginia, 1819–1919* (5 vols.; New York, 1920) is the authoritative history.

[83] "Our National Schools of Science," *North American Review,* CV (1867), 520.

[84] Clarke, IV, 734.

NOTES FOR CHAPTER V

[1] The groundwork for any study of women's education in America is in Thomas Woody, *A History of Women's Education in the United States* (2 vols.;

New York, 1929). Woody pays only incidental attention to philanthropy, and what information he has is unorganized and frequently incomplete. Mabel Newcomer's *A Century of Higher Education for American Women* (New York, 1959) includes a short chapter on financing women's education that concerns tuition costs and college expenses as well as philanthropy.

[2] C. W. Bremner, *Education of Girls and Women in Great Britain* (London, 1897), pp. 122–63; Vera Brittain, *The Women at Oxford: A Fragment History* (New York, 1960); Alice Zimmern, *The Renaissance of Girls' Education in England* (London, 1898), pp. 103 ff.

[3] Helene Lange, *Higher Education of Women in Europe*, trans. L. R. Klemm (New York, 1890), pp. 110–19; *Women in Education: Being the Transactions of the Educational Section of the International Congress of Women, London, July, 1899* (London, 1900), pp. 68–89; Ai Hoshino, *The Education of Women*, Western Influences in Modern Japan, No. 11 (Tokyo, 1929); Margaret E. Burton, *The Education of Women in China* (New York, 1911).

[4] For an extended discussion see Merle Curti, *The Social Ideas of American Educators*, 2d ed. (Paterson, N.J., 1959), pp. 169 ff., and Woody, I, 88–123.

[5] Because of difficulty in determining standards for the "genuineness" of a college, historians of women's education in the United States vary widely in their selections of the first institution of collegiate status: Woody, I, 329 ff., II, 137 ff.; James M. Taylor, *Before Vassar Opened* (Boston, 1914), pp. 1–81; I. M. E. Blondin, *History of Higher Education of Women in the South Prior to 1860* (New York, 1909).

[6] "Female Education in Massachusetts," *American Journal of Education*, XXX (1880), 597–600.

[7] Mary Watters, *The History of Mary Baldwin College, 1842–1942* (Staunton, Va., 1942), pp. 14–15.

[8] Charles E. Jones, *Education in Georgia*, U.S. Bureau of Education Circular of Information, No. 4, 1888, Contributions to American Educational History, ed. Herbert B. Adams, No. 5 (Washington), pp. 94 ff.; Rhoda C. Ellison, *The History of Huntingdon College, 1854–1954* (University, Ala., 1954), pp. 4–10.

[9] Mary Watters, *The First Hundred Years of MacMurray College* (Springfield, 1947), pp. 11, 154.

[10] Edward Hitchcock, *The Power of Christian Benevolence Illustrated in the Life and Labors of Mary Lyon*, 7th ed. (Northampton, Mass., 1852), p. 226.

[11] Hitchcock, p. 175.

[12] Sarah D. Stowe, *History of Mount Holyoke Seminary, South Hadley, Massachusetts During its First Half Century, 1837–1887* (South Hadley, Mass., 1887), p. 41.

[13] Arthur C. Cole, *A Hundred Years of Mount Holyoke College: The Evolution of an Educational Ideal* (New Haven, Conn., 1940), p. 26.

[14] Stowe, pp. 59–60. The school existed as a seminary and college after 1888 and in 1893 was renamed Mount Holyoke College.

[15] Cole, p. 32.

[16] Stowe, pp. 222–23. The seminary's largest benefactor was the Williston family of Boston, whose gifts totaled only about $25,000. Mount Holyoke also received a grant of $40,000 from the Massachusetts legislature in 1868.

17 W. Charles Barber, *Elmira College: The First Hundred Years* (New York, 1955), pp. 34–85.

18 Boyd McDowell, "Simeon Benjamin, Founder of Elmira College, 1792–1868," *Elmira College Bulletin*, XXI (1930); Gilbert Meltzer, *The Beginnings of Elmira College* (Elmira, N.Y., 1941), pp. 1–67.

19 *The Autobiography of Matthew Vassar*, ed. Elizabeth H. Haight (New York, 1916), p. 33.

20 As quoted from a manuscript narrative by Jewett dated 1879 in James M. Taylor and Elizabeth H. Haight, *Vassar* (New York, 1915), p. 32.

21 Benson J. Lossing, *Vassar College and Its Founder* (New York, 1867), pp. 91–93.

22 "Matthew Vassar and the Vassar Female College," *American Journal of Education*, XI (1862), pp. 53–56; Lossing, p. 93.

23 A testimony to Vassar's modesty and refusal to interfere in matters unfamiliar to him was made in a letter of the second president, John H. Raymond: *Life and Letters of John Howard Raymond*, ed. Harriet Raymond Lloyd (New York, 1881), p. 513.

24 Taylor, pp. 150 ff.

25 *Life and Letters of Raymond*, pp. 515–16.

26 Ernest Earnest, *Academic Procession: An Informal History of the American College, 1636 to 1953* (Indianapolis, 1953), p. 182.

27 *Life and Letters of Raymond*, p. 503.

28 "Vassar College," *Harper's Monthly*, LII (1876), 36.

29 *Wells College and Its Founder: An Historical Sketch*, comp. Walter I. Lowe (Aurora, N.Y., 1901), p. 3.

30 *Ibid.*, pp. 10–12; *Christian Union*, VIII (Aug. 13, 1873), 131.

31 Elizabeth D. Hanscom and Helen French Greene, *Sophia Smith and the Beginnings of Smith College* (Northhampton, Mass., 1926), pp. 39–40.

32 As recalled by John M. Greene in his "The Origin of Smith College," *Celebration of the Quarter-Centenary of Smith College* (Cambridge, Mass., 1900), p. 91. Sophia Smith had an elementary education in Hatfield and a single term at Catherine E. Beecher's Hartford Female Seminary.

33 Hanscom and Greene, p. 43.

34 Hanscom and Greene, pp. 44–45.

35 Greene's "Plan" is printed in Hanscom and Greene, pp. 60–63.

36 Her complete will appears in L. Clark Seelye, *The Early History of Smith College, 1871–1910* (Boston, 1923), pp. 221–28.

37 Hanscom and Greene, p. 43.

38 Seelye, pp. 15, 16.

39 *Life and Letters of Raymond*, p. 511.

40 L. Clark Seelye, "History of Smith College," *Celebration of the Quarter-Century of Smith College* (Cambridge, Mass., 1900), pp. 105–6.

41 Florence Morse Kinsley, *The Life of Henry Fowle Durant, Founder of Wellesley College* (New York, 1924); Alice Payne Hackett, *Wellesley: Part of the American Story* (New York, 1949), pp. 24–25.

42 Florence Converse, *The Story of Wellesley* (Boston, 1915), p. 7.

43 Converse, pp. 43–44.

44 Kinsley, p. 336.

45 George H. Palmer, *The Life of Alice Freeman Palmer* (Boston, 1908), p. 98.

[46] Palmer, p. 127.

[47] Kinsley, pp. 260–61; Hackett, pp. 48–49, 72–73.

[48] On Taylor and his college see Margaret Taylor MacIntosh, *Joseph Wright Taylor: Founder of Bryn Mawr College* (Haverford, Pa., 1936).

[49] Cornelia Meigs, *What Makes a College? A History of Bryn Mawr* (New York, 1956), pp. 15 ff.

[50] Quoted in MacIntosh, p. 209.

[51] Meigs, pp. 68 ff.

[52] Meigs, pp. 77 ff.

[53] Edith Finch, *Carey Thomas of Bryn Mawr* (New York, 1947), pp. 164, 219, 224, 330 fn. 1.

[54] Kenneth L. Mark, *Delayed By Fire: Being the Early History of Simmons College* (Concord, Mass., 1945); George S. Hale, "The Charities of Boston," *Memorial History of Boston*, ed. Justin Winsor (Boston, 1881), IV, 669.

[55] Edwin Mims, "The South Realizing Itself," *World's Work*, XXII (1911), 14972–87; Anna H. Knipp and Thaddeus P. Thomas, *The History of Goucher College* (Baltimore, 1938); *Atlanta Constitution*, Jan. 23, 1915.

[56] "James Edwin MacMurray: An Appreciation," *MacMurray College Bulletin*, XXXIV (1944), 10.

[57] George R. Grose, *The Man from Missouri* (Los Angeles, 1943) is a biography of MacMurray. See also Robert Johns, "Ten Philanthropies to American Higher Education: A Study of the Philanthropists and Their Influence on the Beneficiaries" (unpubl. diss., Stanford University, 1950), pp. 196–203; *New York Times*, May 3, 1938; and Watters, *MacMurray College*, passim.

[58] See above, Chapter III; Robert S. Fletcher, *A History of Oberlin From Its Foundation Through the Civil War* (Oberlin, 1943), I, 375 ff., II, 904 ff.; and Fletcher, "The First Coeds," *American Scholar*, VII (1938), 78–93.

[59] George W. Knight and John R. Commons, *History of Higher Education in Ohio*, U.S. Bureau of Education Circular of Information, No. 5, 1891, Cont. Am. Ed. Hist., No. 12 (Washington), p. 129; Mary Tyler Mann, *Life of Horace Mann*, 2d ed. (Boston, 1865), pp. 509 ff.
Philanthropy was not the only factor in the development of women's higher education. At the state universities of Iowa, Wisconsin, and Michigan, co-education began early and received the financial support of the state.

[60] *Autobiography of Andrew Dickson White* (New York, 1907), I, 398.

[61] For Sage's life and philanthropic philosophy see Anita Shafer Goodstein, *Biography of a Businessman: Henry W. Sage, 1814–1897* (Ithaca, N.Y., 1962), especially pp. 221–46.

[62] M. Carey Thomas, "Mr. Sage and Co-education," *Memorial Exercises in Honor of Henry William Sage* (Ithaca, N.Y., 1898), pp. 55, 57.

[63] Walter P. Rogers, *Andrew D. White and the Modern University* (Ithaca, N.Y., 1942), p. 85; Morris Bishop, *A History of Cornell* (Ithaca, N.Y., 1962), pp. 143–52.

[64] *Christian Union*, VIII (May 28, 1873), 427.

[65] Ida H. Harper, *The Life and Work of Susan B. Anthony* (Indianapolis, 1908), III, 1221 ff.; Jesse L. Rosenberger, *Rochester: The Making of a University* (Rochester, N.Y., 1927), pp. 264–65; Alma Lutz, *Susan B. Anthony: Rebel, Crusader, Humanitarian* (Boston, 1959), p. 295

[66] A woman received an M.D. from an American institution as early as 1849, and more than a thousand women were in various medical schools by the time Johns Hopkins was opened: Woody, *op. cit.* (above, fn. 1), II, 340 ff.

[67] Finch, *op. cit.* (above, fn. 53), pp. 196 ff.; Elizabeth T. King, "The Admission of Women to the Medical School of The Johns Hopkins University," *Transactions of the National Council of Women of the United States assembled in Washington, D.C., Feb. 22 to 25, 1891* (Philadelphia, 1891), pp. 199–203.

[68] Alan M. Chesney, *The Johns Hopkins Hospital and The Johns Hopkins University School of Medicine* (Baltimore, 1943), I, 197, 219.

[69] Chesney, I, 199.

[70] Chesney, I, 203–4; Bertram M. Bernheim, *The Story of Johns Hopkins: Four Great Doctors and the Medical School They Created* (New York, 1948), p. 31.

[71] Harvey K. Cushing, *The Life of Sir William Osler* (Oxford, 1925), p. 387.

[72] Chesney, I, 216.

[73] Lucy Allen Paton, *Elizabeth Cary Agassiz: A Biography* (Boston, 1919), pp. 192–274; Samuel Eliot Morison, *Three Centuries of Harvard, 1636–1936* (Cambridge, Mass., 1937), p. 392; Woody, II, 307 ff.

[74] Brandt V. B. Dixon, *A Brief History of H. Sophie Newcomb Memorial College, 1887–1919* (n.p., 1928), pp. 13–14.

[75] Dixon, pp. 6–11, 52–53; William Preston Johnston, "Tulane University of Louisiana," in Edwin W. Fay, *The History of Education in Louisiana*, U.S. Bureau of Education Circular of Information, No. 1, 1898, Cont. Am. Ed. Hist., No. 20 (Washington), p. 222.

[76] As quoted in Virginia C. Gildersleeve, *Many a Good Crusade* (New York, 1954), p. 87. See also Marian Churchill White, *A History of Barnard College* (New York, 1954), pp. 17 ff.; *New York Times,* March 21, 1913; Alice Duer Miller and Susan Myers, *Barnard College: The First Fifty Years* (New York, 1939).

NOTES FOR CHAPTER VI

[1] "The Emergence of the American University, 1865–1910" (unpubl. diss., U. of Calif., Berkeley, 1961).

[2] Andrew D. White, "A National University," *National Education Association Addresses and Journal of Proceedings, 1874* (Worcester, Mass., 1874), pp. 58, 59, 72.

[3] Frederick A. P. Barnard, *The Rise of a University: The Later Days of Old Columbia College From the Annual Reports of Frederick A. P. Barnard, President of Columbia College, 1864–1888,* ed. William F. Russell (New York, 1937), I, 153–55.

[4] James Morgan Hart, *German Universities: A Narrative of Personal Experience* (New York, 1874), which had considerable reading and probably came to the attention of the trustees of Johns Hopkins during the planning stage, described the author's experiences during his study of law and linguistics in several German universities.

[5] Barnard, I, 340.

[6] For further discussion of the giving habits of wealthy Americans see Merle Curti, Judith Green, and Roderick Nash, "Anatomy of Giving: Millionaires in the Late 19th Century," *American Quarterly,* XV (1963), 416–35.

[7] Richard Emmons Thursfield, *Henry Barnard's American Journal of Education* (Baltimore, 1945), pp. 112–31.

[8] Franklin Parker, "Influences on the Founder of the Johns Hopkins University and the Johns Hopkins Hospital," *Bulletin of the History of Medicine,* XXXIV (1960), 148–53.

[9] Ch. IV above discusses achievement in practical higher education. Also pertinent is Irvin G. Wyllie's article, "The Business Man Looks at the Higher Learning," *Journal of Higher Education,* XXIII (1952), 295–97.

[10] Carl L. Becker, *Cornell University: Founders and Founding* (Ithaca, N.Y., 1943), p. 111.

[11] G. Stanley Hall, *Life and Confessions of a Psychologist* (New York, 1923), p. 261.

[12] George T. Clark, *Leland Stanford* (Stanford, Calif., 1931), pp. 389, 392.

[13] Daniel Coit Gilman, *The Launching of a University and Other Papers* (New York, 1906), pp. 7 ff., 37–38; Hugh Hawkins, *Pioneer: A History of the Johns Hopkins University, 1874–1889* (Ithaca, N.Y., 1960), pp. 3 ff.; Robert Johns, "Ten Philanthropies to American Higher Education" (unpubl. diss., Stanford University, 1950), pp. 105–184, 259–303.

[14] Philip Dorf, *The Builder: A Biography of Ezra Cornell* (New York, 1952), pp. 255–86.

[15] Milicent W. Shinn, "The Leland Stanford, Junior, University," *Overland Monthly,* XVIII (1891), 337–55; Edith R. Mirrielees, *Stanford: Story of a University* (New York, 1959), pp. 211 ff.

[16] A. E. Tanner, "History of Clark University through the Interpretation of the Will of the Founder" (unpubl. MS in Clark U. Library); Edmund C. Stanford, "Life and Character of Mr. Clark," *Publications of Clark University Library,* VII (1924), 3–8.

[17] Until the forthcoming history of the University of Chicago by Richard J. Storr is available, the most useful accounts of the background of the founding are those in Allan Nevins, *Study in Power: John D. Rockefeller, Industrialist and Philanthropist* (New York, 1953), II, 156–96, and Thomas Wakefield Goodspeed, *A History of the University of Chicago Founded by John D. Rockefeller: The First Quarter Century* (Chicago, 1916).

[18] Thomas W. Goodspeed, *William Rainey Harper* (Chicago, 1928), Ch. IV; John D. Rockefeller, *Random Reminiscences of Men and Events* (New York, 1909), pp. 179–80.

[19] Abraham Flexner, *I Remember* (New York, 1940), p. 49.

[20] John C. French, *A History of the University Founded by Johns Hopkins* (Baltimore, 1946), pp. 74–75, 97–101, 371–73; Hawkins, pp. 187, 189, 316.

[21] David Starr Jordan, *The Story of a Good Woman: Jane Lathrop Stanford* (Boston, 1912); George Edward Crothers, *The Educational Ideals of Jane Lathrop Stanford, Co-Founder of the Leland Stanford Junior University* (San Francisco, 1933); Bertha Berner, *Mrs. Leland Stanford: An Intimate Account* (Stanford, Calif., 1935), *passim.*

[22] Orrin Leslie Elliott, *Stanford University: The First Twenty-Five Years* (Stanford, Calif., 1937), 251 ff.; George E. Crothers, "Historical Outline of

the Founding of Stanford," *Stanford Illustrated Review*, XXIII (n.d.); David Starr Jordan, *The Days of a Man* (Yonkers-on-Hudson, N.Y., 1922), I, 478–510.

[23] Hall, Ch. VII; Calvin Stebbins, "Rev. Calvin Stebbins's Address," *Publications of the Clark University Library*, I (1905), 138–60.

[24] Becker, *op. cit.* (above, fn. 9), pp. 39 ff., 111 ff.; Dorf, *op. cit.* (above, fn. 14) pp. 271 ff., 306 ff.; Andrew D. White, *Reminiscences of Ezra Cornell: An Address Delivered at Cornell University on January 11, 1890* (Ithaca, N.Y., 1890); Morris Bishop, *A History of Cornell* (Ithaca, N.Y., 1962), pp. 69 ff.; *Autobiography of Andrew D. White* (New York, 1907), I, 308 ff.; Walter P. Rogers, *Andrew D. White and the Modern University* (Ithaca, N.Y., 1942), *passim*.

[25] Bishop, p. 188.

[26] White, *Autobiography*, I, 373, 385, 402–6.

[27] Bishop, pp. 224–32; White, *Autobiography*, I, 419 ff.

[28] John Tebbel, *The Marshall Fields: A Study in Wealth* (New York, 1947), pp. 79–80; Box 15, Hanover Bank Philanthropy Collection, Manuscripts Room, Wisconsin State Historical Society, Madison; *Great Men Who Have Added to the Enlightenment of Mankind Through Endowed Professorships at the University of Chicago* (Chicago, n.d.); Goodspeed, *History*, Ch. X and pp. 173–76, 236–37, 307–13.

[29] Edwin Mims, *History of Vanderbilt University* (Nashville, 1946), *passim*; Wheaton J. Lane, *Commodore Vanderbilt: an Epic of the Steam Age* (New York, 1942), pp. 316 ff.

[30] Roderick Nash, "Anna Russell Cole, 1846–1926," to be published in *Notable American Women, 1607–1950: A Biographical Dictionary*, which Edward T. James is editing for Radcliffe College.

[31] William Preston Johnston, "Tulane University of Louisiana," in Edwin W. Fay, *The History of Education in Louisiana*, U.S. Bureau of Education Circular of Information, No. 1, 1898, Contributions to American Educational History, ed. Herbert B. Adams, No. 20 (Washington); Benjamin Brawley, *Doctor Dillard of the Jeanes Fund* (New York, 1930), p. 45.

[32] See above, p. 105.

[33] John W. Jenkins, *James B. Duke: Master Builder* (New York, 1927), pp. 231–78; William K. Boyd, *The Story of Durham: City of the South* (Durham, N.C., 1925), *passim*; Nora Campbell Chaffin, *Trinity College 1839–1892: the Beginnings of Duke University* (Durham, N.C., 1950), pp. 376–77, 396, 496.

[34] Ernest Seeman, "Duke: But Not Doris," *New Republic*, LXXXVIII (1936), 220–22; Ben Dixon MacNeill, "Duke," *American Mercury*, XVII (1929), 430–38. See also Horace Coon, *Money to Burn* (New York, 1938), pp. 181–86; Ernest V. Hollis, *Philanthropic Foundations and Higher Education* (New York, 1938), pp. 82–86; and Abraham Flexner, "Private Fortunes and the Public Future," *Atlantic Monthly*, CLVI (1935), 221.

[35] Henry M. Bullock, *A History of Emory University* (Nashville, 1936), p. 286.

[36] Charles Howard Candler, *Asa Griggs Candler* (Atlanta, 1950), pp. 357 ff.

[37] "Charles Howard Candler: An Obituary and an Appreciation," *The Emory Alumnus* (1957), pp. 4–9, 34–36.

[38] *Dictionary of American Biography*, XVII.

[39] M. P. Dowling, *Creighton University: Reminiscences of the First Twenty-five Years* (Omaha, Neb., 1903), pp. 45 ff.

[40] John Tracy Ellis, *The Formative Years of the Catholic University of America* (Washington, 1946), pp. 96 ff.

[41] Colman J. Barry, *The Catholic University of America, 1903–1909: the Rectorship of Denis J. O'Connell* (Washington, 1950), p. 107 ff.

[42] "The Founder: Remarks by Mr. William M. Rice, Jr.," *Rice Institute Pamphlet*, XVII (1930), 159; "Address by Capt. James A. Baker, Reminiscences of the Founder," *Rice Institute Pamphlet*, XVIII (1931), 127–44; *The Book of the Opening of the Rice Institute* (3 vols.; Houston, n.d.).

[43] Ron Moskowitz, "Houston's University," *Houston Post*, July 6–9, 1958; Ed Kilman and Theon Wright, *Hugh Roy Cullen: A Story of American Opportunity* (New York, 1954), pp. 305 ff.; *New York Times*, July 6, 1957.

[44] *New York Times*, Jan. 20, Feb. 2, 1926.

[45] Herbert C. Cornuelle, *"Mr. Anonymous": The Story of William Volker* (Caldwell, Idaho, 1951), pp. 169–72.

[46] *New York Times*, Dec. 7, 1956; *This Is Your College*, Fairleigh Dickinson College (Rutherford and Teaneck, N.J., n.d.), in Box 21, Hanover Bank Philanthropy Papers.

[47] *New York Times*, June 18, 1950; Israel Goldstein, *Brandeis University: Chapter of its Founding* (New York, 1951), *passim*.

[48] Richard Hofstadter and Walter P. Metzger, *The Development of Academic Freedom in the United States* (New York, 1955), pp. 468–506.

[49] Hall, *op. cit.* (above, fn. 11), p. 292.

[50] Hofstadter and Metzger, pp. 437–38.

[51] Elliott, *op. cit.* (above, fn. 21), pp. 340–41.

[52] Edward A. Ross, *Seventy Years of It* (New York, 1936), pp. 64–65; Jordan, *Days of a Man*, II, 3–4; Hofstadter and Metzger, pp. 438–42; Elliott, pp. 340 ff.

[53] S. Lawrence Bigelow, I. Leo Sharfman, and R. M. Wenley, "Henry Carter Adams," *Journal of Political Economy*, XXX (1922), 205; Henry Carter Adams, "The Labor Problem," Sibley College Lectures, XI, *Scientific American Supplement*, XXII (1886), 8861; E. R. A. Seligman, "Memorial to Former Professor Henry Carter Adams," *American Economic Review*, XII (1922), 405; Bishop, *op. cit.* (above, fn. 23), pp. 193, 217–22; Anita S. Goodstein, *Biography of a Businessman: Henry W. Sage* (Ithaca, N.Y., 1962), p. 245.

Adams refused to allow certain alumni to make a test case of his dismissal and accepted an invitation to join the faculty of the University of Michigan. In 1890 he declined a flattering offer, issued by a unanimous vote of the trustees, to return to Cornell.

For further discussion of the problems that arose when millionaires gave to higher education, including the infringement of academic freedom, see Walter P. Metzger, "College Professors and Big Business Men: A Study of American Ideologies, 1880–1915" (unpubl. diss., State University of Iowa, 1950), especially pp. 177 ff.

[54] Goodstein, pp. 221–46.

[55] Hofstadter and Metzger, pp. 421, 428 ff.

[56] John Spencer Bassett, "Trinity College and Academic Liberty," *South Atlantic Quarterly*, III (1904), 62–73; Paul Neff Garber, *John Carlisle Kilgo:*

President of Trinity College, 1894–1910 (Durham, N.C., 1937); John Franklin Crowell, *Personal Recollections of Trinity College, North Carolina, 1887–1894* (Durham, N.C., 1939).

[57] White, *Autobiography*, I, 413.

NOTES FOR CHAPTER VII

[1] See Ch. IX.

[2] The inaugural address is reprinted in *The Development of Harvard University since the Inauguration of President Eliot, 1869–1929,* ed. Samuel Eliot Morison (Cambridge, 1930), lix–lxxviii.

[3] See pp. 13–18.

[4] *Development of Harvard,* p. lxix.

[5] Charles W. Eliot, "Four Harvard Benefactors," *Harvard Alumni Bulletin,* XVI (March 18, 1914), 405; Morris Hadley, *Arthur Twining Hadley* (New Haven, Conn., 1948), p. 127.

[6] "Summary of Financial Statement," *Development of Harvard,* p. lxxxix.

[7] Henry A. Yeomans, *Abbott Lawrence Lowell, 1856–1943* (Cambridge, Mass., 1948), Ch. XIII.

[8] Robert de Forest to Mrs. Sage, April 5, 1911; Lowell to Mrs. Sage, Jan. 6, 1914; Lowell to Mrs. Sage, Oct. 31, 1914; Lowell to de Forest, May 30, 1914: Papers of Mrs. Russell Sage, Russell Sage Foundation, New York.

[9] Yeomans, p. 170.

[10] See pp. 148–49.

[11] George Wilson Pierson, *Yale College: An Educational History, 1871–1921* (New Haven, Conn., 1952), pp. 62–63.

[12] Timothy Dwight, *Memories of Yale Life and Men, 1854–1890* (New York, 1903), Chs. XVIII–XXV.

[13] Henry Seidel Canby, *Alma Mater: The Gothic Age of the American College* (New York, 1936), *passim.*

[14] John W. Burgess, *Reminiscences of an American Scholar: The Beginnings of Columbia University* (New York, 1934), pp. 161 ff.; John Fulton, *The Memoirs of Frederick A. P. Barnard* (New York, 1896), pp. 400 ff.

[15] Brander Matthews, *Four American Universities* (New York, 1895), pp. 197–98.

[16] Benjamin R. C. Low, *Seth Low* (New York, 1925), p. 64; *A History of Columbia College on Morningside Heights* (New York, 1954), pp. 166 ff.

[17] James E. Russell, *The Founding of Teachers College* (New York, 1937), pp. 8, 23 ff.; Abbie Graham, *Grace H. Dodge, Merchant of Dreams* (New York, 1926), pp. 175 ff.

[18] Nicholas Murray Butler, *Across the Busy Years* (New York, 1939–40), II, 442–43.

[19] *The Rise of a University: The University In Action From the Annual Reports of Nicholas Murray Butler, 1902–1935* (New York, 1937), II, 449–51.

[20] *The Life of James McCosh,* ed. W. M. Sloane (New York, 1896); Thomas Jefferson Wertenbaker, *Princeton, 1746–1896* (Princeton, N.J., 1946), pp. 378–90.

[21] *The Public Papers of Woodrow Wilson: College and State,* ed. Ray Stannard Baker and William E. Dodd (New York, 1925–1927), I, 443–61.

[22] Arthur Walworth, *Woodrow Wilson: American Prophet* (New York, 1958) I, Ch. VIII; Arthur S. Link, *Wilson: The Road to the White House* (Princeton, N.J., 1947), Ch. III.

[23] *Survey,* XXIII (Nov. 6, 1909), 167; XXIII (Nov. 27, 1909), 276–78; *New York Times,* Nov. 1, 1909.

[24] Joseph Bucklin Bishop, *A. Barton Hepburn: His Life and Service to His Time* (New York, 1923), pp. 156–58.

[25] *New York Times,* Jan. 6, 1959.

[26] Lawrence A. Cremin, David A. Shannon, and Mary E. Townsend, *A History of Teachers College, Columbia University* (New York, 1954), pp. 88, 91, 97.

[27] HUB 2434, 2510, Harvard University Archives, Cambridge, Mass.; Yeomans, *op. cit.* (above, fn. 7), pp. 231–35.

[28] See pp. 148–49.

[29] Jacob Schiff and Charles W. Eliot MSS in Harvard University Archives; Frieda Schiff Warburg, *Reminiscences of a Long Life* (New York, 1956), p. 69.

[30] *Bulletin of the Fogg Museum of Art,* I (1931), *passim.*

[31] Burgess, *op. cit.* (above, fn. 14), pp. 186–87.

[32] Edward Washburn Hopkins, *India Old and New* (New York, 1901), pp. 3–19.

[33] See, as examples: "Self-Made Men as Public Benefactors," *Nation,* IX (Nov. 11, 1869), pp. 406–7; "The College and the Professors," *Nation,* XXXII (Jan. 23, 1881), pp. 437–38; Bishop Clark, "Our Colleges," *Christian Union,* V (April 3, 1872), 298; Leonard W. Bacon, "A Direct Way to Christian Collegiate Education," *Christian Union,* XXVI (Oct. 12, 1882); *New York Tribune,* Nov. 29, 1893; J. A. Hobson, "Millionaire Endowments," *Living Age,* CCXLV (1905), 13–21.

[34] Lyman Hotchkiss Bagg, *Four Years at Yale by a Graduate of '69* (New Haven, Conn., 1871), pp. 597–99; Richard J. Storr, *The Beginnings of Graduate Education in America* (Chicago, 1953), p. 32.

[35] *New York Herald Tribune,* Oct. 28, 1951.

[36] *New York Times,* Feb. 18, 1913.

[37] *New York Times,* Dec. 31, 1942; Professor O. W. Eshbach to Merle Curti, Jan. 21, 1958.

[38] *New York Times,* Dec. 17, 1937.

[39] *Development of Harvard,* pp. 202–10; Wilmarth Lewis, *The Yale Collections* (New Haven, Conn., 1948), p. 29.

[40] Eliot, "Four Harvard Benefactors" (above, fn. 5), p. 405.

[41] W. L. R. Gifford, "Edward Mallinckrodt," *Harvard Alumni Bulletin,* XXVI (1924), 956–58.

[42] "Gordon McKay Gift to Practical Science: Perpetuation of His Name" (Harvard Archives, n.p., n.d.), pp. 29 ff.; Hennen Jennings, *The McKay Endowment and Applied Science at Harvard* (n.p., 1918). In a similar opinion the court held that the intentions of the 19th-century benefactors who had established and strengthened the Andover Theological Seminary as a buttress against liberalism would be thwarted if a union were effected between it and the Harvard Divinity School, a sensible proposal dear to Lowell's heart. The

failure of attempts to merge Harvard's specialized programs in engineering and theology with those of M.I.T. and the Andover Seminary emphasized the limitations involved in restricted gifts: Yeomans, *op. cit.* (above, fn. 7), pp. 259 ff.

[43] *New York Herald Tribune*, Jan. 30, 1932.

[44] George Harvey, *Henry Clay Frick, the Man* (New York, 1928), pp. 344–45.

[45] "The Harvey S. Firestone Memorial Library," *Princeton Alumni Weekly* (April 22, 1949), pp. 1–28.

[46] Abraham Flexner, *I Remember* (New York, 1940), pp. 356–80.

[47] Francis H. Stoddard, *The Life and Letters of Charles Butler* (New York, 1903), pp. 304–16.

[48] *New York Times*, Nov. 16, 1890; *New York Tribune*, Dec. 9, 1890; Jackson Guy, "The Fayerweather Will Litigation," *University of Virginia Alumni Bulletin*, IV n.s. (1904), 297–303.

[49] *New York Times*, Sept. 29, 1930, Oct. 25, 1934.

[50] *Boston Evening Globe*, July 20, 1931; *New York Times*, June 15, 1940.

[51] Mrs. Sarah W. Flannery to Merle Curti, Aug. 14, 1963; *New York Times*, June 8, 1939.

[52] *Christian Century*, XXVIII (Nov. 15, 1883), 427.

[53] *New York Herald Tribune*, Jan. 30, 1932.

[54] *New York Times*, Nov. 1, 1938; *New York Herald Tribune*, Oct. 7, 1947.

[55] Thus Mrs. Levy Mayer gave Northwestern $500,000 for a home for the law school and Mrs. Montgomery Ward contributed to the same institution $3,000,000 to be used for a medical center, the largest single gift made during the lifetime of the donor by a Chicago citizen: Estelle F. Ward, *The Story of Northwestern University* (New York, 1924), pp. 346–49.

[56] *New York Times*, Nov. 4, 5, 7, 14, 1918; Mrs. Russell Sage Papers, Russell Sage Foundation.

[57] *New York Herald Tribune*, Nov. 1, 1957.

[58] Blake McKelvey, *Rochester, The Flower City, 1855–1890* (Cambridge, Mass., 1949), pp. 313–15; Jesse L. Rosenberger, *Rochester: The Making of a University* (Rochester, N.Y., 1927), pp. 185 ff.; *Rochester Times-Union*, Aug. 6, 1934; Historical Subject File, Eastman Kodak Co., Rochester, N.Y.

[59] John R. Slater, *Rhees of Rochester* (New York, 1946), Chs. IX, X.

[60] Carl W. Ackerman, *George Eastman* (London, 1930), *passim*.

[61] Rhees to Eastman, April 3, 1904, Letters, Chronological File, 1904, George Eastman Papers, Eastman Kodak Co., Rochester, N.Y.

[62] Eastman to George B. Selden, March 18, 1904, Personal Letter Book 4, Eastman Papers.

[63] Eastman to Fran L. Babbott, June 27, 1908, Personal Letter Book 6, Eastman Papers.

[64] Eastman to Rhees, March 14, 1912, Personal Letter Book 5, Eastman Papers.

[65] Rhees to Eastman, Dec. 13, 1912, Letters, Chronological File, 1912, Eastman Papers.

[66] Eastman to Rhees, Feb. 14, 1919; Eastman to H. A. Strong, March 12, 1919; Eastman to Eugene Goosens, May 14, 1925; Eastman to Rhees, June 2, 1919, Personal Letter Books 12, 13, 14, Eastman Papers.

[67] Flexner, *op. cit.* (above, fn. 46), pp. 284–90.

[68] Rhees to Eastman, May 25, 1920; Rhees to Eastman, Aug. 15, 1920, Letters, Chronological File, 1920, Eastman Papers.

[69] Raymond B. Fosdick, *Adventures in Giving: The Story of the General Education Board* (New York, 1962), p. 169.

[70] Flexner, p. 288.

[71] Rhees to Eastman, Aug. 15, 1920, Letters, Chronological File, 1920; Eastman to Rhees, July 7, 1923, Eastman to McKim, Mead and White, July 18, 1923, Personal Letter Book 18, Eastman Papers.

[72] Eastman to Rhees, July 13, 1923, Personal Letter Book 18, Eastman Papers; Ackerman, pp. 440 ff.

[73] *St. Louis Globe-Democrat*, Jan. 7, 8, 1912; Hermann Hagedorn, *Brookings: A Biography* (New York, 1936), pp. 58–59, 122, 133 ff.

[74] [William Wilson Corcoran], *Grandfather's Legacy; Containing a Sketch of His Life and Obituary Notices of some Members of his Family, together with Letters from his Friends* (Washington, 1879), 472; Corcoran Collection, XIX, Div. of Manuscripts, Library of Congress; *Washington Post*, Feb. 25, 1888; *Evening Star*, Washington, Feb. 24, 1888.

[75] Sarah Bolton, *Famous Givers and Their Gifts* (New York, 1896), pp. 331 ff.

[76] Bishop, *op. cit.* (above, note 24), pp. 180–81. Hepburn gave almost $5,000,000 to higher education. His recipients included Princeton and Columbia as well as St. Lawrence University, Williams, Middlebury, and Wellesley, which his daughter attended. Barton favored the small college because it seemed freer than the large, privately endowed universities from "plutocratic" interference with educational programs and freer than the state universities from political pressure.

[77] John H. Harris, *Thirty Years as President of Bucknell* (Washington, 1926), pp. 11 ff.; Lewis E. Theiss, *Centennial History of Bucknell University, 1846–1946* (Williamsport, Pa., 1946), pp. 165 ff.

[78] See below, Ch. X, and Burton J. Hendrick, *Life of Andrew Carnegie* (Garden City, N.Y., 1932), II, 261.

[79] Edward F. Williams, *The Life of Dr. D. K. Pearsons: Friend of the Small College and of Missions* (New York, 1911), pp. 10 ff., 240; Edward D. Eaton, "Dr. Pearsons at Close Range," *The Congregationalist*, XCVII (1912), 649. Pearsons especially singled out for aid Whitman, Pomona, Lake Forest, Knox, Yankton, Beloit, Mount Holyoke, and Berea; he also generously supported the Chicago Theological Seminary, the Chicago Y.M.C.A., and the American Board of Commissioners for Foreign Missions. See also "A Giver who Gave All," *Literary Digest* (May 11, 1912), pp. 1003–5, and the *Chicago Evening Post*, April 27, 1912.

[80] *Endowment of the Terrell Professorship of Agriculture in the University of Georgia* (Athens, Ga., 1854), p. 4; *Men of Mark in Georgia*, ed. William T. Northern (Atlanta, Ga., 1907–12), II, 377; Albert L. Demaree, *The American Agricultural Press, 1819–1860* (New York, 1941), pp. 67, 363; Ellis M. Coulter to Merle Curti, Oct. 22, 1957.

[81] Wallace P. Reed, *History of Atlanta, Georgia* (Syracuse, N.Y., 1889), pp. 90–91.

[82] George Foster Peabody Papers, Subject File Peace-Philanthropy, Library of Congress.

[83] Burton Myers, *History of Indiana University* (Bloomington, Ind., 1940),

pp. 38 ff. In 1925 Ball Brothers gave $500,000 for the Riley Hospital, which was associated with the university. In 1931 James B. Nelson of Indianapolis gave $200,000 for an endowment for the teaching of philosophy, subsequently enlarged to $293,000.

[84] Box 114, Hanover Bank Philanthropy Collection, Manuscripts Room, Wisconsin State Historical Society, Madison; Bus Entsminger to Merle Curti, July 19, 1963.

[85] J. C. Penney, "The American Way," address before the Rotary Club of New York, Aug. 29, 1949, Box 118, Hanover Bank Collection; *New York Herald Tribune*, Sept. 7, 1952.

[86] *New York Times*, Nov. 13, 1938.

[87] James Marsh, *The Remains of the Rev. James Marsh, D.D.* (Boston, 1843), pp. 105–6, 108.

[88] James B. Angell, *The Reminiscences of James B. Angell* (New York, 1912), pp. 122–27.

[89] *Burlington Free Press*, Dec. 17, 1958, Jan. 21, 22, 1959, Jan. 25, 1961; *Montpelier Evening Argus*, Dec. 5, 1958.

[90] Kent Sagendorph, *Michigan: The Story of the University* (New York, 1948), pp. 38, 82, 87, 116, 148, 173, 174; Wilfred B. Shaw, "Support of the University of Michigan from Sources Other than Public Funds or Student Fees, 1817–1934," *University of Michigan Official Publication*, XXV (1934), 1–52; Wilfred B. Shaw, *Support of the University of Michigan from Sources Other than Public Funds or Student Fees, 1931–1939* (Ann Arbor, Mich., 1940), *passim*.

[91] *Horace H. Rackham and Mary A. Rackham Fund*, ed. Frances H. Miner (Ann Arbor, Mich., 1940); Sheridan W. Baker, Jr., *The Rackham Funds of the University of Michigan, 1933–1953* (Ann Arbor, Mich., 1955). Michigan State University, which had few private gifts in its early history, received in 1957 an impressive one from Mrs. Alfred B. Wilson, widow of a cofounder of the Dodge Brothers Motor Company. Mrs. Wilson gave an estate near Pontiac, Michigan, along with a cash endowment of $2,000,000 to underwrite construction of academic buildings. The gift was estimated to total $10,000,000; *New York Times*, Jan. 4, 1957.

[92] *New York Herald Tribune*, Feb. 20, 1951; Mablon M. Day, Head of the Mathematics Department, University of Illinois, to Merle Curti, July 5, 1963; H. R. Brahana, "George Abram Miller, 1863–1950," *National Academy of Sciences Biographical Memoirs*, XXX (1957), 257–312.

[93] William W. Ferrer, *Origin and Development of the University of California* (Berkeley, Calif., 1930), pp. 411–48.

[94] Lick, noted for eccentricity, did not marry and, except for a $150,000 legacy to a "natural" son, left his fortune to several institutions and charities, including the California Academy of Science and the Society of California Pioneers. For the story of the observatory see E. S. Holden, *A Brief Account of the Lick Observatory* (Sacramento, Calif., 1895).

[95] For an evaluation of the significance of Mrs. Hearst's support of ethnology and archaeology: *Phoebe Apperson Hearst Memorial Volume*, ed. Alfred L. Kroeber, University of California Publications in American Archaeology and Ethnology, XX (1923). See also Regent Winifred Black Bonfils, *The Life and Personality of Phoebe Apperson Hearst* (San Francisco, 1928), and *San Francisco Chronicle*, April 14, 1919.

⁹⁶ Ferrier, pp. 538–40.

⁹⁷ "Andrew McMicken," *The Biographical Cyclopedia and Portrait Gallery with an Historical Sketch of the State of Ohio* (Cincinnati, 1883–95), VI, 1520–21; Box 18, Hanover Bank Philanthropy Collection; John B. Shotwell, *A History of the Schools of Cincinnati* (Cincinnati, 1902), pp. 210–22.

⁹⁸ Alpheus T. Mason, *Brandeis: A Free Man's Life* (New York, 1946), pp. 587–93, 639.

⁹⁹ For example, Emanuel Boasberg in 1925 donated $100,000 to the University of Buffalo to establish a professorship in American history; *New York Times*, July 3, 1925.

¹⁰⁰ Elmer M. Kenyon, "Dangers and Drawbacks in Endowments," *Dial*, XXIX (1900), 47–48; Abraham Flexner, *Universities: American, English, German* (New York, 1930), p. 196.

¹⁰¹ James Bryce, *The American Commonwealth* (New York, 1909), II, 723.

¹⁰² In 1960 the Hanover Bank gave the entire collection of more than 100 file boxes to the University of Wisconsin History of Philanthropy Project. It is currently in the manuscripts division of the Wisconsin State Historical Society.

¹⁰³ Wheeler Sammons, Jr., Marquis-Who's Who, Inc., to Merle Curti, July 11, 1958.

¹⁰⁴ "Self Made Men as Benefactors," *The Nation*, IX (Nov. 11, 1869), 406–7.

¹⁰⁵ See pp. 97–99 and 120–21 for examples.

¹⁰⁶ Hobson, *loc. cit.* (above, note 33).

¹⁰⁷ Thorstein Veblen, *The Higher Learning in America: A Memorandum on the Conduct of Universities by Business Men* (New York, 1918), made the most incisive criticism on these lines.

¹⁰⁸ Flexner, *Universities*, pp. 196 ff. While most reviewers felt that Flexner overstated his thesis and failed to appreciate the relation of trends in higher education to specifically American needs, conditions, and characteristics, the general reaction was surprisingly favorable.

¹⁰⁹ "The Goose-Step and the Golden Egg," *New Republic*, XLI (1924), pp. 106–8.

NOTES FOR CHAPTER VIII

¹ Enough colleges admitted Negroes before 1860 to produce twenty-eight graduates with degrees. Avery College (1849), Ashmun Institute (1856)—later known as Lincoln University—in Pennsylvania, and Wilberforce University (1856) in Ohio were the first institutions devoted exclusively to Negroes. Avery received part of the estate of the Rev. Charles Avery, a Methodist minister and skillful investor, who bequeathed about $300,000 for the education and Christianization of the black race: Carter G. Woodson, *The Education of the Negro Prior to 1861* (New York, 1915), pp. 270–72; Leon F. Litwack, *North of Slavery: The Negro in the Free States, 1790–1860* (Chicago, 1961), pp. 139–52.

² As quoted in Horace Mann Bond, *The Education of the Negro in the American Social Order* (New York, 1934), p. 146.

[3] Augustus Field Beard, *A Crusade of Brotherhood* (Boston, 1909); Wesley A. Hotchkiss, "Congregationalists and Negro Education," *Journal of Negro Education*, XXIX (1960), 289–98; Dwight O. W. Holmes, *The Evolution of the Negro College*, Teachers College, Columbia University, Contributions to Education, No. 609 (New York, 1934), pp. 76–92.

[4] *Annual Report of the American Missionary Association, 1888* (New York), pp. 67–72.

[5] A. A. McPheeters, "Interest of the Methodist Church in the Education of Negroes," *Phylon*, X (1949), 343–50; Isaac E. Clarke, *Arts and Industry: Education in the Industrial and Fine Arts in the United States* (Washington, 1898), IV, 552–54; Lucius S. Merriam, *Higher Education in Tennessee*, U.S. Bureau of Education Circular of Information, No. 5, 1893, Contributions to American Educational History, ed. Herbert B. Adams, No. 16 (Washington), p. 272; Josiah H. Shinn, *History of Education in Arkansas*, U.S. Bureau of Education Circular of Information, No. 1, 1900, Cont. Am. Ed. Hist., No. 26 (Washington), p. 120.

[6] *Bulletin of Gammon Theological Seminary*, LXXIV (1957), 14–19; Charles S. Johnson, *The Negro College Graduate* (Chapel Hill, N.C., 1938), pp. 290–91.

[7] James S. Thomas, "The Rationale Underlying Support of Negro Private Colleges by the Methodist Church," *Journal of Negro Education*, XXIX (1960), 255; Holmes, p. 112.

[8] Ullin W. Leavell, *Philanthropy in Negro Education*, George Peabody College for Teachers Contributions to Education, No. 100 (Nashville, 1930), pp. 43–44.

[9] Edwin W. Fay, *The History of Education in Louisiana*, U.S. Bureau of Education Circular of Information, No. 1, 1898, Cont. Am. Ed. Hist., No. 20 (Washington), pp. 149–50.

[10] Willard Range, *The Rise and Progress of Negro Colleges in Georgia, 1865–1949* (Athens, Ga., 1951), pp. 49–53.

[11] For a fuller discussion see Amory Dwight Mayo, "The Work of Certain Northern Churches in the Education of the Freedman, 1861–1900," *Report of the Commissioner of Education, 1902* (Washington), I, 285–314, and George S. Dickerman, "History of Negro Education," and Julius H. Parmelee, "Freedmen's Aid Societies, 1861–1871," in Thomas Jesse Jones, *Negro Education: A Study of the Private Schools for Colored People in the United States*, I, U.S. Bureau of Education Bulletin, No. 38 (Washington, 1916), pp. 248–95.

[12] Edward T. Ware, "Higher Education of Negroes in the United States, *Annals of the American Academy of Political and Social Science*, XLIX (1913), p. 209; George R. Bentley, *A History of the Freedmen's Bureau* (Philadelphia, 1955).

[13] G. D. Pike, *The Jubilee Singers and their Campaign for Twenty Thousand Dollars* (Boston, 1873); Alphonso A. Hopkins, *The Life of Clinton Bowen Fisk* (New York, 1910), pp. 114–19.

[14] J. B. T. Marsh, *The Story of the Jubilee Singers* (London, 1878).

[15] Merriam, p. 264; Marsh, pp. 49–76; *The Story of Music at Fisk University* (n.p., n.d.).

[16] Francis Greenwood Peabody, *Education for Life: The Story of Hampton Institute* (Garden City, N.Y., 1919), p. 110.

[17] Edith Armstrong Talbot, *Samuel Chapman Armstrong: A Biographical*

Study (New York, 1904). See also *Report of the Hampton Normal and Agricultural Institute, 1874* (Hampton, Va.) for lists of donations entirely from Northern communities and in large part from New York, Boston, and Philadelphia.

[18] *Proceedings of the Trustees of the Peabody Education Fund From Their Organization on the 8th of February, 1867* (Boston, 1875), I, 3; Franklin Parker, "George Peabody: Founder of Modern Philanthropy" (unpubl. diss., George Peabody College, Nashville, 1956).

[19] Franklin Parker, "George Peabody's Influence on Southern Educational Philanthropy," *Tennessee Historical Quarterly,* XX (1961), 65–74; Daniel Coit Gilman, "Five Great Foundations," *Outlook,* LXXXVI (1907), 652; George D. Wilson, "The Contribution of the Educational Funds to Negro Higher Education," *A Century of Municipal Higher Education* (Chicago, 1937), pp. 312 ff.; Jabez L. M. Curry, *A Brief Sketch of George Peabody and a History of the Peabody Education Fund Through Thirty Years* (Cambridge, Mass., 1898).

[20] *Documents Relating to the Origin and Work of the Slater Trustees, 1882–1894,* Trustees of the John F. Slater Fund Occasional Papers, No. 1 (Baltimore, 1894); Benjamin Brawley, *Doctor Dillard of the Jeanes Fund* (New York, 1930), pp. 67 ff.

[21] *Documents of the Slater Trustees,* pp. 9–10; Leavall, *op. cit.* (above, fn. 9), pp. 64, 126; and Holmes, *op. cit.* (above, fn. 3), pp. 168, 170, present statistics on the Slater Fund's benefactions to higher education.

[22] George A. Wilcox, *A Sketch of the Life of Mr. Daniel Hand and of His Benefaction to the American Missionary Association for the Education of the Colored People in the Southern States of America* (New York, 1889); *Charleston News and Courier,* Oct. 7, 26, 1888; *Dictionary of American Biography,* VIII; Bond, *op. cit.* (above, fn. 2), p. 144.

[23] For the Jeanes Fund see Brawley, pp. 55 ff., and Will W. Alexander, *The Slater and Jeanes Funds: An Educator's Approach to a Difficult Social Problem,* Trustees of the John F. Slater Fund Occasional Papers, No. 28 (Washington, 1934).

[24] A more detailed discussion of the General Education Board and its support of higher education may be found on pp. 215–19 and 233.

[25] *The General Education Board: An Account of Its Activities, 1902–1914* (New York, 1915), p. 216. The definitive history, based on the uncompleted manuscript of Henry F. and Katherine Douglas Pringle, is Raymond B. Fosdick, *Adventure in Giving: The Story of the General Education Board* (New York, 1962).

[26] *Annual Report of the General Education Board, 1917–1918* (New York), pp. 84–85.

[27] Johnson, *op. cit.* (above, fn. 6), pp. 290–91, lists the larger gifts and their source.

[28] Vivid demonstration may be found in the Philanthropies File, George Foster Peabody Papers, Library of Congress, Washington, D.C., and in Jabez L. M. Curry, *Difficulties, Complications, and Limitations Connected with the Education of the Negro,* Trustees of the John F. Slater Fund Occasional Papers, No. 5 (Baltimore, 1895).

[29] *General Education Board: An Account,* pp. 205–8.

[30] Holmes, pp. 44–45. For a full treatment of Curry's thought see Merle

Curti, *Social Ideas of American Educators,* 2d ed. (Paterson, N.J., 1959), pp. 264–80. Jessie Pearl Rice, *J. L. M. Curry: Southerner, Statesman and Educator* (New York, 1949), pp. 87–121, discusses Curry's work with the Peabody Fund.

[31] John Hope Franklin, *From Slavery to Freedom* (New York, 1947), pp. 385. For further evidence see Harvey Lee Swint, *The Northern Teacher in the South, 1862–1870* (Nashville, 1941) and Yoshimitsu Ide, "The Significance of Richard Hathaway Edmunds and his *Manufacturers Record* in the New South" (unpubl. diss., U. of Fla., Gainesville, 1959), pp. 256 ff.

[32] Carter G. Woodson, *The Mis-Education of the Negro* (Washington, 1933), p. 24.

[33] Louis R. Harlan, *Separate and Unequal: Public School Campaigns and Racism in the Southern Seaboard States, 1901–1915* (Chapel Hill, N.C., 1958), p. 8; Lester W. Jones, "The Agent as a Factor in the Education of Negroes in the South," *Journal of Negro Education,* XIX (1950), 28–34; Bond, pp. 132–33; Charles H. Thompson, dean of the Graduate School, Howard University, to the authors, March 10, 1958.

[34] Fosdick, *op. cit.* (above, fn. 25), pp. 7, 80–87, 113–14, 324, evaluates the board's policy from a sympathetic viewpoint consistent with his position as its long-time president.

[35] Harlan, *passim,* asserts that the philanthropic agencies surrendered to the idea of white supremacy. For a more favorable assessment see Joseph C. Kiger, "The Large Foundations in Southern Education," *Journal of Higher Education,* XXVII (1956), 125–32, 172.

[36] Curti, pp. 288–309; Samuel R. Spencer, Jr., *Booker T. Washington and the Negro's Place in American Life* (Boston, 1959); interview with John Hope Franklin, Professor of History, University of Chicago, March 1, 1958.

[37] Booker T. Washington, *Up From Slavery: An Autobiography* (Garden City, N.Y., 1944), p. 178.

[38] W. E. Burghart DuBois to the authors, June 4, 1958; Curti, pp. 304–9; Francis L. Broderick, *W. E. B. DuBois: Negro Leader in a Time of Crisis* (Stanford, Calif., 1959).

[39] Jones, *op. cit.* (above, fn. 11), II (Bulletin No. 39, 1917), 16–18. The Jones survey was made possible by the bequest of Caroline Phelps Stokes of New York: Olivia Egleston Phelps Stokes, "The Story of Caroline Phelps Stokes" (MS in the possession of the Phelps-Stokes Fund, New York).

[40] *Annual Report of the General Education Board, 1918–1919,* pp. 55–56. Additional information on the board's policy was obtained in interviews with Frederick Douglass Patterson, president of the Tuskegee Institute, Feb. 26, 1958, and Charles H. Thompson, dean of the Graduate School of Howard University, March 10, 1958.

[41] Fosdick, pp. 190–93. While James Dalles Burrus was unable to match the Rockefeller benefactions in amount, his bequest of $100,000 to Fisk in 1929 must have been immensely satisfying. Burrus was Fisk's first graduate and the first Negro to receive a B.A. in the South: Thomas E. Jones, *Progress at Fisk University* (Nashville, 1930), p. 45; *New York Times,* July 2, 1927, Jan. 3, 1929.

[42] Fosdick, pp. 179–80, 328.

[43] The Julius Rosenwald Fund was established in 1917 for the "well-being of mankind" by the creator of the Sears, Roebuck mail-order business. In

the field of Negro higher education it followed the General Education Board's policy of supporting selected promising institutions, among which were Fisk, Meharry, Atlanta, and Dillard. The last named received more than $1,000,000: Edwin R. Embree, *Investment in People: The Story of the Julius Rosenwald Fund* (New York, 1949), *passim.*

[44] "Dillard University," *Quarterly Review of Higher Education Among Negroes,* I (1933), 47–48; Fosdick, pp. 205–7; Embree, pp. 97–100.

[45] Range, *op. cit.* (above, fn. 10), p. 196.

[46] Holmes, *op. cit.* (above, fn. 3), pp. 194–97; Fosdick, pp. 196–205.

[47] *Christian Advocate,* July 30, 1891; *Bulletin of Gammon Theological Seminary,* LXXIV (1957), 14–19.

[48] Woodson, *op. cit.* (above, fn. 32), p. 33.

[49] "Endowed by the Creator," *Report of the President of Talladega College, 1940–41,* pp. 9 ff.; Holmes, pp. 97–100; *Annual Report of the General Education Board, 1927–1928,* p. 24.

[50] Charles C. McCracken, "Results," *Quarterly Review of Higher Education Among Negroes,* IV (1936), 59; T. E. McKinney, "In Memoriam: Henry Lawrence McCrorey, 1863–1951," *Quarterly Review of Higher Education Among Negroes,* XIX (1951), 171–73; Holmes, p. 133.

[51] John K. Winkler, *Tobacco Tycoon: The Story of James Buchanan Duke* (New York, 1942), p. 294–95; *New York Times,* Dec. 9, 1924.

[52] Eastman to Rosenwald, May 22, 1913, Personal Letter Book 8, George Eastman Papers, Eastman Kodak Co., Rochester, N.Y.

[53] Hampton misc. leaflets, Wisconsin State Historical Society, Madison, Wis.; *New York Times,* Dec. 9, 19, 28, 1924, Dec. 31, 1925.

[54] *Annual Report of the General Education Board, 1931–1932,* p. 34; *Annual Report of the General Education Board, 1932–1933,* p. 16; *Annual Report of the General Education Board, 1933–1934,* p. 37; D. O. W. Holmes, "The Negro College Faces the Depression," *Journal of Negro Education,* II (1933), 16–25; Henry G. Badger, "Finances of Negro Colleges, 1929–1939," *Journal of Negro Education,* IX (1940), 162–70.

[55] Fosdick, pp. 266, 329–32.

[56] Charles H. Thompson, "The Critical Situation in Negro Higher and Professional Education," *Journal of Negro Education,* XV (1946), 579–84.

[57] William J. Trent, Jr., "The Problems of Financing Private Negro Colleges," *Journal of Negro Education,* XVIII (1949), 115.

[58] It was also expected that the Southern states would aid Negro higher education as a result of the Gaines case in 1938, in which the Supreme Court ruled that state governments were required to provide educational facilities for Negroes equal to those for whites or else admit Negroes to the white institutions. As a direct result of the decision Missouri appropriated $200,000 for Negro graduate and professional education and Alabama began giving Tuskegee an annual grant of $100,000, which was later raised to $225,000: W. Sherman Savage, "The Influence of the Gaines Case on Negro Education in the Post-War Period," *Quarterly Review of Higher Education Among Negroes,* XI (1943), 1–5; *New York Times,* June 27, 1943, Nov. 9, 1948.

[59] United Negro College Fund, *The Biography of an Idea* (n.p., n.d.); Calvin H. Ravellerson, U.N.C.F., to the authors, April 11, 1958; Charles H. Wesley, president of Central State College, Wilberforce, Ohio, to the authors, March 6, 1958; Charles H. Thompson, dean of the Graduate School, Howard

University, to the authors, March 10, 1958; interview with Frederick Douglas Patterson, president of the Tuskegee Institute, Feb. 26, 1958.

[60] Charles H. Thompson, "The Control and Administration of the Negro College," *Journal of Educational Sociology*, XIX (1946), pp. 484–95.

[61] Fosdick, pp. 210–11, 329–32.

[62] National chairmen included Walter Hoving, president of Lord and Taylor (1944); Frank M. Totton, vice-chairman of Chase National Bank (1948); John R. Suman, vice-president and director of the Standard Oil Co. of New Jersey (1949); and Charles D. Jackson of *Fortune* and *Time* (1952 and 1953). The advisory committee numbered such men as Harvey S. Firestone, Jr., David Dubinsky, Charles E. Hughes, Jr., and John D. Rockefeller, Jr. The New York women's committee, which Mrs. Chauncey L. Waddell, daughter of former Chief Justice Charles Evans Hughes, headed, included Mrs. Clare Booth Luce, Mrs. Theodore Roosevelt, Jr., and Miss Cornelia Otis Skinner. The tradition of Northern white philanthropy to the Southern Negro was continued in the United Negro College Fund. During the first three years Negroes contributed only 13% of the fund's total: *New York Times*, March 8, July 13, 1947. However, Negroes controlled the administration of the funds as never before.

[63] William J. Trent, Jr., "The United Negro College Fund," *Journal of Negro Education*, XIV (1945), 115–17; Trent, "Cooperative Fund Raising for Higher Education," *Journal of Negro Education*, XXIV (1955), 11; Trent, "The Relative Adequacy of Sources of Income of Negro Church-Related Colleges," *Journal of Negro Education*, XXIX (1960), 362–63; *New York Times*, March 4, 1946, Jan. 25, 1947, April 2, 1961.

[64] *New York Times*, May 16, 20, 1945.

[65] *New York Times*, April 1, 1947.

[66] Trent, "Cooperative Fund Raising," p. 11.

[67] *New York Times*, Nov. 30, Dec. 4, 1947.

[68] *New York Times*, March 6, 1951.

[69] Carnegie Corporation of New York, *Report of Officers for the Fiscal Year Ended September 30, 1952* (New York), p. 20.

[70] William J. Trent, executive director of the U.N.C.F., to the authors, July 2, 1963.

NOTES FOR CHAPTER IX

[1] *Gifts and Bequests to Dartmouth College in the Amount of $5,000 or More* (Hanover, N.H., 1956), p. 5.

[2] William Graham Sumner, "The 'Ways and Means' for our Colleges," *Nation* (Sept. 8, 1870), pp. 153–54.

[3] James B. Angell, *Selected Addresses* (New York, 1912), pp. 25–26.

[4] Quoted in Trevor Arnett, *Recent Trends in Higher Education in the United States*, General Education Board Occasional Paper, No. 13 (New York, 1940), pp. 27–28.

[5] *The Dartmouth*, IV (1883), p. 329.

[6] Canby, *Alma Mater, The Gothic Age of the American College* (New York, 1936), pp. 223 ff.

[7] Tucker, *My Generation: An Autobiographical Interpretation* (Boston, 1919), pp. 321–23.

[8] Box 16, Hanover Bank Philanthropy Collection, Manuscripts Room, Wisconsin State Historical Society, Madison.

[9] Stanley King, *A History of the Endowment of Amherst College* (Amherst, Mass., 1950), pp. 186–87, 194.

[10] King, pp. 130, 143, 151–53, 164–66; *New York Times*, April 5, 13, 1929.

[11] Tucker, pp. 319 ff.; *New York Times*, Oct. 4, 1913; Leon Burr Richardson, *History of Dartmouth College* (Hanover, N.H., 1932), pp. 685 ff., 772.

[12] *New York Herald Tribune*, March 3, 1947, May 5, 1951, June 17, 1955; *New York Times*, Oct. 22, 1948.

[13] Philip Jessup, *Elihu Root* (New York, 1938), II, 486; *New York Times*, July 20, 1941.

[14] *New York Times*, Dec. 7, 1947; *New York Herald Tribune*, Jan. 24, 1948.

[15] *Who's Who in America*, 26th edition (1950–1951), p. 3211.

[16] *New York Times*, June 9, 1929, May 21, 1958.

[17] *Who's Who in America*, 27th edition (1952–1953), p. 2077; *New York Times*, Jan. 17, 1951; Box 122, Hanover Bank Philanthropy Collection.

[18] *Reports of the President and of the Treasurer of Swarthmore College, 1956–1957* (Swarthmore, Pa., 1957), pp. 25–26.

[19] Carnegie Corporation of New York, *Report of the President, the Secretary and the Treasurer for the Year Ended September 30, 1943*, pp. 34–35; Dr. Algo D. Henderson to Merle Curti, Dec. 24, 1957; *Journal of the National Education Association of the United States*, XXVIII (1939), 61.

[20] Bettis A. Garside, *One Increasing Purpose: The Life of Henry Winters Luce* (New York, 1948), p. 186; "Charles Martin Hall," *Dictionary of American Biography*, VIII; *New York Times*, Dec. 28, 1914.

[21] *New York Times*, April 9, 1939; *Who's Who in America*, 21st edition (1940), p. 17.

[22] George Wilson Pierson, *Yale College: an Educational History, 1871–1921* (New Haven, Conn., 1952), p. 371; John A. Garver, *John William Sterling: A Biographical Sketch* (New Haven, Conn., 1929), p. 106.

[23] HU B2602, Harvard University Archives, Cambridge, Mass.; *Christian Science Monitor*, March 23, 1928; *New York Times*, March 14, 1947.

[24] *New York Tribune*, Feb. 16, 1880; Henry A. Yeomans, *Abbott Lawrence Lowell, 1856–1943* (Cambridge, Mass., 1948), p. 248.

[25] Yeomans, pp. 184 ff.; *New York Herald Tribune*, Jan. 30, 1940; HU B2447Z, Harvard Archives; *Harvard Alumni Bulletin*, XXXI (1928), pp. 187–91; *Yale Alumni Weekly*, XLIII (1933), p. 280.

[26] Bliss Perry, *Life and Letters of Henry Lee Higginson* (Boston, 1921), pp. 327 ff.

[27] *New York Times*, July 8, 1956.

[28] Garver, pp. 110 ff.; Pierson, p. 371n. The Sterling philanthropy almost doubled Yale's resources.

[29] Edward Potts Cheyney, *History of University of Pennsylvania* (Philadelphia, 1940), p. 337; *Dictionary of American Biography*, VIII.

[30] *New York Times*, Jan. 6, Feb. 19, 1959.

[31] *New York Times*, Nov. 29, 1952.

[32] *Letters and Recollections of Alexander Agassiz with a Sketch of His Life and Work*, ed. George R. Agassiz (Boston, 1913), pp. 127 ff., 399.

[33] *New York Times,* May 5, 1963.

[34] James K. Finch, *A History of the School of Engineering, Columbia University* (New York, 1954), p. 104.

[35] *New York Times,* June 24, 1937.

[36] See pp. 73–75 and 218–19.

[37] Box 122, Hanover Bank Philanthropy Collection.

[38] *New York Times,* May 31, 1950.

[39] *New York Herald Tribune,* March 3, 1944; Carnegie Corporation, *Annual Report, 1937* (New York), p. 39.

[40] Samuel Eliot Morison, *The Development of Harvard University, since the Inauguration of President Eliot, 1869–1929* (Cambridge, Mass., 1930), p. 449.

[41] Wilmarth S. Lewis, *The Yale Collections* (New Haven, Conn., 1946), p. 15 ff.; *Yale College: A Sketch of its History,* ed. William L. Kingsley (New York, 1879), I, 140 ff.

[42] *Harvard Graduates Magazine,* XV (1906), 21–27.

[43] John Tasker Howard, *Our American Music: Three Hundred Years of It* (New York, 1931), pp. 395–402. The lectures MacDowell gave at Columbia were in part published in *Critical and Historical Essays* (New York, 1912). See also Lawrence Gilman, *Edward MacDowell: A Study* (New York, 1909).

[44] *New York Herald Tribune,* Nov. 30, 1952. Thomas N. McCarter of Newark gave Princeton $25,000 for a well-equipped theater, while a Yale alumnus made it possible for his alma mater to develop a department of theater presided over by George P. Baker, who had developed this work at Harvard but who found little support from President Lowell or Harvard alumni.

[45] A. S. W. Rosenbach, *A Catalog of the Books and Manuscripts of Harry Elkins Widener* (Philadelphia, 1918).

[46] The Houghton Library housed rare books and manuscripts. The Lamont, built and stocked at a cost of $1,500,000, was designed for undergraduate study. It represented only a small part of Lamont's gifts to Harvard, which by 1949 reached $5,000,000: Robert W. Lovett, "The Undergraduate and the Harvard Library, 1877–1937," *Harvard Library Bulletin,* I (1947), 221–37.

[47] Dumbarton Oaks Research Library and Collection, *Bulletin,* I (1950); *New York Times,* Nov. 3, 1950.

[48] *New York Times,* June 7, 1931, Nov. 26, 1932; Wilfred B. Shaw, "Support of the University of Michigan from Sources Other Than Public Funds or Student Fees, 1817–1934," *University of Michigan Official Publication,* XXV (1934), 1–52.

[49] *New York Times,* May 11, 1929; *Science,* LXIX (1929), 519; Box 113, Hanover Bank Philanthropy Collection.

[50] *New York Times,* Nov. 26, 1927; Paul H. Price, Director, Geological and Economic Survey, and State Geologist of West Virginia, to Merle Curti, July 17, 1963.

[51] Ernest T. Stewart, Jr., "Alumni Support and Annual Giving, "*Annals of the American Academy of Political and Social Science,* CCCI (1955), 129.

[52] *Gifts and Endowments to the University of Wisconsin, 1865–1931,* Bulletin of the University of Wisconsin, No. 1851 (Madison, Wis., 1932), *passim;* Charles R. Van Hise, "William Freeman Vilas and the University," *Wisconsin Alumni Magazine,* X (1908), 83; *Wisconsin Alumnus,* LXI (1960), 19.

[53] The authors are indebted to Dr. E. B. Fred, former president of the University of Wisconsin, for access to his unpublished history of WARF and

to Gail Bremer for her unpublished study of philanthropy to Wisconsin. See also *Wisconsin Alumnus,* XLI (1948), 21–22.

⁵⁴ Merle Curti and Vernon Carstensen, *The University of Wisconsin: A History, 1848–1925* (Madison, Wis., 1949), II, 224–28.

⁵⁵ *New York Times,* March 16, 1956.

⁵⁶ For example, Thomas Davies Jones, Princeton '76, a prominent Chicago lawyer and capitalist, having contributed generously to endowment while he was living, left $500,000 at his death in 1930 for improving Princeton salaries: *New York Times,* Sept. 28, 1930.

⁵⁷ Hanover Bank of New York, *Philanthropy and the College* (New York, ca. 1955). The replies of the presidents to the bank's query are in Box 124, Hanover Bank Philanthropy Collection.

⁵⁸ Some donors who favored more than one college did so because they had taken a second degree at another institution or had been given honorary degrees elsewhere. Sometimes religious commitments influenced diversified giving. John W. Hamilton, a bishop of the Methodist Episcopal Church, left his alma mater, Mount Union College, $200,000 and the same amount each to American University, the University of Southern California, and the College of the Pacific, all church-connected institutions. The fact that a spouse had graduated from an institution other than one's own also explained some instances of diversified giving. Business connections as well as family considerations and academic loyalties also were in the picture. Thus James A. Gray, a graduate of the University of North Carolina and an executive officer of the R. J. Reynolds Company, in 1947 gave gifts ranging from $25,000 to $900,000 in the form of common stock of his company to eleven North Carolina colleges. Similar associations led William R. Perkins, attorney for the Duke tobacco interests, to will $150,000 to Washington and Lee, his alma mater, and the same amount to Duke University, of which he was a trustee. Edward Harkness, it will be recalled, gave munificently not only to Yale, his alma mater, but to Harvard and other institutions as well.

⁵⁹ Donald E. Smith, "A Short History of Private Educational Philanthropy," Box 15, Hanover Bank Philanthropy Collection.

⁶⁰ *Boston Globe,* June 14, 1963.

⁶¹ William Lawrence, *Memories of a Happy Life* (New York, 1926), pp. 215–16.

⁶² George A. Brakely, "Higher Education Endowments: Their Past and Future from the Point of View of Fund-Raising Methods," *Association of American Colleges Bulletin,* XX (1934), 262–78; Irene H. Gerlinger, "College and University Financing," *Association of American Colleges Bulletin,* XXV (1939), 426–27; Stewart, p. 125.

⁶³ Association of Alumni Secretaries, *Report of the First Conference* (Ann Arbor, 1913), *passim,* and subsequent reports, along with the *American Alumni Council News,* tell the story.

⁶⁴ Scott M. Cutlip, *Fund-Raising in the United States: Its Role in America's Philanthropy* (New Brunswick, N.J., 1965) discusses these developments in detail.

⁶⁵ John Price Jones to Thomas Nelson Perkins, Sept. 20, 1919, John Price Jones Collection, Baker Library, Harvard Graduate School of Business Administration, Cambridge, Mass.

⁶⁶ "John Price Jones Corporation History," John Price Jones Collection; *Report of the Seventh Conference of the Association of Alumni Secretaries*

(Bethlehem, Pa., 1920), pp. 89–95. See David McCord, "The Harvard Fund," *Report of the Seventeenth Annual Conference of the American Alumni Council* (Ithaca, N.Y., 1930), pp. 116–25 for the way in which the Harvard Fund developed from the Harvard Endowment Fund campaign of 1919.

[67] "John Price Jones Corporation History"; Cutlip, Ch. VII.

[68] *Ibid.*

[69] John Price Jones, "College Endowment Campaigns," *Report of the Tenth Annual Conference of the Association of Alumni Secretaries* (Ithaca, N.Y., 1923), pp. 98–103.

[70] Box 14, Hanover Bank Philanthropy Collection; *New York Times,* April 5, Nov. 5, 1933; *New York Herald Tribune,* June 27, 1933.

[71] *New York Herald Tribune,* Oct. 1, Dec. 3, 1939; Harry J. Casey, Jr., "Objectives of the 75th Anniversary Fund Endowment," reprinted from *Goucher Alumnae Quarterly* (1958), in Box 21, Hanover Bank Philanthropy Collection.

[72] *"Now Press You On": The Story of a Program for Harvard College* (ca. 1957), in Box 21, Hanover Bank Philanthropy Collection; *Newsletter: A Program for Harvard College,* Jan. 1959, May, 1959; *New York Times,* June 13, 1958, June 12, 1959; "The Program—What Actually Happened," *Harvard Alumni Bulletin,* LXII (1960), *passim.*

[73] Stewart, pp. 123–25; Vanderbilt University Pamphlet, Box 31, Hanover Bank Philanthropy Collection; American Alumni Council, *Bulletin of Information and Memberships List, 1957–1958,* Box 14, Hanover Bank Philanthropy Collection; *Association of Alumni Secretaries and Magazines 1921 Convention* (Columbus, Ohio, 1921), p. 76; *Report of the Ninth Annual Conference of the Association of Alumni Secretaries* (Ithaca, N.Y., 1922), pp. 117 ff.

[74] The report of the Harvard College Fund for 1962–63, a year in which receipts from alumni slumped more than $1,000,000 behind Yale, printed below the comparative statistics an anonymous reaction: "It was something of a shock to read that the Fund ranked below Yale. Harvard is too important to be anything less than first." Harvard College Fund, *37th Annual Report, 1962–1963* (n.p., 1963), p. 4.

[75] *New York Herald Tribune,* Aug. 10, 1951; *School and Society,* LXXVII (1953), 251; *American Alumni Council News,* April, 1957; *New York Times,* Jan. 10, 1958; American Alumni Council, *Annual Giving and Alumni Support, 1960–1961* (Washington, 1962), p. 3

[76] John D. Millett, *Financing Higher Education in the United States* (New York, 1952), pp. 306 ff.; Stewart, p. 129.

[77] Ernest T. Stewart, Jr., "Philanthropy and the College," *School and Society,* LXXXVI (1958), p. 44.

[78] Stewart, "Alumni Support," p. 133.

[79] Harold Flack, "The Cornell University Bequest Program," *Association of American Colleges Bulletin,* XVIII (1932), 313–16; Thomas A. Gonser, "The Story of Some Colleges," *Association of American Colleges Bulletin,* XIX (1933), 218–20; Neal Dow Becker, "Successful Financing Through Wills," *Association of American Colleges Bulletin,* XIX (1933), 214–17; Archie M. Palmer, "Cultivating 'Will-ful' Giving," *Educational Record,* XVIII (1937), 107–24.

[80] *School and Society,* XVI (1935), 795; *Association of American Colleges Bulletin,* XX (1934), 310–12.

[81] Council for Financial Aid to Education, *Guide Lines to Voluntary Support*

of American Higher Education, Supplemental Report, No. 2 (New York, 1963), pp. 11, 23.
⁸² C.F.A.E., *1962–1963 Voluntary Support of America's Colleges and Universities* (New York, 1964), p. 4.

NOTES FOR CHAPTER X

¹ See below, Ch. XI; F. Emerson Andrews, *Corporation Giving* (New York, 1952), pp. 101–12; Frank M. Andrews, *A Study of Company-Sponsored Foundations* (New York, 1960).

² John D. Rockefeller, *Random Reminiscences of Men and Events* (New York, 1909), p. 147.

³ Allan Nevins, *John D. Rockefeller: The Heroic Age of American Enterprise* (New York, 1940), II, 148.

⁴ *The Foundation Directory*, ed., Ann D. Walton and F. Emerson Andrews (New York, 1960), lists many of them along with their fields of activity.

⁵ Allan Nevins, *Study in Power: John D. Rockefeller, Industrialist and Philanthropist* (New York, 1953) I, 31, 340, II, 91.

⁶ *The General Education Board: An Account of Its Activities, 1902–1914* (New York, 1915), p. 216.

⁷ See above, pp. 172–73.

⁸ Rockefeller, p. 165.

⁹ Rockefeller, pp. 159–60.

¹⁰ See above, pp. 116–17.

¹¹ The authoritative history of the founding and work of the General Education Board, based on the uncompleted manuscript of Henry F. and Katherine Douglas Pringle, is Raymond B. Fosdick, *Adventure in Giving: The Story of the General Education Board* (New York, 1963).

¹² *General Education Board: An Account*, pp. 218–19.

¹³ *Ibid.*, pp. 109, 111.

¹⁴ *Ibid.*, pp. 116, 119.

¹⁵ Fosdick, p. 130.

¹⁶ *General Education Board: An Account*, pp. 119–42.

¹⁷ Fosdick, p. 133.

¹⁸ *General Education Board: An Account*, p. 143. A complete listing of the grants, which averaged about $100,000, and the supplemental sums raised by the colleges appears on pp. 155–59.

¹⁹ John S. Brubacher and Willis Rudy, *Higher Education in Transition* (New York, 1958), pp. 360–67; Ernest Victor Hollis, *Philanthropic Foundations and Higher Education* (New York, 1938), pp. 44, 127 ff., 268 ff.

²⁰ *Annual Report of the General Education Board, 1925–26* (New York), p. 3.

²¹ Abraham Flexner, *Medical Education in the United States and Canada*, Carnegie Foundation for the Advancement of Teaching Bulletin, No. 4 (New York, 1910), and Flexner's *I Remember* (New York, 1940), pp. 113–32, give his own account of preparing the report.

²² Fosdick, *Adventure in Giving*, pp. 150–72; Raymond B. Fosdick, *The Story of the Rockefeller Foundation* (New York, 1952), pp. 93–104; *General Education Board: An Account*, pp. 160–72.

[23] See pp. 155–57.

[24] Hollis, pp. 209–12; Fosdick, *Adventure in Giving*, pp. 166–73.

[25] Abraham Flexner, *Funds and Foundations: Their Policies Past and Present* (New York, 1952), p. 126.

[26] "Wealth," *North American Review*, CXLVIII (1889), 653–64. For an expanded discussion of the philanthropy of wealthy Americans at this time, in part to higher education, see Merle Curti, Judith Greene, and Roderick Nash, "Anatomy of Giving: Millionaires in the Late 19th Century," *American Quarterly*, XV (1963), 416–35.

[27] Carnegie, *op. cit.*, and Carnegie, "The Best Fields for Philanthropy," *North American Review*, CXLIX (1889), 682–98. See also Burton J. Hendrick, *The Life of Andrew Carnegie* (New York, 1932), I, 330–51.

[28] *Autobiography of Andrew Carnegie* (Boston, 1920), p. 268.

[29] Howard J. Savage, *Fruit of an Impulse: Forty-five Years of the Carnegie Foundation, 1905–1950* (New York, 1953), pp. 3 ff.; Theron F. Schlabach, *Pensions for Professors* (Madison, Wis., 1963), pp. 1–17; Robert M. Lester, *Forty Years of Carnegie Giving* (New York, 1941), pp. 45–50, 152–60.

[30] Hollis, pp. 53–57, 129–36; Robert L. Duffus, *Democracy Enters College* (New York, 1936), *passim;* Savage, pp. 102–4.

[31] Hollis, pp. 136–41; Abraham Flexner, *Henry S. Pritchett: A Biography* (New York, 1943), *passim.*

[32] Warren Akin Candler, *Dangerous Donations and Degrading Doles* (Atlanta, Ga., 1909).

[33] J. McKeen Cattell, *Carnegie Pensions* (New York, 1919), is a compilation of this variety of criticism.

[34] Schlabach's *Pensions for Professors* is a superb presentation of the Carnegie Foundation's relation with the public universities.

[35] Hans Zinser, "The Perils of Magnanimity: A Problem in American Education," *Atlantic Monthly*, CLIX (1927), 246–50.

[36] Carnegie, "Wealth," p. 655.

[37] Schlabach, pp. 49, 86–91.

[38] Henry S. Pritchett, *A Comprehensive Plan of Insurance and Annuities for College Teachers*, Carnegie Foundation for the Advancement of Teaching Bulletin, No. 9 (New York, 1916). Horace Coon, *Money to Burn: What the Great American Philanthropic Foundations Do With Their Money* (New York, 1938), pp. 177 ff., criticizes Pritchett's early policy and discusses his change. Pensions have remained the major interest of the Carnegie Foundation. As of the present time about $75,000,000 of the foundation's money has been put into the program to swell the payments of professors and the colleges: Carnegie Foundation for the Advancement of Teaching, *Fifty-seventh Annual Report, 1961–62* (New York), and previous reports tell the story.

[39] Palmer O. Johnson, "Educational Research and Statistics: The Benefactions of Philanthropic Foundations and Who Receive Them," *School and Society*, XXXV (1932), 264–68.

[40] Dalo O. Patterson and Malcolm M. Willey, "Philanthropic Foundations and Their Grants to Institutions of Higher Education During the Depressed Years," *School and Society*, XLV (1937), 661–64; Ernest V. Hollis, "Are You Seeking Foundation Aid?", *School and Society*, LII (1940), 1–4.

[41] Fosdick, *Adventure in Giving*, pp. 140–49.

[42] Lester, *op. cit.* (above, fn. 29), p. 166.

[43] *Ibid.*, pp. 57–63; Robert M. Lester, *Review of Grants to Colleges and*

Universities in the United States, 1911–1932, Carnegie Corporation of New York Review Series, No. 12 (New York, 1933); Carnegie Endowment for International Peace, *A Manual of the Public Benefactions of Andrew Carnegie* (Washington, 1919), pp. 201–14.

[44] Lester, *Carnegie Giving*, p. 166.

[45] Carnegie Corporation of New York, *Report of the Acting President for the Year Ended September 30, 1922* (New York), p. 38; Carnegie Corporation, *Report*, 1931, p. 12. The titles of the reports vary slightly over the years and will hereafter be cited as *Report*.

[46] Carnegie Corporation, *Report*, 1923, p. 55; 1928, p. 19.

[47] Carnegie Corporation, *Report*, 1926, p. 23; 1939, p. 16.

[48] Carnegie Corporation, *Report*, 1932, p. 30; 1931, p. 19; 1926, pp. 15 ff.; Central Hanover Bank and Trust Company, *The Fine Arts in Philanthropy* (New York, 1937), pp. 17 ff.; *Appreciations of Frederick Paul Keppel by Some of His Friends* (New York, 1951), pp. 60 ff.

[49] Carnegie Corporation, *Report*, 1929, p. 12; 1936, pp. 26 ff.; Thomas R. Barcus, *Carnegie Corporation and College Libraries, 1938–1943* (New York, 1943).

[50] Carnegie Corporation, *Report*, 1930, p. 11; 1939, pp. 48–49. For a complete listing of corporation grants from 1911 to 1941 see Robert M. Lester, *A Thirty Year Catalog of Grants* (New York, 1942). Of a more specialized nature is Carnegie Corporation of New York, *Summary of Grants in Education During the Period January 1, 1913 to December 31, 1931*, Carnegie Corporation of New York Review Series, No. 5 (New York, 1932).

[51] Hollis, *Philanthropic Foundations*, p. 153.

[52] *Ibid.*, p. 61; Carnegie Corporation, *Report*, 1935, p. 33; 1938, pp. 31 ff.

[53] Fosdick, *Adventure in Giving*, pp. 230 ff., 262.

[54] *Ibid.*, pp. 236–37; Fosdick, *Rockefeller Foundation*, pp. 238 ff.; Carnegie Corporation, *Report*, 1932, pp. 25–26.

[55] Merle Curti, *American Philanthropy Abroad: A History* (New Brunswick, N.J., 1963), pp. 227 ff., discusses in detail its overseas activities.

[56] Fosdick, *Rockefeller Foundation*, pp. 152–64, 172–77, 192–239; *The Rockefeller Foundation: A Condensed Record of Activities from 1913 to 1963* (New York, 1963), *passim;* Rockefeller Foundation, *Annual Report, 1936* (New York), pp. 33 ff.

[57] Howard J. Savage *et al.*, *American College Athletics*, Carnegie Foundation for the Advancement of Teaching Bulletin, No. 23 (New York, 1929); *New York Times*, March 10, 1924.

[58] Savage, *Fruit of an Impulse*, pp. 161–62, 217 ff., 221 ff., 286 ff.

[59] G. Harold Duling, "Giving Away Money is a Difficult Job," *Association of American Colleges Bulletin*, XLII (1956), 73–77.

[60] *The Commonwealth Fund: Historical Sketch, 1918–1962* (New York, 1962), pp. 113–22.

[61] Kresge Foundation, *The First Thirty Years, 1924–1953* (Detroit, 1954), *passim;* Howard C. Baldwin, "The Work and Policies of the Kresge Foundation," *Association of American Colleges Bulletin*, XLII (1956), 68–72.

[62] "The Foundations and the Universities," *Journal of Higher Education*, XI (1940), pp. 178, 230.

[63] Carnegie Corporation, *Report*, 1937, pp. 42, 37.

[64] Carnegie Corporation, *Report*, 1941, pp. 43–44.

[65] Carnegie Corporation, *Report*, 1944, pp. 16–17; 1948, pp. 23–24.

[66] The most widely read criticisms of the foundations were Eduard C. Lindeman, *Wealth and Culture: A Study of One Hundred Foundations and Community Trusts and Their Operation During the Decade 1921–1931* (New York, 1936); Ferdinand Lundberg, *America's 60 Families* (New York, 1937); and Harold J. Laski, *The Dangers of Obedience and Other Essays* (New York, 1930).

[67] Most prominent of these attacks were the congressional investigations Rep. Eugene E. Cox and Senator B. Carroll Reece conducted in the early 1950's: John E. Lankford, *Congress and the Foundations in the Twentieth Century* (River Falls, Wis., 1964) summarizes the proceedings. René A. Wormser, *Foundations: Their Power and Influence* (New York, 1958) presents the charges of the Reece Committee from a position sympathetic to the Committee.

[68] Flexner, *Funds and Foundations*, pp. 129 ff.

[69] "Timid Billions: Are the Foundations Doing Their Job?", *Harper's Magazine*, CXCVIII (1949), 28–37.

[70] William H. Whyte, Jr., "What Are the Foundations Up To?", *Fortune*, LII (Oct., 1955), 110–13, 254, 256, 258, 260.

[71] Allan Nevins and Frank Ernest Hill, *Ford: Decline and Rebirth, 1933–1962* (New York, 1963), pp. 411–13; Dwight Macdonald, *The Ford Foundation: The Men and the Millions* (New York, 1956), pp. 130–33.

[72] H. Rowan Gaither, Jr., *et al.*, *Report of the Study for the Ford Foundation on Policy and Program* (Detroit, 1949).

[73] Clarence H. Faust, "The Role of the Foundation in Education: 2. Opportunities," *Saturday Review*, XXXV (1952), 13–14. Faust amplified his ideas in Fund for the Advancement of Education, *Annual Report for 1951–52* (New York), pp. 3–28. See also Robert M. Hutchins, *Freedom, Education and the Fund* (New York, 1956).

[74] *Decade of Experiment: The Fund for the Advancement of Education, 1951–61* (New York, 1961), pp. 19–37.

[75] Faust, p. 14.

[76] Robert S. Donaldson, *Fortifying Higher Education: A Story of College Self-Studies* (New York, 1959).

[77] "Four Universities to Admit Male Students at Age 16½ Years," *School and Society*, LXXIII (1951), 316; *Decade of Experiment*, 38–39.

[78] A recent illustration is G. K. Hodenfield, "Fear Tinges Educators' Desire for Foundation Money," *Syracuse Post-Standard*, July 7, 1963, which appeared as an Associated Press dispatch in many newspapers.

[79] Fund for the Advancement of Education, *Report, 1957–1959* (New York), p. 32. Recent publications of the Ford philanthropic organizations leave no doubt that a sober discussion of the advantages and disadvantages in new educational techniques rather than their championship is the foundation's line: John W. Meany, *Televised College Courses* (New York, 1962); Wilbur Schramm, *Programmed Instruction: Today and Tomorrow* (New York, 1962); *Decade of Experiment*, pp. 59 ff.

[80] "The Ford Foundation's 'Academic Monastery,'" *Fortune*, LII (1955), 220.

[81] Macdonald, pp. 4–5, 167 ff.; Olga Hoyt, "Ford's $260,000,000 College Grants: What Happened," *Saturday Review*, XLI (1958), 11–13, 74.

[82] Harrison Brown, "The $500,000,000 Question: What Will the Ford Foundation Grant Do for Education?", *Saturday Review*, XXXIX (1956), 10.

[83] Courtney C. Brown, "A Reply to Harrison Brown: Support Without Influence," *Saturday Review*, XXXIX (1956), 11. See also "The Foundations and Freedom," *Colliers*, CXXXVIII (1956), 86.

[84] "Colleges and Foundations," *Christian Century*, LXXIII (1956), pp. 1286–87.

[85] Ford Foundation, *Annual Report, 1962* (New York), pp. 106–7.

[86] *New York Times*, June 28, 1962; "Ford Grants to Liberal Arts Colleges," *School and Society*, LXXXIX (1961), 388; Wellesley College, *Ford Foundation: Matching Challenge* (n.p., 1962), *passim*.

[87] *The Ford Foundation in the 1960's: Statement of the Board of Trustees on Policies, Programs, and Operations* (New York, 1962), p. 16.

[88] Fosdick, *Adventure in Giving*, pp. 293–94; Wilmer S. Rich, "Foundation Support for Higher Education," *The Impact of Foundations on Higher Education* (n.p., 1954), p. 18.

[89] Rockefeller Foundation, *Annual Report, 1961*, pp. 39 ff.

[90] Fosdick, *Adventure in Giving*, pp. 318–19; "For Future Generations . . . ," Box 24, Hanover Bank Philanthropy Collection.

[91] Carnegie Corporation, *Report*, 1945, pp. 16 ff.

[92] Carnegie Corporation, *Report*, 1947, p. 14.

[93] Alfred P. Sloan Foundation, Inc., *Report for 1953–54* (New York), pp. 63 ff. and *Report for 1959–60*, pp. 11–24, 53–54.

[94] Sloan Foundation, *Report for 1953–54*, p. 1.

[95] A. W. Mellon Educational and Charitable Trust, *Report, 1930–1945* (Pittsburgh), *passim;* Rich, pp. 17, 18; *New York Times*, June 1, 1958.

[96] "Million Dollar Grant to the University of Pittsburgh," *School and Society*, LXXXII (1955), 60–61.

[97] *Commonwealth Fund*, pp. 59–60, 60–70.

[98] Council for Financial Aid to Education, *Guide Lines to Voluntary Support of American Higher Education*, Supplemental Report, No. 2 (New York, 1963), is a summary of the council's biennial statistical surveys of philanthropic support of American higher education. About 80% of all contributions are represented.

[99] Laski, *op. cit.* (above, fn. 66), pp. 164 ff.

[100] Whyte, "Where the Foundations Fall Down," *Fortune*, LII (1955), pp. 140–41, 211–12, 214, 216, 219–20, which is elaborated in Whyte's *The Organization Man* (New York, 1956), pp. 254–65.

[101] Barzun, *The House of Intellect* (New York, 1959), p. 191.

[102] Schlesinger, "The Historian and the Research Foundation," mimeographed paper delivered at the American Historical Association, New York, Dec. 30, 1957.

[103] John J. Parker and Frank E. Sellers, "The University and the Independent Foundation or Trust," *Educational Record*, XXVI (1945), 241–51; Walter A. Morton, "Freedom of Research," *School and Society*, LXXXVIII (1956), 127–29.

NOTES FOR CHAPTER XI

[1] F. Emerson Andrews, *Philanthropic Foundations* (New York, 1956), pp. 29 ff.; F. Emerson Andrews, *Corporation Giving* (New York, 1952), pp. 101–

12, and Frank M. Andrews, *A Study of Company-Sponsored Foundations* (New York, 1960) are the authoritative works in the field.

[2] Thomas C. Cochran, *Railroad Leaders 1845–1890* (Cambridge, Mass., 1953), pp. 174, 177, 210.

[3] Clarke A. Chambers, "Social Welfare Policies and Programs on the Minnesota Iron Range, 1880–1930" (unpubl. paper, University of Minnesota Conference on Education, Oct., 1963).

[4] Edward G. Hartmann, *The Movement to Americanize the Immigrant* (New York, 1948), pp. 131–32, 151n., 152–53, 176–77n., 183; Lewis Paul Todd, *Wartime Relations of the Federal Government and the Public Schools, 1917–1919* (New York, 1945), Ch. II.

[5] Philanthropic motivation of this variety is suggested in the following writings of industrial leaders: Leston P. Faneuf, "All Must Defend Free Enterprise," *Vital Speeches*, XXIII (1957), 655–57; Frank W. Abrams, "Businessman Looks at Education," *Saturday Review*, XXXV (1952), 13–14, 71; Clarence B. Randall, "The Businessman and the Professor," *Freedom's Faith* (Boston, 1953), pp. 77–95.

In unpublished documents: Irving S. Olds, "Remarks . . . at the Dinner of the Workshop of the Commission of Colleges and Industry of the Association of American Colleges . . . April 14, 1953," mimeographed text in Box 31, Arthur W. Page Papers, Manuscripts Room, Wisconsin State Historical Society, Madison; Robert E. Wilson, "A Businessman Looks at Higher Education," address at Indianapolis, Nov., 1953, in Box 14, Hanover Bank Philanthropy Collection, Manuscripts Room, Wisconsin State Historical Society; Arthur W. Page to A. Crawford Greene, June 21, July 26, Aug. 27, 1951, and Greene to Page, July 23, Sept. 22, 1951, Box 26, Page Papers; Arthur W. Page to A. Whitney Griswold, April 20, 1953, Box 31, Page Papers.

[6] Boris Emmet and John E. Jeuck, *Catalogues and Consumers: A History of Sears, Roebuck and Company* (Chicago, 1950), pp. 642–43, and Theodore V. Houser, *Big Business and Human Values* (New York, 1957), pp. 47, 55–56. Sears, Roebuck allocated its scholarships for farm boys and girls to 48 land-grant colleges, which administered them; its city scholarships, also allocated principally to state-supported institutions, were administered by high schools. At a later date its Merit Scholarships (100 a year), administered through the Merit Scholarship Corporation, established by the Ford Foundation, sent young men and women to small, independent, privately supported colleges.

[7] Thomas F. Devine, *Corporate Support for Education: Its Bases and Principles*, The Catholic University of America Educational Research Monographs, Vol. XIX, No. 2 (Washington, 1956), p. 175.

[8] John D. Millett, *Financing Higher Education in the United States* (New York, 1952), p. 454.

[9] U.S., Congress, Senate, Committee on Finance, *Hearings Revenue Act of 1935*, 74th Cong., 1st Sess., 1935 (Washington, 1935), pp. 111–18; *Congressional Record*, 74th Cong., 1st Sess., LXXIX, Part II (Washington, 1935), 12418–12445. See also Robert C. Sullivan, *Memorandum Relating to Reasons Advanced for Granting Corporations an Income Tax Reduction on Contributions to Charities, as Recorded in the Congressional Committee Reports, Transcripts of Hearings, and the Congressional Record* (June, 1953), in Box 32, Page Papers.

[10] "A. P. Smith Manufacturing Company v. Barlow, *et al.*," *Reports of Cases Argued and Determined in the Supreme Court of New Jersey*, XIII (Newark, N.J., 1954), 147–49. For a detailed discussion of the arguments in the case and the important testimony of Irving S. Olds and Frank W. Abrams see Devine, pp. 77–125.

[11] *New Jersey Superior Court Reports*, XXVI (Newark, N.J., 1953), 114.

[12] *New York Times*, May 24, 1953, Sec. 4, p. 10.

[13] Douglas Williams to Arthur W. Page, July 30, 1953, Box 32, Page Papers.

[14] Arthur Page to C. D. Jackson, Nov. 25, 1953, Box 33, Page Papers. For a discussion of the relationship of the man of business and the colleges see Irvin G. Wyllie, "The Businessman Looks at the Higher Learning," *Journal of Higher Education*, XXIII (1952), 295–300, 344.

[15] Public Relations Dept., Standard Oil Company of California, *Report: Corporate Attitude on Support of Liberal Arts Institutions* (San Francisco, 1953), in Box 33, Page Papers.

[16] A. C. Monteith, "Proposed Contribution to Westinghouse Educational Foundation," mimeographed memorandum in Box 29, Page Papers. For similar examples see Lloyd F. Tannhouser to Charles M. O'Hearn, Jan. 29, 1953, Box 33, Page Papers, and Albert E. Thiele and C. T. Ulrich to Arthur W. Page, Sept. 28, 1953, Box 32, Page Papers.

[17] Opinion Research Corporation, "Stockholders Give Their Views on What Companies Should Do About Aid to Colleges," *The Public Opinion Index for Industry* (May, 1953), p. 7, in Box 31, Page Papers.

[18] Arthur Page, Memorandum, Dec. 23, 1953, Box 33, Page Papers; Council for Financial Aid to Education, *Reference Book: Corporation Aid to American Higher Education* (New York, 1955) [p. 15].

[19] Frank H. Sparks, "Federal Aid to Education," *Association of American Colleges Bulletin*, XXXIII (1947), 84–85. The italics are Sparks's.

[20] Furthermore, the graduated income tax created a situation where corporations in the higher income tax brackets could contribute at less cost to the company. The Revenue Act of 1951 taxed corporations 30 percent on the first $25,000 of net income, and 52 percent on other income; excess profits it assessed an additional 30 percent, or a total of 82 percent. Under these high rates of taxation, corporations in the excess-profits brackets could contribute "more than five and a half times the amount it could have retained for its own uses." Andrews, *Corporation Giving*, p. 247. Andrews furnished the following illustrative chart:

NET COST OF CONTRIBUTIONS MADE BY CORPORATIONS
IN VARIOUS PROFIT BRACKETS, 1952

Taxed Income	Amount of Gift	Tax Saved	Net Cost
$25,000 or less	$100	$ 30	$ 70
Over 25,000	100	52	48
Excess Profits	100	82	18
$25,000 or less	142.86	42.86	100
Over 25,000	208.33	108.33	100
Excess profits	555.56	455.56	100

[21] Biographical information on Sparks and material on the Indiana, Ohio, and Michigan organizations can be found in Joe Alex Morris, "The Small Colleges Fight for Their Lives," *Saturday Evening Post,* CCXXVI (May 15, 1954), pp. 42 ff. Figures come from the Educational Dept., National Association of Manufacturers, *Our Private Colleges: Our Heritage . . . Our Investment* (New York, 1958), p. 6, in Box 15, Hanover Bank Philanthropy Collection. See also Carter Davidson, "Commission on Colleges and Industry," *Liberal Education,* XIV (1959), 82–84.

[22] Frank D. Fackenthal to Arthur W. Page, Oct. 17, 1952, Box 29, Page Papers.

[23] Laird Bell to Arthur Page, May 28, 1951, in Box 26, Page Papers.

[24] John D. Millett, "Shall Corporations Contribute to Higher Education? Report of a Discussion at the University Club, New York City, June 12, 1951, under auspices of the Commission on Financing Higher Education," mimeographed report attached to letter from Laird Bell to Arthur Page, July 9, 1951, in Box 26, Page Papers. This memorandum also has names of the participants at the conference.

[25] Council for Financial Aid to Education, *The Meaning of the Council for Financial Aid to Education, Inc.–Objectives, Policies and Scope* (New York, ca. 1953); Alfred P. Sloan Foundation, *Report, 1957–58* (New York), pp. 63–67. The council is hereafter referred to as C.F.A.E.

[26] C.F.A.E., *The Function of the Council for Financial Aid to Education, Inc.* (New York, 1958), p. 5.

[27] For example, see C.F.A.E., *Reference Book* [pp. 59–61], where the council urged preservation of the "dual system" of higher education, which meant preserving private institutions.

[28] C.F.A.E., *Information Bulletin for University Trustees and Business Executives* (New York, 1956), pp. 1–8.

[29] Memorandum for discussion at Conference on Financing Higher Education attached to letter from Alvin C. Eurich to Arthur Page, April 15, 1952, Box 28, Page Papers. "Minutes: Meeting of Corporation Executives Concerned with the Problem of Corporation Giving to Higher Education, June 12, 1952, New York, New York," attached to letter from India Horton to Arthur W. Page, June 24, 1952, Box 29, Page Papers.

[30] A. H. Raskin, "The Corporation and the Campus," *New York Times Magazine,* April 17, 1955, p. 63.

[31] Frank W. Abrams, *Education is Everybody's Business* (New York, ca. 1959), in Box 15, Hanover Bank Philanthropy Collection.

[32] See p. 234.

[33] "Twenty Businessmen Set Out to Start a New Trend in Financing Education," *Business Week* (Sept. 13, 1958), p. 79.

[34] *Ibid.,* pp. 78–79.

[35] Devereux C. Josephs, "The Corporation's Debt to the Great Schools," *Fortune,* LIX (1959), 142.

[36] Josephs, pp. 142–43, 152; "Twenty Businessmen," pp. 82, 84.

[37] Raskin, p. 63.

[38] A. V. Wikker, "Your Education Dollar," undated typescript, Box 15, Hanover Bank Philanthropy Collection; Harlow H. Curtice, "Industry and Education in a Free Society," *Journal of Higher Education,* XVI (1955), pp. 357–58; David A. Shepard, *Liberal Education in an Industrial Society,* Public

Affairs Pamphlet, No. 248 (n.p., 1957); Alfred P. Sloan, Jr., "Big Business Must Help Our Colleges," *Colliers*, CXXVII (1951), pp. 13–15.

[39] "The Rationale of Corporate Philanthropy," *Vital Speeches*, XXIII (1957), 220. See also Eells, *Corporation Giving in a Free Society* (New York, 1956), *passim*.

[40] Olds, *op. cit.* (above, fn. 5).

[41] "Should Business Support the College?" *Fortune*, XLIV (1951), p. 74, being a report of Olds's speech at the 250th anniversary of Yale University.

[42] For example: Education Dept., N.A.M., *op. cit.* (above, fn. 22); Sloan; Robert E. Wilson, *Industry and the Private Liberal Arts College* (Chicago, 1953), pamphlet in Box 33, Page Papers; Courtney C. Brown, "Focusing on the Problem of Business Aid to Higher Education," in C.F.A.E., *Reference Book* [pp. 6–9]; Henning W. Prentis, Jr., *The Stake of Business in Higher Education* (San Francisco, 1955), in Box 15, Hanover Bank Philanthropy Collection.

[43] Abrams, *op. cit.* (above, fn. 5), p. 71.

[44] Randall, *op. cit.* (above, fn. 5), pp. 77–95; Courtney C. Brown, "Economic Peace," *Saturday Review of Literature*, XXXIX (1956), 20; Faneuf, *op. cit.* (above, fn. 5). Laird Bell dissented from the fear of radicalism in the colleges in a letter to A. Crawford Greene, July 10, 1951, copy in Box 26, Page Papers.

[45] Abrams, p. 71.

[46] A. Crawford Greene, memorandum attached to his letter to Arthur Page, Sept. 22, 1951, in Box 26, Page Papers.

[47] Arthur Page to A. Crawford Greene, June 21, 1951, in Box 26, Page Papers.

[48] James B. Conant, "Confidential Report of the President of the University to the Two Governing Boards of the Department of Economics of the Faculty of Arts and Sciences," and Page to Conant, Jan. 9, 1952, Box 28, Page Papers.

[49] "Grove City College," *New Republic*, CXLVI (1962), 3–4.

[50] University of California, *Free Enterprise and University Research: A Record of Public Service by Business, Industry, Private Associations, and Foundations Through Support of the Research Activities of the University of California* (n.p., ca. 1954), *passim*.

[51] Quoted in C.F.A.E., *Reference Book* [p. 61].

[52] See the materials for Indiana, Illinois, and Maryland associations in Box 14, and for the Southern California association in Box 15 of the Hanover Bank Philanthropy Collection.

[53] Harding College, *The College That Speaks to the Nation* (Searcy, Ark., ca. 1957).

[54] "Corporate Support of Higher Education," *Harvard Alumni Bulletin*, LVII (1955), 621.

[55] A *Special Presentation From the University of Vermont* (ca. 1956), pamphlet in Box 31, Hanover Bank Philanthropy Collection.

[56] C.F.A.E., *Reference Book* [p. 57]; F. Emerson Andrews to the authors, December 26, 1963.

[57] C.F.A.E., *Reference Book* [p. 58].

[58] C.F.A.E., *The Upward Trend Continues: 1960 Corporation Support of Higher Education* (New York, 1962), p. 8.

[59] C.F.A.E., *Guide Lines to Voluntary Support of American Higher Educa-*

tion, Supplemental Report, No. 2 (New York, 1963), p. 11; C.F.A.E., *Voluntary Support for America's Colleges and Universities, 1962–1963* (New York, 1964), p. 4. About 80% of all contributions are represented.

[60] C.F.A.E., *1960 Corporation Support,* pp. 3–4, 24–25.

[61] *Ibid.,* pp. 5, 12.

[62] *Ibid.,* p. 29; C.F.A.E., *Who Uses Our Manpower?: A Survey Report on the Employment of College Alumni* (New York, 1961).

[63] As quoted in U. of Cal., *op. cit.* (above, fn. 50), p. 117. For a general discussion see Devine, *op. cit.* (above, fn. 7), pp. 126–86.

[64] C.F.A.E., *Upward Trend,* pp. 25–26.

[65] *Ibid.,* p. 26.

[66] July 7, 1963.

[67] *New York Times,* Oct. 16, 1963. Frederick Rudolph, *The American College and University: A History* (New York, 1962), points out that the federal government now furnishes 70% of the support for all university research and 20% of the operating expenses. See, in addition, Homer D. Babbidge, Jr. and Robert Rosenzweig, *The Federal Interest in Higher Education* (New York, 1962), and Richard G. Axt, *The Federal Government and Financing Higher Education* (New York, 1952).

[68] C.F.A.E., *Guide Lines,* pp. 24–27.

A Note on the Sources

Indicated below are the types of sources, with representative examples, that we found most useful in the research for this book. The footnotes to the text furnish a more complete listing.

General Works: We decided upon the subject of this study after discovering the lack of any extensive recent treatment of the overall impact of philanthropy on American higher education. The only comprehensive study was Jesse B. Sears's 1919 doctoral dissertation, published slightly condensed as *Philanthropy in the History of American Higher Education* (Department of the Interior, Bureau of Education Bulletin, No. 26; Washington, 1922). In the author's words it is "quite largely quantitative," and its strict adherence to chronology does not permit much interpretation. Other secondary material is limited and fragmentary. Robert H. Bremner, *American Philanthropy* (Chicago, 1960) and Frederick Rudolph, *The American College and University: A History* (New York, 1962) give only cursory attention to philanthropy and higher education. There is valuable material on one of the most crucial of the relationships between colleges and philanthropists in Richard Hofstadter and Walter P. Metzger, *The Development of Academic Freedom in the United States* (New York, 1955). Metzger's "College Professors and Big Business Men: A Study of American Ideologies, 1880–1915" (unpublished doctoral dissertation, University of Iowa, 1950) discusses a related subject. The uses of their respective indexes will lead to pertinent portions of George P. Schmidt, *The Liberal Arts College: A Chapter in American Cultural History* (New Brunswick, N.J., 1957); John S. Brubacher and Willis Rudy, *Higher Education in Transition* (New York, 1958); Ernest Earnest, *Academic Procession: An Informal History of the American College, 1636–1953* (Indianapolis, 1953); Richard J. Storr, *The Beginnings of Graduate Education in America* (Chicago, 1953); John Dale Russell, *The Finance of Higher Education* (rev. ed.; Chicago, 1954); and John D. Millet, *Financing Higher Education in the United States* (New York, 1952). An excellent unpublished study which sacrifices scope for depth is Robert Johns's "Ten Philanthropies to American Higher Education" (unpublished doctoral dissertation, Stanford University, 1950).

Several secondary works exist on various topics within the general field. Beverly McAnear's "The Raising of Funds by the Colonial Colleges," *Mississippi Valley Historical Review*, XXXVIII (March, 1952), 591–612 is well done and important. Scott M. Cutlip's book-length study of American fund-raising techniques, *Fund Raising in the United States* (New Brunswick, N.J., 1965), provides many additional insights into this and later periods. Louis Shores discusses an aspect of the colonial college with which philanthropy was closely associated in *Origins of the American College Library, 1638–1800* (George Peabody College for Teachers Contributions to Education, No. 134; Nashville, 1934). Gifts and bequests to women's colleges received unorganized treatment in Thomas Woody, *A History of Women's Higher Education in the United States* (2 vols.; New York, 1929) and is the subject of a short chapter in Mabel Newcomer's *A Century of Higher Education for American Women* (New York, 1959). Lawrence Ross Veysey's "The Emergence of the American University, 1865–1910" (unpublished doctoral dissertation, University of California, Berkeley, 1961) deals in part with the role of philanthropy. Although published before the crucial development of the last three decades, Ullin W. Leavell, *Philanthropy in Negro Education* (George Peabody College for Teachers Contributions to Education, No. 100; Nashville, 1930) and Dwight O. W. Holmes, *The Evolution of the Negro College* (Teachers College, Columbia University, Contributions to Education, No. 609; New York, 1934) are extremely valuable for the earlier period. For the influence of alumni contributions there is only Ernest T. Stewart, Jr.'s "Alumni Support and Annual Giving," *Annals of the American Academy of Political and Social Science*, CCCI (Sept., 1955), 123–38. In spite of the fact that foundation philanthropy has altered considerably since Ernest Victor Hollis published *Philanthropic Foundations and Higher Education* (New York, 1938), the book remains the basis for investigation in this field. Abraham Flexner, *Funds and Foundations: Their Policies Past and Present* (New York, 1952) is a cursory historical survey, while F. Emerson Andrews, *Philanthropic Foundations* (New York, 1956) is primarily concerned with the inner workings of foundations. Andrews's *Corporation Giving* (New York, 1952) along with Frank M. Andrews, *A Study of Company-Sponsored Foundations* (New York, 1960) and especially Thomas F. Devine, *Corporate Support for Education: Its Bases and Principles* (The Catholic University of America Educational Research Monographs, Vol. XIX, No. 2; Washington, 1956) furnish an insight into the recent surge of corporation gifts to colleges and universities.

Especially for the recent period, relevant secondary articles frequently appear in *School and Society, Journal of Higher Education, Educational Record,* and the *Association of American Colleges Bulletin.* A useful guide in cumulative form to these and other periodicals, which includes entries for philanthropy, is the *Educational Index. Fortune, Business Week* and similar magazines occasionally carry pertinent articles for which the *Readers' Guide to Periodical Literature* provides a comprehensive index. Newspapers, in particular the *New York Times,* whose national coverage and detailed index make it of special importance to the researcher, can be used to ascertain facts about most of the major philanthropies to higher education in the present century.

Colleges and Universities: Almost every institution of higher learning has at least one published history. They vary greatly in quality and in the attention paid to philanthropy. Some lack even an index entry for the subject. Others, however, like Josiah Quincy's *The History of Harvard University* (2 vols.; Boston, 1860), give such wide coverage to gifts and bequests as to become in effect philanthropic histories. Examples of competent studies with adequate discussion of philanthropy are Samuel Eliot Morison, *Harvard College in the Seventeenth Century* (2 vols.; Cambridge, Mass., 1936); Robert Fletcher, *A History of Oberlin College from its Foundation through the Civil War* (2 vols.; Oberlin, Ohio, 1943); Arthur C. Cole, *A Hundred Years of Mount Holyoke College: The Evolution of an Educational Ideal* (New Haven, Conn., 1940); Frederick Rudolph, *Mark Hopkins and the Log: Williams College, 1836–1872* (New Haven, Conn., 1956); Hugh Hawkins, *Pioneer: A History of the Johns Hopkins University, 1874–1889* (Ithaca, N.Y., 1960); and Morris Bishop, *A History of Cornell* (Ithaca, N.Y., 1962). The histories of institutions made possible through the generosity of a single person usually include a full discussion of the impact of the donation, as is the case with Orrin Leslie Elliot, *Stanford University: The First Twenty-Five Years* (Stanford, Calif., 1937); Elizabeth D. Hanscom and Helen French Greene, *Sophia Smith and the Beginnings of Smith College* (Northampton, Mass., 1926); and Palmer C. Ricketts, *History of the Rensselaer Polytechnic Institute, 1824–1894* (New York, 1895). The "Contributions to American Educational History" that Herbert B. Adams edited in the 1890's for the United States Bureau of Education should not be ignored in the search for information about donations to colleges. A book-length volume exists for every state and includes a detailed discussion of its major institutions.

While usually reliable as to fact, college histories are frequently uncritical and, in regard to philanthropy, laudatory. Most useful are the detailed investigations of the influence of donations on individual institutions, but Stanley King's *A History of the Endowment of Amherst College* (Amherst, Mass., 1950) is unique. Comparable studies need to be undertaken. College and university records are a fruitful source of information for such investigations, but few are as accessible as the early ledgers of Harvard, which have been printed and indexed in the *Colonial Society of Massachusetts Collections*, XV, XVI (1925). With their help Margery Somers Foster wrote *"Out of Small Beginnings . . .": An Economic History of Harvard College in the Puritan Period, 1636–1712* (Cambridge, Mass., 1962), which contains an excellent analysis of philanthropy's role. The financial records of other institutions are, in the main, available only in their respective archives, although recently the annual reports of presidents and treasurers are becoming more widely distributed. For only a few schools are there published breakdowns of receipts from voluntary donors. Students of the history of the University of Michigan are especially fortunate in having Wilfred B. Shaw's "Support of the University of Michigan from Sources Other than Public Funds or Student Fees, 1817–

1934," *University of Michigan Official Publication*, XXV (April 25, 1934), 1–52, and Shaw's *Support of the University of Michigan from Sources other than Public Funds or Student Fees, 1931–1939* (Ann Arbor, Mich., 1940). In addition there is Sheridan W. Baker, Jr., *The Rackham Funds of the University of Michigan, 1933–1953* (Ann Arbor, Mich., 1955). Dartmouth has listed its larger philanthropic receipts in *Gifts and Bequests to Dartmouth College in the Amount of $5,000 or More* (Hanover, N.H., 1956), and a comparable study exists for the University of Wisconsin: *Gifts and Endowments to the University of Wisconsin, 1865–1931* (Bulletin of the University of Wisconsin, No. 1851; Madison, Wis., 1932). Less comprehensive but valuable for the recent period is the University of California's *Free Enterprise and University Research: A Record of Public Service by Business, Industry, Private Associations, and Foundations through Support of the Research Activities of the University of California* (n.p., ca. 1954). Most colleges and universities have library bulletins and alumni magazines that frequently publish articles of relevance to philanthropy at the particular institution.

Educators: Another way to approach the subject of philanthropy to higher education is through the biographies and autobiographies of educators and educational administrators. As a rule these accounts are more candid than the institutional histories and do not hesitate to discuss the limitations as well as the advantages of accepting large donations. Difficulties that arose at Wellesley, Clark, and Stanford respectively are dramatized in George H. Palmer, *The Life of Alice Freeman Palmer* (Boston, 1908); G. Stanley Hall, *Life and Confessions of a Psychologist* (New York, 1923); and David Starr Jordan, *The Days of a Man* (2 vols.; Yonkers-on-Hudson, N.Y., 1922). More harmonious relations between university president and philanthropist came about at Cornell, Johns Hopkins and Vassar: *Autobiography of Andrew Dickson White* (2 vols.; New York, 1907) along with Walter P. Rodgers, *Andrew D. White and the Modern University* (Ithaca, N.Y., 1942); Daniel Coit Gilman, *The Launching of a University and Other Papers* (New York, 1906); and Harriet Raymond Lloyd, ed., *Life and Letters of John Howard Raymond* (New York, 1881).

Autobiographies often illuminate the impact of philanthropy on institutions of various types as with Philander Chase, *Bishop Chase's Reminiscences: An Autobiography* (2d ed., 2 vols.; Boston, 1848) for Kenyon; Nicholas Murray Butler, *Across the Busy Years* (2 vols.; New York, 1939–40) for Columbia; Emory R. Johnson, *Life of a University Professor: An Autobiography* (Philadelphia, 1943) for the Wharton School of Finance and Commerce at the University of Pennsylvania; James B. Angell, *The Reminiscences of James B. Angell* (New York, 1912) for Vermont and Michigan; and William Jewett Tucker, *My Generation: An Autobiographical Interpretation* (Boston, 1919) for Dartmouth. Still more examples might easily be added.

There are a number of distinguished biographies of educators that include insights into the way gifts were solicited and the effects they had on the college. Reuben A. Guild, *Early History of Brown University Including the Life, Times and Correspondence of President Manning, 1756–1791* (2d rev. ed.; Providence, R.I., 1897) and Varnum Lansing Collins, *President Witherspoon: A Biography* (2 vols.; Princeton, N.J., 1925) are cases in point for the colonial period. Thomas W. Goodspeed, *William Rainey Harper* (Chicago, 1928) and Henry A. Yeomans, *Abbott Lawrence Lowell, 1856–1943* (Cambridge, Mass., 1948) go a long way toward telling the philanthropic histories of the University of Chicago and Harvard during the incumbency of these presidents. The biographies of three educators who pioneered in new directions illustrate the problems of finding and using philanthropy on behalf of practical higher education and the training of women and Negroes: Ethel M. McAllister, *Amos Eaton: Scientist and Educator* (Philadelphia, 1941) for Rensselaer Polytechnic Institute; Edith Finch, *Carey Thomas of Bryn Mawr* (New York, 1947); and Samuel R. Spencer, Jr., *Booker T. Washington and the Negro's Place in American Life* (Boston, 1959). In addition Washington has written his personal reminiscences: *Up From Slavery: An Autobiography* (Garden City, N.Y., 1944).

Individual Philanthropists: The biographies, personal memoirs, and manuscript collections of those who have given to higher education are the best way of approaching the difficult subject of philanthropic motivation. In addition, they usually contain insights into what the donor hoped to accomplish through his benefaction as well as his reaction to what actually transpired. As with institutional histories, however, philanthropists' accounts frequently present only one side of controversial matters.

The lives of the large-scale givers who founded colleges or universities are usually the best documented. Mrs. Leland Stanford, for instance, has three biographies: David Starr Jordan, *The Story of a Good Woman: Jane Lathrop Stanford* (Boston, 1912); George Edward Crothers, *The Educational Ideals of Jane Lathrop Stanford: Co-Founder of the Leland Stanford Junior University* (San Francisco, 1933); and Bertha Berner, *Mrs. Leland Stanford: An Intimate Account* (Stanford, Calif., 1935). Supplementing these is her husband's life: George T. Clark, *Leland Stanford* (Stanford, Calif., 1931). Representative of the work that has been done on other major educational philanthropists are: Hiram Bingham, "Elihu Yale: Governor, Collector and Benefactor," *American Antiquarian Society Proceedings*, XLVII, n.s. (April, 1937), 93–144; Edward C. Mack, *Peter Cooper: Citizen of New York* (New York, 1949); Florence Morse Kinsley, *The Life of Henry Fowle Durant, Founder of Wellesley College* (New York, 1924); Margaret Taylor MacIntosh, *Joseph Wright Taylor: Founder of Bryn Mawr College* (Haverford, Pa., 1936); Philip Dorf, *The Builder: A Biography of Ezra Cornell* (New York, 1952); and Charles Howard Candler, *Asa Griggs Candler* (Atlanta, 1950). Sarah Bolton's *Famous Givers and Their Gifts* (New York, 1896), although badly outdated, is still unique in gathering under one cover brief biographical sketches of many philanthropists who do not appear in standard references.

Fortunately for two of the largest benefactors of higher education there exist firsthand statements as well as biographical accounts. John D. Rockefeller, *Random Reminiscences of Men and Events* (New York, 1909) along with Allan Nevins, *John D. Rockefeller: The Heroic Age of American Enterprise* (2 vols.; New York, 1940) and the sequel volumes *Study in Power: John D. Rockefeller Industrialist and Philanthropist* (2 vols.; New York, 1953) provide a complete if somewhat uncritical presentation. Andrew Carnegie has written two articles that are probably the most incisive self-analysis of philanthropic motivation in print: "Wealth," *North American Review*, CXLVIII (June, 1889), 653–64, and "The Best Fields for Philanthropy," *North American Review*, CXLIX (Dec.,

1889), 682–98. His personal memoirs, *Autobiography of Andrew Carnegie* (Boston, 1920), and a biography, Burton J. Hendrick, *The Life of Andrew Carnegie* (2 vols.; New York, 1932), help complete the picture. Elizabeth H. Haight, ed., *The Autobiography of Matthew Vassar* (New York, 1916) is an example of the revealing personal accounts that sometimes exist for less munificent donors.

We were particularly interested in the manuscript collections in existence for several noteworthy philanthropists. The George Eastman Papers at the Eastman Kodak Company, Rochester, New York are a rich source of information about one of the most generous and diverse givers of his time. The "Personal Letter Books" contain the correspondence of Eastman and various college presidents about his gifts. Additional files document Eastman's interests and suggest the reasons behind his philanthropies. The "Historical Subject File" of the Eastman Kodak Company and a published biography, Carl W. Ackerman, *George Eastman* (London, 1930), round out the picture. The papers of Amos Lawrence and his two equally generous sons, Abbott Lawrence and Amos Adams Lawrence, are contained in the Lawrence Family Manuscripts, Massachusetts Historical Society, Boston. Of special interest are the journals in which the elder Lawrence confessed his inmost attitudes toward philanthropy and the Mark Hopkins-Amos Lawrence correspondence, which documents the relation of the philanthropist with Williams College. The benefactions of a remarkable woman are the subject of a large part of the Papers of Mrs. Russell Sage, Russell Sage Foundation, New York. Where they exist, the manuscripts of other philanthropists might be expected to prove equally useful.

Philanthropic Organizations: In the past, colleges and universities have frequently received money from or through organizations rather than from individuals. There are almost always published reports. The Society for the Promotion of Collegiate and Theological Education at the West issued annual accounts of its activities from 1844 to 1874, including the texts of fund-raising speeches. More recently, the yearly reports of the foundations provide the best means of assessing their impact on higher education. John D. Rockefeller's General Education Board published *The General Education Board: An Account of Its Activities, 1902–1914* (New

York, 1915) as an initial statement and subsequently issued annual summaries of its donations. Since 1922 the annual reports of the Carnegie Corporation have been a reliable index of trends in foundation philanthropy to higher learning. The Ford Foundation's Fund for the Advancement of Education and the parent organization as well have published yearly reports, but rely, in the main, on irregular brochures such as *Decade of Experiment: The Fund for the Advancement of Education, 1951–61* (New York, 1961). Files of the reports of most foundations as well as facilities for answering numerous questions pertaining to their relations with higher education are available at the Foundation Library Center, 444 Madison Avenue, New York.

A number of excellent organizational histories exist. C. Harve Geiger, *The Program of Higher Education of the Presbyterian Church in the United States of America* (Cedar Rapids, Iowa, 1940) concerns one of the most active churches in the support of colleges. Jabez L. M. Curry's *A Brief Sketch of George Peabody and a History of the Peabody Education Fund through Thirty Years* (Cambridge, Mass., 1898) describes the work of this pioneer foundation in Negro education from the viewpoint of its director. Supplementing the Curry history is his biography, Jessie Pearl Rice, *J. L. M. Curry: Southerner, Statesman and Educator* (New York, 1949), and an analysis of his social theory, Merle Curti, *Social Ideas of American Educators* (2d ed., Paterson, N.J., 1959), pp. 264–80. In addition, Franklin Parker's "George Peabody: Founder of Modern Philanthropy" (unpublished doctoral dissertation, George Peabody College, 1956) has considerable relevance.

There are secondary studies for most of the great twentieth century foundations. Raymond B. Fosdick's *Adventure in Giving: The Story of the General Education Board* (New York, 1962), based on the uncompleted manuscript of Henry F. and Katherine Pringle is a model of its kind and, although the work of a former president of the board, does not hesitate to judge candidly the philanthropy of its subject. Fosdick's history of another Rockefeller philanthropic enterprise, *The Story of the Rockefeller Foundation* (New York, 1952) is also excellent but, like the foundation, is concerned only slightly with higher education in the United States. The work of the Carnegie Foundation for the Advancement of Teaching is documented in Howard J. Savage, *Fruit of an Impulse: Forty-five Years of the Carnegie Foundation, 1905–1950* (New York, 1953) and in the biography of its long-time president: Abraham Flexner, *Henry S. Pritchett: A Biography* (New York, 1943). Robert M. Lester takes a broad look at Carnegie's many philanthropies in *Forty Years of Carnegie Giving* (New York, 1941) and focuses specifically on higher education in *Review of Grants to Colleges and Universities in the United States, 1911–1932* (Carnegie Corporation of New York Review Series, No. 12; New York, 1933). For the Ford Foundation there is a critical, popularly written history, Dwight Macdonald, *The Ford Foundation: The Men and the Millions* (New York, 1956. In contrast is Allan Nevins and Frank Ernest Hill's *Ford: Decline and Rebirth, 1933–1962* (New York, 1963). Abraham Flexner's *I Remember* (New York, 1940) deserves special mention as the autobiography of a person who was behind the scenes at the headquarters of several foundations.

There is a dearth of published material on the philanthropic activities of individual corporations, but the Arthur W. Page Papers, Manuscripts Room, Wisconsin State Historical Society, Madison, tell in large part the story of the advent of corporation giving after World War II. Page was a vice-president of the American Telephone and Telegraph Company and an officer of several organizations concerned with corporation support of higher education.

While not directly involved in giving or receiving philanthropy, several organizations have been so close to the process as to merit attention. The American Alumni Council, sometimes known as the Association of Alumni Secretaries, has published reports of its annual conferences since 1913 that contain material pertinent to alumni giving. The council also began in 1957–58 a *Survey of Annual Giving and Alumni Support* with an institution-by-institution breakdown. The Council for Financial Aid to Education, 6 East 45th Street, New York, was organized in 1952 and has become a center of information relating to philanthropy and higher education, especially in regard to corporations. Starting with the academic year 1954–55, it has published biennial surveys under the title *Voluntary Support of America's Colleges and Universities* tabulating in meaningful form the statistics for more than eighty percent of the nation's institutions. The council's *Guide Lines to Voluntary Support of American Higher Education* (Supplemental Report, No. 2; New York, 1963) is an extremely useful summary of the previous surveys. In addition the council has published special studies, such as *The Upward Trend Continues: 1960 Corporation*

Support of Higher Education (New York, 1962) and *Where's the Money Coming From? A Study of Changes in the Sources of Income of America's Colleges and Universities 1943–44 to 1957–58* (New York, 1959).

Another source of statistical information, although not as comprehensive as the C.F.A.E. surveys for the period covered, are the annual compilations since 1920–21 made by the John Price Jones Company, which appear under the running title *American Philanthropy for Higher Education: Gifts and Bequests to Fifty Selected Colleges and Universities.* There are also occasional summaries of statistics for several decades. The John Price Jones Company, one of the nation's leading fund-raising and public-relations firms, also has published since 1954 *Philanthropic Digest,* a weekly newsletter in which major gifts, including those to higher education, are summarized. The John Price Jones Collection at the Baker Library, Harvard Graduate School of Business Administration, Cambridge, Mass., contains additional information about the work of the company. The United States Office of Education's *Biennial Survey of Education in the United States* began in 1917–18 to make available statistical breakdowns of the income, including philanthropy, of most American colleges and universities. In the early 1940's the detailed analysis was discontinued, but bulk listings of the philanthropic receipts of all institutions continued. In spite of the scope of the *Biennial Survey,* its methods of classifying and reporting statistics have varied so frequently that numerous difficulties arise in attempting to use the reports to detect long-range trends.

Especially in regard to developments in the last several decades, we have drawn on the Hanover Bank Philanthropy Collection, Manuscripts Room, Wisconsin State Historical Society. Amounting to more than one hundred file boxes, it comprises the material that the Hanover Bank of New York City collected to help it advise its patrons in matters of philanthropy. Included is fund-raising literature of most major American colleges and universities as well as correspondence with educators, donors, and potential donors. Of special interest are the records of the miscarriages of philanthropic intentions and the replies of college and university presidents in answer to the bank's questionnaire on the importance and role of philanthropy.

Index